WHO
RULES
AMERICA?

WHO
RULES
AMERICA?

POWER AND POLITICS
IN THE YEAR 2000

THIRD EDITION

G. WILLIAM DOMHOFF
University of California, Santa Cruz

Mayfield Publishing Company
Mountain View, California
London • Toronto

Library of Congress Cataloging-in-Publication Data

Domhoff, G. William.
    Who rules America? : power and politics in the year
    2000 / G. William Domhoff—3rd ed.
        p.   cm.
    Updated ed. of: Who rules America now?
    Includes index.
    ISBN 1-55934-973-5
    1.   Elite (Social sciences)—United States.   2. Power
(Social sciences)—United States.   3. Social classes—
United States.   4. United States—Politics and
government—1993–   5. United States—Economic
conditions—1981–   6. United States—Social
conditions—1980–   I. Domhoff, G. William. Who
rules America now?   II. Title.
HN90.E4D654   1998
305.5'.2'0973—DC21   97-31049
                                                                     CIP

Manufactured in the United States of America
10   9   8   7   6   5   4   3   2

Mayfield Publishing Company
1280 Villa Street
Mountain View, CA 94041

Sponsoring editor, Serina Beauparlant; production editor,
Julianna Scott Fein; manuscript editor, Mary Anne
Shahidi; art director, Jeanne M. Schreiber; text designer,
Leigh McLellan; cover designer, Laurie Anderson; art
manager, Amy Folden; illustrator, Judith Ogus; manufac-
turing manager, Randy Hurst. The text was set in 10/12
New Aster by ExecuStaff and printed on acid-free 50#
Amherst Matte by Malloy Lithographing, Inc.

To the newest members of our family,
Glenallen Hill,
a wonderful son-in-law,
and Lorrynn Hamel-Domhoff,
an equally wonderful granddaughter

Preface

Another chance. That's what many of us hope for on this, that, or the other, so I am elated to have this new opportunity to try to convince people that there are strong arguments and systematic evidence to support my theory of who rules America.

Although the main title is borrowed from an earlier version, *Who Rules America Now?* (1983), this book is completely fresh. Three-fourths of the writing and information is new; the rest is updated and rewritten. Two old chapters are gone, and three new ones take their place. This time I discuss what could happen in the future in addition to analyzing the present. The book is written in a style meant to be accessible to those who are new to the topic, but it holds back nothing when it comes to ideas and theory.

I am very grateful to John L. Campbell, Dartmouth College; Howard Kimeldorf, University of Michigan; Shirley Kolack, University of Massachusetts, Lowell; Jeff Manza, Pennsylvania State University; Judith Stepan-Norris, University of California, Irvine; and Ann R. Tickamyer, Ohio University for providing me with their critiques of the second edition and suggestions for this new version. I thank Dick Flacks, Walter Goldfrank, and Harvey Molotch for useful comments on specific chapters, and Val Burris for a discussion that helped frame chapter 5. I deeply appreciate Richard Zweigenhaft for his detailed editorial comments on the entire manuscript that tightened the sentence structure, removed numerous redundancies, and saved me from many small errors, and to Howard Kimeldorf and Jeff Manza for substantive comments on my first draft that led me to sharpen several of my analyses.

Judy Burton, Zoey Sodja, and Cheryl Van De Veer did their usual fast and accurate work in entering the manuscript into the word processor, and Mary Anne Shahidi did great work with her careful editing of the final manuscript.

Most of all, my thanks to Rhonda F. Levine for discussions that strengthened the presentation of the argument and for a critical reading of the manuscript, and to Serina Beauparlant, a superb editor at Mayfield Publishing, who suggested that I undertake the project and provided much-needed perspective and encouragement.

Contents

ix

1

Power and Class in the United States

Power and *class* are terms that make Americans a little uneasy, and concepts like *power elite* and *dominant class* immediately put people on guard. The idea that a relatively fixed group of privileged people might shape the economy and government for their own benefit goes against the American grain. Nevertheless, this book argues that the owners and top-level managers in large income-producing properties are far and away the dominant power figures in the United States. Their corporations, banks, and agribusinesses come together as a *corporate community* that dominates the federal government in Washington. Their real estate, construction, and land development companies form *growth coalitions* that dominate most local governments. Granted, there is competition within both the corporate community and the local growth coalitions for profits and investment opportunities, and there are sometimes tensions between national corporations and local growth coalitions, but both are cohesive on policy issues affecting their general welfare, and in the face of demands by organized workers, liberals, environmentalists, and neighborhoods.

As a result of their ability to organize and defend their interests, the owners and managers of large income-producing properties have a very great share of all income and wealth in the United States, greater than in any other industrial democracy. Making up at best 1 percent of the total population, by the early 1990s they earned 15.7 percent of the nation's yearly income and owned 37.2 percent of all privately held wealth, including 49.6 percent of all corporate stocks and 62.4 percent of all bonds.[1] Due to their wealth and the lifestyle it makes possible, these owners and managers draw closer as a common social group. They belong to the same exclusive social clubs, frequent the same summer and winter resorts, and send their children to a relative handful of private schools. Members of the corporate community thereby become a *corporate rich* who create a nationwide *social upper class* through their social interaction. (A detailed explanation of the term *social class* is provided at the beginning of chapter 3.) Members of the growth coalitions, on the other hand, are *place entrepreneurs*, people who sell locations and buildings. They come together as local upper classes in their respective cities and sometimes mingle with the corporate rich in educational or resort settings.

The corporate rich and the growth entrepreneurs supplement their small numbers by developing and directing a wide variety of nonprofit organizations, the most important of which are a set of tax-free charitable foundations, think tanks, and policy-discussion groups. These specialized nonprofit groups constitute a *policy-formation network* at the national level. Chambers of commerce and policy groups affiliated with them form similar policy-formation networks at the local level, aided by a few national-level city development organizations that are available for local consulting.

Those corporate owners who have the interest and ability to take part in general governance join with top-level executives in the corporate community and the policy-formation network to form the *power elite*, which is the leadership group for the corporate rich as a whole. The concept of a power elite makes clear that not all members of the upper class are involved in governance; some of them simply enjoy the lifestyle that their great wealth affords them. At the same time, the focus on a leadership group allows for the fact that not all those in the power elite are members of the upper class; many of them are high-level employees in profit and nonprofit organizations controlled by the corporate rich. The relationship between the power elite and the three overlapping networks from which it is drawn is shown in figure 1.1. The power elite, in other words, is based in both ownership and in organizational positions. It is specified more exactly in later chapters after the methodological framework for the book has been explained. The point here is that this book presents a synthesis of the class and organizational perspectives sometimes seen as competing viewpoints in the social sciences.

The power elite is not united on all issues because it includes both moderate conservatives and ultraconservatives. Although both factions favor minimal reliance on government on all domestic issues, the moderate conservatives sometimes agree to legislation advocated by liberal elements of the society, especially in times of social upheaval like the Great Depression of the 1930s and the Civil Rights Movement of the early 1960s. Except on defense spending, ultracon-

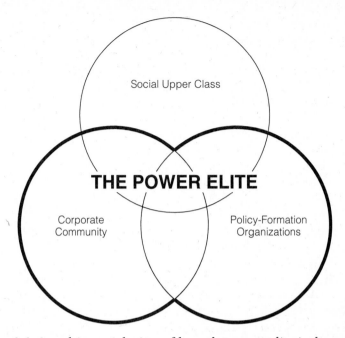

Figure 1.1 A multinetwork view of how the power elite is drawn from three overlapping networks of people and institutions: the corporate community, the social upper class, and the policy-formation network. The power elite is defined by the thick lines.

servatives are characterized by a complete distaste for any kind of government programs under any circumstances—even to the point of opposing government support for corporations on some issues. Moderate conservatives often favor foreign aid, working through the United Nations, and making attempts to win over foreign enemies through patient diplomacy, treaties, and trade agreements. Historically, ultraconservatives have opposed most forms of foreign involvement, although they have become more tolerant of foreign trade agreements over the past thirty or forty years. At the same time, their hostility to the United Nations continues unabated.

Members of the power elite enter into the electoral arena as the leaders within a *corporate-conservative coalition,* where they are aided by a wide variety of patriotic, antitax, and other single-issue organizations. These conservative advocacy organizations are funded in varying degrees by the corporate rich, direct-mail appeals, and middle-class conservatives. This coalition has played a large role in both political parties at the presidential level and usually succeeds in electing a conservative majority to both houses of Congress. Historically, the conservative majority in Congress was made up of most Northern Republicans and most Southern Democrats, but that arrangement has been changing gradually since the 1960s as the conservative Democrats of the South are replaced by even more conservative Southern Republicans. The corporate-conservative coalition also has access to the federal government in Washington through lobbying and the appointment of its members to top positions in the executive branch.

During the past twenty-five years the corporate-conservative coalition has formed an uneasy alliance within the Republican Party with what is sometimes called the "New Right" or "New Christian Right," which consists for the most part of middle-level religious groups concerned with a wide range of "social issues," such as teenage sexual and drinking behavior, abortion, and prayer in school. I describe the alliance as an "uneasy" one because the power elite and the New Right do not have quite the same priorities, except for a general hostility to government and liberalism, and because it is not completely certain that the New Right is helping the corporate-conservative coalition as much as its publicists and fund-raisers claim. Nevertheless, ultraconservatives within the power elite help to finance some of the single-issue organizations and publications of the New Right, as illustrated in chapter 4.

Despite their preponderant power within the federal government and the many useful policies it carries out for them, members of the power elite are constantly critical of government as an alleged enemy of freedom and economic growth. Although their wariness toward government is expressed in terms of a dislike for taxes and government regulations, I believe their underlying concern is that government could change the power relations in the private sphere by aiding average Americans through a number of different avenues: (1) creating government jobs for the unemployed; (2) making health, unemployment, and welfare benefits more generous; (3) helping employees gain greater workplace rights and protections; and (4) helping workers organize unions. All of these initiatives are opposed by members of the power elite because they would increase wages and taxes, but the deepest opposition is toward any government support for unions because unions are a potential organizational base for advocating the whole range of issues opposed by the corporate rich. Evidence for this supposition appears in a variety of contexts throughout the book.

WHERE DOES DEMOCRACY FIT IN?

The argument I present in this book, although contrary to some generally held beliefs, starts with the assumption that everyone is equal before the law and has opportunities for social mobility. I believe that there is freedom of expression, the possibility of political participation, and public conflict over significant issues. Furthermore, the class system is an open and changing one, and the political system is democratic. Thus, the challenge I face is to demonstrate that a dominant class and power elite can persist despite the political conflict and social change that are an inherent part of American society.

Moreover, to claim that the corporate rich have enough power to be considered a dominant class does not imply that lower social classes are totally powerless. *Domination* means the power to set the terms under which other groups and classes must operate, not total control. Highly trained professionals with an interest in environmental and consumer issues have been able to couple their technical information and their understanding of the legislative and judicial processes with well-timed publicity, lobbying, and lawsuits to win governmental restrictions on some corporate practices. Wage and salary employees, when they are organized into unions and have the right to strike, have been able to gain pay increases, shorter hours, better working conditions, and social benefits such as health insurance. Even the most powerless of people—the very poor and those discriminated against—sometimes develop the capacity to influence the power structure through sit-ins, demonstrations, social movements, and other forms of social disruption, and there is evidence that such activities do bring about some redress of grievances, at least for a short time.[2]

More generally, the various challengers to the power elite sometimes work together on policy issues as a *liberal-labor coalition* that is based in unions, local environmental organizations, some minority group communities, university and arts communities, liberal churches, and small newspapers and magazines. Despite a decline in membership over the past twenty years, unions are the largest and best-financed part of the coalition, and the largest organized social force in the country (aside from churches). They also cut across racial and ethnic lines more than any other institutionalized sector of American society. They have 16.3 million members, 80 percent of them in the seventy-eight unions affiliated with the American Federation of Labor-Congress of Industrial Organizations (known as the AFL-CIO). They spend over $5 billion a year on routine operations, most of it from membership dues, and have about $10 billion in assets. During the 1990s they spent approximately $50 million a year on political campaigns.[3] The twelve largest unions in the AFL-CIO and their membership figures for 1995 are listed in table 1.1. Membership figures for 1975 and 1985 are also included, along with the percentage of increase or decrease, to show the decline in membership in traditional industrial unions and the rise in service and government-employee unions.

Table 1.1 The 12 Largest AFL-CIO Unions and Their Membership Figures (in thousands)

Union	1975	1985	1995	% Change
Teamsters	1,889	1,161	1,285	−32
State, county, and municipal employees (AFSCME)	647	997	1,183	+83
Service Employees International Union (SEIU)	480	688	1,027	+114
Food and commercial workers (UFCW)	1,150	989	983	−15
Automobile, aerospace, and agriculture workers (UAW)	1,358	974	751	−45
Electrical workers (IBEW)	856	971	679	−21
American Federation of Teachers (AFT)	396	470	613	+55
Communication workers (CWA)	476	524	478	+.4
Machinists	780	520	448	−43
Steelworkers	1,062	572	403	−62
Carpenters	700	609	378	−46
Laborers	475	383	352	−26

Source: *Statistical Abstracts of the United States*, 1978, p. 429; 1986, p. 423; 1996, p. 436.

The liberal-labor coalition also includes a few sons and daughters from well-to-do business and professional families who are critical of the power elite and the corporate-conservative coalition despite their comfortable financial upbringings. The presence of people from privileged social backgrounds in the liberal-labor camp suggests that religious and social values can sometimes be as important as class in shaping political orientations, and historically there are many examples of liberal, reformist, and even revolutionary leaders who come from high levels of the social ladder in their countries.

The liberal-labor coalition enters the electoral arena through the liberal wing of the Democratic Party. Contrary to conservative political activists, liberal journalists, and some social scientists, this coalition never has had a major voice in the Democratic Party at the national level, although it probably had more impact from the late 1930s to the early 1970s than it has had since. It could, however, gain much greater influence in the party in the future due to social changes, which are examined in the final chapter.

The policy conflicts between the corporate-conservative and liberal-labor coalitions are best described as *class conflicts* because they primarily concern the distribution of profits and wages, the rate and progressivity of taxation, the usefulness of labor unions, and the degree to which business should be regulated by government. The liberal-labor coalition wants corporations to pay higher wages to employees and higher taxes to government. It wants government to regulate a wide range of business practices, including many that are related to the environment, and help employees to organize unions. The corporate-conservative coalition resists all these policy objectives to a greater or lesser degree, claiming they endanger the freedom of individuals and the efficient workings of the economic marketplace. The conflicts these disagreements generate can manifest themselves in many different ways: workplace protests, industrywide boycotts, massive demonstrations in cities, pressure on Congress, and the outcome of elections.

Neither the corporate-conservative nor the liberal-labor coalition includes a very large percentage of the American population, although each has the regular support of about 25–30 percent of the voters. Both coalitions are made up primarily of financial donors, policy experts, political consultants, and party activists. Members of the rival coalitions share an intense interest in policy issues and elections, and both include individuals ambitious for political office, but the coalitions disagree greatly in their values, policy prescriptions, and general ideology.*

The two coalitions are in constant competition for the allegiance of the general citizenry, most of whom pay little attention to politics, or hold views somewhere between those of the two coalitions, or entertain a mixture of views that seem "contradictory" to activists on both sides of the fence. This means that as many as 40–50 percent of the electorate may be open to an attractive candidate or well-crafted policy appeal from one coalition or the other. More often than not, however, the corporate-conservative coalition triumphs in both the electoral and policy arenas. The hows and whys of these triumphs are the key issues of this book.

To help familiarize readers with the main differences among various political orientations in the United States, table 1.2 presents a brief characterization of six groups on the issues that unite and divide them. The most central issues are the value of trade unions,

---

*An ideology is the complex set of rationales and rationalizations through which a group, class, or nation interprets the world and justifies its actions within it. An ideology usually is fervently believed by those who espouse it. Although the emphasis at this point is on ideological differences between the two coalitions, Chapter 5 describes the commonalties in the general ideology that most Americans share.

Table 1.2 The Policy Preferences on Several Key Issues for Six Political Orientations

	Anti-market Pro Planning?	Pro Union?	For Environmental Regulation?	Pro Social Benefits?	Pro Social Issues?
New right	No	No	No	No	No
Ultraconservatives	No	No	No	No	Sometimes
Moderate Conservatives	No	No	Somewhat	Somewhat	Often
Trade unionists*	No	Yes	Sometimes	Yes	Maybe
Liberals	No	Yes	Yes	Yes	Yes
Leftists/socialists	Yes	Yes	Yes	Yes	Yes

*Some trade unionists are also liberals or leftists.

greater government involvement in economic and environmental regulation, the usefulness of government social benefit programs like Social Security, and government support for a liberal agenda on social issues like affirmative action, abortion, and civil rights for gays and lesbians. Although those who now call themselves "leftists" or "progressives" make up only a few percent of the American population, the table also includes their views because they are highly vocal critics of both the corporate community and the liberal-labor coalition—especially in university and literary settings—and often have their greatest appeal to college students and readers of books such as this one.

Historically, leftists differed sharply from liberals in that most of them wanted to replace the market economy and private business ownership with a comprehensive system of government ownership and planning called "socialism," in which citizens would participate through involvement in the planning process and the election of government officials. At the same time, they held a range of views on how much planning and government ownership was necessary, and on how these objectives might be obtained. More recently, the differences between leftists and liberals have narrowed as more leftists have come to advocate a mixture of private and public ownership, and the use of planning within a system of markets. However, many leftists still work in opposition to the liberal-labor coalition, and most of them favor one or another of several socialist or progressive third parties, arguing vigorously among themselves about which party has the best analysis and strategy.

THE MAIN ALTERNATIVE THEORIES

There are several other theories concerning the location and concentration of power in the United States. Three of these alternative frameworks are discussed at relevant points throughout the following chapters. They are (1) pluralism, (2) state-centered theory, and (3) institutional elitism. This section presents a brief overview of the main tenets of each of them and explains how they differ from my class-dominance perspective.

Pluralism

The main alternative theory addressed in this book claims that power is more widely dispersed among groups and classes than a class-dominance theory allows. This general perspective is usually called *pluralism*, meaning there is no one dominant power group. It is the theory most favored by social scientists. In its strongest version, pluralism holds that power is held by the general public through the pressure that public opinion and voting put on elected officials. According to this version, citizens form voluntary groups and pressure groups that shape public opinion, lobby elected officials, and back sympathetic political candidates in the electoral process. Evidence against this public-opinion version of pluralism is presented in chapters 5 (the role of public opinion) and 6 (parties and elections).

The second version of pluralism sees power as rooted in a wide range of well-organized "interest groups" that are often based in economic interests (e.g., industrialists, bankers, labor unions), but also in other interests as well (e.g., environmental, consumer, and civil rights groups). These interest groups join together in different coalitions depending on the specific issues. Proponents of this version of pluralism sometimes concede that public opinion and voting have only a minimal or indirect influence, but they see business groups as too fragmented and antagonistic to form a cohesive dominant class. They also claim that some business interest groups occasionally join coalitions with liberal or labor groups on specific issues, and that business-dominated coalitions sometimes lose. Furthermore, some proponents of this version of pluralism believe that the Democratic Party is responsive to the wishes of liberal and labor interest groups.

In contrast, I argue that the business interest groups are part of a tightly knit corporate community that is able to develop classwide cohesion on the issues of greatest concern to it: opposition to unions, high taxes, and government regulation. When a business group loses on a specific issue, it is often because other business groups have been opposed; in other words, there are arguments within the corporate community, and these arguments are usually settled within the governmental arena. I also claim that liberal and labor groups are rarely part of coalitions with business groups and that for most of its history the Democratic Party has been dominated by corporate and agribusiness interests in the Southern states, in partnership with the growth coalitions in large urban areas outside the South. Finally, I show that business interests rarely lose on labor and regulatory issues except in times of extreme social disruption like the 1930s and 1960s, when differences of opinion between Northern and Southern corporate leaders made victories for the liberal-labor coalition possible.

State-Centered Theory

While pluralists put their greatest emphasis on the way in which private citizens and interest groups influence government, state-centered theorists start with the potential power of government to dominate or shape private groups. This potential state independence, usually called *autonomy*, is due to several intertwined factors: (1) its monopoly on the legitimate use of force within the country, (2) its unique role in defending the country from foreign rivals, and (3) its regulatory and taxing powers.

For some state-centered theorists, the potential for state autonomy is more or less realized in the United States. Contrary to this "strong" version of state-centered theory, I argue that the potential for state autonomy does not manifest itself in the United States for a variety of historical reasons that include the rivalries among the original thirteen colonies that formed the American government, the great power of business leaders and plantation owners at the time the government was founded, and the absence of any strong nearby countries once the nation was established. Chapters 6 and 7 explain how a majority of elected officials become beholden to the corporate rich in order to win elections and how the corporate rich can ensure that policies generated in their policy-formation network are enacted.

There is a second, less controversial version of state-centered theory that is not disputed in this book. It notes that the institutional structure of the state—the nature of its legislative, executive, regulatory, and judicial systems and the relationships among them—plays a very important role in shaping party systems and political strategies. Further, it emphasizes that some institutions within the state can have a greater capacity for autonomy than others and that state institutions sometimes strive for independence from one another.

I agree with state-centered theorists that the institutional structure of the state shapes the way in which political power is organized
and exercised in the United States. There is no inherent incompatibil-
ity between this point and a class-domination theory. From a class-
domination perspective, the issue is to see whether and how government
can be influenced. For example, the division of the American government into national, state, and local levels helps to explain why growth
coalitions can be so powerful in most cities. The lack of large planning
staffs in most departments of the executive branch made it possible
for a private policy-formation network to flourish. The existence of an
independent executive branch and the election of Congress on a state-
by-state and district-by-district basis accounts for the strength of the
two-party system, a topic addressed in chapter 6.

Institutional Elitism

A third alternative view, institutional elitism, claims that power is
lodged in the largest organizations of the society, whether aimed toward making a profit or not. The theory contends that elites are inevitable in any large-scale society based in bureaucratic organizations,
but it does not contend that these elites are necessarily unified and
highly self-conscious, or intellectually or morally superior to nonelites.
Nor does it say that nonelites are powerless; they sometimes have the
ability to set limits on the actions of elites. Empirical work by elite
theorists has demonstrated variations in the interdependence between elites and nonelites in different countries.[4]

Although the comparative and historical studies by elite theorists hold considerable interest, the emphasis in this book is on a variant of elite theory by political scientist Thomas R. Dye that focuses
exclusively on the United States and elaborates in considerable empirical detail. Dye's 1976 book, *Who's Running America?*, written in
reaction to the 1967 version of *Who Rules America?*, has gone through
six editions, updated most recently in 1995 to include the first Clinton
Administration. His book is even more critical of pluralism than this one
is. It stresses the great power of a few hundred large corporations and
nonprofit groups, and shows the many common directors shared among
them, but nonetheless sees government officials as powerful as well. It
borrows an earlier version of the policy-formation network presented in
chapter 4 of this book, albeit with the addition of the mass media.[5]

Despite some similarities between Dye's views and class-dominance
theory, this book shares more in common with the interest-group
version of pluralism than it does with his institutional elitism. Dye's
analysis underestimates the role of classes and class conflict, overem-
phasizes the degree of social mobility, and presents a truncated view

of the corporate community. It overstates the independence of the mass media and the size of the federal government. The following chapters include a conceptual and empirical critique of Dye's variant of institutional elitism as well as a critique of pluralism and state autonomy theory.

In general, this book is situated between interest-group pluralism on the one hand and institutional elitism on the other. It tries to show that interest groups aggregate into conflicting social classes and that the institutions stressed by Dye are directed by a leadership group based in the ownership and control of large income-producing property.

WHAT ABOUT MARXISM?

So far, the most controversial power theory of the nineteenth and twentieth centuries, Marxism, has not been mentioned. It is a wide-ranging system of thought that includes a philosophy of history, a critique of capitalism as an economic and social system, and a theory of power that emphasizes the clash between social classes rooted in opposing economic interests. Marxism is also a call to political action in the name of a new social order that abolishes private ownership of income-producing property and replaces the economic marketplace with government planning.

Although I do not accept the key theoretical tenets of Marxism, which are briefly explained in the following paragraphs, I do share Marxism's focus on class domination and class conflict as central to an understanding of the distribution and workings of power in America. I use the term *class conflict* rather than the Marxian term *class struggle*, however, to emphasize that I do not agree with Marxists that a sustained challenge to the capitalist system by the nonowning classes is either inevitable or certain of victory.

To make these differences clear, an overview of Marxism and its major concepts is necessary. *Marxism* is the term for a comprehensive theory of Western history created by Karl Marx (1818–1883) and Friedrich Engels (1820–1895). Shorn to its barest essentials, the theory states that history begins when the creative labor of human beings acts upon nature to serve human needs. The creation of tools and machinery ("forces of production") leads to more goods being produced than can be individually consumed, and hence to the potential for conflict over how to distribute the surplus. As the forces of production develop, there is an increasing division of labor as well as increasing conflict over the ownership and control of the machinery ("relations of production"). As people divide into owners and nonowners, there is both greater overall productivity and increasing exploitation of the nonowners (who, at different stages of history, were slaves, serfs, peasants, and most recently "workers"). This framework, known as historical materialism, assumes that the level of development of the "forces of production" shapes the basic structure of the "relations of production." The relations of production, in turn, shape the "superstructure," which includes political institutions, organized religion, customs, and ideas about the world. Historical materialism thus claims that the historically specific way in which people create goods and services is the basis for their political, religious, and philosophic systems, thereby giving primacy to the "economic" and material aspects of human existence.[6]

Within the context of this exploitative and volatile economic structure, a "state" is developed by the owners to protect themselves and their private ownership of the means of production. When the socioeconomic system reaches the highly productive stage of development called capitalism, the economic surplus is "appropriated" from workers as "profits" through the seemingly fair social institution known as the "market," which replaces the direct and coercive forms of appropriation used in earlier social systems. However, Marxists argue that the market system is not really fair because it has a strong tendency to push wages to a subsistence level due to the fact that there are always more workers than are necessary. In other words, the powerlessness of workers, which forces them to sell their labor power in order to survive, underlies what most economists celebrate as a "free" market and makes profits possible.

For all the market's usefulness as a method of organizing a highly productive and flexible economy, Marxism claims that it also generates increasing discontent in workers, both in terms of psychological alienation (their creative energies are controlled by owners) and sociological despair (low wages and poor working conditions). As workers come to realize their common plight, they join together to form unions and political parties. In the context of increasing economic crises, such as depressions and runaway inflation, they decide that they are capable of organizing a fairer and more humane social system. They struggle to replace the capitalist system with a cooperative one called "socialism" in which the means of production are owned by everyone through cooperatives and government. In particular, the market is replaced by democratic planning through government.

Although workers do not understand the fact at first, socialism, and then communism—a more advanced stage of socialism—is inevitable because the economic problems and social conflicts that develop within a fully mature capitalist system are unsolvable. Capitalism thus contains within it the seeds of its own destruction, but the apparent fairness of the market and the pervasiveness of capitalist ideology mask this fact from workers. It creates in them a "false consciousness" about their best interests that is only gradually overcome. The aim of Marxist political parties is to help workers overcome their false consciousness and undertake the task that has been assigned them by the historical process—the overthrow of capitalism.

I see the foregoing Marxian analysis as too narrow and restrictive, although it contains useful insights about capitalism as a social system. The concept of historical materialism does not give independent weight to political, military, and religious organizations in explaining social structure. History is driven by more than class struggle, especially in the centuries before the development of capitalism. Moreover, the best present archeological and historical evidence suggests that states emerged before private property or class conflict and therefore have a more basic role than Marxists claim. Also, the problems of a fully developed capitalist economy may not be unsolvable, and there seems to be nothing inevitable about the historical process. The theory underestimates the strength of patriotic sentiments and ignores the common social bonds between the social classes in a country. As for the political movements arising from Marxism, they are discussed in the final chapter where the future of American politics is considered.[7]

THERE ARE NO CONSPIRACIES

Few social scientists would agree, but there are some people who believe that power in the United States is exercised from behind the scenes by a small secretive group of private citizens who want to change the government system or put the country under the control of a world government. In the past, the conspirators were usually said to be secret Communist sympathizers who were intent on bringing the United States under a common world government in conjunction with the Soviet Union, but the collapse of the Soviet Union in 1991 changed the focus to the United Nations as the likely controlling force in a "new world order." For a smaller group of conspiratorial thinkers, a secret group of operatives located in the government itself, especially the CIA, has been responsible for many terrible tragedies since the 1960s, including the assassination of President John F. Kennedy.

From my standpoint, no conspiracy theory is credible on any issue. If there is anything to the theory presented here, the leaders in visible positions in the corporate community, the policy-formation network, and the government are the real leaders, and the processes that lead to class domination are the same mundane ones that social scientists have documented for other levels of the socioeconomic system. The group said by some conspiratorial thinkers to be at the center of the alleged conspiracy in the United States, the Council on

Foreign Relations, is in fact a mere policy discussion forum (with nearly 3,000 members) that issues annual reports, allows access to its historical archives, and has a very different role in the overall power structure than what is claimed by conspiratorial theorists. As seen in later chapters, it has been studied in great detail by historians and social scientists.

The conspiratorial view is different in several ways from the theory presented in this book. First, it is based on psychological assumptions, not sociological ones. The main version assumes that some wealthy and highly educated private citizens develop an extreme psychological desire for power that takes precedence over their normal economic and political interests. In my theory, on the other hand, leaders act for understandable sociological reasons, such as profit-seeking motives and institutional roles. Second, the conspiratorial view assumes that the behind-the-scenes leaders are extremely clever and knowledgeable, whereas I assume that leaders often make short-sighted or ill-informed decisions due to the limits placed on their thinking by their social backgrounds and institutional roles. Third, the conspiratorial view places power in the hands of only a few dozen or so people, often guided by one strong leader, whereas I believe there is a leadership group of many thousands for a corporate rich that numbers several million. Finally, the conspiratorial view assumes that illegal plans to change the government or assassinate people can be kept secret for long periods of time, but all evidence shows that secret groups in the United States are uncovered by civil liberties groups, infiltrated by reporters or government officials, and written about in the press.[8] Assassinations and bombings in the United States have been the acts of individuals or small groups with no power.

All this said, it is also true that government officials sometimes take illegal actions or try to deceive the public. During the 1960s, for example, government leaders claimed that the Vietnam War was easily winnable, even though they knew otherwise. In the 1980s the Reagan Administration defied a Congressional ban on support for antigovernment rebels in Nicaragua (the "contras") through a complicated scheme that raised money from foreign countries for the rebels. The plan included an illegal delivery of armaments to Iran in exchange for money and hostages. But deceptions and illegal actions are usually uncovered, if not immediately, then in historical records.

In the case of the Vietnam War deception, the unauthorized release in 1971 of government documents *(The Pentagon Papers)* revealing the true state of affairs caused the government great embarrassment and turned more people against the war. It also triggered the creation of a secret White House operation to plug leaks, which led in turn to an illegal entry into Democratic Party headquarters during the 1972 elections, an attempted cover-up of high-level approval of the operation, and the resignation of President Richard M. Nixon in the face of impeachment charges. As for the Reagan Administration's illegal activities, they were unraveled in widely viewed congressional hearings that led to a six-month imprisonment for the president's national security adviser for his part in an unsuccessful cover-up, along with convictions or guilty pleas for several others for obstruction of justice or lying to Congress. The secretary of defense was indicted for his part in the cover-up but was spared a trial when he was pardoned by President George Bush on Christmas Eve, 1992.[9]

It is also true that the CIA has been involved in espionage, sabotage, and the illegal overthrow of foreign governments and that the FBI spied on and attempted to disrupt Marxist third parties, the Civil Rights Movement, and the Ku Klux Klan. But careful studies show that all these actions were authorized by top government officials, which is the critical point here. There was no "secret team" or "shadow government" committing illegal acts or ordering government officials to deceive the public and disrupt social movements.[10] Such a distinction is crucial in differentiating all sociological theories of power from a conspiratorial one.

THE CONCEPT OF POWER

American ideas about power have their origins in the struggle for independence, but they owe as much to the conflict within each colony about the founding of a new government as they do to the war itself. Every high school textbook and every Fourth of July speech sets forth the idea that people fought in the Revolutionary War because of a desire to have a voice in how they were governed—and especially in how they were taxed. But it is often lost from sight that the average citizens were making revolutionary political demands on their leaders as well as helping in the fight against the British.

Due to their own experience, those yeoman farmers and artisans who supported the Revolution gradually developed the new idea that power is the possession of all the people and is delegated to government with their consent. They also created a way to implement the idea when they insisted not only that special conventions be elected to frame constitutions, but that the constitutions then be ratified by the vote of all free white males without regard to their property holdings. In the past, governments had been founded on the basis of the power and legitimacy of religious leaders, kings, self-appointed conventions, or parliaments. The American revolutionary leaders who drafted the constitutions for the thirteen states between 1776 and

1780 expected their handiwork to be debated and voted on by state legislatures, but they did not want to involve the general public in a direct way.

It was members of the "middling" classes who pressured for special conventions and for the right to vote on acceptance or rejection. They were steeled in their resolve by their participation in the revolutionary struggle and by a fear of the property laws and taxation policies that might be written into the constitutions by those who were known at the time as their "betters." "The idea of the people as the constituent power," argues historian Robert R. Palmer in his history of democratic revolutions, "arose locally, from the grass roots." He therefore concludes that the American Revolution was "a political revolution, concerned with liberty, and with power."[11]

The middle-level insurgents won the right to both a constitutional convention of elected delegates and a vote on subsequent ratification in only one state, Massachusetts, but from that time forth it was widely agreed that power in the United States belonged to "the people." Since then every liberal, radical, populist, or ultraconservative political group has claimed that it represents "the people" in its attempt to wrest allegedly arbitrary power from the "vested interests," the "cultural elite," or the "bureaucrats." Even the Founding Fathers, who were far removed from the general population in their wealth, income, education, and political experience, did not consider putting forth a new constitution designed to more fully protect private property and commerce without asking for the consent of the governed, and they were forced to add the Bill of Rights to ensure its acceptance. In a very profound sense, then, no group or class has "power" in America, but only "influence."

Reflecting general American beliefs, some social scientists prefer to avoid using the term *power* at all, or to define power and influence to mean the same thing. Whatever their definition, however, all social scientists use the term in the sense of great or preponderant influence, not in the sense of absolute control. The most widely used definition of power in the social sciences is a variation of one suggested by Max Weber (1864–1920), a German sociologist. Weber wrote that "we understand by 'power' the chance of a man or a number of men to realize their own will in a social action even against the resistance of others who are participating in the action."[12] In a similar vein, an American political scientist who has written extensively on power and democracy, Robert Dahl, concludes his discussion of the concept by noting that definitions usually rest on the "intuitive idea" that "A has power over B to the extent that he can get B to do something that B would not otherwise do." He also decides that the terms *power* and *influence* can be used interchangeably.[13]

Despite the partiality shown to this definition by most social scientists, it has a major disadvantage. It harbors within it the implicit theory that the basis of power is the ability to use force or coercion on the other person or group. Since the basis of power should be an issue for empirical study, I prefer a new definition suggested by sociologist Dennis Wrong after a thorough consideration of every major discussion of the subject: "Power is the capacity of some persons to produce intended and foreseen effects on others."[14] This definition has another advantage. It does not try to reduce the various types of power to any basic type that is said to have "ultimate primacy." Rather than seeing military force, economic ownership, political control, or religious/cultural values as the primary source from which all other forms of power develop (as the rival "grand theories" of nineteenth-century sociology and politics tended to do), this definition allows for the possibility that the different types of power may combine in different ways in different times and places. Indeed, the possibility of such varying combinations is one of my basic premises. As philosopher Bertrand Russell wrote sixty years ago in his classic historical and cross-national study of power:

> The fundamental concept in social science is power in the sense in which energy is the fundamental concept in physics. Like energy, power has many forms, such as wealth, armaments, influence on opinion. No one of these can be regarded as subordinate to any other, and there is no form from which the others are derivable.[15]

However, to say that power is the ability to produce intended and foreseen effects on others, and that no one form of power is more basic, does not mean it is a simple matter to study the power of a group or social class. A formal definition does not explain how a concept is to be measured. In the case of power, it is seldom possible to observe interactions that reveal its operation even in small groups, let alone to see one "class" producing "effects" on another. It is therefore necessary to develop what are called *indicators* of power.

CONCEPTS AND INDICATORS

For research purposes, power can be thought of as an underlying trait or property of a collectivity. As with any social trait, it is measured by a series of indicators, or signs, that bear a probabilistic relationship to it. This means the indicators do not necessarily appear each and every time the trait manifests itself. This way of thinking about such sociological concepts as power and morale was developed by social psychologist Paul Lazarsfeld. In a detailed discussion of the relationship between concepts and measurement in the social sciences, he showed that the traits of a social collectivity are similar in their logical structure to the idea of personality traits developed by psychologists to understand individual behavior and the abstract concepts developed by philosophers of science to explain the nature of scientific theory. Whether a theorist is concerned with friendliness, as in psychology, or magnetism, as in physics, or power, as in sociology, the underlying structure of the investigatory procedure is the same. In each case there is an underlying concept whose presence can be inferred only through a series of diagnostic signs or indicators that vary in their strength under differing conditions. Research proceeds, in this view, through a series of "if-then" statements. "If" a group is powerful, "then" it should be expected that certain indicators of this power will be present.[16]

The indicators of a concept such as power are not perfect. For this reason, it is especially important to have more than one indicator. Ideally, indicators will be of very different types so that the irrelevant components of each will cancel one another out. In the best of all possible worlds, these multiple indicators will point in the same direction, giving greater confidence that the underlying concept has been measured correctly. This point is most convincingly argued by five methodologists in social psychology and sociology:

> Once a proposition has been confirmed by two or more independent measurement processes, the uncertainty of its interpretation is greatly reduced. The most persuasive evidence comes through a triangulation of measurement processes. If a proposition can survive the onslaught of a series of imperfect measures, with all their irrelevant error, confidence should be placed in it.[17]

Working within this framework, four different types of power indicators are used in this book. They can be called: (1) "Who benefits?" (2) "Who governs?" (3) "Who wins?" and (4) "Who shines?"

Who Benefits?

In every society there are experiences and material objects that are highly valued. If it is assumed that everyone in the society would like to have as great a share as possible of these experiences and objects, then their distribution in that society can be used as a power indicator. Those who have the most of what people want are, by inference, the most powerful. Put another way, the distribution of valued experiences and objects within a society can be viewed as the most visible and stable outcome of the operation of power within that social system.

In the United States society, for example, wealth and well-being are highly valued. People seek to own property, to earn high incomes, to have interesting and safe jobs, to enjoy the finest in travel and leisure, and to live long and healthy lives. All of these "values" are unequally distributed, and all can be employed as power indicators. In this book, however, the primary focus is on the wealth and income distributions. This does not mean that wealth and income are the same thing as power, but that the possession of great wealth and income is a visible sign that one class has power in relation to other classes.

The argument for using value distributions as power indicators is strengthened by empirical studies showing that such distributions vary from country to country depending on the relative strength of rival political parties and trade unions. In one study, it was found that since 1945, the degree of inequality in the income distribution in Western democracies varied inversely with the percentage of social democrats who had been elected to the country's legislature.* The greater the social democratic presence, the greater the amount of income that went to the lower classes.[18] In another study of eighteen Western democracies, it was reported that the presence of strong trade unions and successful social democratic parties correlated with greater equality in the income distribution, progressivity in the tax structure, and a higher level of welfare spending.[19] Thus, there is evidence that value distributions do vary depending on the relative power of contending groups or classes. In western Europe, these findings suggest, the working class has greater power than it does in the United States. Several reasons for this difference are presented in later chapters.

Who Governs?

Power also can be inferred from studies of who occupies important institutional positions and takes part in important decision-making groups. If a group or class is highly overrepresented or underrepresented in relation to its proportion of the population, it can be inferred that the group is relatively powerful or powerless, as the case may be. For example, when women are in only a small percentage of the leadership positions in business and government, even though they make up a majority of the population, it can be inferred that they

---

*"Social democrats" come from a tradition that began with a socialist orientation and then moved in a more reformist direction. For the most part, social democratic parties have only slightly more ambitious goals than the liberal-labor coalition in the United States; the liberal-labor coalition in the United States would feel at home in a social democratic party in western Europe.

are relatively powerless in these arenas. Similarly, when a minority group has only a small percentage of its members in leadership positions, even though it comprises 10 to 20 percent of the population in a given city or state, then the basic processes of power—inclusion and exclusion—are inferred to be at work.

This indicator also can be shown to vary over time and place. The decline of landed aristocrats and the rise of business leaders in Great Britain has been charted through their degree of representation in Parliament, for example. Then, too, as women, African-Americans, Latinos, and Asian-Americans began to demand a greater voice in the United States in the 1960s and 1970s, their representation in positions of authority began to increase.[20]

Who Wins?

There are many issues over which groups or classes disagree. In the United States, different policies are proposed by the corporate-conservative and liberal-labor coalitions on foreign policy, taxation, unionization, business regulation, welfare, and the environment. Power can be inferred from these issue conflicts by determining who successfully initiates, modifies, or vetoes policy alternatives. This indicator, by focusing on actions within the decision-making process, comes closest to approximating the process of power contained in the formal definition. It is the indicator most preferred by pluralists. For many reasons, it is also the most difficult to use accurately. Aspects of a decision process may remain hidden, some informants may exaggerate or downplay their roles, and people's memories about who did what often become cloudy shortly after the event. These are just three among several problems.[21]

Who Shines?

The fourth and final indicator, "Who shines?", is derived from a person's or group's reputation for being powerful, as determined by a series of interviews. In addition to being a good way to discover a power group when there is little information available on value distributions or social backgrounds, it is valuable for learning about the interactions among the top leaders within a power group and about the settings within which they operate. The sociologist who developed this approach, Floyd Hunter, in an allusion to anthropological studies in little-known areas of the world, often called it the "take-me-to-your-leader" method. The process begins with nominations by a cross-section of observers who are thought to be knowledgeable about the powerful on the basis of their occupational roles (e.g., reporter, administrator,

Table 1.3 Hypothetical Membership Network

Individuals	Organizations			
	A	B	C	D
1	X	X		
2	X		X	
3	X			X
4			X	X
5				

Note: Person 5 is an "isolate" with no connections.

fund-raiser). The people nominated by this cross-section of observers are then interviewed and asked for their nominations as well as their opinions regarding the power of the other people on the original list. Any new nominees are then interviewed and asked for their opinions. The process ends, usually within three or four rounds, when the same names keep coming up and no new names are added to the list. This approach, called the reputational method, probably works best at the community or city level, where it is less expensive and time-consuming to apply, but it has been used with good results in two studies of national power in the United States.[22]

All four of these power indicators have proven to be useful in a wide range of studies, but each has its strengths and weaknesses, as with any indicators in the social sciences. Not only do studies of who wins and loses on specific issues have risks, as pointed out earlier in this section, but the value distributions that determine "who benefits" may be in part determined by unintended consequences or by actions of the powerful to extend some benefits downward.[23] In the case of the "Who governs?" indicator, people in leadership positions sometimes have only formal authority and no "real" power. As for the reputational method, bias might be introduced by the way the original cross-section of informants is chosen, by the wording of the questions asked, by unwarranted newspaper publicity for some people, or by a strong leadership role on only a single issue.[24]

However, these potential weaknesses present no serious problem if the perspective of multiple indicators outlined earlier is used because each indicator involves different kinds of information drawn from very different types of investigatory procedures. The case is considered most convincing if all four types of indicators point to one particular group or social class. The way in which the power indica-

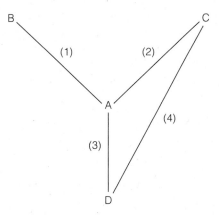

Figure 1.2 Hypothetical Organization Network Created by Overlapping Members (for example, A and B are connected by Person 1)

tors fit into the general study of power is explained at the end of the next section.

METHODS: NETWORK ANALYSIS AND CONTENT ANALYSIS

The empirical study of social power begins with a search for connections among the people and organizations that are thought to constitute the powerful group or class. This procedure is called *membership network analysis*. The results of a membership network analysis are usually presented in the form of a matrix, as shown in table 1.3. The people are listed from top to bottom, and the organizations are arrayed from left to right. The "cells" or boxes created by the intersection of a person and organization are filled with "relational" information such as "member," "director," "owner," or "financial donor." The attitudes the person has toward any given organization in the matrix also can be included, such as "supporter" or "opponent." The information used in filling the cells of the matrix is obtained in a variety of ways described in the next section.

The information contained in the matrix is used to create two different kinds of networks: *organizational* and *interpersonal*. An organizational network displays the relationships among organizations as determined by their common (or "overlapping") members. These member-created ties among organizations are sometimes called *interlocks*, especially in studies of relationships among corporations. Figure 1.2 displays an organizational network based on the overlapping members in table 1.3. It shows that organization A is at the center of

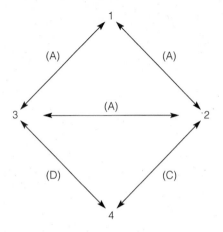

Figure 1.3 Hypothetical Interpersonal Network Created by Common Organizational Affiliations (for example, persons 1 and 3 are connected through organization A)

the network. An interpersonal network, on the other hand, reveals the relationships among individuals as determined by their common organizational affiliations. It is the organizational network turned inside-out, so to speak. Figure 1.3 shows the interpersonal network that emerges from table 1.3. Note that no one person is at the center of the network even though the organizational network had a center. Note also that one person is an "isolate," with no connections, a common situation for most Americans in terms of power networks.

A membership network is in principle very simple, but it is theoretically important because it contains the two types of human relationships of concern in sociological theorizing: interpersonal relations and memberships in organizations. In the words of sociologist Ronald Brieger, one of the first to recognize the implications of membership networks, they contain a "duality of persons and groups." For analytical purposes, the organizational and interpersonal networks are often treated separately, but in reality there is always a "duality of persons and groups."[25]

Large, complicated membership networks have been analyzed using computer software based on sophisticated mathematical techniques such as graph theory, matrix algebra, and Boolean algebra (an algebra that detects "hierarchies" or "levels" in a large complex network). Analyses using these methods are presented in later chapters.

Once the membership networks have been established, a second step can be taken: the tracing of the size and direction of money flows in the network. In theory, money flows are another kind of relationship between people or institutions, but in practice it is a good idea to consider them separately because they are socially distinct in most people's minds. There are four kinds of money flows:

1. people to people (e.g., gifts, loans, campaign donations);
2. people to institutions (e.g., taxes to government, individual or family gifts to foundations);
3. institutions to people (e.g., corporate dividends to stockholders, foundation grants to research experts);
4. institutions to institutions (e.g., foundation grants to policy discussion groups, corporate donations to foundations).

The first finding from network analyses using relational data or money flows is whether the group or class under consideration actually exists as a social reality. If no connections among corporations are found, for example, then it makes no sense to speak of a "corporate community." If there are few or no overlapping memberships among exclusive social clubs in different cities, then it is less likely that there is a nationwide "upper class." If there are no money flows from wealthy people to foundations or from foundations to policy discussion groups, then there is very little basis for talking about a "policy-formation network."

The second finding from membership network analysis concerns various characteristics of organizational and interpersonal networks, such as their density and the existence of central points or subgroups. Some parts in a social network may have more interconnections than others, for example, or some types of businesses might be more central in the corporate community, or there might be moderately conservative and extremely conservative subgroups within the overall policy-formation network. In fact, findings of these kinds are reported in later chapters.

Once a membership network is constructed, it is possible to take the next necessary step in the study of social power: an analysis of the ideology and policy preferences of the group or class under scrutiny. This is done by studying the verbal and written "output" of strategically located people or organizations in the network—that is, speeches, policy statements, campaign literature, and proposed legislation. Technically speaking, such studies are called *content analysis* in the social sciences. Content analyses are not always done formally, but content analysis is what investigators are doing when they infer on the basis of a speech or policy statement that a person or organization has specific values or policy preferences. That is, many content analyses are informal and intuitive, based on implicit categories that exist in the culture. To ensure against personal biases, however, an objective and systematic content analysis is far more useful.[26]

A systematic content analysis usually begins with the creation of carefully defined categories that relate to the attitude or issue being studied. Categories can be constructed, for example, to determine a person or organization's stance toward corporations, environmental regulation, or the ideal role for the federal government in dealing with racial injustices. Once the categories are developed, relevant texts are studied to determine the frequency and intensity of elements that fit into one or more of the categories. Then the various frequencies are analyzed by calculating averages or percentages. Finally, the averages or percentages for two or more groups are compared. Using this approach, for example, the attitudes toward government expressed in institutional advertisements by various types of corporations have been analyzed, finding that large corporations are more prone to talk of a partnership with government than smaller ones, and the speeches of a wide range of corporate executives have been studied for possible differences in concern for consumer rights and corporate social responsibility, revealing that corporate executives whose firms sell directly to the public are far more likely to be supportive on these issues than executives from firms that sell primarily to other corporations.[27]

Thanks to computers, content analyses now can be done without a set of predefined categories by using programs that determine what concepts or phrases are interconnected in documents, a technique known as semantic network analysis. Applying this technique to aspects of the annual reports from thirty-five American and Japanese corporations, it was found that American reports discussed financial and structural information, while Japanese reports focused on organizational operations.[28]

Now that membership network analysis and content analysis have been explained, a generic definition of the term *power structure* can be provided: A power structure is a network of people and institutions that stands at the top of the four power indicators in the city or nation being studied. This definition can be employed by researchers of any theoretical persuasion because the methodological approach outlined in this section makes it possible to discover any concentration or configuration of power. It is not biased toward any given theory. It can show that power is highly concentrated or more dispersed, depending on the degree of difference between rival networks on the power indicators. It can show that some groups or classes have power in one arena, some in another arena. It can show changes in a power structure over time by changes in the power indicators.

Although the methodological approach described in this section can be used in a generic way, in this book it is used to answer what is, in effect, a series of specific questions that follow one from the other: Are there (1) a corporate community, (2) a social upper class, and (3) a policy-formation network that (4) intersect with each other and (5) score at the top in terms of all four power indicators?

THE SOURCES OF INFORMATION

I used several different sources of information to construct membership networks and answer the five questions just posed. First, a wide variety of biographical reference volumes, magazines, and newspapers provided relational information. They include the eighteen different *Who's Who*s published by Marquis, which contain 770,000 names on a CD-ROM; the hundreds of magazines on MAGS in the University of California's computerized library information system (Melvyl); and the five newspapers included in NEWS on the same system (*New York Times, Los Angeles Times, Washington Post, Wall Street Journal*, and *Christian Science Monitor*). Also, I consulted *Who Knows Who*, Standard and Poor's *Register of Corporations and Directors*, the *Foundation Directory*, the *Foundation Grants Index*, and the annual reports of many organizations.

The second major source of information for this book is the large number of network and content studies done by other social scientists. Research on power is a cumulative effort, and it would not be possible to construct a general picture without the dozens of specific studies by others on a wide range of topics. Third, the book draws on interview and observational studies by other social scientists and me. Such studies are necessary when published information is not available and to flesh out the personal and subjective dimensions in the exercise of power.

Finally, to establish the importance of the policy-formation network in shaping government policy, the book sometimes draws on detailed historical case studies. Such studies do not have the immediacy and personal relevance that many readers prefer, but they are necessary for a full understanding of the American power elite's impact. It is often difficult to do complete and accurate studies of contemporary issues, especially, for example, when some of the key decision makers believe it might compromise their current power roles to talk freely or allow researchers to see their personal and governmental papers, or when they don't want to hurt the feelings of other participants. Also, some commentators reporting on current policy issues on the basis of "inside sources" may be misinformed or self-serving. What is said in best-selling books or on television about the here-and-now by Washington observers is often proven wrong later in historical studies.

WHAT LIES AHEAD

Because the argument in this book challenges some basic American beliefs as well as prevailing theories in the social sciences, it is necessary to proceed in a deliberate fashion, defining each concept as it is introduced and providing empirical examples of how each part of the system works. By approaching the problem in this manner, readers can draw their own conclusions at each step of the way and decide for themselves if they think the argument fails at some point.

Each chapter presents one aspect of a cumulative argument. In the second chapter, evidence is presented for the existence of a nationwide corporate community that includes corporate lawyers, military contractors, and agribusinesses as well as large and well-known corporations like General Motors, General Electric, Exxon, and IBM. It also explains the nature of local growth coalitions.

Chapter 3 shows that the owners and top-level executives in the corporate community form a socially cohesive and clearly demarcated upper class that has created its own social institutions and a distinctive lifestyle. I argue that the social bonds developed by the corporate rich combine with their common economic interests to make it easier to overcome policy disagreements when they meet in the policy-formation network.

Chapter 4 demonstrates that the corporate rich finance and direct the foundations, think tanks, and policy discussion groups that make up the policy-formation network. Through involvement in the policy-formation network, members of the power elite gain an understanding of general issues beyond the confines of their own narrow business problems and discuss policy alternatives that are in their interests as a class.

Chapter 5 describes how several of the organizations in the policy-formation network interact with public relations firms, the public affairs departments of large corporations, and middle-class volunteer groups in an effort to reinforce the individualistic and anti-government dimensions of the American value system and to influence public opinion on specific issues.

Chapter 6 explains the nature of the American electoral system and why it always has had only two major political parties at the national level. It also shows how campaign donations play a critical role in American politics, making support from wealthy donors essential for a successful candidacy at the national level and in highly populated states. The chapter also analyzes the use of citywide elections and the elimination of partisan politics in many cities as a strategy that growth entrepreneurs created to defeat the challenges they were facing from socialists and the Democratic Party in the late nineteenth and early twentieth centuries. Information on the social and occupational backgrounds of presidents and members of Congress is presented, and the reasons for the preponderance of lawyers in elected offices is discussed.

Chapter 7 examines the processes through which the power elite is able to dominate the federal government in Washington. They include the appointment of corporate leaders to important positions in the executive branch under both Democratic and Republican presidents, lobbying Congress and departments of the executive branch on issues of concern to specific corporations or business sectors, and convincing government leaders that policies developed in the policy-formation network are in the best interests of everyone. The conflicts between the corporate-conservative and liberal-labor coalitions on several major issues in the 1980s and 1990s are examined. Classic and widely cited case studies of alleged victories for the liberal-labor coalition are dissected and found wanting.

The eighth and final chapter discusses the future of American politics in light of the previous chapters and ongoing social changes. I suggest that the Civil Rights Movement has not been fully appreciated for the major change it triggered in Southern politics—namely, the gradual movement of Southern white conservatives into the Republican Party, which makes it possible for a nationwide liberal-labor coalition to utilize the Democratic Party as an educational and power base for the first time in American history. Still, the possibility of a transformed Democratic Party does not mean it is certain to happen. It would require the creation of workable government programs, the emergence of new leaders, the crafting of larger and more liberal black-white voting coalitions in the South than have been developed to date, and an appeal to nonvoters to join the electorate and support a liberal-labor program.

Even if a nationwide liberal-labor coalition were able to transform the Democratic Party, there would be no guarantee of success in changing government policies. The power elite described in this book commands great wealth, the best advice money can buy, and direct access to government officials. It has polished antigovernment ideology and rags-to-riches success stories to a small science. Its allies in "New Right" organizations know how to use divisive social issues to recruit new activists and put liberals on the defensive.

But power structures, no matter how strong or cohesive, are not immutable. No one predicted the New Deal in the face of the Great Depression or the emergence of a massive Civil Rights Movement. No one would have believed in the 1980s that the Soviet Union would give up its Eastern European satellites without a war and then collapse without a violent internal struggle, or that there would be a relatively peaceful transformation of the repressive apartheid system in South Africa, with a long-imprisoned black freedom fighter taking over as president.

All we know for sure is that societies do change and that no one can predict the future. It is in this spirit that the present book unfolds.

NOTES

1. Edward Wolff, *Top Heavy* (New York: The New Press, 1996), pp. 64, 67.
2. Robert R. Alford and Roger Friedland, "Political Participation and Public Policy," *Annual Review of Sociology*, 1 (1975); William A. Gamson, *The Strategy of Social Protest* (Homewood, IL: Dorsey Press, 1975); Frances Piven and Richard Cloward, *Regulating the Poor*, updated ed. (New York: Pantheon, 1993); Frances Piven and Richard Cloward, *Poor People's Movements* (New York: Random House, 1977).
3. David Moberg, "The Resurgence of American Unions: Small Steps, Long Journey," *Working USA*, vol. 1, no. 1 (1997): 22.
4. For the most cogent and clear general statements of institutional elitism in its modern-day form, see G. Lowell Field and John Higley, *Elitism* (London: Routledge and Kegan Paul, 1980); and Michael Burton and John Higley, "Invitation to Elite Theory: The Basic Contentions Reconsidered," in *Power Elites and Organizations*, eds. G. William Domhoff and Thomas R. Dye (Beverly Hills: Sage Publications, 1987), pp. 219–238.
5. Thomas Dye, *Who's Running America? The Clinton Years*, 6th ed. (Englewood Cliffs, NJ: Prentice-Hall, 1995).
6. For clear and insightful discussions of Marxism, see Paul M. Sweezy, *The Theory of Capitalist Development* (New York: Modern Reader Paperbacks, 1942/1968); Bertell Ollman, *Alienation: Marx's Conception of Man in Capitalist Society*, 2d ed. (New York: Cambridge University Press, 1976); Ralph Miliband, *Marxism and Politics* (New York: Oxford University Press, 1977); and Gary Teeple, *Marx's Critique of Politics, 1842–1847* (Toronto: University of Toronto Press, 1984).
7. For thoughtful criticisms of Marxism, see Robert Heilbroner, *Marxism For and Against* (New York: W. W. Norton, 1980); C. Wright Mills, *The Marxists* (New York: Dell, 1962); Michael Mann, *The Sources of Social Power*, vol. 1 (New York: Cambridge University Press, 1986). For my critique of Marxism, see my *The Power Elite and the State* (Hawthorne, NY: Aldine de Gruyter, 1990), chapters 1–4.
8. For a detailed critique of the conspiratorial view, see G. William Domhoff, *The Higher Circles* (New York: Random House, 1970), chapter 8.

9. On the Pentagon Papers, see George Herring, ed., *The Pentagon Papers* (New York: McGraw Hill, 1997). For the effects of the Pentagon Papers on the Nixon Administration, see Fred Emory, *Watergate* (New York: Random House, 1994). On the Iran-contra scandal, see Peter Kornbluh and Malcolm Byrne, eds., *The Iran-contra Scandal: The Declassified History* (New York: The New Press, 1993); Theodore Draper, *A Very Thin Line: The Iran-Contra Affair* (New York: Hill and Wang, 1991); and Lawrence Walsh, *Firewall: The Iran-Contra Conspiracy and Cover-up* (New York: W. W. Norton, 1997).

10. Morton Halperin, Jerry Erman, Robert Borosage, and Christine Marwick, *The Lawless State: The Crimes of U.S. Intelligence Agencies* (New York: Penguin Books, 1976); James K. Davis, *Spying on America* (New York: Praeger, 1992).

11. Robert Palmer, *The Age of the Democratic Revolution*, vol. 1 (Princeton: Princeton University Press, 1959), pp. 213, 222. See also Gordon S. Wood, *The Radicalism of the American Revolution* (New York: Alfred A. Knopf, 1992), chapter 14, and Michael Mann, *The Sources of Social Power*, vol. 2 (New York: Cambridge University Press, 1993), chapter 5.

12. Dennis Wrong, *Power: Its Forms, Bases, and Uses* (New York: Harper & Row, 1979), p. 21.

13. Robert A. Dahl, "The Concept of Power," *Behavioral Science*, 2 (1957): 202–203.

14. Wrong, *Power*, p. 2.

15. Bertrand Russell, *Power: A New Social Analysis* (London: George Allen & Unwin, 1938), pp. 10–11; Michael Mann, op. cit., vol. 1, is the most eloquent current sociological voice against the claim for "primacy" for any one form of power.

16. Paul Lazarsfeld, "Concept Formation and Measurement," in *Concepts, Theory, and Explanation in the Behavioral Sciences*, ed. Gordon J. DiRenzo (New York: Random House, 1966).

17. Eugene T. Webb, Donald T. Campbell, Richard D. Schwartz, Lee Sechrest, and Janet Belew Grove, *Nonreactive Measures in the Social Sciences*, 2d ed. (Boston: Houghton Mifflin, 1981), p. 35.

18. Christopher Hewitt, "The Effect of Political Democracy and Economic Democracy on Equality in Industrial Societies," *American Sociological Review*, 42 (1977). The strength of this relationship has declined in recent years, but that does not negate the methodological point made here.

19. John Stephens, *The Transition from Capitalism to Socialism* (Atlantic Highlands, NJ: Humanities Press, 1980), chapter 4.

20. W. L. Guttsman, *The British Political Elite* (New York: Basic Books 1963); Dahl, *Who Governs?*, chapters 1–5; Ralph Miliband, *The State in Capitalist Society* (New York: Basic Books, 1969), p. 177. For the increasing number of women and minorities in positions of authority in the United States, see Richard L. Zweigenhaft and G. William Domhoff, *Diversity in the Power Elite* (New Haven: Yale University Press, 1998).

21. See G. William Domhoff, *Who Rules America?* (Englewood Cliffs, NJ: Prentice-Hall, 1967), pp. 6–7, 144–146, and Raymond Bauer, "Social

Psychology and the Study of Policy Formation," *American Psychologist*, 21 (1966) for detailed comments on the difficulties of decision-making studies of power.

22. The two national studies are by Floyd Hunter, *Top Leadership USA* (Chapel Hill: University of North Carolina Press, 1957), and Gwen Moore, "The Structure of a National Elite Network," *American Sociological Review*, 44 (1979): 673–692. For excellent abstracts of all studies of community power using the reputational method, see Willis D. Hawley and James H. Svara, *The Study of Community Power: A Bibliographic Review* (Santa Barbara, CA: American Bibliographic Center/Clio Press, 1972). There were very few reputational studies done at the community level after 1972.

23. Nelson Polsby, *Community Power and Political Theory*, 2d ed. (New Haven, CT: Yale University Press, 1980), p. 132.

24. Raymond Wolfinger, "Reputation and Reality in the Study of Community Power," *American Sociological Review*, 25 (1960): 636–644. For empirical evidence gathered by a skeptical pluralist showing that the method is far better than Wolfinger claimed, see M. Kent Jennings, *Community Influentials: The Elites of Atlanta* (New York: Free Press, 1964), pp. 24, 25, 156, 164.

25. Ronald Breiger, "The Duality of Persons and Groups," *Social Forces*, 53 (1974): 181–190. The distinction between interpersonal contacts and common membership is also central to social identity theory within social psychology. On this point, see the critique of studies on the nature of small groups by Michael Hogg, *The Social Psychology of Group Cohesiveness* (New York: New York University Press, 1992).

26. Robert Weber, *Basic Content Analysis*, 2d ed. (Newbury Park, CA: Sage Publications, 1990).

27. Francis Sutton, *The American Business Creed* (Cambridge: Harvard University Press, 1956); Maynard Seider, "Big Business Ideology: A Content Analysis of Executive Speeches," *American Sociological Review*, 39 (1974): 802–815; Maynard Seider, "Corporate Ownership, Control and Ideology: Support for Behavioral Similarity," *Sociology and Social Research*, 62 (1977): 113–128.

28. Ha-Yong Jang, "Cultural Differences in Organizational Communication: A Semantic Network Analysis," *Bulletin de Methodologie Sociologique*, 44 (1994): 31–59. For a general discussion of methods of analyzing texts, see Carl Roberts, ed., *Text Analysis for the Social Sciences* (Mahwah, NJ: Erlbaum, 1997).

2

The Corporate Community and the Growth Coalitions

This chapter describes the nationwide corporate community and the local growth coalitions that are at the center of power in American society. It explains the role of corporate boards of directors. It shows that corporate lawyers, military contractors, and agribusinesses are part of the corporate community, and that the large number of small businesses do not provide an organized counterweight to the corporate community. The relationship between the corporate community and the growth coalitions is analyzed.

The corporate community is defined as all those profit-seeking organizations connected into a common network. For research purposes, the most visible and useful ties are those created by people who sit on two or more corporate boards. There are other types of links as well, such as common ownership, long-standing patterns of supply and purchase, and the use of the same legal, accounting, advertising, and public relations firms. Large corporations, banks, and other interconnected firms also come together as a corporate community—despite the competition among them—because they share the same goals and values, especially the profit motive. Finally, and just as important as any other factor, they develop a closeness because they are all opposed and criticized to some degree by the labor movement, environmentalists, liberals, leftists, and other types of anticorporate activists.

The corporate community and growth coalitions maintain two types of organizations for purposes of relating to each other and government. First, they have trade associations made up of all the businesses in a specific industry or sector of the economy. Thus, there is the American Petroleum Institute, the American Bankers Association, the National Association of Home Builders, and hundreds of similar organizations that focus on the narrow interests of their members. Second, there are more general organizations like the National Association of Manufacturers, the Chamber of Commerce of the United States, and the Business Roundtable that look out for the general interests of the corporate community and the growth coalitions. In the case of the National Association of Manufacturers and its many state affiliates, for example, one of its foremost concerns for over ninety years has been all-out opposition to labor unions in any part of the economy. As for the Business Roundtable, it has coordinated the corporate community against a wide range of challenges from the liberal-labor coalition since the 1970s. For growth coalitions, as noted in the first chapter, it is usually the local chapter of the Chamber of Commerce that focuses on general issues; in larger cities, however, there is often a smaller and more prestigious organization representing the biggest real estate owners and developers as well.

The corporations and banks in the corporate community control a great proportion of the country's economic activity. According to useful calculations by Dye, just five giant corporations—General Electric, General Motors, Ford Motor, IBM, and Exxon—have 28 percent of all industrial assets, and the top 100 have almost 75 percent. Eleven banks have 33 percent of all commercial banking assets; the top fifty have 62 percent. The levels of concentration are roughly the same for other major business sectors, such as insurance and public utilities, although retailing is somewhat less concentrated.[1] These figures reflect a gradual increase in economic concentration over the space of the twentieth century. A merger movement between 1895 and 1904 gave the corporate community its current configuration. The history of the corporate community is discussed later in the chapter.

THE BOARD OF DIRECTORS

The board of directors is the official governing body of the corporation. Usually composed of from ten to fifteen members, but including as many as twenty-five in the case of commercial banks, it meets for a day or two at a time about ten times a year and receives reports and other information between meetings. Various board committees meet from time to time with top managers as well. A smaller executive committee of the board often meets more frequently, and its most important individual members are sometimes in regular contact with the top management that handles the day-to-day affairs of the corporation. The most important duty of the board of directors is to hire and fire top management, but it also is responsible for accepting or rejecting major policy changes. Boards seem to play their most important role when there is conflict within management, the corporation is in economic distress, or there is the possibility of a merger or acquisition.[2]

Although the board is the official governing body, it is often the case that the company executives on the board, who are called "inside directors," play a great role in shaping the board's decisions. These inside directors, perhaps in conjunction with two or three of the non-management directors (called "outside directors"), are able to set the agenda for meetings, shape board thinking on policy decisions, and select new outside directors. When the company is doing well, the board may become little more than a sounding board and source of advice for management, with the top managers having great influence in naming their successors in running the company.

The exact role of the board may vary from corporation to corporation, but boards of directors in general nonetheless embody the complex power relations within the corporate community. In addition to their role in selecting top management and dealing with crises, their importance manifests itself in a number of ways. They speak for the corporation to the rest of the corporate community and to the public at large. New owners demand seats on boards to consolidate their positions and to have a "listening post." Conflicts over hostile merger attempts may be concluded by electing the top officers of the rival corporations to each other's boards. Commercial bankers may seek seats on boards to keep track of their loans and to ensure that future business will be directed their way. The chief executives of leading companies take time from their busy schedules to be on two or three other boards because it is a visible sign that their advice is respected outside their home company, and board memberships provide them with general intelligence on the state of the business world as well. Also, the presence of investment bankers, corporate lawyers, and academic experts on a board is a sign that their expertise is respected by the corporations. The appointment of a university president, former government official, well-known woman, or highly visible minority group leader is a sign that their high status and respectability are regarded as valuable to the image of the corporation.

There is evidence that corporate officials recognize the symbolic importance of the board of directors. As one president told business professor Myles Mace in his interview study with top executives:

> When I look at a company, I look at who is on the board. I don't know how good a criterion it is, but I form a judgment—is it a responsible kind of outfit, or is it a marginal high-flyer? The type of people on a board does, in a series of informal and intangible

ways, have a great deal to do with what the character of a company is. Is it a respectable and conservative company, or is it highly speculative? The investing public, you know, really cares who is on the board.[3]

Another said: "You want to communicate to the various publics that if any large company is good enough to attract the president of a large New York bank as a director, for example, it just has to be a great company."[4]

Boards of directors are important for another reason. In the broadest sense, they are the interface between individual corporations and the general society. More specifically, I see them as the intersection between organized bureaucracies and social classes. As such, they are one of the means by which I attempt to create a synthesis of class-dominance theory and several major insights from organizational theory.

The organizational perspective is represented on the board of directors by the inside directors who are full-time employees of the corporation. They are concerned that the organization survive and that any new initiatives have a minimal effect on routine functioning. They see outside directors as "ambassadors" of the organization who help to reduce uncertainty in the organization's environment by linking with other corporations and government. The class perspective is represented by those outside directors who own a significant percentage of the company's stock or are members of the upper class. Such directors want to ensure that any given corporation fits well with their other investments and profit-making opportunities and does not jeopardize new policy initiatives or general public acceptance in the political realm. Outside directors have a number of "resources" that make it possible for them to represent a class perspective; these include their own wealth, their directorships at other corporations and nonprofit organizations, their general understanding of business and investment, and their many relationships with other wealthy people, fund-raisers, and politicians. Such resources make it possible for them to have a very real impact when new leadership must be selected or new policy directions must be undertaken.[5]

THE CORPORATE COMMUNITY

As noted at the outset of the chapter, the corporate community is indexed for purposes of this book in terms of interlocking directorates, even though common stock ownership and other factors are also important in shaping it. Two studies, the first by sociologist Peter Mariolis for the 1970s, the other by me on the 1990s for this book, provide a detailed analysis of the modern-day corporate community.

Table 2.1 Number of Network Connections
for 1,029 Corporations in 1996

Number of Connections	Frequency	Cumulative Percent
28–45	28	2.7
20–27	65	9.0
15–19	102	19.0
10–14	146	33.1
5–9	226	55.1
2–4	241	78.5
1	93	87.6
0	128	100.0

Source: *Who Knows Who* (Detroit: Gale Research, Inc., 1997), chap. 4.

Other studies make it possible to trace the origins of interlocking directorates to the early nineteenth century and the contours of corporate community as it exists today to the turn of the twentieth century.

The corporate community is very large, encompassing 90 percent of the 800 corporations Mariolis studied for the 1970s, 87.6 percent of the 1,029 I looked at for 1996. Furthermore, most corporations are within three or four "steps" of any other, but for practical purposes only the first two steps are relevant because most directors, like people in any setting, cannot see beyond the "friends of friends" level.[6] Although large, the network is not generally very dense because most corporations have only one to nine connections to the rest of the network. On the other hand, the largest corporations usually have ten or more connections, and some have as many as twenty-eight to forty-five. The exact figures for the number of connections among the top 1,029 corporations in 1996 are presented in table 2.1.

Generally speaking, the corporations with the most connections are also the corporations that are in the center of the network. This point is demonstrated by studying the number of connections that the most highly connected firms have with each other. Table 2.2 presents the interconnections for the twenty-eight companies with twenty-eight or more interlocks. Twenty-four of the twenty-eight have three or more connections with one another; American Express and Sara Lee head the list with nine ties each in the top group; Chase Manhattan Bank, General Motors, and Procter and Gamble have eight; and Prudential Insurance, Minnesota Mining and Manufacturing, and Mobil Oil have seven. Of the four companies with two or fewer connections within the top twenty-eight, two are banks in San Francisco

Table 2.2 The 28 Most Connected Corporations for 1996 and Their Connections to One Another (Financial Companies Marked by Asterisks)

Company	Total Number of Connections	Connections among the Top 28
Chase Manhattan Bank*	45	8
Wells Fargo Bank*	41	2
American Express*	40	9
Prudential Insurance*	39	7
Sara Lee Foods	39	9
Minnesota Mining and Manufacturing	37	7
General Motors	33	8
Kroger Stores	33	5
Ashland Oil	32	3
Bank of America*	32	1
CSX (railroad)	32	2
Bell Atlantic	31	6
Coca-Cola	31	3
Procter and Gamble	31	8
Spring Industries	31	6
AMR	30	4
Mobil Oil	30	7
TRW	30	3
Xerox	30	4
Ameritech	29	5
Bell South	29	3
Union Pacific	29	6
Westinghouse Electric	29	4
Burlington Northern	28	2
Cummins Engine	28	4
Kellogg	28	6
Kmart	28	4
Time Warner	28	6

Source: *Who Knows Who* (Detroit: Gale Research, Inc., 1997), p. 749. Reprinted with permission of Gale Research.

Table 2.3 Examples of How Corporations with One Connection Link to the Top 28

Company	Linking Corporation	Linking Corporation's Connection to the Top 28
A. G. Edwards	Helig-Meyers	CSX
Ascend	Silicon Graphics	Mobil, Prudential, Sara Lee
Bally Co.	First Union Bank	Bell Atlantic
Dimm Co.	First Union Bank	Bell Atlantic
Big Flowers Press	Host Marriott	AMR
First Federal Savings	Teledyne	Wells Fargo & Co. Bank
Glendale Federal Savings	Teledyne	Wells Fargo & Co. Bank
Unitrin	Teledyne	Wells Fargo & Co. Bank

that have most of their many connections to corporations located on the West Coast. The other two are railroad companies.

The most highly connected corporations are usually financial ones—banks, insurance companies, and credit card companies. The centrality of financial companies is one of the network's most striking and consistent features, dating back to the earliest years for which information can be assembled. Contrary to the claim by pluralist sociologist Gerald Davis, financial companies did not decline in centrality due to the takeover movement of the 1980s. Three of the ten most interlocking companies were financials in 1989, six in 1991 and 1993, and five in 1996.[7]

The centrality of the 28 firms with the most connections also is shown by their links to other highly interlocked corporations. Of the 313 firms with between ten and twenty-seven connections, 226 (72.2 percent) have at least one tie to the top 28. In addition, every one of the 81 corporations without a link to the top 28 has at least one connection (and most have three or more) to the 226 with a link. More generally, a representative sample of 400 companies in the overall network showed that 39 percent of them had at least one direct tie to the central group of 28. This means that the network tends to radiate out in concentric circles from its central core, but even that image does not capture the full picture because some corporations with only two or three connections are linked directly to the top 28 and still more are only one step removed from it. Examples of this two-step relationship for 8 corporations with only one network tie are given in table 2.3.

Aside from some tendency to regional concentrations, there are no subgroups or "cliques" within the corporate community, at least as measured by director interlocks. Instead, as the findings in the previous paragraphs reveal, there tends to be a very general core with smaller corporations around the periphery. Further evidence for this conclusion comes from the fact that corporate connections "broken" by the death or retirement of a director are not very often "restored" by a new director from closely related companies, which is what would be expected if the companies were part of a subgroup. New directors usually come from a small general pool of people who are highly visible in the corporate community; they often have several directorships already. Thus, the main constants in the network are its large size, the centrality of financial firms and top industrials, and slight shifts in the degree of a corporation's interlocks when directors are replaced.[8]

THE ORIGINS OF THE CORPORATE COMMUNITY

The corporate community had its origins in the earliest jointly owned companies in the textile industry in New England in the late eighteenth and early nineteenth centuries. At that time the common directors reflected the fact that a small group of wealthy Boston merchants were joining together in varying combinations to invest in new companies. By 1845 a group of eighty men, known to historians as the "Boston Associates," controlled thirty-one textile companies that accounted for 20 percent of the nation's textile industry. Seventeen served as directors of Boston banks that owned 40 percent of the city's banking capital, twenty were directors of six insurance companies, and eleven sat on the boards of five railroad companies.[9]

Meanwhile, wealthy investors were creating commonly owned and directed companies in other cities as well, as shown for New York in detailed archival work by economist David Bunting. For 1816, the earliest year for which Bunting could assemble systematic information from the few surviving records, he found that the ten largest banks and ten largest insurance companies were linked into one network; ten of the companies had from eleven to twenty-six interlocks, six had six to ten interlocks, and four had one to five interlocks. The figures are not much different for 1836, when the twenty largest banks, ten largest insurance companies, and ten largest railroads could be determined: thirty-eight of the forty were linked into one common network, with twelve of the thirty-eight having eleven to twenty-six interlocks, ten having six to ten interlocks, and sixteen having one to five interlocks. Some sense of the economic potency of this network can be found in the concentration of banking assets that Bunting discovered for 1842: The ten largest banks had 70 percent of the bank assets in New York City and 40 percent of the bank assets in the entire state.[10]

Further work by Bunting and sociologist William Roy shows that this network of financial companies and railroads persisted in roughly its mid-century form until it was transformed between 1895 and 1904 by a massive merger movement, creating huge industrial corporations that were drawn into the formal network for the first time.[11] Until that point, industrial companies had been organized as partnerships among a few men or families. They tended to stand apart from the financial institutions and the stock market. Roy's careful study of the development of the enlarged corporate community found no economic efficiencies that might explain the relatively sudden incorporation of industrial companies. Instead, it seems more likely that industrials had to adopt the "corporate" form of organization and merge into larger companies for a variety of historical, legal, and sociological reasons. The most important of these reasons was a need to (1) regulate the competition among the industrialists that was driving down profits and (2) gain better legal protection against the middle-class reformers, populist farmers, and socialists who had mounted an unrelenting critique of "the trusts"—meaning agreements among industrialists to fix prices, divide up markets, and/or share profits. When such agreements were outlawed by the Sherman Anti-Trust Act of 1890, and a major economic depression and worker strikes followed in the early 1890s, the stage was set for industrialists to resort to the legal device called a "corporation."[12]

These findings on nineteenth-century corporate networks and the reasons for their enlargement at the turn of the twentieth century have major implications for standard historical accounts. First, they call into question theories claiming that American business evolved from family ownership to banking control to managerial and then general institutional control. In fact, the first large American businesses were owned and controlled by groups of well-to-do merchants who shared common economic interests and social ties even more than kinship ties. Moreover, banks and insurance companies were providing investment capital from the start, even if it was not the very large sums that were raised in the second half of the century by the investment bankers who played a central role in the merger movement. That is, "other people's money"—meaning the deposits and premiums held by banks and insurance companies—was part of the system from the beginning, not a later addition.

Also, control of corporations by directors and high-level executives was an early feature of the American business system, not a change that occurred when stockholders allegedly lost control of companies to bankers or managers in the first half of the twentieth century. Finally, these findings challenge the usual claim that corporate mergers and restructuring are sensible and efficient responses to changing technology and markets, a claim that leaves little room for a concern with power. Instead, both are at least in part responses to class conflict and legal changes, even though it is also true that improvements in transportation and communication made such changes possible. If the conventional economic view is called into question by these findings, then an analysis of American society based in class and power becomes more plausible as a challenge to those social scientists who claim that "rational choices" by individuals in a wide variety of "marketplaces" are the best starting point for social analysis.

THE CORPORATE COMMUNITY IN THE TWENTIETH CENTURY

Separate studies by Bunting, Roy, and sociologist Mark Mizruchi, each using different methods, reveal that the corporate community has been remarkably stable since it became nationwide during the merger movement. It always includes the largest corporations and banks, and financial companies are always at the center. The three main changes found in a study by Mizruchi covering the years 1904 to 1974 seem to reflect a gradual economic and financial transformation. First, railroads became more peripheral as they gradually declined in economic importance. Second, manufacturing firms became more central as they increased in economic importance. Third, as corporations became more independent of banks, the banks became less likely to place their top officers on nonbank boards and more likely to receive officers of nonbank corporations on their own boards. According to Mizruchi, this reversal of flow may reflect the gradual transformation of banks from major power centers to places of coordination and communication.[13]

Although there have been only minor adjustments in the structure of the corporate community in terms of interlock patterns, there have been changes within the corporations themselves. Tracing the importance of different divisions within corporations, as most directly reflected by the previous corporate positions held by those who rose to the top at different times in the twentieth century, sociologist Neil Fligstein argues that corporations have had three different internal orientations through which their owners and managers have gauged success. They began with a manufacturing orientation that led to a calculation of success and efficiency by means of production costs.

They then turned to a sales orientation in the 1920s because of a concern with the loss of market share, which led to the measurement of success and efficiency in terms of gross revenues. Still later, a financial definition of success and efficiency was adopted, as measured by stock price and average earnings per share of stock. Like other sociologists who have studied corporations, Fligstein stresses that these changes were due not to rational economic calculations, but to issues of power and control that were created by changes in laws—especially antitrust laws—and by internal struggles for power within corporations. Rather than reflecting an inevitable economic search for an unquestioned something called "efficiency," the changes within the corporations led to new definitions of what was meant by efficiency.[14]

THE DIRECTOR NETWORK AS AN "INNER CIRCLE"

Who are the directors who create a corporate community through their presence on boards of directors? They are 90–95 percent men, 95 percent white, 3–4 percent African-American, and 1–2 percent Latino and Asian-American. Most are business executives, commercial bankers, investment bankers, and corporate lawyers, but there are also a significant minority of university administrators, foundation presidents, former elected officials, and representatives of ethnic and racial minorities.

Compared to three or four decades ago, there is somewhat greater diversity in the corporate community in terms of the number of women and minorities, a response to the social movements that emerged in the 1960s. There is irony in this diversity, however, because the social class and educational backgrounds of the women and minorities tend to be similar to those of their white male counterparts. They also share the Christian religion and Republican politics with most of the white males. In the case of African-American and Latino corporate directors, they tend to have lighter skin color than leaders within their own communities. Based on this and other information, there is reason to believe that white male directors select new women and minority directors who are similar to them in class, education, and skin color. There is also evidence that women and minority directors usually share the same perspectives on business and government as other directors.[15] (The next chapter presents information on the social and educational backgrounds of all corporate directors and executives.)

Approximately 15–20 percent of all directors sit on two or more corporate boards. These people have been labeled the "inner circle" of the corporate community by sociologists Maurice Zeitlin and

Michael Useem. They do not differ demographically from other directors, but they do tend to sit on more nonprofit boards and to be appointed more frequently to government positions, as shown in chapter 7. Thus, the inner circle contributes disproportionately to the activities of the power elite.[16]

The percentage of directors who qualify as members of the inner circle has been very stable over time. The figure was 24 percent in Bunting's study of New York banks and insurance companies in 1816, 18 percent in his 1836 findings. For the fifty-five companies Bunting used in 1891 and 1912, the figures were 13 percent and 17 percent, respectively. Roy reports a figure of 12 percent for a larger sample of companies between 1898 and 1905.[17]

A small number of corporate directors sit on three or more corporate boards. They tend to be major investors, highly successful chief executive officers from large corporations, highly visible women with experience in government, or African-Americans with legal or business backgrounds. It is likely that they have important coordinating roles and therefore gain general prominence in the corporate community.

THE ROLE OF THE CORPORATE NETWORK

Historically, as noted, interlocking directorships reflected shared ownership, and they often expressed power relationships as well. More recently, they seem to serve more diffuse purposes, such as helping corporate leaders to develop common perspectives and gain new insights into how to manage their own companies. Mizruchi, for example, found that interlocked firms tended to support the same political candidates through political action committee (PAC) contributions and to give similar testimony to Congressional committees. According to another study, interlocked firms adopted policies to ward off takeovers in the 1980s more quickly than did other firms.[18]

But the role of specific relationships in the corporate network should not be overstated when it comes to the economic and political issues facing corporations. Interlocks seem to have little or no correlation with the economic performance of companies. They do not link suppliers and producers or co-opt rivals. Instead, the corporate network is of primary use to individual directors as a source of general information. As Useem puts it, corporate directors develop a "business scan" through serving on boards of directors, especially when they are on several.[19]

In short, the corporate network provides a general framework within which common business and political perspectives can gradually develop. I see it as a starting point for a deeper class consciousness that emerges in the social settings and policy groups discussed in the next two chapters. Put another way, knowledge about interlocking directors and the corporate network is useful in understanding corporate power, but it is no substitute for showing how policy views are formed and how government is influenced on specific issues where there is conflict.

STRATEGIC ALLIANCES/PRODUCER NETWORKS

Firms in the corporate community have numerous complex ties not only to one another, but also to multinational firms in other countries and smaller firms in both the United States and abroad. The relations to the multinationals are called "strategic alliances"; the relations with smaller companies create "producer networks." Both types of ties developed more rapidly in the 1970s than they had in the past, perhaps due to increasing world economic competition, including competition within the United States from Japanese and Western European producers of automobiles and steel. This new competition forced American corporations to seek greater flexibility through internal reorganizations, changes in labor relations, and new relations with other companies.[20]

Strategic alliances with foreign multinationals usually focus on a very specific issue, such as research and development, or the creation of one particular product. Thus, IBM, Toshiba (Japan), and Siemens (Germany) entered into an alliance for research and development on a new kind of microchip. General Motors and Toyota developed a joint venture to produce small cars in a plant in Fremont, California, using advanced technology and improved labor relations. The several different types of alliances that five separate American companies created with Siemens are shown in figure 2.1. Such alliances make it possible for large corporations to bypass political barriers blocking their entry into new foreign markets, create new products more quickly by pooling technical know-how, and avoid the expense of start-up costs and head-on competition.

Producer networks, on the other hand, provide supplies and services that give the big corporations at the center the flexibility to rearrange bureaucracies and cut back on employees. In particular, they allow corporations to subcontract or "outsource" for many of the parts and services they need; they thereby outflank unions, which often have difficulty organizing when there are many small companies. Eliminating unions has the effect of lowering wage and benefit costs and allowing less costly health, safety, and work rules. Due to outsourcing, the large corporations continue to hold on to or enlarge

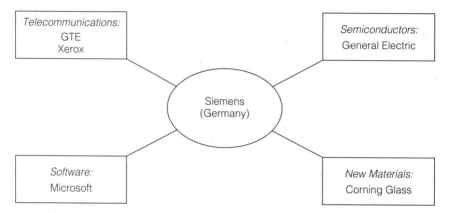

Figure 2.1 Types of Alliances Developed with Siemens by Five American Corporations. Source: Bennett Harrison, *Lean and Mean* (New York: Basic Books, 1994), p. 137. Copyright © 1994 by Bennett Harrison. Reprinted by permission of Basic Books, a division of HarperCollins Publishers, Inc.

their share of sales and profits, but the number of employees has leveled off or declined. Even with outsourcing, however, the largest 1 percent of manufacturing companies still account for 70 percent of all manufacturing jobs. Nor does outsourcing reduce the power of the big corporations. As economist Bennett Harrison concludes after a detailed investigation of all new corporate strategies, "Production may be decentralized into a wider and more geographically far-flung number of work sites, but power, finance, and control remain concentrated in the hands of the managers of the largest companies in the global economy."[21]

As far back as 1961, outsourcing seemed to be a feasible option for cutting union power, but it took a decade for corporations to realize its potential in the face of liberal-labor opposition. The conflict began when the federal government's National Labor Relation Board (NLRB), dominated at the time by Republican appointees, ruled that this practice did not violate union contracts. The ruling was vigorously opposed by liberals and union leaders and was overturned one year later by the liberal appointees of Democratic president John F. Kennedy. Convinced that this new ruling was the opening round in a liberal-labor attack on "management prerogatives," the entire corporate community began to mobilize against any further growth in union power; this mobilization included companies that had maintained formally positive relations with unions for over a decade. Top executives from these companies claimed they were willing to bargain with unions over wages, hours, and working conditions, but not over an issue that involved their rights as managers—

including their right to weaken unions. Their successful battle, won through both court cases and influence on NLRB appointments by the Nixon Administration, culminated in 1971 with a series of rulings against any collective bargaining on management decisions that concerned outsourcing, plant relocations, and plant closings. The Business Roundtable, which has coordinated the corporate community on policy issues since the 1970s, originated in the committees set up to overturn the NLRB's 1961 pro-union ruling on outsourcing.[22]

THE CORPORATE LAWYERS

Some lawyers specialized in corporate law from the beginnings of American corporations. Making up only a few percent of all lawyers, they generally practice in large firms with hundreds of partners and even more "associates," recent law school graduates who work for a salary and aspire to an eventual partnership. Partners routinely earn several hundred thousand dollars each year, and top partners may make several million.

Corporate law firms grew in size and importance in tandem with the large corporations that developed in the second half of the nineteenth century. Their partners played a central role in creating the state-level laws in New Jersey and Delaware that made the corporate form an attractive and safe haven for businesses under pressure from the reformers and socialists trying to pass national laws that would break up or socialize large businesses.[23]

In more recent times, corporate lawyers prepare briefs for key legal cases but rarely appear in court. They advise corporations on how widely or narrowly to interpret requests for information when facing lawsuits over the dangers of their products. They are central to mergers and acquisitions by corporate executives. They also serve as important go-betweens with government, sometimes as heads of major departments of the executive branch, sometimes as White House counsel. After government service, they return to their private practices with new knowledge and contacts that make them even more valuable to their corporate clients.[24]

Corporate lawyers were central figures in the fight over outsourcing discussed in the previous section. Brought together from several major corporations and independent law firms, they formed a committee that drafted new amendments to the existing labor laws and urged government hearings on labor issues. Many drew on experience as former employees or appointees at the National Labor Relations Board. They coordinated discussions with the White House and Congress concerning new appointments to the NLRB. They then helped turn the labor law committees into the Business Roundtable so that the same kind of focused concentration could be brought to bear on other policy issues[25] (several of which are discussed in chapters 4 and 7).

Some social scientists have argued that corporate lawyers, despite these close ties with corporations, are "professionals" with a code of ethics and a commitment to the larger society that set them apart from the corporate community. Dye expresses this sentiment by including them as part of his chapter on "civic associations," discussing them along with directors of cultural institutions and universities.[26] A detailed analysis by sociologist Robert Nelson of four large corporate law firms in Chicago provides the best evidence that these lawyers are an integral part of the corporate community—with a strong loyalty to their clients, not to their profession or code of ethics. As he concludes:

> My central thesis is that lawyers in large firms adhere to an ideology of autonomy, both in their perception of the role of legal institutions in society and the role of lawyers vis-à-vis clients, but that this ideology has little bearing in practice. In the realm of practice these lawyers enthusiastically attempt to maximize the interests of clients and rarely experience serious disagreements with clients over the broader implications of a proposed course of conduct. The dominance of client interests in the practical activities of lawyers contradicts the view that large-firm lawyers serve a mediating function in the legal system.[27]

Nelson finds that corporate lawyers, although closely tied to their clients, and in that sense not independently powerful, are nonetheless important in shaping law schools, the American Bar Association, courts, and political institutions. He concludes that they "maintain and make legitimate the current system for the allocation of rights and benefits," and that they do so for the benefit of their clients: "The influence of these organizations in the legal system derives from and can only serve the interests of corporate clients."[28]

The socialization that creates the mentality found in corporate lawyers has been studied in great detail at Harvard Law School by sociologist Robert Granfield. Based on interviews and classroom observations, he concludes that as a result of a grueling process in which students are stripped of their certainties about their identities and values, they end up actively participating in building "collective identities within law school that all but guarantee that they will become members of America's power elite." More specifically,

> the habits and tastes developed by these students direct the vast majority away from lower status legal positions. In fact, affiliating with the social network at Harvard demands that students

gravitate toward positions in large urban law firms, in spite of the reservations they may harbor.[29]

As a key part of this socialization, students learn that there is no such thing as right or wrong, only differing shades of gray. They need not worry about the guilt or innocence of a client; that is for a judge or jury to decide, so it is their obligation to give their clients the best defense they possibly can. In addition, summer internships provide the students with a taste of the corporate world. They come to feel they must be special to be attending a high-status law school and be sought after by powerful law firms that offer starting salaries of up to $100,000 a year. So, even though a high percentage of students enter prestigious law schools with an interest in public interest law, all but a few percent end up in corporate law firms. Of 11,000 graduates of the eight most prestigious law schools between 1983 and 1987, only 243 took public interest positions.[30]

Not all young lawyers follow the corporate path, of course, and those from lower-status schools are very unlikely to do so. Some become trial lawyers who represent aggrieved or injured individuals or groups in cases against corporations; they are often viewed as the major enemies of corporate lawyers. Other young lawyers work for the government as prosecutors and public defenders. Still others focus on environmental, civil rights, or labor law—in effect siding with the liberal-labor coalition in many instances.

Given this diversity of interests and viewpoints, it makes little sense in terms of a power analysis to talk about lawyers in general as part of a profession that is separate from business and other groups in society, as pluralists and state autonomy theorists often do. Although lawyers do share some qualities that make them useful mediators and politicians (a topic that is discussed at the end of chapter 6), it is important to ascertain, for purposes of power studies, what kind of law a person practices and to realize that corporate lawyers are the hired guns of the corporate community.

DO PENSION FUNDS HAVE CORPORATE POWER?

About half of the stock issued by large corporations is now owned by what are called *institutional investors*. The term encompasses a mixture of entities such as mutual funds, bank trust departments, corporate pension funds, union pension funds, and public employee pension funds that are responsible for investing other people's money in a financially responsible manner. Although public employee pension funds have grown dramatically, most institutional funds are controlled by organizations in the corporate community, as table 2.4

Table 2.4 Percentage of Market Value Held by Five Major Categories for All Corporate Stock in the United States

Type of Holder	1975	1985	1994
Households (privately held)	57	51	48
Personal bank trust funds	11	7	3
Mutual funds	4	5	12
Corporate pension funds	13	20	18
Public pension funds	3	5	8
Total for five categories	88	88	89

Source: Mary Blair, *Ownership and Control* (Washington, DC: The Brookings Institution, 1995), p. 46, table 2.1.

Note: The percentages do not add up to 100 percent because the holdings of commercial banks, savings and loans, insurance companies, closed-end funds, brokers and dealers, and foreign groups are not included.

shows. During the late 1980s and early 1990s, several public employee and union pension funds seemed to be flexing their muscles in corporate meeting rooms, attempting to force policy changes and even changes in management. Their actions raised the possibility of an "investor capitalism" in which government employees and unions could challenge the prerogatives and power of the traditional owners and executives inside the corporate community. But other pension fund managers never joined the effort, and such a challenge seems less and less likely since the high point in the early 1990s.[31]

The idea of public pension fund managers as active participants in corporate governance arose in the mid-1980s when partners at the investment firm of Kohlberg, Kravis, Roberts convinced the head of the pension fund in the state of Oregon to contribute major sums to their takeover projects. Other public pension funds were soon drawn into the action. The liberal treasurer of California and the head of the New Jersey Division of Investment took matters in a new direction in 1985 when they encouraged several public employee and union pension funds to form a Council of Institutional Investors that would help them influence corporate governance through their voting power. The leaders of the New York City Employees Retirement System and the State of Wisconsin Investment Board also supported an activist approach. The goal was to convince corporations to be more open and socially responsible on a variety of issues.

The rise and decline of this effort is mirrored in the career of one of its leaders, Dale Hanson, a longtime state employee in Wisconsin who was appointed head of the California State Employees Retirement System (known as Calpers) in 1987. Hanson made several efforts to influence corporate behavior by introducing various shareholder resolutions calling for more responsiveness to stockholders' concerns. All were overwhelmingly defeated, although a few corporations did alter their policies to allow confidentiality in voting on stockholder resolutions.[32] In 1989, at a secret meeting with members of the Business Roundtable, Hanson and other institutional investors were quietly urged to criticize General Motors for its poor profit performance. Shortly after this attack began, the CEO at General Motors was ousted and new policies were put in place. There followed several other successful public campaigns against CEOs whose companies were performing poorly, and the movement seemed to be launched.[33]

But public pension fund managers are beholden to boards of directors that are in part appointed by governors and state legislators, so it was not long before Hanson and other activists were facing criticism at home. Since Calpers was viewed as the leader of the insurgency, business leaders complained directly to the state's Republican governor. Hanson became especially vulnerable when Calpers itself did not do well in its investment returns for a year or two. By 1993 Hanson was taking a quieter approach. In May 1994, he resigned to become head of American Partners Capital, an investment firm funded by a Republican fundraiser, and a director of ICN Pharmaceuticals, a large California company with 2,500 employees.[34] Faced with similar criticisms from politicians and appointed board members, leaders of other public pension funds adopted a slower and quieter approach, simply meeting with individual CEOs or directors to express their concerns or merely publishing lists of underperforming companies.

The reining-in of the public pension funds was reinforced in 1996 by leadership changes at the Council of Institutional Investors, which by then included insurance companies, mutual funds, and corporate pension funds as well as public and union funds. Although pension fund activists opposed the selection of a corporate pension fund representative to preside over the council, the majority of the members expressed their lack of enthusiasm for activism by electing the director of the TRW Pension Fund as president.* The vote was widely interpreted as a rebuff to the leaders of union funds and activists at public employee funds.[35]

Looking back at the most vigorous days of the movement, from roughly 1988 to 1992, very little was changed or accomplished. Not a single stockholder resolution relating to corporate governance came

---

*TRW, a manufacturing company, was the 125th largest corporation in the United States in the mid-1990s.

close to passing. The most dramatic change in management, that at General Motors, had the tacit support of leaders in the Business Roundtable, and some members of the GM board say that the changes were their own idea.[36] In the end, the success of activists in charge of public employee pension funds depends on the success of the liberal-labor coalition in electing legislators and governors who are supportive of—or at least willing to tolerate—challenges to the management of private corporations. When the Republican governor and conservative legislators in California began to question the activities of Hanson and Calpers, it was not long before the pension fund gradually began to lower its profile.

No one can be sure, but it seems unlikely that institutional investors from public employee and union pension funds ever will be able to create a coalition of institutional investors that could do anything more than chide, chastise, or confer with directors and executives from the large corporations in which they invest. Institutional investors are not a threat to the current power relations in the corporate community. They play their largest role when rival private investors vie for their voting support in takeover battles.[37]

IS THERE A SEPARATE MILITARY-INDUSTRIAL COMPLEX?

Unlike the countries of Europe, which had to have big armies from the fifteenth century onward to defend themselves against one another, the United States did not have a large military establishment until World War II. This fact goes a long way toward explaining the small size of the federal government and the major role of the power elite within it. However, the large amount of defense spending since World War II has led a few social scientists to believe that there now exists a separate military-industrial complex able to win the budgetary allocations it needs to maintain at least some degree of independence from the corporate community. It is said to consist of the Pentagon, congressional committees concerned with military budgets, and a few dozen companies that specialize in weapons manufacturing. There are three major findings that contradict this notion.

First, several of the largest defense contractors, such as Boeing, General Electric, and United Technologies, are also among the largest corporations in the country, irrespective of their military contracts. That is, the very large contracts they receive from the Pentagon are only a small percentage of their overall business.

Second, sociologist Stephen Johnson showed that the companies that focused on defense contracts in the years following World War II are completely integrated into the corporate community through their

Table 2.5 The Nine Leading Military Contractors by the Size of Their 1995 Prime Contracts, Along with Their Ties to the Corporate Network

Company	Contracts (billions)	% of Business in Defense	Network Ties	Ties to Central 28
Lockheed Martin	12.45	39.5	20	3
Boeing	9.80	30.0	20	3
Raytheon	5.91	23.3	14	0
Newport News Shipbuilding*	3.71	100.0	14	2
Northrop Grumman†	2.91	42.7	22	4
General Electric	2.10	3.0	20	2
United Technologies	1.77	7.8	13	3
General Dynamics	1.70	55.4	14	3
Litton Industries	1.24	34.3	1	0

Source: *New York Times*, Jan. 17, 1997, p. C6, and *Who Knows Who*, 1997.

*Newport News Shipbuilding was spun off from Tenneco in December 1996. It is Tenneco that has fourteen connections overall in the corporate network and two in the top twenty-eight.

†Purchased by Lockheed Martin in July 1997.

bank connections and interlocking directors; in addition, their directors went to the same universities and belong to the same social clubs as other corporate directors.[38]

Third, the claim of a separate military-industrial complex is contradicted by the fact that the defense budget rises and falls in terms of foreign policy crises and military threats. This does not fit with the idea that defense contractors and their Pentagon allies have the power to obtain for themselves all the defense spending they would like to have. Budgetary decline was significant after World War II, the Korean War, and the Vietnam War.[39] The drop in defense spending since the end of the Cold War has been substantial as well, although it remains true that the defense budget is still a major portion of all government spending (as shown in table 7.3 in chapter 7).

The argument over the existence of a separate and independent military-industrial complex became less revelant during the 1990s when the Clinton Administration decided to adopt new contracting policies advocated by the largest defense companies. These new policies in effect eliminated most defense companies because of declining defense needs and placed a greater emphasis on competition in the marketplace among a few large corporations as the means to ensure the continued development of sophisticated weapons systems. The result was a massive merger movement that downsized the defense industry by hundreds of thousands of employees and left the bulk of the defense contracts in the hands of a small number of corporations that also have large nondefense business operations.[40] Table 2.5 lists these companies, the percentage of their sales coming from defense contracts, and the extent of their interlocking connections within the corporate community.

FARMERS: TOO FEW, TOO SMALL TO MATTER

In the last half of the nineteenth century, when the farm vote was critical in state and national elections, farmers often provided major opposition to the rising national corporations. Many angry small farmers were part of an anticorporate populist movement that started in the 1870s and formed its own political party in the 1880s to challenge both Democrats and Republicans. Several of the reforms advocated by the populists—such as a government commission to set railroad rates, the direct election of senators, and the federal income tax—were eventually adopted.

But the day of farmers as any kind of challenge to the corporate community is long past. The rural populists were defeated at the turn of the twentieth century by a coalition of prosperous farmers and local business leaders. As the farm population declined and the average size of farms increased, farm owners became an interest group rather than a large popular movement. Moreover, the large-scale family farmers of the Midwest and Great Plains increasingly joined with the plantation owners of the South and the ranchers of California as employers of wage labor, especially part-time migrant labor, and identified themselves as business owners. The periodic attempts since the 1930s by farm workers to organize labor unions, often aided and encouraged by liberals and leftists, have intensified the farm owners' sense of opposition to the liberal-labor coalition.[41]

Although most of the 2 million farms in existence today are still family owned and managed, with less than 1 percent owned by large corporations in other businesses, the overwhelming majority of them are extremely small. Approximately 66 percent of farms earn less than $40,000 a year in sales and account for only 7.3 percent of net cash from farm sales. The people on these small farms earn over 90 percent of their income in off-farm jobs, many in manufacturing and service firms that relocated to rural areas to take advantage of lower wages.[42] At the other end of the farm ladder, a mere 2.5 percent of farms, those with sales of $500,000 a year or more, receive 45.9 percent of all net

Table 2.6 Percent of Net Cash Income and Government Payments Received by Farms in Five Size Classes

Sales Class	No. of Farms	% of All Farms	% Net Cash	% Government Payments
Less than $40,000	1,359,000	65.9	7.3	8.5
$40,000 to $99,999	313,000	15.2	12.0	19.9
$100,000 to $499,999	339,000	16.4	34.8	56.8
$500,000 to $999,999	35,000	1.7	10.7	9.8
Over $1 million	17,000	0.8	35.2	5.0
Total no. of farms	2,063,000			

Source: United States Department of Agriculture, Economic Research Service, *Economic Indicators of the Farm Sector: National Financial Summary*, 1994, p. 70, Table 49.

cash from farm sales. These large farms received 14.8 percent of the government support payments that went to farmers until 1996, when a program that had its origins in the farm crisis of the early 1930s was repealed by Congress. Information on the net cash and government payments for farms in five general categories can be found in table 2.6.

For all the persistence of family-owned farms, many of the largest farms are part of agribusiness complexes, particularly for farm commodities in which a few companies control most of the market. Roughly 85 percent of all eggs and poultry, for example, come from 20 corporations and the farmers under contract to them.[43] Just 43 farm companies control one-third of the American market for pork; they own 1.74 million sows that produce over 30 million pigs each year.[44] More generally, there are 400 companies with $10 million or more in farm sales each year: 114 produced beef, 75 produced poultry, 70 raised vegetables, and 54 produced eggs.[45] The farm sales for the ten largest farms in the United States are presented in table 2.7, along with their primary products and state location.

The "well-to-do" among farmers, the 18.9 percent with sales of $100,000 a year or more, are organized into a wide variety of associations that look out for their interests. Some of these organizations are "commodity groups," made up of those who produce a particular crop. There are also two or three general farm groups, the most important of which is the American Farm Bureau Federation. The Farm Bureau, as it is known, and most other farm groups usually ally themselves with business trade associations in the political arena. The Farm

Table 2.7 The Ten Largest Farms by Farm Sales, with Primary Products, and State (in millions of dollars)

Farm Name	Farm Sales	Products	State
1. Tyson Foods	1,701.23	broilers, pork	AR
2. ConAgra	1,458.01	beef, broilers, turkeys	NE
3. Gold Kist	899.00	poultry, pork	GA
4. Continental Grain	893.00	beef, broilers	IL
5. Perdue Farms	545.76	broilers, turkeys	MD
6. Pilgrims Pride	434.15	broilers, eggs	TX
7. Cargill	374.76	beef, turkeys, broilers	MN
8. U.S. Sugar	365.00	sugar, citrus, vegetables	FL
9. Hudson Foods	350.69	broilers, eggs, turkeys	AR
10. Cactus Feeder	310.00	beef	TX

Source: *Successful Farming*, April 1992, p. 21. Used with permission of the publisher.

Bureau in particular is an important part of the corporate-conservative coalition and includes related agribusinesses and local businesses among its members. There is, however, one farm organization, the National Farmers Union, that usually has allied itself with the liberal-labor coalition. Its historical origins are in wheat farming in the Great Plains.[46]

Farmers, then, are no longer an independent base of power in the United States. They are few in number, and most of those few do not have enough income from their farms to have any political impact. On the other hand, the small percent of farmers who produce most of the cash crops are integrated into the agribusiness complex within the corporate community through commodity groups and the Farm Bureau. Their fate is closely tied to the same policies favored by large businesses in general.

SMALL BUSINESS: NOT A COUNTERWEIGHT

There are about 22 million small businesses in the United States, defined as businesses with fewer than 500 employees. Because they make 52 percent of all sales and employ 54 percent of the private labor force, they are sometimes claimed to be a counterweight to the power of the corporate community. They have an important place in the American belief system because they are thought to embody the independence and initiative of all Americans, and since the 1980s they have been extolled as the primary force in creating new jobs in the economy.[47] But the owners of small businesses are too large in number, too diverse in size, and too lacking in financial assets to have any collective power that could challenge the corporate community. One-third of American businesses are part-time and another one-third are one-person operations. Others operate in immigrant ethnic enclaves and have no contacts with businesspeople outside their community. In addition, attitudinal surveys suggest that the political orientation of small business owners varies greatly by income, religion, ethnicity, and type of business.[48] As a result of all these factors, small business-people have not formed their own associations to lobby for them.

There are organizations that claim to represent small business, especially the National Federation of Independent Business, which has 560,000 members. In fact, these organizations are actually businesses created by political entrepreneurs as a way to make profits on "dues" and lobby for their policy preferences at the same time. The National Federation of Independent Business is actually an extremely conservative lobbying organization that is part of the corporate-conservative coalition, drawing much of its leadership and staff from the Republican Party. Although it is now a nonprofit organization, it was created in 1943 as a for-profit organization and controlled by its founder until his retirement. Now it is controlled by a small board of directors made up of wealthy business owners who pay the top officers several hundred thousand dollars a year to manage 700 employees and oversee $58 million in revenue. There are no general meetings or votes for officers. Memberships are sold by traveling sales representatives who receive a commission for each new member they recruit. The turnover in membership is very great. At best, the organization reflects the opinions of the most conservative of small business owners.[49]

The claims by small business organizations notwithstanding, the small businesses that go beyond the part-time and one-person levels are most often part of trade associations that receive most of their funding and direction from the large corporations in the industry. They are also part of the two largest general business organizations in the country: the Chamber of Commerce, which claims 180,000 companies and 2,800 state and local chambers as members, and the National Association of Manufacturers, which claims 12,500 companies and subsidiaries as members. These are figures that go well beyond the several hundred companies in the corporate community and the mere 14,000 companies with 500 or more employees.

Many small businesses are also part of economic networks that have large corporations at the center, or else they are part of local growth coalitions (discussed in the next section of this chapter). The most visible and long-standing examples of small businesses tied to large corporations are the many franchise businesses that sell retail products to the general public—gas stations, car dealerships, convenience stores, fast-food outlets, and mall shops. Between 1967 and the 1990s, the percentage of all sales made by franchises grew from 10 to 41 percent.[50]

As for the small manufacturing companies sometimes said to be the sources of innovation and new jobs, they are often part of the producer networks that sell parts and services to large corporations. The fact that many of these firms start with 100 or more employees suggests just how important their subcontracts from large corporations are for their existence and survival. Not all small manufacturing firms are directly tied to large corporations, however. Some are in business sectors like furniture making, where there are no economic advantages to bigness. Many are part of what one author calls "the minor industrial revolution" that brought small firms into Southern states in search of low-wage, non-unionized labor.[51] Still others owe their origins to discoveries and patents that were developed in large universities, especially in the electronic and biotechnology industries.

Therefore, there is no "small business community" in the United States to provide any opposition to the corporate community. Many of the relatively few small businesses that are full-time operations and have more than a handful of employees are incorporated into the power networks of the corporate community (1) by belonging to trade associations dominated by larger businesses, (2) as franchise outlets for larger businesses, and (3) as suppliers and service providers for big corporations. These ties place severe market and political constraints on most small businesses in relation to the large corporations. Moreover, the people who claim to speak for small business as a whole are in fact wealthy conservatives using the problems of small business as part of their efforts to keep the government small and under their dominance. Small business is too poor and fragmented to be a counterweight to the .3 percent of businesses that have 59 percent of total business assets.[52]

LOCAL GROWTH COALITIONS

The most important small businesses in the United States are organized into local growth coalitions whose members share a common interest in intensifying land use in their area. The most typical way of intensifying land use is growth, which usually expresses itself in a constantly rising population. In economic terms, these place entrepreneurs are trying to maximize "rents" from land and buildings, which is a little different from the goal of the corporate community—maximizing profits from the sale of goods and services. As sociologists John R. Logan and Harvey Molotch explain in *Urban Fortunes*, their seminal book about local growth coalitions, the term *rent* is used in their theory as a way to describe all payments to landowners and related businesses: "We use the term broadly to include outright purchase expenditures as well as payments that home buyers or tenants make to landlords, realtors, mortgage lenders, title companies, and so forth."[53] This distinction between rents and profits is important because it emphasizes that the economics of land and buildings is different from the economics of goods and services in a wide variety of ways that need not be discussed for purposes of this book but that make for subtle differences between the objectives of the corporate community and the growth coalitions.

Local growth coalitions and the corporate community, as owners of income-producing properties, have much in common and often work together, but their somewhat different ways of making money means that there are some political tensions and conflicts between them. They are different "segments" of the ownership class. That is, as owners and as employers of wage labor, they are in the same general economic category and share more in common than with nonowners, but they nonetheless are to some extent rivals because their interests in business dealings are not always exactly the same.*

The basis for cooperation between the corporate community and the local growth coalitions is found in the fact that the primary way to intensify land use is to attract corporate investments to the area. Thus the place entrepreneurs in the growth coalitions are very much attuned to the needs of corporations, working hard to provide them with the physical infrastructure, municipal services, labor markets, and political climate they find attractive. At the same time, the growth coalitions also try to win new government buildings, new university campuses, and other capital investments that bring more people to an area. The growth caused by such investments then leads to housing

---

*Historically, Northern manufacturers and Southern plantation owners were the two main rival segments within the ownership class. In the first sixty years of the twentieth century there also was conflict between an internationalist segment of corporations, which derived a large part of their profits from overseas sales and investments, and a nationalist segment that produced for regional and local domestic markets. By the 1980s, however, these differences had largely disappeared. The South is now industrialized, and its plantations have been transformed into agribusinesses. Nor are there any disagreements within the corporate community about the need to develop global markets for all American companies through lower tariffs and any other means possible. Even the conflicts between the corporate community and local growth coalitions have been ameliorated to some extent with the arrival of national and international developers and the creation of land development divisions in some large corporations.[54]

development, increased financial activity, and increased consumer spending—all of which make land and buildings even more valuable.

But, as already noted, the relationship between the growth coalitions and the corporate community is not without its tensions. Corporations can move if they think that regulations are becoming too stringent or taxes and wages too high. A move by a major corporation can have a devastating impact on a local growth coalition. Moreover, this ability to move contributes to the constant competition among rival cities for new capital investments, creating tensions between growth coalitions as well as between individual growth coalitions and the corporate community. The net result is often a "race to the bottom" as rival cities offer tax breaks, less environmental regulation, and other benefits to corporations in order to tempt them to relocate. Ironically, most studies of plant location suggest that environmental laws and local taxes are of minor importance in corporate decisions concerning the location or relocation of production facilities. A union-free environment and low-cost raw materials are the major factors.[55]

Local growth coalitions face a third source of tension and conflict: disagreements with neighbors about expansion and development. Neighborhoods are places to be used and enjoyed in the eyes of those who live in them, but they are often sites for further development from the point of view of those in the growth coalitions. Thus, neighborhood residents often end up opposing freeways, wider streets, high-rises, and commercial buildings. This conflict between "use value" and "exchange value" becomes a basic one in most successful cities, especially when developers try to expand the central business district, often at the expense of established low-income and minority neighborhoods. For example, from 1955 to 1975 a government program called "urban renewal" removed housing on thousands of acres of land so that central business districts and downtown universities could be expanded.[56]

The success rate of neighborhoods in conflict with the growth coalitions is not high. Since the primary focus of residents is on their everyday lives, they often do not persist in their protests and seldom join larger coalitions with other neighborhoods in the city. Moreover, as explained in chapter 6, local elections were reorganized early in the twentieth century to minimize the impact of neighborhood politics. As a result, neighborhood activists usually lose after bringing about some delays and some changes in the plans. Sometimes the neighborhood groups formed to oppose developers end up serving as paid liaisons between the growth coalitions and neighborhood residents.[57]

Although the growth coalitions are based on land ownership and the maximization of rents, they include all those local interests that profit from the intensification of land use, including developers, contractors, mortgage bankers, and related real estate businesses. Executives from the local bank, the savings and loan, the telephone company, the gas and electric company, and the local department stores are often quite prominent as well because they, too, have a strong stake in the growth of the local community. As in the case of the corporate community, the central meeting points of the growth coalitions are most often banks, where executives from the utility companies and the department stores join with the largest landlords and developers as members of the boards of directors.[58]

There is one other important component of the local growth coalition—the newspaper. Newspaper publishers are committed to local growth so that their circulation—and even more importantly their pages of advertising—will continue to rise. No better expression of this commitment can be found than a statement by the publisher of the main newspaper in the booming city of San Jose, California. When asked why he had consistently favored development on beautiful orchard lands that had turned the city into one of the largest in California within a period of two decades, he replied, "Trees do not read newspapers."[59] The unique feature of the newspaper is that it is not committed to growth on any particular piece of land or in any one area of the city, so it often becomes the mediator among any competing interests within the growth machine.

A local growth coalition sometimes includes a useful junior partner—the unions of the building trades. Despite a general allegiance to the liberal-labor coalition at the national level, these unions see their fate tied to the growth coalition in the belief that growth creates jobs. They are often highly visible on the side of the growth coalition in battles against neighborhood groups, environmentalists, and university faculty, staff, and students. Although local growth does not create new jobs in the economy as a whole—which is a function of corporate and governmental decisions beyond the province of any single community—it does determine where the new jobs will be located. Thus local construction unions find it in their interest to help the growth coalition in its competition with other localities.

Jobs are the ideal unifying theme for bringing the whole community together behind just about any growth project. The goal of the growth coalition is never said to be moneymaking, but jobs for the citizens of the community:

> Perhaps the key ideological prop for the growth coalition, especially in terms of sustaining support from the working class majority, is the claim that growth "makes jobs." This claim is aggressively promulgated by developers, builders, and chambers of commerce; it becomes part of the statesman talk of editorialists and

political officials. Such people do not speak of growth as useful to profits—rather, they speak of it as necessary for making jobs.[60]

Although a concern with growth in general is at the basis of each developed local area, every city enters into the competition with a different set of priorities and strategies for achieving it. Calculations have to be made about what investment prospects are the most desirable and plausible based on such factors as the availability of natural resources; the nature of the climate; the proximity of oceans, lakes, and rivers; the skills of the workforce; and the history of successes and failures in growth competition. There is a clear preference for clean industries that require highly paid skilled workers over dirty industries that use unskilled workers. Attractive beachfront towns are not as likely as inland cities to seek out just any type of industry; beachfront property can bring in more money as a site for tourist resorts and convention centers.

Historical factors also enter into growth strategies. If one locale captures a once-in-a-generation opportunity—such as a stockyard or a railroad—over which competition was very fierce in the nineteenth century, then nearby communities have to settle for lesser opportunities even though they have very similar natural conditions. On the other hand, earlier successes may lock an area into relationships and obligations that make it very difficult for it to take advantage of new opportunities. The rise of Sunbelt cities is due not only to cheaper labor costs, the availability of land, and good weather, but also to the previous lack of heavy industry that made growth coalition leaders there more alert to the possibilities in electronics and information processing.

It is worth noting that there is variation from country to country in the importance of local growth coalitions. They are strongest in the United States because the movement of settlers to the West in search of land gave it the freest markets in land, and hence the most intense speculation in it, and because local governments are not controlled by the federal government. Although the influence of the United States and the globalization of markets are leading to the gradual development of independent place entrepreneurs in some countries that did not have them, the existence of both a corporate community and local growth coalitions is one of many unique features of the United States.[61]

CONCLUSION

This chapter shows that the national economy is dominated by a few hundred interlocked corporations that constitute a majority of all manufacturing and banking assets. The picture is similar at the local level, where landed and real estate interests work together to attract investments by the corporate community, government agencies, and universities. Farmers and small business owners are not in a position to challenge corporate power; in fact, the most successful are integrated into corporate networks. Although there are sometimes tensions between the corporate community and local growth coalitions, they work together more often than not.

In short, none of the other economic interests studied in this chapter provide the organizational base for any significant opposition to the corporate community. To the degree that the corporate community faces any challenges, they come from the union movement and the relatively small number of liberals and leftists. Members of this liberal-labor opposition are often highly visible and vocal through their writing and media appearances, giving an initial appearance of considerable strength, and the constant criticisms of them in the media by ultra-conservatives as powerful and dangerous reinforces this impression. Whether this impression is true is the topic of several later chapters.

On the other hand, the power that can be exercised by corporate leaders through their companies is considerable. For example, they can invest their money when and where they choose. If they feel threatened by new laws or labor unions, they can close or move their factories and offices, often leaving an economically shattered community or city behind. Unless restrained by union contracts, which in the 1990s covered only 10–12 percent of workers in the private sector, they can hire, promote, and replace workers as they see fit, often laying off employees on a moment's notice. These economic powers give them a direct influence over the great majority of Americans, who are dependent on wages and salaries for their incomes and therefore often hesitant to challenge corporations politically. They also give the corporate rich indirect influence over elected and appointed officials because the growth and stability of a city, state, or the country as a whole can be jeopardized by a lack of business confidence in government.

One of the clearest statements of the way in which economic power influences government without any effort on the part of corporate leaders is provided by economist Charles Lindblom. The crux of his argument is that businesspeople have to be induced to invest their funds because in a Western capitalist society they have the legal right to spend their money when and as they wish. Since the government cannot take over the investment function, its main job is therefore to cater to business. If government officials do not carry out this task, there are likely to be economic difficulties that would lead people to desire new political leadership. Since most government officials do not want to lose their positions, they do what is necessary to satisfy business leaders and maintain a healthy economy.[62]

In other words, private control over the investment function provides leaders within the corporate community and the growth coalitions with a "structural" power that is independent of any attempts by them to influence government officials directly. While such power is very great, I do not find it sufficient in and of itself, especially in times of economic or political crisis. First, it does not preclude the possibility that government officials might turn to nonbusiness constituencies to support new economic arrangements. As Lindblom rightly points out, there is no necessary relationship between private ownership and markets, contrary to claims by conservative economists. Improbable though it may seem, it would be possible for government to create firms to compete in the market system and thereby revive a depressed economy, or to hire unemployed workers in order to increase their ability to spend. A legislative effort of roughly this sort by the liberal-labor coalition in the mid-1940s is discussed in chapter 7.

Second, structural power does not guarantee that employees will accept continuing economic depression without taking over factories or destroying private property. In such situations, however rare, the corporate leaders need government to protect their private property. As philosopher Bertrand Russell notes in criticizing "the undue emphasis on economics" in understanding power, "The power of the industrialist rests, in the last analysis, upon the lockout, that is to say, upon the fact that the owner of a factory can call upon the forces of the State to prevent unauthorized persons from entering it."[63] In short, Lindblom's structural theory, which views the issue as between owners and government officials, ignores the volatile power conflict built into the economy between owners and workers and the critical role that government plays in determining the outcome of that conflict. In fact, such conflicts did arise in the 1930s, leading to both new labor legislation and the frequent use of police forces to subdue strikers and union organizers.[64]

Because there is no guarantee that the underlying population and government officials will accept the viewpoint of corporate owners under all economic circumstances, there is uncertainty in the relationship between the corporate community and government. This makes it risky for corporate officials to refuse to invest or to remain passive in an economic depression. Leaders within the corporate community and the growth coalitions thus feel a need to have direct influence on both the public at large and elected and appointed government officials, and they have developed a number of ways to realize those objectives. As a top corporate leader said when a sociologist suggested to him that his company probably had enough economic power to dispense with its efforts to influence elected officials, "I'm not sure, but I'm not willing to find out."[65]

Before explaining how the corporate rich attempt to shape public opinion, elect politicians they trust, and influence government officials on specific policies, it is necessary to see if there is a relationship between the corporate community and the social upper class. An affirmative resolution of that question provides another way to distinguish between a class-domination theory and interest-group pluralism.

NOTES

1. Thomas R. Dye, *Who's Running America: The Clinton Years* (Englewood Cliffs, NJ: Prentice-Hall, 1995), pp. 15–22.
2. Mayer Zald, "The Power and Functions of Boards of Directors," *American Journal of Sociology*, 75 (1969): 97–117; William Bowen, *Inside the Boardroom* (New York: Wiley, 1994). For a study that uses women directors as "strategic informants" to learn more about how boards operate, see Beth Ghiloni, "New Women of Power," Ph.D. Dissertation, University of California, Santa Cruz, 1986, chapters 6 and 7.
3. Myles Mace, *Directors: Myth and Reality* (Cambridge: Harvard University Press, 1971), p. 90.
4. Ibid.
5. Zald, op. cit.; Ghiloni, op. cit.; Susan Ostrander, "Elite Domination in Private Social Agencies: How It Happens and How It Is Challenged," in *Power Elites and Organizations*, eds. G. William Domhoff and Thomas Dye (Beverly Hills: Sage Publications, 1987), pp. 85–102.
6. Peter Mariolis, "Interlocking Directorates and Control of Corporations," *Social Sciences Quarterly*, 56 (1975): 425–439.
7. Gerald Davis, "The Corporate Elite and the Politics of Corporate Control," *Current Perspectives in Social Theory*, Supplement 1 (Greenwich, CT: JAI Press, 1994), pp. 215–238.
8. Beth Mintz and Michael Schwartz, "Interlocking Directorates and Interest Group Formation," *American Sociological Review*, 46 (1981): 852–869; Beth Mintz and Michael Schwartz, "Financial Interest Groups and Interlocking Directorates," *Social Science History*, 7 (1983): 183–204; Beth Mintz and Michael Schwartz, *The Power Structure of American Business* (Chicago: University of Chicago Press, 1986); Thomas Koenig and Robert Gogel, "Interlocking Directorates as a Social Network," *American Journal of Economics and Sociology*, 40 (1981): 37–50; Donald Palmer, "Interpreting Corporate Interlocks from Broken Ties," *Social Science History*, 7 (1983): 217–231.
9. Robert F. Dalzell, Jr., *Enterprising Elite: The Boston Associates and the World They Made* (New York: W. W. Norton & Co., 1987), pp. 79–81 and Appendix.
10. David Bunting, "Origins of the American Corporate Network," *Social Science History*, 7 (1983): 129–142.

11. Ibid., William Roy, "Interlocking Directorates and the Corporate Revolution," *Social Science History,* 7 (1983): 143–164.

12. William Roy, *Socializing Capital: The Rise of the Large Industrial Corporation in America* (Princeton, NJ: Princeton University Press, 1997). See Martin Sklar, *The Corporate Reconstruction of American Capitalism, 1890–1916* (New York: Cambridge University Press, 1988), pp. 163–167, for the factors triggering the corporate merger movement. Further support for an emphasis on power dynamics in understanding the American corporate community can be found in the work of legal scholar Mark Roe, *Strong Managers, Weak Owners: The Political Roots of American Corporate Finance* (Princeton, NJ: Princeton University Press, 1994). Roe shows that banks are less important in the United States than in some European countries because of American banking laws, which are rooted in people's fears of bank power.

13. Bunting, op. cit.; Roy, "Interlocking Directorates and the Corporate Revolution," op. cit.; Mark Mizruchi, *The Structure of the American Corporate Network, 1904–1974* (Beverly Hills: Sage Publications, 1982); Mark Mizruchi, "Relations among Large Corporations, 1904–1974," *Social Science History,* 7 (1983): 165–182; Mark Mizruchi and David Bunting, "Influence in Corporate Networks: An Examination of Four Measures," *Administrative Science Quarterly,* 26 (1981): 475–489.

14. Neil Fligstein, *The Transformation of Corporation Control* (Cambridge: Harvard University Press, 1990).

15. Richard L. Zweigenhaft and G. William Domhoff, *Diversity in the Power Elite* (New Haven, CT: Yale University Press, 1998).

16. Maurice Zeitlin, "Corporate Ownership and Control: The Large Corporations and the Capitalist Class," *American Journal of Sociology,* 79 (1974): 1071–1119; Michael Useem, *The Inner Circle* (New York: Oxford University Press, 1984).

17. Bunting, op. cit.; Roy, "Interlocking Directorates and the Corporate Revolution," op. cit. For a similar finding in Norway, where 17.6 percent of 527 corporate directors sat on two or more boards, see John Higley, G. Lowell Field, and Knut Groholt, *Elite Structure and Ideology: A Theory with Applications to Norway* (Oslo, Norway: Universitetsforlaget, 1976), p. 141.

18. Mark Mizruchi, *The Structure of Corporate Political Action* (Cambridge: Harvard University Press, 1992); Davis, op. cit.

19. Useem, op. cit.; for further interview evidence supporting Useem's point, see Ghiloni, op. cit. For an overview on the significance of corporate interlocks, see Mark Mizruchi, "What Do Interlocks Do?," *Annual Review of Sociology,* 22 (1996): 271–298.

20. Bennett Harrison, *Lean and Mean: The Changing Landscape of Corporate Power in the Age of Flexibility* (New York: Basic Books, 1994). This section draws heavily on Harrison's seminal work.

21. Ibid., p. 47. For a review of evidence suggesting that dependence places constraints on a firm's political behavior, see Mizruchi, 1992, op. cit., pp. 57–59, 80.

22. James Gross, *Broken Promise: The Subversion of U.S. Labor Relations Policy, 1947–1994* (Philadelphia: Temple University Press, 1995), chapters 11–12. Gross shows there never was a live-and-let-live "social contract" between the corporate community and organized labor in the years after World War II.

23. For excellent accounts of how corporate law firms developed in the years between 1870 and 1915 in response to the needs of industrial corporations, see the original empirical studies in Gerald W. Gawalt, ed., *The New High Priests: Lawyers in Post–Civil War America* (Westport, CT: Greenwood Press, 1984). For a detailed study of corporation law in one state, see Rachel Parker Gwin and William Roy, "Corporate Law and the Organization of Property in the United States: The Origins and Institutionalization of New Jersey Corporation Law, 1888–1903," *Politics and Society,* 24 (1996): 111–135.

24. For a detailed critique of the involvement of corporate lawyers on behalf of their clients on specific issues involving citizen complaints or governmental attempts to redress grievances, see Ralph Nader and Wesley J. Smith, *No Contest: Corporate Lawyers and the Perversion of Justice in America* (New York: Random House, 1996). For the threatening attempts to scare off citizen complaints through countersuits known as SLAPPs, see pages 159–181 of *No Contest* as well as George W. Pring and Penelope Canan, *SLAPPs: Getting Sued for Speaking Out* (Philadelphia: Temple University Press, 1996).

25. Gross, op. cit., pp. 234–239.

26. Dye, op. cit., pp. 127–131.

27. Robert Nelson, *Partners with Power* (Berkeley: University of California Press, 1988), p. 232.

28. Ibid., pp. 264, 269.

29. Robert Granfield, *Making Elite Lawyers: Visions of Law at Harvard and Beyond* (New York: Routledge, 1992), p. 202, for both quotes. For a survey of other studies of the socialization of lawyers that come to conclusions similar to those of Granfield, see Mark Miller, *The High Priests of American Politics* (Knoxville: University of Tennessee Press, 1995), chapter 2.

30. Granfield, op. cit., p. 41.

31. For a full discussion of this new movement until 1994, see Michael Useem, *Investor Capitalism* (New York: Basic Books, 1996).

32. Ibid., p. 64.

33. Judith Dobrzynski, "Tales from the Boardroom Wars," *Business Week* (June 6, 1994): 71–72.

34. Jack Egan, "The Elephant That Roared," *U.S. News and World Report* (October 7, 1991): 95; Martha Groves, "Used to Giving Heat, Fund Chief Is Now Getting Some," *Los Angeles Times* (June 23, 1991): D1; Judith Dobrzynski, "Is Pete Wilson Trying to Mute a Shareholder Activist?," *Business Week* (July 1, 1991): 29; George Anders, "Restless Natives; While Head of Calpers Lectures Other Firms, His Own Board Frets," *Wall Street Journal* (Jan. 29, 1993): A1; Mary Blair, *Ownership and Control* (Washington, DC: Brookings Institution, 1995), p. 165.

35. Judith Dobrzynski, "Shareholder-Rights Group Faces a Fight over Its Own Leadership," *New York Times* (April 1, 1996): A1; Judith Dobrzynski, "Investor Group's Leadership Vote Is a Rebuff to Union Members," *New York Times* (April 2, 1996): C2.

36. Blair, op. cit., p. 170.

37. For a detailed analysis of why public employee pension funds are not likely to have much influence on corporate governance, see Blair, op. cit., pp. 167 and 184ff.

38. Stephen Johnson, "How the West Was Won: Last Shootout for the Yankee Cowboy Theory," *Insurgent Sociologist*, 6 (1976): 61–93. For a detailed critique of the idea of a military-industrial complex, along with all relevant evidence, see my *State Autonomy or Class Dominance?* (Hawthorne, NY: Aldine de Gruyter, 1996), chapter 6. For a good analysis of defense spending in a power context, see John Boies, *Buying for Armageddon* (New Brunswick, NJ: Rutgers University Press, 1994).

39. Ted Goertzel, "Militarism as a Sociological Problem," *Research in Political Sociology*, 1 (1985): 119–139.

40. James Sterngold, "A Swift Transformation," *New York Times* (Dec. 16, 1996): 1; James Sterngold, "Boeing's Deal Quickens Pace for Arms Industry Takeovers," *New York Times* (Dec. 17, 1996): 1; James Sterngold, "G.M. Sells Unit to Raytheon as Arms Mergers Continue," *New York Times* (Jan. 17, 1997): 1.

41. Grant McConnell, *The Decline of Agrarian Democracy* (Berkeley: University of California Press, 1953); Cindy Hahamovitch, *The Fruits of Their Labor* (Chapel Hill: University of North Carolina Press, 1997). For a detailed account of class conflict in agriculture during the New Deal, see G. William Domhoff, *State Autonomy or Class Dominance,* op. cit., chapter 3.

42. William P. Browne, Jerry R. Skees, Louis E. Swanson, Paul P. Thompson, and Laurian J. Unnevehr, *Sacred Cows and Hot Potatoes* (Boulder: Westview Press, 1992), pp. 22, 46.

43. John Shover, *First Majority, Last Minority* (DeKalb: Northern Illinois University Press, 1976), p. 144.

44. Betty Freese, "Pork Powerhouses 1996," *Successful Farming* (October 1996): 27–32.

45. Jennifer Erickson, "The 400 Largest Farms in the U.S.," *Successful Farming* (April 1992): 18–27.

46. Wesley McCune, *Who's Behind Our Farm Policy?* (New York: Praeger, 1956), chapter 4, for the origins of the National Farmers Union. Although dated in its details on farm organizations, this book still provides the best account of how well-to-do farmers and the corporate community work together through a wide range of organizations. For a thorough account of agribusiness, see A. V. Krebs, *The Corporate Reapers: The Book of Agribusiness* (Washington, DC: Essential Books, 1992).

47. Small Business Administration, *The Facts About Small Business* (Washington, DC: Small Business Administration, 1996), p. 1.

48. Richard Hamilton, *Restraining Myths* (New York: Wiley, 1975), chapter 2.

49. Ibid.; L. Harmon Zeigler, *The Politics of Small Business* (Washington, DC: Public Affairs Press, 1961); G. William Domhoff, "Who Killed Health

Care Reform in Congress, Small Business or Rich Conservatives, and Why Did They Do It?" (paper presented to the annual meetings of the American Sociological Association, Washington, DC, August 21, 1995).

50. Mansel Blackford, *A History of Small Business in America* (New York: Twayne Publishers, 1991), pp. 104, 112.

51. Browne, op. cit., p. 24.

52. *Handbook of Small Business Data* (Washington, DC: Small Business Administration, 1988), p. 6.

53. John R. Logan and Harvey Molotch, *Urban Fortunes* (Berkeley: University of California Press, 1987), p. 23.

54. Maurice Zeitlin, "On Classes, Class Conflict, and the State," in *Classes, Class Conflict, and the State,* ed. Maurice Zeitlin (Cambridge: Winthrop Publishers, 1980), has an excellent discussion of the concept of class segments. For a detailed application, see Maurice Zeitlin and Richard Ratcliff, *Landlords and Capitalists: The Dominant Class of Chile* (Princeton: Princeton University Press, 1988). For a discussion of class segments in the United States, see G. William Domhoff, *The Power Elite and the State,* op. cit., pp. 22–24, 38–39.

55. Harrison, op. cit., pp. 38–40; Barry Bluestone and Bennett Harrison, *The Deindustrialization of America: Plant Closings, Community Abandonment, and the Dismantling of Basic Industry* (New York: Basic Books, 1982).

56. G. William Domhoff, *Who Really Rules? New Haven and Community Power Re-examined* (New Brunswick, NJ: Transaction Books, 1978), pp. 49–75, for the conflict between growth coalitions and liberals over housing and redevelopment in urban areas after World War II. For two excellent studies of the conflicts between the growth coalition and neighborhoods in Atlanta, see Clarence Stone, *Neighborhood and Discontent* (Chapel Hill: University of North Carolina Press, 1976); and Clarence Stone, *Regime Politics* (Lawrence: University of Kansas Press, 1989).

57. Logan and Molotch, op. cit., pp. 134–140 and chapter 6.

58. Floyd Hunter, *Community Power Structure* (Chapel Hill: University of North Carolina Press, 1953); Domhoff, *Who Really Rules?,* op. cit., chapter 5; Logan and Molotch, op. cit.

59. Leonard Downie, *Mortgage on America* (New York: Praeger, 1974), p. 112.

60. Harvey Molotch, "The City as a Growth Machine," *American Journal of Sociology,* 82 (1976): 320.

61. Harvey Molotch, "The Political Economy of Growth Machines," *Journal of Urban Affairs,* 15 (1993): 29–53.

62. Charles Lindblom, *Politics and Markets* (New York: Basic Books, 1977).

63. Bertrand Russell, *Power: A New Social Analysis* (London: George Allen and Unwin, 1938), pp. 123–124. For my critique of Lindblom's theory, see *The Power Elite and the State,* op. cit., chapter 7.

64. For example, see Irving Bernstein, *The Turbulent Years* (Boston: Houghton Mifflin, 1970), for a highly readable account of labor conflict in the 1930s.

65. Dan Clawson, Alan Neustadtl, and Denise Scott, *Money Talks: Corporate PACs and Political Influence* (New York: Basic Books, 1992), p. 121.

3

The Corporate Community and the Upper Class

This chapter has three main points; all three relate to claims made by pluralists in rejecting a class-dominance theory. First, it shows there is a nationwide social upper class in the United States that has its own exclusive social institutions and is based in the ownership of great wealth. Second, it demonstrates that this upper class is closely intertwined with the corporate community. Third, it argues that the social cohesion that develops among members of the upper class is another basis for the creation of policy agreements within the policy-formation network.

The demonstration of an upper class that is tightly interconnected with the corporate community is relevant because it contradicts the idea that there has been a separation between corporate ownership and control in the United States. According to that view, there is on the one hand a wealthy but powerless upper class that is a mere "status group," and on the other a "managerial class" that has power independent of wealthy owners by virtue of its expertise in running corporations. Due to this division between high-society owners and well-trained independent managers, pluralists say it no longer makes sense to think in terms of a dominant class whose general interest in profits transcends the fate of any one corporation or business sector. They therefore prefer to think of corporations as one type of "interest group."

Contrary to this pluralist view, the evidence in this chapter shows that (1) members of the upper class own almost half of all privately held stock, (2) many large stockholding families in the upper class continue to be involved in the direction of major corporations through family offices, investment partnerships, and holding companies, (3) members of the upper class are disproportionately represented on the boards of large corporations, which is evidence for upper-class power on the "Who governs?" indicator, and (4) the professional managers of middle-level origins are assimilated into the upper class both socially and economically and share the values of upper-class owners.

In addition to refuting the pluralist claim about a managerial revolution, this chapter shows that the corporate rich are drawn together by bonds of social cohesion as well as their common economic interests. This social cohesion is based in the two types of relationships found in a membership network: common membership in specific social institutions and friendships based on social interactions within those institutions. Research on small groups in laboratory settings by social psychologists suggests that social cohesion is greatest when (1) the social groups are seen to be exclusive and of high status, and (2) the interactions take place in relaxed and informal settings.[1] This chapter shows that many of the social institutions of the upper class fit these specifications very well. From the viewpoint of social psychology, the people who make up the upper class can be seen as members of numerous small groups that meet at private schools, social clubs, retreats, resorts, and social gatherings.

Social cohesion is important from a class-dominance perspective because the most socially cohesive groups are the ones that do best in arriving at consensus when dealing with a problem. The members are proud of their identification with the group and come to trust each other through their friendly interactions, so they are more likely to listen to each other and seek common ground.[2] If these findings can be generalized beyond the social psychology laboratory, as seems very likely, then social bonding can be seen as another reason why the corporate rich are cohesive enough to dominate the rest of society despite their small numbers.

The more extravagant social activities of the upper class—the expensive parties, the trips to spas and vacation spots all over the world, the involvement with exotic entertainers—are often viewed by pluralists as superfluous trivialities best left to society page writers. However, there is reason to believe that these activities play a role both in solidifying the upper class and in maintaining the class structure. Within the upper class itself, these occasions provide an opportunity for members to show that they are similar to one another and superior to the average citizen. As political scientist Gabriel Almond concluded in his study of the New York upper class and its involvement in city politics: "The elaborate private life of the plutocracy serves in considerable measure to separate them out in their own

Table 3.1 Hypothetical Membership Network Showing Overlap of the Corporate Community and the Upper Class

	Corporate Community			Upper Class			
	Corporation 1	*Bank 1*	*Law Firm 1*	*School 1*	*School 2*	*Club 1*	*Club 2*
Person:							
One	X	X		X		X	
Two			X	X		X	X
Three	X				X	X	
Four	X	X		Not part of upper class			
Five	Not part of corporate community			X		X	X

consciousness as a superior, more refined element."[3] Even more relevant, the values on which the class system is based are conveyed to the rest of the population in this conspicuous consumption. Such activities make clear that there is a gulf between members of the upper class and ordinary citizens, reminding everyone of the hierarchical nature of the society. Social extravaganzas bring home to everyone that there are great rewards for success, helping to stir up the personal envy that can be a goad to competitive striving.

In sociological terms, the upper class comes to serve as a "reference group." Sociologist Harold Hodges, in a discussion of his findings concerning social classes in the suburban areas south of San Francisco, expresses the power of the upper class as a reference group in the following way: "Numerically insignificant . . . the upper class is nonetheless highly influential as a 'reference group': a membership to which many aspire and which infinitely more consciously or unconsciously imitate."[4] Exhibiting high social status, in other words, is a way of exercising power. This "status power" operates by creating respect, envy, and deference in others.

The social institutions discussed in this chapter are important in one other way. They provide what are called "indicators" of upper-class standing. These indicators are useful starting points in determining the involvement of members of the upper class in the corporate community, the policy-formation network, and politics. These indicators are not perfect, for reasons explained throughout the chapter, but they are satisfactory for large-scale studies in which the various sources of error tend to cancel each other out.

In effect, the chapter is based on a membership network analysis that seeks to determine the degree of overlap between (1) the social institutions thought to make up the upper class, and (2) the corporate community and the upper class. The *hypothetical* membership matrix presented in table 3.1 demonstrates the general nature of the findings in this chapter. Note that the social institutions are not perfectly connected and that some members of the upper class are not part of the corporate community. Nor are all corporate executives originally part of the upper class. The executives not from the upper class are the kinds of leaders focused on by pluralists. The gradual assimilation of these rising executives into the upper class is explained later in the chapter.

Before turning to the social institutions of the upper class, and the involvement of leaders of the corporate community in them, it is necessary to explain the several meanings of the term *social class*.

THE IDEA OF SOCIAL CLASS

Most Americans do not like the idea that there are social classes. Classes imply that people have relatively fixed stations in life. They fly in the face of beliefs about equality of opportunity and seem to ignore the evidence of upward social mobility. Even more, Americans tend to deny that social classes are based in wealth and occupational roles but then belie that denial through a fascination with rags-to-riches stories and the trappings of wealth.

American dislike for the idea of class is deeply rooted in the country's colonial and revolutionary history. Because it was a rapidly expanding frontier country with no feudal aristocracy, colonial America seemed very different from other countries to its new inhabitants, most of whom wanted to escape the fixed stations that were their fate in Europe. The sense of difference was heightened by the need for solidarity among all classes in the nationalistic war for freedom from England. Revolutionary leaders from the higher classes had to concede greater freedom and equality for common people to gain their support. Historian Robert Palmer states the situation succinctly: "Leaders who did not fight for equality accepted it in order to win."[5]

Although large differences in wealth, income, and lifestyle already existed in revolutionary America, particularly in port cities and the South, these well-understood inequalities were usually explained away or downplayed by members of the middle classes as well as by the merchants, plantation owners, and lawyers who were at the top of the social ladder. As a detailed historical study of diaries, letters, newspapers, and other documents of the period demonstrates, Americans instead emphasized and took pride in the fact that "class distinctions were minor in comparison with Europe." They recognized that there were rich and poor, but they preferred to think of their country "as one of equality and proudly pointed to such features as the large middle class, the absence of beggars, the comfortable circumstances of most people, and the limitless opportunities for those who worked hard and saved their money."[6] The fact that nearly 20 percent of the population was held in slavery, and that 100,000 Native Americans lived in the western areas of the colonies, was not part of this self-definition. It is clear, however, that the free white majority also defined itself in terms of the potentially dangerous slaves on the one hand and the warlike "savages" on the other, leading to a concern with guns and a level of violence that remain prominent features of American society.

Even members of the upper class preferred this more democratic class system to what had existed for many centuries in Europe. To emphasize this point, Palmer begins his two-volume work on the age of the democratic revolution in North America and Europe with a letter written from Europe in 1788 by a young adult member of a prominent American upper-class family. After noting his disgust with the hereditary titles and pomp of the European class system, and with the obsequiousness of the lower classes, the young man stated his conviction that "a certain degree of equality is essential to human bliss." He then went on to argue that the greatness of the United States was that it had provided this degree of equality "without destroying the necessary subordination."[7] As if to make sure the limits of his argument were clear, he underlined the words *a certain degree of equality*.

Two hundred years later, in response to sociologists who wanted to know what social class meant to Americans, a representative sample of the citizenry in Boston and Kansas City expressed ideas similar to those of the first Americans. Although most people were keenly aware of differences in social standing and judged status levels primarily in terms of income, occupations, and education (but especially income), they emphasized the openness of the system and the opportunity for advancement. They also argued that a person's social standing was in good part determined by such individual qualities as initiative and the motivation to work hard. Moreover, many of them felt that the importance of class was declining. This belief was partly due to their conviction that people of all ethnic and religious backgrounds were being treated with greater respect and decency whatever their occupational and educational levels, but even more to what they saw as material evidence for social advancement in the occupations and salaries of their families and friends. In the words of sociologists, social mobility and a formal system of equality in all areas of political and social life make class a relatively unimportant idea for Americans. People are very aware of basic economic and educational differences, and they can size up social standing fairly well from such outward signs as speech patterns, mannerisms, and style of dress, but the existence of social classes is nonetheless passed over as quickly as possible.[8]

People of the highest social status share the general distaste for talking about social class in an open and direct way. In a classic study of social classes in New Haven, Connecticut, a person in the top category in terms of neighborhood residence and educational background seemed startled when asked about her class level. After regaining her composure, she replied: "One does not speak of classes; they are felt."[9] In the study of Boston and Kansas City residents, an upper-class Bostonian said: "Of course social class exists—it influences your thinking." Then she added: "Maybe you shouldn't use the word 'class' for it, though—it's really a niche that each of us fits into."[10] As part of a study of thirty-eight upper-class women in a large Midwestern city, sociologist Susan Ostrander bluntly asked her informants at the end of the interview if they were members of the upper class. The answers she received had the same flavor of hesitation and denial:

> I hate [the term] upper class. It's so non-upper class to use it. I just call it "all of us," those of us who are wellborn.

> I hate to use the word "class." We're responsible, fortunate people, old families, the people who have something.

> We're not supposed to have layers. I'm embarrassed to admit to you that we do, and that I feel superior at my social level. I like being part of the upper crust.[11]

Social scientists mean much the same things by the term *social class* as do typical Americans, but their definitions emphasize that class is a double-edged concept, denoting both the relationship between categories of people and the specific categories within the overall relationship. Large-scale employers and wage earners both can be considered classes, for example, but the idea of classes also encompasses the relationship between them. In defining classes for research purposes, however, sociologists and other social scientists tend to stress the similarities and interconnections among families and individuals at a given social level more than they do the relationship between levels. In one of the first empirical investigations of social class in America, a study of caste and class in a Southern city in the 1930s, the sociological researchers defined a social class as:

> The largest group of people whose members have intimate access to one another. A class is composed of families and social cliques.

The interrelationships between these families and cliques, in such informal activities as visiting, dances, receptions, teas, and larger informal affairs, constitute the structure of the social class. A person is a member of the social class with which most of his or her participations, of this intimate kind, occur.[12]

Similar definitions are provided by researchers from other disciplines. One social psychology textbook defines a social class as "a division of a society, made up of persons possessing certain common social characteristics which are taken to qualify them for intimate equal-status relations with one another, and which restrict their interaction with members of other social classes."[13] Political scientist Robert Dahl defines equal "social standing" in terms of

the extent to which members of that circle would be willing— disregarding personal and idiosyncratic factors—to accord the conventional privileges of social intercourse and acceptance among equals; marks of social acceptability include willingness to dine together, to mingle freely in intimate social events, to accept membership in the same clubs, to use forms of courtesy considered appropriate among social equals, to intermarry, and so on.[14]

A definition of social class based on various types of social interactions also is used by Marxian social scientists, even though their primary emphasis is on the relational dimension of the concept. Economist Paul Sweezy, raised in an upper-class family, concludes that classes are "obstinate facts and not mere logical categories" and that "the fundamental unit of class membership is the family and not the individual." He closes by saying: "A social class, then, is made up of freely intermarrying families."[15]

There is a general consensus, then, on what is meant by the term *social class*. Indeed, it may be the only concept on which there is widespread agreement when it comes to studying power in the United States. The real problem begins with the question of whether an upper social class exists in the United States that is based in the corporate community.

THE INSTITUTIONAL INFRASTRUCTURE

If there is an American upper class, it must exist not merely as a collection of families who feel comfortable with each other and tend to exclude outsiders from their social activities. It must exist as a set of interrelated social institutions. That is, there must be patterned ways of organizing the lives of its members from infancy to old age that create a relatively unique style of life, and there must be mechanisms for socializing both the younger generation and new adult members who have risen from lower social levels. If the class is a reality, the names and faces may change somewhat over the years, but the social institutions that underlie the upper class must persist with remarkably little change over several generations. This emphasis on the institution-alized nature of the upper class, which reflects a long-standing empiri-cal tradition in studies of it, is compatible with the theoretical focus of the "new institutionalists" within sociology and political science.[16]

Four different types of empirical studies establish the existence of an interrelated set of social institutions, organizations, and social activities. They are historical case studies, quantitative studies of biographical directories, open-ended surveys of knowledgeable ob-servers, and interview studies with members of the upper-middle and upper classes.

The first and most detailed historical study of the upper class was carried out by sociologist E. Digby Baltzell. A member of the upper class himself, Baltzell drew together all previous historical and anecdotal data on the subject and then turned his attention to the his-torical development of the upper class in Philadelphia. He was able to demonstrate in this way that the people of highest status and great-est wealth gradually created a set of exclusive neighborhoods, expen-sive private schools, restricted social clubs, and such unique social occasions as debutante balls and fox hunts.[17] Building from his Philadelphia materials, Baltzell was able to show that in the late nine-teenth and early twentieth centuries, members of the city's upper class began to frequent the same resorts as the people of highest status in other Eastern cities. They sent their children to boarding schools in New England and Virginia that catered to the wealthy from other cities across the country, and they joined the social clubs of their counter-parts in other cities.

Baltzell also found that they were listed in great numbers in an exclusive intercity address and telephone book called the *Social Reg-ister*, symbolizing the interconnectedness of the families in many dif-ferent cities. Founded in 1887, *Social Register*s existed for thirteen major cities and contained approximately 65,000 families from the 1950s to 1976, when they were consolidated into one large volume because of declining interest on the part of upper-class listees. Since that time, the *Social Register* has been pared back to the point where it includes only about 30,000 families, mostly of long-standing wealth on the East Coast. It is still very useful for some purposes, but it is now too narrow to be used as an indicator of upper-class standing.[18]

In effect, Baltzell showed the relationships among these institu-tions and activities by demonstrating that the same few people created and belonged to all of them. To test and extend his findings, I did the same kind of study in an ahistorical and quantitative way with information on school attendance and club membership from 3,000 randomly selected *Who's Who in America* biographies, along with listings in the *Social Register.* The memberships and affiliations were analyzed with a statistical technique known as *contingency analysis.* This technique provides a way to uncover relationships between two or more affiliations by determining whether their appearance together is greater than would be expected by chance.[19] The findings of this study fully supported Baltzell's claim that a relationship exists among listing in the *Social Register,* attendance at prep schools, and membership in one or more of several social clubs.

A very different method—using newspaper editors as informants—provided further support for these findings and also greatly extended the list of clubs and schools. For this study, I sent a questionnaire to editors of women's pages and society pages at newspapers in the 317 cities with a chapter of the Junior League, an exclusive women's service organization. It was used as a starting point because it is one of the few nationwide organizations known to have a great many upperclass members. In essence, the questionnaire asked if there was a set of high-status schools and clubs in the city and if their members were also members of the Junior League or listed in the *Social Register.* In all, 128 questionnaires were returned. Some had very little information, but most were quite informative. In twelve cases, replies were received from two different newspapers in a city, and in all but one instance there was complete agreement. The replies of these well-placed observers also produced strong agreement with the findings of Baltzell's historical study and my contingency analysis.[20]

Intensive interviews with a cross-section of citizens provide the fourth way of establishing the existence of upper-class institutions. The most detailed study of this type was conducted in Kansas City. The study concerned people's perceptions of the social ladder as a whole, from top to bottom, but it is the top level that is of relevance here. Although most people in Kansas City could point to the existence of exclusive neighborhoods in suggesting that there was a class of "blue bloods" or "big rich," members of the upper-middle class and the upper class itself demonstrated that clubs and other social institutions as well as neighborhoods gave the class an institutional existence.[21]

The schools and clubs discovered by these and related investigations are listed in Appendix 1 because they have been used as indicators of upper-class standing in past studies. The *Social Register* and other directories are listed as well but are now utilized primarily for historical investigations. These indicators are criteria by which it can be determined in a general way how many people in a given group, organization, or agency are members of the upper class. Such information is useful when the "Who sits?" indicator of power is being employed.

As noted in the first chapter, no indicators in the social sciences are perfect, and these are no exception. As Baltzell emphasizes, constructing any set of indicators involves simplifications. Indicators must be seen as "only a convenient tool which is constructed to approximate" the concept being studied.[22] They are subject to two different kinds of errors that tend to cancel each other out in group data.

"False positives" are those people who qualify as members of the upper class according to the indicators even though further investigation would show that they are not really members. Scholarship students at private secondary schools are one example of a false positive. Honorary and performing members of social clubs, who usually are members of the middle class, are another important type of false positive. "False negatives" are people who do not seem to meet any of the criteria of upper-class standing but are in fact members of the upper class. Such people probably are much more prevalent than false positives because researchers are dependent on published biographical sources and newspapers that may or may not include the necessary information on the person's schools and clubs.

Private schools are especially underreported. Prominent political figures of the past such as Governor Averell Harriman of New York, Governor Adlai Stevenson of Illinois, President John F. Kennedy, and Mayor John V. Lindsay of New York never listed their private secondary schools in *Who's Who in America*, for example, and President George Bush removed his from the 1980–1981 edition when he became vice president. More generally, a study of 168 Hotchkiss alumni listed in *Who's Who in America* found that 37 percent did not list their graduation from that prestigious boarding school.[23] Similar findings are reported in a study of corporate officers and directors listed in *Who's Who in America:* Of 177 executives and directors on the alumni lists of eleven top prep schools, 55 percent did not list their school affiliation.[24]

Membership in social clubs may also go unreported in *Who's Who in America*. I found that neither President Reagan nor President Bush ever listed membership in the prominent Bohemian Club of San Francisco (discussed later in the chapter). But they are not the only ones who omitted this information. Of the 326 Bohemians listed in *Who's Who in America* for 1980–1981, 29 percent did not include this affiliation.

There are other problems that produce false negatives. Social registers and social directories exist for only a relative handful of cities, and there are some people who choose not to be included in those directories. Also, a substantial number of people prefer to keep their children close to home in small private schools that are little known and hardly ever listed in standard biographical sources. In a few exclusive neighborhoods, the suburban high schools are considered quite adequate for upper-class children, and only more subtle cues, such as debutante parties, separate the upper-middle from the upper class. Finally, some upper-class people belong only to specialized clubs for fox hunting or horse showing, which are not uncovered in statistical attempts to establish upper-class indicators.

None of these points casts any doubt on the usefulness of the indicators, however. They show only that the indicators must be used with caution. Moreover, these points all raise interesting empirical questions deserving of systematic studies. Why are scholarship students sought by some private schools, and are such students likely to become part of the upper class? Why aren't private schools and clubs listed in biographical sources by some members of the upper class? Why are some middle-class people taken into upper-class clubs? Why do some upper-class people decline to be listed in a social directory? Merely to ask these questions is to suggest the complex social and psychological reality that lies beneath this seemingly dry catalogue of upper-class indicators. More generally, the information included or excluded in a social register or biographical directory is a "presentation of self" that social psychologist Richard Zweigenhaft has shown to be highly revealing concerning religious, ethnic, and class identifications.[25]

These indicators are the beginning, not the end, of sociological studies of the upper class. They could be expanded greatly by a computerized analysis of all the major biographical sources using the statistical technique of contingency analysis. They could be made even more accurate by assigning weights to each indicator through factor analysis or discriminant analysis. Until a mathematical sociologist develops a deep interest in research on power, however, they are more than adequate for most studies of the upper class.

PREPPING FOR POWER

From infancy through young adulthood, members of the upper class receive a distinctive education. This education begins early in life in preschools that frequently are attached to a neighborhood church of high social status. Schooling continues during the elementary years at a local private school called a day school. During the adolescent years the student may remain at day school, but there is a strong chance that at least one or two years will be spent away from home at a boarding school in a quiet rural setting. Higher education will take place at one of a small number of heavily endowed private colleges and universities. Large and well-known Ivy League schools in the East and Stanford in the West head the list, followed by smaller Ivy League schools in the East and a handful of other small private schools in other parts of the country. Although some upper-class children may attend public high school if they live in a secluded suburban setting, or go to a state university if there is one of great esteem and tradition in their home state, the system of formal schooling is so insulated that many upper-class students never see the inside of a public school in all their years of education.

This separate educational system is important evidence for the distinctiveness of the mentality and life-style that exists within the upper class because schools play a large role in transmitting the class structure to their students. Surveying and summarizing a great many studies on schools in general, sociologist Randall Collins concludes: "Schools primarily teach vocabulary and inflection, styles of dress, aesthetic tastes, values and manners."[26] His statement takes on greater significance for studies of the upper class when it is added that only 1 percent of American teenagers attend independent private high schools of an upper-class nature.[27]

The training of upper-class children is not restricted to the formal school setting, however. Special classes, and even tutors, are a regular part of their extracurricular education. This informal education usually begins with dancing classes in the elementary years, which are seen as important for learning proper manners and the social graces. Tutoring in a foreign language may begin in the elementary years, and there are often lessons in horseback riding and music as well. The teen years find the children of the upper class in summer camps or on special travel tours, broadening their perspectives and polishing their social skills.

The linchpins in the upper-class educational system are the dozens of boarding schools founded in the last half of the nineteenth and the early part of the twentieth centuries. Baltzell concludes that these schools became "surrogate families" that played a major role "in creating an upper-class subculture on almost a national scale in America."[28] The role of boarding schools in providing connections to other upper-class social institutions is also important. As one informant explained to Ostrander in her interview study of upper-class women: "Where I went to boarding school, there were girls from all over the country, so I know people from all over. It's helpful when you move to a new city and want to get invited into the local social club."[29]

It is within these few hundred schools that are consciously modeled after their older and more austere British counterparts that a distinctive style of life is inculcated through such traditions as the initiatory hazing of beginning students, the wearing of school blazers or ties, compulsory attendance at chapel services, and participation in esoteric sports such as squash and crew. Even a different terminology is adopted to distinguish these schools from public schools. The principal is a headmaster or rector, the teachers are sometimes called masters, and the students are in forms, not grades. Great emphasis is placed on the building of "character." The role of the school in preparing the future leaders of America is emphasized through the speeches of the headmaster and the frequent mention of successful alumni. Thus, boarding schools are in many ways the kind of highly effective socializing agent that sociologist Erving Goffman calls "total institutions," isolating their members from the outside world and providing them with a set of routines and traditions that encompass most of their waking hours.[30] The end result is a feeling of separateness and superiority that comes from having survived a rigorous education. As a retired business leader told one of my research assistants: "At school we were made to feel somewhat better [than other people] because of our class. That existed, and I've always disliked it intensely. Unfortunately, I'm afraid some of these things rub off on one."[31]

Almost all graduates of private secondary schools go on to college, and almost all do so at prestigious universities. Graduates of the New England boarding schools, for example, historically found themselves at one of four large Ivy League universities: Harvard, Yale, Princeton, and Columbia. However, that situation changed somewhat after World War II as the boarding schools grew and provided more scholarships. An analysis of admission patterns for graduates of fourteen prestigious boarding schools between 1953 and 1967 demonstrated this shift by showing that the percentage of their graduates attending Harvard, Yale, or Princeton gradually declined over those years from 52 to 25 percent. Information on the same fourteen schools for the years 1969 to 1979 showed that the figure had bottomed out at 13 percent in 1973, 1975, and 1979, with some schools showing very little change from the late 1960s and others dropping even more dramatically.[32] Now many upper-class students attend a select handful of smaller private liberal arts colleges, most of which are in the East, but there are a few in the South and West as well.

Graduates of private schools outside of New England most frequently attend a prominent state university in their area, but a significant minority go to Eastern Ivy League and top private universities in other parts of the country. For example, the Cate School, a boarding school near Santa Barbara, California, is modeled after its New England counterparts and draws most of its students from California and other Western states. In the four years between 1993 and 1996, 35 percent of the 245 graduates went to one of fifteen prestigious Eastern schools, with Middlebury (12), Harvard (10), and Brown (7) topping the list. The other leading destinations for Cate graduates were the University of California (27), Stanford (9), University of Colorado (9), Georgetown (8), Duke (7), Vanderbilt (6), and University of Chicago (5). Or, to take another example, St. John's in Houston is a lavishly endowed day school built in the Gothic architecture typical of many universities. From 1992 through 1996, 22 percent of its 585 graduates went to the fifteen Eastern schools used in the Cate analysis, with Princeton (27), the University of Pennsylvania (15), Cornell (13), Harvard (12), and Yale (12) the most frequent destinations. As might be expected, the most graduates attended the University of Texas (105). Rice (49), Vanderbilt (33), and Stanford (15) were high on the list. Few graduates of either Cate or St. John's went to non-prestigious state schools.[33]

A majority of private school graduates pursue careers in business, finance, or corporate law. For example, a classification of the occupations of a sample of the graduates of four private schools—St. Mark's, Groton, Hotchkiss, and Andover—showed that the most frequent occupation for all but the Andover graduates was some facet of finance and banking. Others became presidents of medium-size businesses or were partners in large corporate law firms. A small handful went to work as executives for major national corporations.[34]

The business-oriented preoccupations of upper-class men is demonstrated in greater detail in a study of the careers of all those who graduated from Hotchkiss between 1940 and 1950. Using the school's alumni files, one researcher followed the careers of 228 graduates from their date of graduation until 1970. Fifty-six percent of the sample were either bankers or business executives, with 80 of the 91 businessmen serving as president, vice president, or partner in their firms. Another 10 percent of the sample were lawyers, mostly as partners in large firms closely affiliated with the business community. Outside the world of business, the most frequent occupations of the remaining one-third of the Hotchkiss graduates studied were physician (7 percent), engineer (6 percent), and public official (3 percent).[35]

Although finance, business, and law are the most typical occupations of upper-class males, there is no absence of physicians, architects, museum officials, and other professional occupations. This fact is demonstrated most systematically in Baltzell's study of Philadelphia: 39 percent of the Philadelphia architects and physicians listed in *Who's Who* for the early 1940s were also listed in the *Social Register,* as were 35 percent of the museum officials. These figures are close to the 51 percent for lawyers and the 42 percent for businessmen, although they are far below the 75 percent for bankers—clearly the most prestigious profession in Philadelphia at that time.[36]

The involvement of private school graduates on boards of directors is demonstrated in my detailed study of all alumni over the age of 45 in 1980 from one of the most prestigious Eastern boarding schools, St. Paul's. Using *Poor's Register of Corporations, Directors and Executives* and *Who's Who in America*, it showed that 303 of these several thousand men were serving as officers or directors in corporations in general and that 102 were directors of ninety-seven corporations in the Fortune 800. Their involvement was especially great in the financial sector. Most striking of all, 21 graduates of St. Paul's were either officers or directors at J. P. Morgan Bank, one of the five largest banks in the country. This finding suggests that the alumni of particular schools may tend to cluster at specific banks or corporations.

A Better Chance

As noted in the discussion of upper-class indicators and "false positives" in the previous section, private schools sometimes include scholarship students in their programs. The largest and most extensive of these programs, called A Better Chance, shows how private schools can be used to assimilate low-income minorities into the upper class in times of social turmoil. Founded in 1963 as a reaction to the Civil Rights Movement, the program, known as ABC, has graduated nearly 11,000 minority-group teenagers from 100 prestigious private schools and a few select public schools, about 70 percent of whom are African-Americans from Northern ghettos and impoverished rural areas of the South. The program is based primarily on scholarship money from the corporate and individual charitable foundations (discussed in Chapter 4), but in its first few years it had government money as well.[37]

Virtually all ABC graduates have gone on to a higher education; Harvard, Dartmouth, Tufts, and the University of Pennsylvania were the most popular universities for the students who participated during the first twenty years of the program. Lengthy interviews with thirty-eight early graduates by Zweigenhaft, along with information from written sources, suggest that most graduates of the program have done extremely well—although there are, of course, a small percentage of failures, as there are among any group of private school or university graduates. Many of those studied by Zweigenhaft are now moving into senior positions in corporations, banks, and corporate law firms, and even more work in a wide range of professions. The highest ranking graduate of the program to date is Deval Patrick, a corporate lawyer from Boston, who served as Assistant Attorney General for Civil Rights in the first Clinton Administration, but the most famous ABC graduate is singer and songwriter Tracy Chapman, who sings about revolution and is not likely to join the power elite.[38]

The way in which such programs are viewed depends at least in part on a person's political orientation. For Baltzell, who favored the class system because of the opportunities and incentives he thought it provides, programs like ABC are useful because they prepare a broader range of talented people of all racial and ethnic backgrounds for possible leadership roles. For Sweezy, also raised in the upper class and educated at Exeter and Harvard, but a Marxist, such programs are to be deplored as "recruiters for the ruling class, sucking upwards the ablest elements of the lower classes and thus performing the double function of infusing new brains into the ruling class and weakening the potential leadership of the working class."[39]

From kindergarten through college, then, schooling is very different for members of the upper class and it teaches them to be distinctive in many ways. In a country where education is highly valued and nearly everyone attends public schools, this private system benefits primarily members of the upper class and provides one of the foundations for the old-boy and old-girl networks that will be with them throughout their lives.

SOCIAL CLUBS

Just as private schools are a pervasive feature in the lives of upper-class children, so, too, are private social clubs a major point of orientation in the lives of upper-class adults. These clubs also play a role in differentiating members of the upper class from other members of society. According to Baltzell, "the club serves to place the adult members of society and their families within the social hierarchy." He quotes with approval the suggestion by historian Crane Brinton that the club "may perhaps be regarded as taking the place of those extensions of the family, such as the clan and the brotherhood, which have disappeared from advanced societies."[40] Conclusions similar to Baltzell's resulted from an interview study in Kansas City: "Ultimately, say upper-class Kansas Citians, social standing in their world reduces to one issue: where does an individual or family rank on the scale of private club memberships and informal cliques?"[41]

The clubs of the upper class are many and varied, ranging from family-oriented country clubs and downtown men's and women's clubs to highly specialized clubs for yacht owners, gardening enthusiasts, and fox hunters. Many families have memberships in several different types of clubs, but the days when most of the men by themselves were in a half dozen or more clubs faded before World War II. Downtown men's clubs originally were places for having lunch and dinner, and occasionally for attending an evening performance or a weekend party. But as upper-class families deserted the city for large suburban estates, a new kind of club, the country club, gradually took over some of these functions. The downtown club became almost entirely a luncheon club, a site to hold meetings, or a place to relax on a free afternoon. The country club, by contrast, became a haven for

all members of the family. It offered social and sporting activities ranging from dances, parties, and banquets to golf, swimming, and tennis.
Special group dinners were often arranged for all members on Thurs-
day night—the traditional maid's night off across the United States.

Sporting activities are the basis for most of the specialized clubs
of the upper class. The most visible are the yachting and sailing clubs,
followed by the clubs for lawn tennis or squash. The most exotic are the
several dozen fox hunting clubs. They have their primary strongholds in
rolling countrysides from southern Pennsylvania down into Virginia,
but they exist in other parts of the country as well. Riding to hounds
in scarlet jackets and black boots, members of the upper class sustain
over 130 hunts under the banner of the Masters of Fox Hounds Association. The intricate rituals and grand feasts accompanying the event, including the Blessing of the Hounds by an Episcopal bishop in the Eastern
hunts, go back to the eighteenth century in the United States.[42]

Initiation fees, annual dues, and expenses vary from a few thousand dollars in downtown clubs to tens of thousands of dollars in
some country clubs, but money is not the primary barrier in gaining
membership to a club. Each club has a very rigorous screening process before accepting new members. Most require nomination by one
or more active members, letters of recommendation from three to six
members, and interviews with at least some members of the membership committee. Names of prospective members are sometimes posted
in the clubhouse, so all members have an opportunity to make their
feelings known to the membership committee. Negative votes by two
or three members of what is typically a ten- to twenty-person committee often are enough to deny admission to the candidate. The careful-
ness with which new members are selected extends to a guarding of
club membership lists, which are usually available only to club members. Older membership lists are sometimes given to libraries by
members or their surviving spouses, but for most clubs there are no
membership lists in the public domain.

Not every club member is an enthusiastic participant in the life
of the club. Some belong out of tradition or a feeling of social necessity. One woman told Ostrander the following about her country club:
"We don't feel we should withdraw our support even though we don't
go much." Others mentioned a feeling of social pressure: "I've only
been to [the club] once this year. I'm really a loner, but I feel I have to
go and be pleasant even though I don't want to." Another volunteered:
"I think half the members go because they like it and half because they
think it's a social necessity."[43]

People of the upper class often belong to clubs in several cities,
creating a nationwide pattern of overlapping memberships. These
overlaps provide evidence for social cohesion within the upper class.

An indication of the nature and extent of this overlapping is revealed by sociologist Philip Bonacich's study of membership lists for twenty clubs in several major cities across the country, including the Links in New York, the Century Association in New York, the Duquesne in Pittsburgh, the Chicago in Chicago, the Pacific Union in San Francisco, and the California in Los Angeles. Using his own original clustering technique based on Boolean algebra, his study revealed there was sufficient overlap among eighteen of the twenty clubs to form three regional groupings and a fourth group that provided a bridge between the two largest regional groups. The several dozen men who were in three or more of the clubs—most of them very wealthy people who also sat on several corporate boards—were especially important in creating the overall pattern. At the same time, the fact that these clubs often have from 1,000 to 2,000 members makes the percentage of overlap within this small number of clubs relatively small, ranging from as high as 20 to 30 percent between clubs in the same city to as low as 1 or 2 percent in clubs at opposite ends of the country.[44]

The overlap of this club network with corporate boards of directors provides evidence for the intertwining of the upper class and corporate community. In one study, the club memberships of the chairs and outside directors of the twenty largest industrial corporations were counted. The overlaps with upper-class clubs in general were ubiquitous, but the concentration of directors in a few clubs was especially notable. At least one director from twelve of the twenty corporations was a member of the Links Club, which Baltzell calls "the New York rendezvous of the national corporate establishment."[45] Seven of General Electric's directors were members, as were four from Chrysler, four from Westinghouse, three from IBM, and two from U.S. Steel. In addition to the Links, several other clubs had directors from four or more corporations. A study I did using membership lists from eleven prestigious clubs in different parts of the country confirmed and extended these findings. A majority of the top twenty-five corporations in every major sector of the economy had directors in at least one of these clubs, and several had many more. For example, all of the twenty-five largest industrials had one or more directors in these eleven clubs. The Links in New York, with seventy-nine connections to twenty-one industrial corporations, had the most.

The Bohemian Grove As a Microcosm

The Bohemian Club is the most unusual and widely known club of the upper class. Its annual two-week retreat seventy-five miles north of San Francisco brings together members of the upper class, corporate leaders, celebrities, and government officials for relaxation and entertainment. They are joined by several hundred "associate" members, who pay lower dues in exchange for producing plays, skits, artwork, and other forms of entertainment. Fifty to 100 professors and university administrators, most of them from Stanford University and campuses of the University of California, are also included in the associate category. The encampment provides the best possible insight into the role of clubs in uniting the corporate community and the upper class. It is a microcosm of the world of the corporate rich.[46]

The 2,700-acre pristine forest setting called the Bohemian Grove was purchased by the club in the 1890s after twenty years of holding the retreat in rented quarters. Bohemians and their guests number anywhere from 1,500 to 2,500 for the three weekends in the encampment, which is always held during the last two weeks in July. However, there may be as few as 400 men in residence in the middle of the week because most return to their homes and jobs after the weekends. During their stay the campers are treated to plays, symphonies, concerts, lectures, and political commentaries by entertainers, musicians, scholars, corporate executives, and government officials. They also trapshoot, canoe, swim, drop by the Grove art gallery, and take guided tours into the outer fringe of the mountain forest. But a stay at the Bohemian Grove is mostly a time for relaxation and drinking in the modest lodges, bunkhouses, and even teepees that fit unobtrusively into the landscape along the two or three dirt roads that join the few "developed" acres within the Grove. It is like a summer camp for the power elite and their entertainers.

The men gather in little camps of from ten to thirty members during their stay—although the camps for associate members are often larger. Each of the approximately 120 camps has its own pet name, such as Sons of Toil, Cave Man, Mandalay, Toyland, Owl's Nest, Hill Billies, and Parsonage. A group of men from Los Angeles named their camp Lost Angels, and the men in the Bohemian chorus call their camp Aviary. Some camps are noted for special drinking parties, brunches, or luncheons to which they invite members from other camps. The camps are a fraternity system within the larger fraternity.

There are many traditional events during the encampment, including plays called the High Jinx and the Low Jinx. The most memorable event, however, is an elaborate ceremonial ritual called the Cremation of Care, which is held the first Saturday night. It takes place at the base of the forty-foot Owl Shrine constructed out of poured concrete and made even more resplendent by the mottled forest mosses that cover much of it. The Owl Shrine is only one of many owl symbols and insignias to be found in the Grove and the downtown clubhouse. The owl was adopted early in the club's history as its mascot, or totem animal. According to the club's librarian—who is also a historian at a large university—the event "incorporates druidical ceremonies, elements of medieval Christian liturgy, sequences directly inspired by the Book of Common Prayer, traces of Shakespearean drama and the seventeenth-century masque, and late nineteenth-century American lodge rites."[47] Bohemians are proud that the ceremony had been carried out 125 consecutive years as of 1997.

The opening ceremony is called the Cremation of Care because it involves the burning of an effigy named Dull Care, who symbolizes the burdens and responsibilities that these busy Bohemians now wish to shed temporarily. More than 250 Bohemians take part in the ceremony as priests, elders, acolytes, shore patrols, brazier bearers, boatmen, and woodland voices. After many flowery speeches and a long conversation with Dull Care, the high priest lights the fire with the flame from the Lamp of Fellowship, located on the "Altar of Bohemia" at the base of the shrine. The ceremony, which has the same initiatory functions as those of any fraternal or tribal group, ends with fireworks, shouting, and the playing of "There'll Be a Hot Time in the Old Town Tonight." The attempt to create a sense of cohesion and in-group solidarity among the assembled is complete. The laughter, drinking, and storytelling can now begin.[48]

But the retreat sometimes provides an occasion for more than fun and merriment. Although business is rarely discussed except in an informal way in groups of two or three, the retreat provides members with an opportunity to introduce their friends to politicians and hear formal noontime speeches (called Lakeside Talks because they take place across the lake from the Owl Shrine) from political candidates. Every Republican president of the twentieth century has been a member or guest at the Bohemian Grove. President Herbert Hoover (1929–1933) was the first Republican president to be a member, which gave him the honor of giving the final Lakeside Talk from the 1930s until his death in 1964. He was a member of Cave Man Camp, as was President Nixon. President Ford is in Mandalay, President Reagan in Owl's Nest, and President Bush in Hill Billies.

In 1995, House Speaker Newt Gingrich delivered the Lakeside Talk on the middle Saturday of the encampment and President Bush gave it on the final Saturday. The featured Saturday speakers in 1996 were the Republican governor of California and a former Republican secretary of state. Perhaps the most striking change in the Lakeside Talks in the 1990s is the absence of any leading Democrats. Although a Democratic president has never been a member or guest at the Grove, cabinet members from the Kennedy, Johnson, and Carter Administrations were prominent guests and Lakeside speakers in the past.[49]

An exhaustive analysis of the members and guests at the Bohemian Grove in 1970 and 1980 demonstrates the way in which one club intertwines the upper class with the entire corporate community. In

Table 3.2 Corporations with Three or More Directors Who Were Members of the Bohemian Club in 1991

Corporation	Number of Directors in Bohemian Club
Bank of America	7
Pacific Gas and Electric	5
AT&T	4
Pacific Enterprises	4
First Interstate Bank	4
McKesson Corporation	4
Carter-Hawley-Hale Stores	3
Ford Motor	3
FMC	3
Safeco Insurance	3
Potlatch Industries	3
Pope and Talbot	3
General Motors	3
Pacific Bell Telephone	3

Source: Peter Phillips, *A Relative Advantage: Sociology of the San Francisco Bohemian Club*. Ph.D. Dissertation, University of California, Davis, 1994, p. 77.

1970, 29 percent of the top 800 corporations had at least one officer or director at the Bohemian Grove festivities; in 1980, the figure was 30 percent. As might be expected, the overlap was especially great among the largest corporations, with twenty-three of the top twenty-five industrials represented in 1970, fifteen of twenty-five in 1980. Twenty of the twenty-five largest banks had at least one officer or director in attendance in both 1970 and 1980. Other business sectors were represented somewhat less.[50]

An even more intensive study by sociologist Peter Phillips, which includes participant-observation and interviews as well as membership network analysis, extends the sociological understanding of the Bohemian Grove into the 1990s. Using a list of 1,144 corporations—well beyond the 800 used in the studies for 1970 and 1980—Phillips nonetheless found that 24 percent of these companies had at least one director who was a member or guest in 1993. For the top 100 corporations outside of California, the figure was 42 percent, compared to 64 percent in 1971.[51] The companies with three or more directors who were members of the Bohemian Club in 1991 are listed in table 3.2.

As the case of the Bohemian Grove and its theatrical perfor-
mances rather dramatically illustrates, there seems to be a great deal
of truth to the earlier-cited suggestion by Crane Brinton that clubs
may function within the upper class the way that the clan or brotherhood does in tribal societies. With their restrictive membership policies, initiatory rituals, private ceremonials, and great emphasis on
tradition, clubs carry on the heritage of primitive secret societies.
They create among their members an attitude of prideful exclusive-
ness that contributes greatly to an in-group feeling and a sense of fraternity within the upper class.

In concluding this discussion of the Bohemian Club and its retreat as one small example of the intersection of the upper class and
corporate community, it needs to be stressed that the Bohemian
Grove is not a place of power. No conspiracies are hatched there, nor
anywhere else. Instead, it is a place where powerful people relax,
make new acquaintances, and enjoy themselves. It is primarily a place
of social bonding. The main sociological function of the Bohemian
Club and other clubs is stated by sociologist Thomas Powell, based on
his own interview study of members in upper-class clubs:

> The clubs are a repository of the values held by the upper-level
> prestige groups in the community and are a means by which
> these values are transferred to the business environment. The
> clubs are places in which the beliefs, problems, and values of the
> industrial organization are discussed and related to the other
> elements in the larger community. Clubs, therefore, are not only
> effective vehicles of informal communication, but also valuable
> centers where views are presented, ideas are modified, and new
> ideas emerge. Those in the interview sample were appreciative of
> this asset; in addition, they considered the club as a valuable
> place to combine social and business contacts.[52]

THE FEMALE HALF OF THE UPPER CLASS

During the late nineteenth and early twentieth centuries, women of
the upper class carved out their own distinct roles within the context
of male domination in business, finance, and law. They went to separate private schools, founded their own social clubs, and belonged to
their own volunteer associations. As young women and party goers,
they set the fashions for society. As older women and activists, they
took charge of the nonprofit social welfare and cultural institutions
of the society, serving as fund-raisers, philanthropists, and directors
in a manner parallel to what their male counterparts did in business
and politics. To prepare themselves for their leadership roles, in 1901

they created the Junior League to provide internships, role models, mutual support, and training in the management of meetings.

Due to the general social changes of the 1960s—and in particular the revival of the feminist movement—the socialization of wealthy young women has changed somewhat in recent decades. Many private schools are now coeducational. Their women graduates are encouraged to go to major four-year colleges rather than finishing schools. Women of the upper class are more likely to have careers; there are already two or three examples of women who have risen to the top of their family's business. They are also more likely to serve on corporate boards. Still, due to its emphasis on tradition, there may be even less gender equality in the upper class than there is in the professional stratum; it is not clear how much more equality will be attained.

The female half of the upper class has been studied by several sociologists. Their work provides an important window into the upper class and class consciousness in general as well as a portrait of the socialization of wellborn women. But before focusing on their work, it is worthwhile to examine one unique institution of the upper class that has not changed very much in its long history—the debutante party that announces a young woman's coming of age and eligibility for marriage. It contains general lessons on class consciousness and the difficulties of maintaining traditional socializing institutions in a time of social unrest.

The Debutante Season

The debutante season is a series of parties, teas, and dances that culminates in one or more grand balls. It announces the arrival of young women of the upper class into adult society with the utmost of formality and elegance. These highly expensive rituals—in which great attention is lavished on every detail of the food, decorations, and entertainment—have a long history in the upper class. They made their first appearance in Philadelphia in 1748 and Charleston, South Carolina, in 1762, and they vary only slightly from city to city across the country. They are a central focus of the Christmas social season just about everywhere, but in some cities debutante balls are held in the spring as well.

Dozens of people are involved in planning the private parties that most debutantes have before the grand ball. Parents, with the help of upper-class women who work as social secretaries and social consultants, spend many hours with dress designers, caterers, florists, decorators, bandleaders, and champagne importers, deciding on just the right motif for their daughter's coming out. Most parties probably cost between $25,000 and $75,000, but sometimes the occasion is so extraordinary that it draws newspaper attention. Henry Ford II spent $250,000 on a debutante party for one of his daughters, hiring a Paris designer to redo the Country Club of Detroit in an eighteenth-century chateau motif and flying in 2 million magnolia boughs from Mississippi to cover the walls of the corridor leading to the reception room. A Texas oil and real estate family chartered a commercial jet airliner for a party that began in Dallas and ended with an all-night visit to the clubs in the French Quarter of New Orleans.[53]

The debutante balls themselves are usually sponsored by local social clubs. Sometimes there is an organization whose primary purpose is the selection of debutantes and the staging of the ball, such as the Saint Cecelia Society in Charleston, South Carolina, or the Allegro Club in Houston, Texas. Adding to the solemnity of the occasion, the selection of the season's debutantes is often made by the most prominent upper-class males in the city, often through such secret societies as the Veiled Prophet in St. Louis or the Mardi Gras krewes in New Orleans.

Proceeds from the balls are usually given to a prominent local charity sponsored by members of the upper class. "Doing something for charity makes the participants feel better about spending," explains Mrs. Stephen Van Rensselear Strong, a social press agent in New York and herself a member of the upper class.[54] It also makes at least part of the expense of the occasion tax deductible.

Evidence for the great traditional importance attached to the debut is to be found in the comments Ostrander received from women who thought the whole process unimportant but made their daughters go through it anyhow: "I think it's passé, and I don't care about it, but it's just something that's done," explained one woman. Another commented: "Her father wanted her to do it. We do have a family image to maintain. It was important to the grandparents, and I felt it was an obligation to her family to do it." When people begin to talk about doing something out of tradition or to uphold an image, Ostrander suggests, then the unspoken rules that dictate class-oriented behavior are being revealed through ritual behavior.[55]

Despite the great importance placed on the debut by upper-class parents, the debutante season came into considerable disfavor among young women as the social upheavals of the late 1960s and early 1970s reached their climax. This decline reveals that the reproduction of the upper class as a social class is an effort that must be made with each new generation. Although enough young women participated to keep the tradition alive, a significant minority refused to participate, which led to the cancellation of some balls and the curtailment of many others. Stories appeared on the women's pages across the country telling of debutantes who thought the whole process was "silly" or that the money should be given to a good cause. By 1973, however, the situation began to change again, and by the mid-1970s things were back to normal.[56]

The decline of the debutante season and its subsequent resurgence in times of domestic tranquillity reveal very clearly that one of its latent functions is to help perpetuate the upper class from generation to generation. When the underlying values of the class were questioned by a few of its younger members, the institution went into decline. Attitudes toward such social institutions as the debutante ball are one indicator of whether adult members of the upper class have succeeded in insulating their children from the rest of society.

The Role of Volunteer

The most informative and intimate look at the adult lives of traditional upper-class women is provided in three different interview and observation studies, one on the East Coast, one in the Midwest, and one on the West Coast. They reveal the women to be both powerful and subservient, playing decision-making roles in numerous cultural and civic organizations but also accepting traditional roles at home vis-à-vis their husbands and children. By asking the women to describe a typical day and to explain which activities were most important to them, sociologists Arlene Daniels, Margot McLeod, and Susan Ostrander found that the role of community volunteer is a central preoccupation of upper-class women, having significance as a family tradition and as an opportunity to fulfill an obligation to the community. One elderly woman involved for several decades in both the arts and human services told Ostrander: "If you're privileged, you have a certain responsibility. This was part of my upbringing; it's a tradition, a pattern of life that my brothers and sisters do too."[57]

This volunteer role is institutionalized in the training programs and activities of a variety of service organizations, especially the Junior League, which is meant for women between 20 and 40 years of age, including some upwardly mobile professional women. "Voluntarism is crucial and the Junior League is the quintessence of volunteer work," said one woman. "Everything the League does improves the situation but doesn't rock the boat. It fits into existing institutions."[58]

Quite unexpectedly, Ostrander found that many of the women serving as volunteers, fund-raisers, and board members for charitable and civic organizations viewed their work as a protection of the American way of life against the further encroachment of government into areas of social welfare. Some even saw themselves as bulwarks against socialism. "There must always be people to do volunteer work," one said. "If you have a society where no one is willing, then you may as well have communism where it's all done by the government." Another commented: "It would mean that the government would take over, and it would all be regimented. If there are no volunteers, we would live in a completely managed society which is quite the opposite to our history of freedom." Another equated government support with socialism: "You'd have to go into government funds. That's socialism. The more we can keep independent and under private control, the better it is."[59]

Despite this emphasis on volunteer work, the women placed high value on family life. They arranged their schedules to be home when children came home from school (thirty of the thirty-eight in Ostrander's study had three or more children), and they emphasized that their primary concern was to provide a good home for their husbands. Several wanted to have greater decision-making power over their inherited wealth, but almost all wanted to take on the traditional roles of wife and mother, at least until their children were grown.

In recent years, thanks to the pressures on corporations from the women's movement, upper-class women have expanded their roles to include corporate directorships. A study of women in the corporate community by former sociologist Beth Ghiloni, now a corporate executive, found that 26 percent of all women directors had upper-class backgrounds, a figure very similar to overall findings for samples of predominantly male directors. The figure was even higher, about 71 percent, for the one-fifth of directors who described themselves as volunteers before joining corporate boards. Many of these women told Ghiloni that their contacts with male corporate leaders on the boards of women's colleges and cultural organizations led to their selection as corporate directors.[60]

Women of the upper class are in a paradoxical position. They are subordinate to male members of their class, but they nonetheless exercise important class power in some institutional arenas. They may or may not be fully satisfied with their ambiguous power status, but they bring an upper-class, antigovernment perspective to their exercise of power. There is thus class solidarity between men and women toward the rest of society. Commenting on the complex role of upper-class women, feminist scholar Catherine Stimson draws the following stark picture: "First they must do to class what gender has done to their work—render it invisible. Next, they must maintain the same class structure they have struggled to veil."[61]

MARRIAGE AND FAMILY CONTINUITY

The institution of marriage is as important in the upper class as it is in any level of American society, and it does not differ greatly from other levels in its patterns and rituals. Only the exclusive site of the occasion and the lavishness of the reception distinguish upper-class marriages. The prevailing wisdom within the upper class is that children should marry someone of their own social class. The women interviewed by Ostrander, for example, felt that marriage was difficult enough without differences in "interests" and "background," which seemed to be the code words for class in discussions of marriage. Marriages outside the class were seen as likely to end in divorce.[62]

The original purpose of the debutante season was to introduce the highly sheltered young women of the upper class to eligible marriage partners. It was an attempt to corral what Baltzell calls "the democratic whims of romantic love," which "often play havoc with class solidarity."[63] But the day when the debut could play such a role was long past, even by the 1940s. The function of directing romantic love into acceptable channels was taken over by fraternities and sororities, singles-only clubs, and exclusive summer resorts.

However, in spite of parental concerns and institutionalized efforts to provide proper marriage partners, some upper-class people marry members of the upper-middle and middle classes. Although there are no completely satisfactory studies, and none that are very recent, what information is available suggests that members of the upper class are no more likely to marry within their class than people of other social levels. The most frequently cited evidence on upper-class marriage patterns appears as part of biographical studies of prominent families. Though these studies demonstrate that a great many marriages take place within the class—and often between scions of very large fortunes—they also show that some marriages are to sons and daughters of middle-class professionals and managers. No systematic conclusions can be drawn from these examples.

Wedding announcements that appear in major newspapers provide another source of evidence on this question. In a study covering prominent wedding stories on the society pages on Sundays in June for two different years one decade apart, it was found that 70 percent of the grooms and 84 percent of the brides had attended a private secondary school. Two-thirds of the weddings involved at least one participant who was listed in the *Social Register,* with both bride and groom listed in the *Social Register* in 24 percent of the cases.[64] However, those who marry far below their station may be less likely to have wedding announcements prominently displayed, so such studies must be interpreted with caution.

A study that used the *Social Register* as its starting point may be indicative of rates of intermarriage within the upper class, but it is very limited in its scope and therefore can only be considered suggestive. It began with a compilation of all the marriages listed in the

Philadelphia *Social Register* for 1940 and 1960. Since the decision to list these announcements may be a voluntary one, a check of the marriage announcements in the *Philadelphia Bulletin* for those years was made to see if there were any marriages involving listees in the *Social Register* that had not been included, but none was found. One in every three marriages for 1940 and one in five for 1961 involved partners who were both listed in the *Social Register*. When private-school attendance and social club membership as well as the *Social Register* were used as evidence for upper-class standing, the rate of intermarriage averaged 50 percent for the two years. This figure is very similar to that for other social levels.[65]

The general picture for social class and marriage in the United States is suggested in a statistical study of neighborhoods and marriage patterns in the San Francisco area. Its results are very similar to those of the Philadelphia study using the *Social Register*. Of eighty grooms randomly selected from the highest-level neighborhoods, court records showed that 51 percent married brides of a comparable level. The rest married women from middle-level neighborhoods; only one or two married women from lower-level residential areas. Conversely, 63 percent of eighty-one grooms from the lowest-level neighborhoods married women from comparable areas, with under 3 percent having brides from even the lower end of the group of top neighborhoods. Completing the picture, most of the eighty-two men from middle-level areas married women from the same types of neighborhoods, but about 10 percent married into higher-level neighborhoods. Patterns of intermarriage, then, suggest both stability and some upward mobility through marriage into the upper class.[66]

Turning now to the continuity of the upper class, there is evidence that it is very great from generation to generation. This finding conflicts with the oft-repeated folk wisdom that there is a large turnover at the top of the American social ladder. Once in the upper class, families tend to stay there even as they are joined in each generation by new families and by middle-class brides and grooms who marry into their families. One study demonstrating this point began with a list of twelve families who were among the top wealthholders in Detroit for 1860, 1892, and 1902. After demonstrating their high social standing as well as their wealth, it traced their Detroit-based descendants to 1970. Nine of the twelve families still had members in the Detroit upper class; members from six families were directors of top corporations in the city. The study cast light on some of the reasons why the continuity is not even greater. One of the top wealthholders of 1860 had only one child, who in turn had no children. Another family dropped out of sight after the six children of the original 1860 wealthholder's only child went to court to divide the dwindling estate of $250,000 into six equal parts. A third family persisted into a fourth generation of four great-granddaughters, all of whom married outside of Detroit.[67]

Comprehensive evidence on the issue of continuity is presented in a study of iron and steel manufacturers of the late nineteenth century. Using a directory of iron and steel manufacturing plants for the years 1874 to 1901 to identify 696 steel manufacturers in six Midwestern cities, historian John Ingham studied their social origins as well as traced their descendants into the mid-twentieth century. Seventy percent of the men in the sample were the sons of well-to-do businesspeople and another 13 percent were the sons of professional men. Only 10 percent were the sons of blue-collar workers, and only 6 percent the sons of farmers. Although there are some variations from city to city, these overall findings are very similar to those of earlier studies on the social origins of nineteenth-century business leaders.

Tracing the families of the steel executives into the twentieth century, Ingham determined that most were listed in the *Social Register*, were members of the most exclusive social clubs, lived in expensive neighborhoods, and sent their children to Ivy League universities. He concludes that "there has been more continuity than change among the business elites and upper classes in America," and he contrasts his results with the claims made by several generations of impressionistic historians that there has been a decline of aristocracy, the rise of a new plutocracy, or a passing of the old order.[68]

A study of listings in the *Social Register* for 1940, 1977, and 1995 demonstrates the continuing presence of families descended from the largest fortunes of the nineteenth and early twentieth centuries. Using a list of eighty-seven families from Gustavus Myers' *History of the Great American Fortunes* and sixty-six from Ferdinand Lundberg's *America's Sixty Families*, sociologist David Broad found that 92 percent of the Myers families were still represented in 1977, with the figure falling only to 87 percent in 1995. In similar fashion, 88 percent of the Lundberg families were represented in 1977 and 83 percent in 1995. Broad also found that the men in over half of these families signaled their connection to the founder of the fortune by putting IV, V, or VI after their names. Almost half had the last name of their wealthy mothers as their first name, once again demonstrating the families' concern with continuity.[69]

It seems likely, then, that the American upper class is a mixture of old and new members. There is both continuity and social mobility, with the newer members being assimilated into the life-style of the class through participation in the schools, clubs, and other social institutions described in this chapter. There may be some tensions between those newly arrived and those of established status—as novelists and journalists love to point out—but what they have in common soon outweighs their differences.[70]

UPWARD MOBILITY: HORATIO ALGER
AND THE FORBES 400

Americans always have believed that anyone can rise from rags to riches if they try hard enough, but in fact a rise from the bottom to the top is very rare and often a matter of luck—being at the right place at the right time. In the late nineteenth century, a wealthy upper-class Bostonian with a Harvard education, Horatio Alger, became a best-selling author by writing short fictional books about young boys who had gone from penniless adversity to great wealth, and in real life the commentators of the day pointed to three or four actual examples. Subsequent research showed that most of the business leaders of that era did not fit the Horatio Alger myth. As one historian noted, Horatio Alger stories "have always been more conspicuous in American history books than in the American business elite."[71]

Since 1982 the Horatio Alger story line has been taken up by *Forbes*, a business magazine that each year publishes a list of the allegedly 400 richest Americans. "Forget old money," says the article that introduces the 1996 list. "Forget silver spoons. Great fortunes are being created almost monthly in the U.S. today by young entrepreneurs who hadn't a dime when we created this list 14 years ago."[72] Thomas Dye, using the *Forbes* lists as his starting place, stresses the same point with almost equal enthusiasm:

> Today over half of America's top wealth-holders are self-made single-generation tycoons. On the lists of billionaires and centi-millionaires, the names of self-made men and women outnumber heirs to family fortunes, and first- and second-generation immigrants abound. Moreover, in every successive list of top wealth-holders over the decades there are as many dropouts and newcomers as holdovers.[73]

But the Horatio Alger story is no less rare today than it was in the 1890s. A study of all those on the *Forbes* lists for 1995 and 1996 showed that at least 56 percent came from millionaire families and that another 14 percent came from the top 10 percent of the income ladder.[74] But even these figures are probably an underestimate because it is so difficult to obtain accurate information on family origins from those who want to obscure their pasts. Even those in the upwardly mobile 30 percent often had excellent educations or other advantages. As for the immigrants, they too sometimes came from wealthy families; contrary to the stereotype, not all immigrants to the United States arrive poor, at least not anymore.[75]

For example, consider the social background of Wayne Huizenga, owner of the professional football, baseball, and hockey teams in

Miami, estimated to be worth $1.4 billion in 1996 through the creation of, first, Waste Management Company, and then Blockbuster Video. As *Current Biography* puts it: "The hero of a real-life Horatio Alger story, in his early twenties, Huizenga worked as a garbage-truck driver."[76] But he was born in a Chicago suburb, graduated from a private high school, and had a grandfather who owned a garbage-collection business in Chicago. His father was a real estate investor. True, Huizenga did start his own garbage company in southern Florida after not showing much aptitude for school, but he also merged it with companies in Chicago that were successors to his grandfather's firm, one of which was headed by a cousin by marriage. This is enterprising behavior, but it is not a Horatio Alger saga.

Forbes also talks about several people on its list as college dropouts, but people who leave a prestigious institution like Harvard or Stanford to pursue a new opportunity in which timing is everything hardly fit the definition of a "college dropout." For example, William Gates, the richest person in the United States in 1996 with $18.5 billion, a graduate of Lakeside School, the top prep school in Seattle, left Harvard early to found Microsoft before someone beat him to what was the next step in the development of personal computers. His father is a corporate lawyer with one of the largest firms in Seattle.

Contrary to *Forbes* and Dye, most upward social mobility in the United States involves relatively small changes for those who are above the lowest 20 percent and below the top 5 percent. In a typical example, the grandfather is a blue-collar worker, the father has a good white-collar job based on a B.A. degree, and one or two of the father's children are lawyers or physicians, but most of the father's grandchildren are white-collar workers.[77]

DROPOUTS, FAILURES, AND CHANGE AGENTS

Not all men and women of the upper class fit the usual molds. A few are dropouts, failures, and even critics of the upper class. These exceptions, when they come to public attention, are sometimes used by pluralists to claim that the upper class is not cohesive enough to be a ruling class. True, some members of the upper class do become playboys and party givers who draw faded European royalty and entertainers into their worldwide social life, but even they can be of some use by providing leisure settings for working members of the upper class. Others turn to a bohemian life-style with an interest in music or writing that takes them away from their old haunts.

With a few long-standing exceptions, however, the anecdotal evidence also suggests that many of the young jet-setters and dropouts return to more familiar pathways. A daughter of upper-class Bostonians, for example, emerged as a celebrity in the early 1940s because she became a dancer in the Ziegfeld Follies and then ran off to Mexico, where she posed in the nude for a portrait by Diego Rivera. By 1947, when she dropped from media attention, she had settled back into the upper class as the wife of a wealthy New Yorker, raising horses and dogs, tending several houses, and gaining attention in the 1970s for her beautiful gardens.[78]

Numerous anecdotal examples also show that some members of the upper class even lead lives of failure, despite all the opportunities available to them. Although members of the upper class are trained for leadership and given every opportunity to develop feelings of self-confidence, there are some who fail in school, become involved with drugs and alcohol, or become mentally disturbed—at least in part because there are negative psychological aspects to an upper-class upbringing.[79] Once again, however, this cannot be seen as evidence for a lack of cohesion in the upper class, for there are bound to be some problems for individuals in any group.

There are even a few members of the upper class who abandon its institutions and values to become part of the liberal-labor coalition or leftists. They participate actively in liberal or leftist causes as well as lend financial support. Several liberal and socialist magazines of the past and present, including *The Nation* and *Mother Jones*, have been supported by such people. Some of the most visible recent examples of this tendency work through a national network of fifteen change-oriented foundations called the Funding Exchange. These foundations gave away about $50 million between their founding in the 1970s and the early 1990s. They receive money from wealthy individuals and then donate it to feminist, environmentalist, low-income, and minority-group activists. They also set up discussion groups for college-age members of the upper class who are working through issues relating to their class backgrounds and thinking about providing money for liberal causes. In the case of the Haymarket Foundation, studied in depth by Ostrander, the committee that makes the donations—which amount to about $400,000 per year—is composed primarily of activists from groups that have been supported by the foundation. Ostrander concludes that this approach provides a way to overcome the usual power relations between donors and recipients and thereby helps to create a potentially egalitarian movement.[80]

The fact that upper-class families produce some liberal and leftist activists is one reason why social psychologists believe it is counterproductive for the leaders of social movements to talk in terms of class categories in seeking adherents, pitting the "greedy ruling class" against the victimized but heroic "working class." Such a strategy makes the assimilation of upper-class liberals and leftists more difficult because an emphasis on class origins heightens the differences among members of the movement, rather than reducing them. It relies on stereotypes and creates "out-groups," which sometimes compounds the problem by creating self-fulfilling negative outcomes. For this reason, most social psychologists favor the approach taken by Martin Luther King, Jr., and the Civil Rights Movement because it emphasizes (1) shared values and (2) "redemption" through the conversion to new beliefs. They point out that people can never rid themselves of the categories they are born into—such as those of race and class—but they can change their values and their practices, which is the actual goal sought by a democratic social movement.[81] The Haymarket Foundation change agents are evidence that a focus on shared values and redemption can be useful in bringing about social change.

WEALTH AND POWER: WHO BENEFITS?

It is obvious that members of the upper class must have large amounts of wealth and income if they can afford the tuition at private schools, the fees at country clubs, and the very high expenses of an elegant social life. Exactly how much they have, however, is a difficult matter to determine because the Internal Revenue Service does not release information on individuals and most people are not willing to volunteer details on this subject.

Direct questions about a person's money are frowned on in America, even in the upper class. One young member of the upper class in Boston told an interviewer: "Money was never talked about. I still don't know how much the family is worth. I have no idea."[82] Nor are the adult members of the upper class likely to talk about their wealth or the distribution of wealth in general. After presenting figures on the wealth distribution, an upper-class society writer notes that "I have never heard a dinner conversation in which figures such as these have been discussed."[83] Instead, she reports, any conversation concerning money is more likely to concern the outrageous starting salaries of bus drivers, police officers, and other working people. Even people with millions of dollars are likely to deny they are rich if they are asked directly. This reaction is in part genuine, for they always know someone else who has much more money and makes them feel poor by comparison. This phenomenon is well-known to social psychologists from studies of other social comparisons: There is always someone who is more knowledgeable, more talented, or richer, and that is what people often focus on.

In considering the distribution of wealth and income in the United States, it must be stressed that they are two separate issues.

Table 3.3 The Distribution of Net Worth, Financial Wealth, and Income for 1983, 1989, and 1992

	Net Worth			Financial Wealth			Income		
	1983	1989	1992	1983	1989	1992	1983	1989	1992
Top 1%	33.8	39.0	37.2	42.9	48.3	45.6	12.8	16.4	15.7
Next 19%	47.6	45.6	46.6	48.4	45.8	46.7	39.0	39.0	40.7
Bottom 80%	18.7	15.4	16.3	8.7	6.1	7.8	48.1	44.5	43.7

Source: Edward Wolff, *Top Heavy* (New York: Twentieth Century Fund, 1996), p. 67. Reprinted with permission from the Twentieth Century Fund, New York.

Net Worth = Total assets minus debts.

Financial Wealth = Net worth minus net equity in owner-occupied housing (a good indication of liquidity).

Wealth distribution has to do with the concentration of ownership of marketable assets, which may include tangible things such as land, machinery, and animals, and intangibles such as stocks, bonds, and copyrights, but also insurance policies, houses, cars, and furniture.[84] Income distribution, on the other hand, has to do with the percentage of wages, dividends, interest, and rents paid out each year to individuals or families at various income levels. In theory, those who own a great deal may or may not have high incomes—depending on the returns they receive from their wealth—but in reality, those at the very top of the wealth distribution also tend to have the highest incomes, mostly from dividends and interest.

For purposes of testing a class-domination theory of power, the most important focus of wealth and income studies is on the highest levels of wealth distribution and the percentage of overall income that is derived from that wealth. Numerous studies show that wealth distribution is extremely concentrated and that it has been very stable over the course of the twentieth century, although there was a temporary decline in wealth concentration in the 1970s (in good part due to a decline in stock prices). By the late 1980s, however, wealth distribution was as concentrated as it had been in 1929, when the top 1 percent had 36.3 percent of all wealth. The percentage of yearly income received by the highest 1 percent of wealthholders also remained constant within the context of some mild fluctuations. In 1958, for example, the top 1.5 percent of wealthholders received 13 percent of yearly income; in 1992, the top 1 percent received 15.7 percent.[85] Table 3.3 presents figures for 1983, 1989, and 1992 for net worth, financial wealth, and income for the wealthiest 1 percent, the next 19 percent, and the bottom 80 percent.

None of the studies on wealth and income distributions include the names of individuals. This means studies have to be done to demonstrate that people of wealth and high income are in fact members of the upper class. The most detailed study of this kind is Baltzell's historical work on Philadelphia, which showed that the wealthiest people are also those who send their children to private schools, live in exclusive neighborhoods, and are listed in the *Social Register*. On the national level, Baltzell reported that nine of the ten wealthiest financiers at the turn of the century had descendants in the *Social Register*, that over 75 percent of the wealthy families in Lundberg's *America's Sixty Families* had descendants in the *Social Register*, and that eighty-seven of the wealthy men in Myers' *History of the Great American Fortunes* also had descendants in those volumes.[86] Supplementing these findings, sociologist C. Wright Mills found that at least one-half of the ninety richest men of 1900 had descendants in the *Social Register*, and my study of ninety corporate directors worth $10 million or more in 1960 found that 74 percent met criteria of upper-class membership.[87] However, the question "Who benefits?" has attracted little further research because the answer seems so obvious to most people.

There are newly rich people who are not yet assimilated into the upper class, and there are highly paid professionals, entertainers, and athletes who for a few years make more in a year than many members of the upper class. However, for the most part it is safe to conclude that the people of greatest wealth and highest income are part of—or are becoming part of—the upper class.

Without a doubt, then, the .5 to 1 percent of the population that makes up the upper class is also the .5 to 1 percent who owned 45.6 percent of the financial wealth in 1992. In terms of the "Who benefits?" indicator of power, the upper class is far and away the most powerful group in society.

THE UPPER CLASS AND CORPORATE CONTROL

Although wealth distribution is a strong indication that the upper class has great power in the United States, it does not follow that members of the upper class control corporations. It may be, as pluralists claim, that members of the upper class simply enjoy the dividends paid by their stocks. To show that members of the upper class have power within the corporate community, it is necessary to look at other types of information, but it is nonetheless noteworthy as a starting point that corporate stock ownership is even more concentrated than net worth or financial wealth. Throughout the twentieth century, between 50 percent and 76 percent of all privately held corporate stock has been owned by the top 1 percent of stockholders, who are surely

Table 3.4 Well-Known Corporations That Are Privately Owned

Name	Rank in Private 500
Mars Candy	6
Levi Strauss & Co.	16
Amway	24
Hallmark Cards	35
Stroh Brewery	113
National Car Rental	138
LL Bean	162
Mary Kay Cosmetics	201
Domino's Pizza	229

Source: "The Private 500," *Forbes*, December 2, 1996, pp. 150–200.

members of the upper class according to the research findings presented in the previous section. In 1992, as stated at the start of the first chapter, the top 1 percent owned 49.6 percent of all privately held corporate stock.

It is also worth noting that not all corporations issue stock that is open to purchase by the general public. There are several hundred very large privately held companies that provide a good starting point for a demonstration of direct involvement by owners in major corporations. Several dozen of these corporations would have been in the *Fortune 500* in the mid-1990s if their assets had been part of the public record. Ninety-two of them are large enough to provide their owners with sufficient wealth to be listed in the Forbes 400.[88] Table 3.4 lists several widely known companies that are privately owned.

Family Ownership

Information presented in the previous chapter shows that not very many companies ever were completely owned by just one family, but family ownership has been the focus of most investigations of corporate control nonetheless. Although these investigations usually rely on public records that are not ideal for research purposes, they provide a good starting point.

Three different studies present detailed evidence on the extent of family involvement in the largest American corporations. The first, by political scientist Philip Burch, used both official documents and the informal—but often more informative—findings of the business press as its sources of information. Burch concluded that 40 percent of the top 300 industrials were probably under family control, using the usual cutoff point of 5 percent of the stock as his criterion.[89] Analyzing the official records that became available in the 1970s, a team of researchers at Corporate Data Exchange provided detailed information on the major owners of most of the top 500 industrials for 1980, showing that significant individual and family ownership continues to exist for all but the very largest of corporations.[90] One individual or family was a top stockholder, with at least 5 percent of the stock, in 44 percent of the 423 profiled corporations not controlled by other corporations or foreign interests. In another 7 percent, from two to four families held at least 5 percent of the stock and had representation on the board of directors. The figures were much lower among the 50 largest, however, where only 17 percent of the 47 companies included in the study showed evidence of major family involvement. The findings on the small percentage of the very largest industrials under individual or family control concur with those in a third study, that by economist Edward S. Herman for the 200 largest corporations among all nonfinancial corporations for 1974–1975.[91] Of the 104 companies common to the two studies, I determined that there were only four disagreements in classifying the nature of their control structure, and some of those may be due to changes in ownership patterns between 1974 and 1980.

These results can be supplemented with more recent information on the ways in which members of the upper class work through family offices, holding companies (a company created only to own stock in operating companies), and investment partnerships in maintaining great influence in the corporate community. In particular, the use of holding companies and investment partnerships in the takeover and merger movement of the late 1980s shows that no company thought to be firmly under the control of management is safe from the greater powers of ownership.

The Family Office

A family office is an informal entity through which members of a family or group of families agree to pool some of their resources in order to hire people to provide them with advice on investments, charitable giving, and even political donations in some cases. Family offices often handle all financial transactions and legal matters as well. Their relevance here is in terms of their potential for maintaining control of corporations founded by an earlier generation of the family. Such offices contradict the belief that corporate control is necessarily lost due to the inheritance of stock by a large number of descendants.

Journalist Shelby White, one of the few people to inquire about family offices at any length, writes that "to a large extent, the wealthy families of America have managed their money by setting up private offices, which then take care of family finances from cradle to grave: activating trusts, dispensing allowances to the younger generations, helping obtain divorces for older family members, and ultimately, managing their estates." However, her strongest emphasis is on the office as a cohesive force in keeping the family a significant economic unit:

> But most of all, family offices have served as a unifying force, keeping the money intact as the families have moved out of the entrepreneurial, risk-taking businesses that formed the basis of the wealth. Without a central office, the fortune would lose its power as it was dispersed over generations. Though each member of a family might be worth several million dollars, it is the collective use of the money that gives the offices the leverage to buy companies, create tax shelters and invest in oil drilling, real estate and the myriad of other ventures favored by the very rich.[92]

It is likely that there are at least several hundred family offices across the country, but no reliable estimate is available.

The most detailed account of a family office is provided by sociologist Marvin Dunn in his study of the Weyerhaeuser family of Saint Paul, Minnesota, and Tacoma, Washington, whose great wealth is concentrated in the lumber industry. By assembling a family genealogy chart that covered five generations, and then interviewing several members of the family, Dunn determined that a family office called Fiduciary Counselors, Inc. (FCI), aids the family in maintaining a central role in two major corporations. By demonstrating that there are several Weyerhaeusers on the boards of these companies who were not known to be Weyerhaeusers by previous investigators, and by aggregating the stock holdings that are managed out of the family office, Dunn shows that Potlatch—thought to be no longer dominated by the Weyerhaeusers—continues to be under the family's control. Table 3.5 presents the corporate directorships for leading members of the Weyerhaeuser family in 1996.

Fiduciary Counselors, Inc., also housed the offices of two Weyerhaeuser holding companies used to make investments for family members as a group and to own shares in new companies established by them. Although the primary focus of the Weyerhaeuser family office is economic matters, the office serves other functions as well. It keeps the books for fifteen different charitable foundations of varying sizes and purposes through which family members give money, and it coordinates political donations by family members all over the country to both candidates and political action committees.[93]

Table 3.5 Weyerhaeuser Family Members on Corporate Boards

Family Member	Corporation
William H. Clapp	Alaska Air Group, Weyerhaeuser
W. John Driscoll	Northern States Power, Weyerhaeuser, St. Paul Companies
George F. Jewett, Jr.	Potlatch
Frederick T. Weyerhaeuser	Potlatch
George H. Weyerhaeuser	Boeing, Weyerhaeuser, Chevron, Safeco
William T. Weyerhaeuser	Potlatch

Source: Director listings in *Who Knows Who 1997*.

Holding Companies

Holding companies can serve the economic functions of a family office if the family is still small and tight-knit. They have the advantage of being incorporated entities that can buy and sell stock in their own names. Because they are privately held, they need report only to tax authorities on their activities. The role of a family holding company can be seen in the case of the Lindner family of Cincinnati, which uses a financial holding company, American Financial Corporation, to control relatively small banks, savings and loans, and insurance companies and to take large ownership positions in a variety of other companies. In 1980, the family was among the top five stockholders in six of the largest 500 industrials through purchases by this company.[94]

The second richest person in the United States in 1996, Warren Buffett, worth $15 billion and the scion of third-generation wealth, operates through a holding company, Berkshire Hathaway. Along with his partners, he sits on the boards of several of the companies in which he invests. Table 3.6 lists the corporate directorships held by Buffett and his partners.[95]

Investment Partnerships

Some wealthy individuals and families use a slightly different financial arrangement, an investment partnership, which gives them more flexibility than the corporate form. Kohlberg, Kravis, Roberts, usually known as KKR, has been the most visible example since the 1980s because it has been involved in many corporate takeovers. The lead partner, Henry Kravis (who is sometimes listed as a self-made person because it is not generally known that his father was worth tens of

Table 3.6 Corporate Directorships Held by Warren Buffett and His Partners in Berkshire Hathaway

Warren Buffett	Howard Buffett	Charles Munger	Walter Scott, Jr.
American Express	Coca-Cola	Salomon	Burlington Resources
Coca-Cola			ConAgra
Geico			Kiewit
Gillette			
Salomon			
Washington Post			
Wells Fargo & Co.			

Source: Director listings in *Who Knows Who 1997*.

millions of dollars), sits on seven corporate boards, including Safeway Stores and Duracell International—all companies that he and his partners acquired in quick succession after 1986. His cousin and partner, George Roberts, joins him on six of those boards. There can be little doubt about who controls these companies, or about the control of any other companies where investment partnerships or holding companies have representatives on the board of directors. The takeovers by KKR and similar partnerships show that corporations allegedly controlled by their managers can be acquired by groups of rich investors, unless they are resisted by a rival group of owners.[96]

These findings on the importance of family ownership, family offices, holding companies, and investment partnerships in large corporations suggest that a significant number of large corporations continue to be controlled by major owners. However, the very largest corporations in several sectors of the economy show no large ownership stake by individuals or families—whether through family offices, holding companies, or other devices. Their largest owners, in blocks of a few percent, are pension funds, bank trust departments, investment companies, and mutual funds. Moreover, interview studies suggest that these fiduciary institutions very rarely take any role in influencing the management of the corporations in which they invest.[97] Upper-class involvement in these corporations is manifested through the presence of upper-class leaders on boards of directors, a point demonstrated earlier in this chapter and again in the next subsection.

While it may seem surprising at first glance that members of the upper class are least involved at the executive level in the very largest corporations, the reasons lie in issues of power and status and have nothing to do with education or expertise. Members of the upper class usually are not interested in a career that means years of working their way up a corporate bureaucracy when there is no incentive for them to do so. They prefer to work in finance, corporate law, or their own family businesses, where they have greater autonomy and more opportunities to exercise power.

With the many ways in which members of the upper class can exert control within the corporate community clearly established, it is now possible to consider the role of upwardly mobile corporate executives.

The Assimilation of Rising Executives

As noted at the outset of the chapter, the middle-level origins of many corporate executives are used by pluralists as part of their argument that ownership and control are separated in the large corporations. Not only is stock ownership allegedly dispersed, with no one family owning a controlling interest, but the leadership is provided by middle-class experts whose primary concern is supposedly not with profits, but with balancing the demands of workers, consumers, and owners. In this view, professional managers are a group distinct from upper-class owners and directors in social origins, skills, and motivations. Contrary to this claim, the evidence presented in this section shows, first, that more executives have high-level origins than is usually realized and, second, that the rising executives are assimilated into the upper class and come to share its values, thereby cementing the relationship between the upper class and the corporate community rather than severing it. The aspirations of professional managers for themselves and for their offspring lead them into the upper class in behavior, values, and style of life, not away from it.

There have been many studies of the class origins of top corporate executives. They most frequently focus on the occupation of the executive's father. These studies show, as Useem suggests in a detailed synthesis, that "between 40 percent and 70 percent of all large corporation directors and managers were raised in business families, which comprised only a tiny fraction of families of that era." One of the studies he cites compared business leaders at thirty-year intervals over the century and found that the percentage whose fathers were businessmen remained constant at 65 percent.[98] In one of the most extensive studies of corporate directors ever undertaken, Dye considered parental occupation, listing in the *Social Register*, and attendance at a prestigious private school to estimate that 30 percent of several thousand directors came from the upper class (the top 1 percent). Approximately 59 percent came from the middle class, which comprises about 21 percent of the population by Dye's definition, and only 3 percent came from the remaining 78 percent of the population (8 percent of the sample was not classifiable).[99]

Very similar backgrounds are found for Latino and Asian-American members of corporate boards. In the case of Latinos, those who are wealthy are most often Cuban-Americans who brought their wealth to the United States when they left Cuba because of Fidel Castro's revolutionary takeover in 1959. Many other well-to-do Latinos on corporate boards come from wealthy or well-educated families in Spain, Puerto Rico, Mexico, or South American countries, although some are the children of upwardly mobile immigrants. Among Asian-Americans, it is Chinese-Americans from the upper class in pre-Communist China who provide a large minority of Asian-American corporate directors. As for Japanese-Americans, they are usually third-generation Americans who are the grandsons and granddaughters of immigrants who began as the owners of small farms or small businesses. For the most part, Japanese-American directors acquired good educations and worked their way up the corporate ladder. As noted in chapter 2, Latino and Asian-American directors often have intermarried with Euro-Americans and are being assimilated into the upper class.[100]

The situation is somewhat different for African-Americans on corporate boards. Although they have excellent educational credentials, they are less likely to be from families of wealth. They come to corporate boards from businesses and organizations outside the corporate community. There is little evidence that they are being assimilated into the upper class. On the basis of these and other findings, Zweigenhaft and I conclude in *Diversity in the Power Elite* that at bottom *white* is the term for the in-group in the United States. Its definition is expanding to include children of immigrants of all racial backgrounds, but not African-Americans, who continue to face subtle forms of stereotyping and racism based on their status as members of a subordinated, nonimmigrant minority group.[101]

Whatever the social origins of corporate executives, most are educated and trained in a small number of private universities and business schools. Useem summarizes the results of several studies by concluding that "approximately one-third of those who oversee the nation's largest firms attended Harvard, Yale, or Princeton, and two-thirds studied at one of the twelve most heavily endowed schools."[102] It is in these schools that people of middle-class origins receive their introduction to the values of the upper class and the corporate community, mingling for the first time with men and women of the upper class to some extent, and sometimes with upper-class teachers and administrators who serve as role models. This modeling continues in the graduate schools of business that many attend before joining the corporation. Minority group members who are not from wealthy families show the same educational patterns as other upwardly mobile corporate executives.

The conformist atmosphere within the corporations intensifies this socialization into upper-class styles and values. As sociologist Rosabeth Kanter explains in her study of managers and secretaries in a large East Coast corporation, the great uncertainty and latitude for decision making in positions at the top of complex organizations creates a situation in which trust among leaders is absolutely essential. That need for trust is what creates a pressure toward social conformity:

> It is the uncertainty quotient in managerial work, as it has come to be defined in the large modern corporations, that causes management to become so socially restricting; to develop tight inner circles excluding social strangers; to keep control in the hands of socially homogeneous peers; to stress conformity and insist upon a diffuse, unbounded loyalty; and to prefer ease of communication and thus social certainty over the strains of dealing with people who are "different."[103]

In this kind of an atmosphere, it quickly becomes apparent to new managers that they must demonstrate their loyalty to senior management by working extra hours, tailoring their appearance to that of their superiors, and attempting to conform in their attitudes and behavior. They come to believe that they have to be part of the "old-boy network" to succeed in the company. Although there are competence criteria for the promotion of managers, they are vague enough or hard enough to apply that most managers become convinced that social factors are critical as well.

Executives who are successful in winning acceptance into the inner circle of their home corporations are invited by their superiors to join social institutions that assimilate them into the upper class. The first invitations are often to charitable and cultural organizations, where they serve as fund-raisers and as organizers of special events. The wives of rising executives, whose social acceptability is thought to be a factor in managers' careers, experience their first extensive involvement with members of the upper class through these same organizations. Also, the social clubs discussed earlier in the chapter are important socializing agents for the rising executive.

The role played by clubs in assimilating rising executives can be seen in my additions to a study of corporate presidents by political scientist Andrew Hacker, who found that the typical president for one of the 100 largest industrial firms in 1958 was born in a middle-class home.[104] Hacker stresses the average socioeconomic origins of these executives in order to criticize class-domination theory and support institutional elite theory, but my analysis showed that 70 percent of these executives had become members of one or more upper-class clubs by the time he studied them.

Upwardly mobile executives also become part of the upper class through the educational careers of their children. As the children go to day schools and boarding schools, the executives take part in evening and weekend events for parents, participate in fund-raising activities, and sometimes become directors or trustees in their own right. The fact that the children of successful managers become involved in upper-class institutions can also be seen in their patterns of college attendance. This is demonstrated very clearly in the 1958 study of executives by Hacker. Whereas only 29 percent of the corporate presidents went to Ivy League colleges, 70 percent of their sons and daughters did so.[105]

Rising executives are assimilated economically at the same time they are assimilated socially. One of the most important of these assimilatory mechanisms is the stock option, an arrangement by which the executive is allowed to buy company stock at any time within a future time period at the price of the stock when the option is granted. If the price of the stock rises, the executive purchases it at the original low price, often with the help of a low-interest or interest-free loan from the corporation. He or she then may sell the stock at the market value, realizing a large capital gain that was taxed at a maximum rate of 28 percent until 1997, when the rate dropped to 18 to 20 percent as part of a tax reform package.[106] Stock-purchasing plans, in conjunction with salaries and bonuses in the millions of dollars, allow some top executives to earn thousands of times more than the average wage earner each year. These high levels of remuneration enable upwardly mobile corporate leaders to become multimillionaires in their own right, and important leaders within the corporate community.

The assimilation of professional executives into the upper class also can be seen in the emphasis they put on profits—the most important of ownership objectives. This point is demonstrated most directly in the performance of the corporations they manage. Several studies comparing owner-controlled companies with companies run by professional managers uncover no differences in profitability.[107]

No studies have asked American executives directly about the emphasis they put on profits as compared with other objectives, but a survey of professional managers in Great Britain, where the corporate structure is very similar, determined that profit was their highest priority.[108] For the United States, the question has been approached by studying the content of speeches by managers of owner-controlled and management-controlled firms. Drawing on a compendium called *Vital Speeches*, sociologist Maynard Seider found that executives from management-controlled firms were no more likely to give speeches emphasizing the social responsibility of corporations than those from owner-controlled companies. Nor were there differences in their attitudes toward government regulation, government spending, or labor relations. Instead, as noted in the first chapter, the content of the speeches tended to differ by business sector. Executives whose companies dealt directly with the general public were more likely to speak in terms of a social responsibility ethic than those selling machinery and services to other companies.[109]

By all accounts, then, the presence of upwardly mobile executives does not contradict the notion that the upper class and the corporate community are closely related. In terms of their wealth, their social contacts, and their values, successful managers become part of the upper class and leaders in the power elite as they rise in the corporate hierarchy.

CONCLUSION

This chapter establishes the existence of a social upper class that is nationwide in scope through private schools, clubs, summer resorts, retreats, and other social institutions, all of which transcend the presence or absence of any given person or family. Families can rise and fall in the class structure, but the institutions of the upper class persist. This upper class makes up from .5 to 1 percent of the population, a rough estimate based on the number of students attending independent private schools, the number of listings in past *Social Register*s for several cities, and detailed interview studies in Kansas City and Boston.[110] The disproportionate share of wealth and income controlled by members of the upper class is evidence for a class-domination theory in terms of the "Who benefits?" indicator of power.

Not everyone in this nationwide upper class knows everyone else, but everybody knows somebody who knows someone in other areas of the country—thanks to a common school experience, a summer at the same resort, or membership in the same social club. With the social institutions described in this chapter as the undergirding, the upper class at any given historical moment consists of a complex network of overlapping social circles knit together by the members they have in common and by the numerous signs of equal social status that emerge from a similar life-style. Viewed from the standpoint of social psychology, the upper class is made up of innumerable face-to-face small groups that are constantly changing in their composition as people move from one social setting to another.

Involvement in these institutions usually instills a class consciousness that includes feelings of superiority, pride, and justified privilege. Deep down, most members of the upper class think they are better than other people and therefore fully deserving of their station in life—an attitude that is very useful in managing employees, even though it is sometimes psychologically debilitating. This class consciousness is ultimately based in the societywide categories of owners and nonowners, but it is reinforced by the shared social identities and interpersonal ties created by participation in social institutions of the upper class.

Above and beyond these specific points, the chapter provides another reason why it makes sense to talk about class domination rather than interest groups: The upper class is based in the ownership and control of profit-producing investments in stocks, bonds, and real estate. In other words, the nationwide upper class rooted in the corporate community is a capitalist class as well as a social class. Its members are not simply concerned with the interests of one corporation or business sector, but with such matters as the investment climate, the rate of profit, and the overall political climate. With the exception of those who have joined the liberal-labor coalition or a leftist movement, members of the upper class have a conservative outlook on economic issues in general. They transcend the interest-group level in their thinking and actions.

The class consciousness generated by economic concerns and an upper-class social existence is strengthened and nuanced within the policy-formation network discussed in the next chapter. The organizations in that network help the corporaate rich to work toward consensus on policy matters in which the potential for misunderstanding and disagreement are great despite the commonalities stressed in this chapter. Human beings are often distrustful or egotistical, and there can be disagreements among corporations for a variety of reasons. Developing a common policy outlook is not automatic for the corporate rich.

NOTES

1. Dorwin Cartwright and Alvin Zander, *Group Dynamics* (New York: Harper and Row, 1960), pp. 74–82; Albert J. Lott and Bernice E. Lott, "Group Cohesiveness as Interpersonal Attraction," *Psychological Bulletin*, 64 (1965): 259–309; Michael Argyle, *Social Interaction* (Chicago: Aldine Publishing Company, 1969), pp. 220–223; Michael Hogg, *The Social Psychology of Group Cohesiveness* (New York: New York University Press, 1992).
2. Cartwright and Zander, op. cit., p. 89; Lott and Lott, op. cit., pp. 291–296.
3. Gabriel Almond, "Plutocracy and Politics in New York City," Ph.D. Dissertation, University of Chicago, 1941, p. 108.

4. Harold M. Hodges, Jr., "Peninsula People: Social Stratification in a Metropolitan Complex," in *Education and Society*, ed. Warren Kallenbach and Harold M. Hodges, Jr. (Columbus, OH: Merrill, 1963), p. 414.
5. Robert R. Palmer, *The Age of the Democratic Revolution*, vol. 1 (Princeton, NJ: Princeton University Press, 1959), p. 203.
6. Jackson Turner Main, *The Social Structure of Revolutionary America* (Princeton, NJ: Princeton University Press, 1965), pp. 239, 284.
7. Palmer, op. cit, p. 3.
8. Richard P. Coleman and Lee Rainwater, *Social Standing in America* (New York: Basic Books, 1978).
9. August B. Hollingshead and Frederick C. Redlich, *Social Class and Mental Illness: A Community Study* (New York: Wiley, 1958), p. 69.
10. Coleman and Rainwater, op. cit., p. 25.
11. Susan Ostrander, "Upper-Class Women: Class Consciousness as Conduct and Meaning," in *Power Structure Research*, ed. G. William Domhoff (Beverly Hills, CA: Sage Publications, 1980), pp. 78–79.
12. Allison Davis, Burleigh B. Gardner, and Mary R. Gardner, *Deep South* (Chicago: University of Chicago Press, 1941), p. 59 n.
13. David Krech, Richard S. Crutchfield, and Egerton L. Ballachy, *The Individual in Society* (New York: McGraw-Hill, 1962), p. 338.
14. Robert A. Dahl, *Who Governs?* (New Haven, CT: Yale University Press, 1961), p. 229.
15. Paul M. Sweezy, "The American Ruling Class," *The Present as History*, ed. Paul Sweezy (New York: Monthly Review Press, 1953), pp. 123–124. For Marxian critiques of the pluralist view of social classes because it does not include a consideration of what Marxists believe to be the inherently exploitative relationship between classes, see James Stolzman and Herbert Gambert, "Marxist Class Analysis versus Stratification Analysis as General Approaches to Social Inequality," *Berkeley Journal of Sociology* (1973–74) and Charles H. Anderson, *The Political Economy of Social Class* (Englewood Cliffs, NJ: Prentice-Hall, 1974).
16. Walter Powell and Paul DiMaggio, eds., *The New Institutionalism in Organizational Analysis* (Chicago: University of Chicago Press, 1991). The emphasis on habits, customs, and culture in "the new institutionalism" is useful in understanding social systems, but the power dynamics that create and sustain institutions are often lost from view by the authors in the Powell and DiMaggio book. For an excellent critique of these authors that gives the right weight to class and power within an institutional framework, see the chapter in the book by Roger Friedland and Robert Alford, "Bringing Society Back In: Symbols, Practices, and Institutional Contradictions," pp. 232–263.
17. E. Digby Baltzell, *Philadelphia Gentlemen: The Making of a National Upper Class* (Glencoe, IL: Free Press, 1958).
18. Brad Edmonson, "Sampling the Upper Crust," *American Demographics*, 12 (1990): 47–48, reports that there are 32,500 people listed in the *Social Register*, 23 percent in New York, 13 percent in Philadelphia, and 8 percent in Boston. The new *Social Register Observer*, published twice a

year, contains useful information on social gatherings, along with biographical information in marriage announcements and obituaries. The *Social Register* received a small flurry of publicity in 1996 when its owner, Steve Forbes, Jr., ran for the presidential nomination in the Republican primaries. His wife, Sabrina Beekman Forbes, is related to the founders of the Social Register Association. See James Perry, "Steve Forbes Is Keeping Tight-Lipped on Family Tie to Blue-Blood Bible," *Wall Street Journal*, January 26, 1996: B12; Joanne Kaufman, "Married Maidens and Dilatory Domiciles," *Wall Street Journal*, May 7, 1996: A16. For a detailed account of the *Social Register* until 1976, see G. William Domhoff, *Who Rules America Now?* (New York: Simon and Schuster, 1983), pp. 20–24.

19. G. William Domhoff, *The Higher Circles* (New York: Random House, 1970), pp. 11–13.

20. Ibid., pp. 14–16.

21. Richard P. Coleman and Bernice L. Neugarten, *Social Status in the City* (San Francisco: Jossey-Bass, 1971), chapters 2 and 6.

22. Baltzell, op. cit., p. 44.

23. Domhoff, *Higher Circles*, p. 31.

24. Michael Useem, personal communication, September 26, 1979.

25. Richard L. Zweigenhaft and G. William Domhoff, *Jews in the Protestant Establishment* (New York: Praeger, 1982), pp. 94–98. Zweigenhaft has also studied the autobiographical entries in 25-year reunion books at prestigious colleges and universities. See, for example, Richard L. Zweigenhaft, "Accumulation of Cultural and Social Capital: The Differing College Careers of Prep School and Public School Graduates," *Sociological Spectrum*, 13 (1993): 365–376; "Prep School and Public School Graduates of Harvard: A Longitudinal Study of the Accumulation of Social and Cultural Capital," *Journal of Higher Education*, 64 (1993): 211–225; and "The Application of Cultural and Social Capital: A Study of the 25th Year Reunion Entries of Prep Schools and Public School Graduates of Yale College," *Higher Education*, 23 (1992): 311–320. For a precursor of Zweigenhaft's approach, see C. Luther Fry, "The Religious Affiliations of American Leaders," *Scientific Monthly*, 36 (1933): 241–249.

26. Randall Collins, "Functional and Conflict Theories of Educational Stratification," *American Sociological Review*, 36 (1971): 1010.

27. "Private Schools Search for a New Role," *National Observer*, August 26, 1968: 5. For an excellent account of major boarding schools, see Peter Cookson and Caroline Hodge Persell, *Preparing for Power: America's Elite Boarding Schools* (New York: Basic Books, 1985).

28. Baltzell, op. cit., p. 339.

29. Susan Ostrander, *Women of the Upper Class* (Philadelphia: Temple University Press, 1984), p. 85.

30. Erving Goffman, *Asylums* (Chicago: Aldine, 1961).

31. Interview conducted for G. William Domhoff by research assistant Deborah Samuels, February 1975; see also Gary Tamkins, "Being Special: A Study of the Upper Class," Ph.D. Dissertation, Northwestern University, 1974.

32. Michael Gordon, "Changing Patterns of Prep School Placements," *Pacific Sociological Review*, vol. 12, no. 1 (Spring 1969): 23–26.

33. These figures were obtained from the Admissions Offices at Cate and St. John's.

34. Steven Levine, "The Rise of the American Boarding Schools," Senior Honors Thesis, Harvard University, 1975, pp. 128–130.

35. Christopher F. Armstrong, "Privilege and Productivity: The Cases of Two Private Schools and Their Graduates," Ph.D. Dissertation, University of Pennsylvania, 1974, pp. 162–163. (The second school in Armstrong's study was Putney, a much newer, smaller, and more liberal school in Vermont.)

36. Baltzell, op. cit., pp. 51–65.

37. Richard L. Zweigenhaft and G. William Domhoff, "Sophisticated Conservatives and the Integration of Prep Schools," *Research in Social Policy*, 5 (1997): 223–240.

38. Richard L. Zweigenhaft and G. William Domhoff, *Blacks in the White Establishment? A Study of Race and Class in America* (New Haven, CT: Yale University Press, 1991).

39. E. Digby Baltzell, *The Protestant Establishment* (New York: Random House, 1964), p. 344; Paul Sweezy, *Power Elite or Ruling Class?* (New York: Monthly Review Press, 1956), Pamphlet Series, No. 13, p. 29.

40. Baltzell, *Philadelphia Gentlemen*, op. cit., p. 373.

41. Coleman and Rainwater, op. cit., p. 144.

42. Sophy Burnham, *The Landed Gentry* (New York: G. P. Putnam's Sons, 1978).

43. Ostrander, *Women of the Upper Class*, op. cit., p. 104.

44. Philip Bonacich and G. William Domhoff, "Latent Classes and Group Membership," *Social Networks*, 3 (1981). The analysis also includes policy groups of the kind that are discussed in chapter 4.

45. G. William Domhoff, *Who Rules America?* (Englewood Cliffs, NJ: Prentice-Hall, 1967), p. 26; E. Digby Baltzell, *The Protestant Establishment*, op. cit, p. 371.

46. G. William Domhoff, *The Bohemian Grove and Other Retreats* (New York: Harper and Row, 1974); G. William Domhoff, "Politics among the Redwoods," *The Progressive* (January 1981): 32–36.

47. *Bohemian Grove 1994: Midsummer Encampment* (San Francisco: Bohemian Club, 1994), p. 19.

48. Domhoff, *The Bohemian Grove and Other Retreats*, op. cit., pp. 1–7 for the details of the Cremation of Care Ceremony.

49. Kevin Wehr, "The Power Elite at the Bohemian Grove: Has Anything Changed in the 1990s?," *Critical Sociology*, 20 (1994): 121–124.

50. Domhoff, *Who Rules America Now?*, op. cit., p. 70.

51. Peter Phillips, "A Relative Advantage: Sociology of the San Francisco Bohemian Club," Ph.D. Dissertation, University of California, Davis, 1994, pp. 77–79, 82.

52. Thomas Powell, *Race, Religion, and the Promotion of the American Executive* (Columbus: Ohio State University Press, 1969), p. 50.

53. Gay Pauley, "Coming-Out Party: It's Back in Style," *Los Angeles Times* (March 13, 1977): section 4, p. 22; "Debs Put Party on Jet," *San Francisco Chronicle* (December 18, 1965): 2.

54. Pauley, "Coming-Out Party," op. cit.
55. Ostrander, "Upper-Class Women: Class Consciousness as Conduct and Meaning," op. cit., pp. 93–94; Ostrander, *Women of the Upper Class*, op. cit., pp. 89–90.
56. "The Debut Tradition: A Subjective View of What It's All About," *New Orleans Times-Picayune* (August 29, 1976): section 4, p. 13; Tia Gidnick, "On Being 18 in '78: Deb Balls Back in Fashion," *Los Angeles Times* (November 24, 1978): part 4, p. 1; Virginia Lee Warren, "Many Young Socialites Want Simpler Debutante Party, or None," *New York Times* (July 2, 1972): 34; Mary Lou Loper, "The Society Ball: Tradition in an Era of Change," *Los Angeles Times* (October 28, 1973): part 4, p. 1.
57. Ostrander, *Women of the Upper Class*, op. cit., pp. 128–129. For three other fine accounts of the volunteer work of upper-class women, see Arlene Daniels, *Invisible Careers* (Chicago: University of Chicago Press, 1988); Margot MacLeod, "Influential Women Volunteers" (paper presented to the meetings of the American Sociological Association, San Antonio, August 1984); and Margot MacLeod, "Older Generation, Younger Generation: Transition in Women Volunteers' Lives" (unpublished manuscript, 1987). For women's involvement in philanthropy and on the boards of nonprofit organizations, see Teresa Odendahl, *Charity Begins at Home: Generosity and Self-Interest among the Philanthropic Elite* (New York: Basic Books, 1990), and Teresa Odendahl and Michael O'Neill, eds., *Women and Power in the Nonprofit Sector* (San Francisco: Jossey-Bass, 1994). For in-depth interviews of both women and men philanthropists, see Francie Ostrower, *Why the Wealthy Give: The Culture of Elite Philanthropy* (Princeton, NJ: Princeton University Press, 1995).
58. Ostrander, *Women of the Upper Class*, pp. 113, 115.
59. Ostrander, "Upper-Class Women," op. cit., p. 84; Ostrander, *Women of the Upper Class*, pp. 132–137.
60. Beth Ghiloni, "New Women of Power," Ph.D. Dissertation, University of California, Santa Cruz, 1986, pp. 122, 159.
61. Daniels, op. cit., p. x.
62. Ostrander, *Women of the Upper Class*, pp. 85–88.
63. Baltzell, *Philadelphia Gentlemen*, p. 26.
64. Paul M. Blumberg and P. W. Paul, "Continuities and Discontinuities in Upper-Class Marriages," *Journal of Marriage and the Family*, vol. 37, no. 1 (February 1975): 63–77; David L. Hatch and Mary A. Hatch, "Criteria of Social Status as Derived from Marriage Announcements in the New York Times," *American Sociological Review*, 12 (August 1947): 396–403.
65. Lawrence Rosen and Robert R. Bell, "Mate Selection in the Upper Class," *Sociological Quarterly*, 7 (Spring 1966): 157–166. I supplemented the original study by adding the information on schools and clubs.
66. Robert C. Tryon, "Identification of Social Areas by Cluster Analysis: A General Method with an Application to the San Francisco Bay Area," *University of California Publications in Psychology*, 8 (1955); Robert C. Tryon, "Predicting Group Differences in Cluster Analysis: The Social Areas Problem," *Multivariate Behavioral Research*, 2 (1967): 453–475.

67. T. D. Schuby, "Class Power, Kinship, and Social Cohesion: A Case Study of a Local Elite," *Sociological Focus*, 8, no. 3 (August 1975): 243–255; Donald Davis, "The Price of Conspicuous Production: The Detroit Elite and the Automobile Industry, 1900–1933," *Journal of Social History*, 16 (1982): 21–46.

68. John Ingham, *The Iron Barons* (Westport, CT: Greenwood Press, 1978), pp. 230–231. For the continuity of a more general sample of wealthy families, see Michael Allen, *The Founding Fortunes* (New York: Truman Talley Books, 1987).

69. David D. Broad, "The Social Register: Directory of America's Upper Class," *Sociological Spectrum*, 16 (1996): 173–181; David Broad, "The Social Register and the Endurance of Upper-Class Values" (paper presented to the annual meetings of the Southern Sociological Society, Atlanta, April 6, 1995).

70. For further evidence of the assimilation of new members into the upper class, see the study of the social affiliations and attitudes of the successful Jewish business owners who become part of the upper class by Zweigenhaft and Domhoff, *Jews in the Protestant Establishment*, op. cit.

71. William Miller, "American Historians and the Business Elite," *Journal of Economic History*, 9 (1949): 184–208. The quote appears on page 208.

72. Ann Marsh, "Meet the Class of 1996," *Forbes* (October 14, 1996): 100.

73. Thomas Dye, *Who's Running America?*, 6th ed. (Englewood Cliffs, NJ: Prentice-Hall, 1995), p. 51.

74. *Born on Third Base: The Sources of Wealth of the 1996 Forbes 400* (Boston: United for a Fair Economy, 1997); Chuck Collins, "Horatio Alger: Where Are You?," *Dollars and Cents* (January/February 1997): 9.

75. Richard Zweigenhaft and G. William Domhoff, *Diversity in the Power Elite* (New Haven, CT: Yale University Press, 1998).

76. "Wayne Huizenga," *Current Biography* (New York: H. H. Wilson, 1995): 260–265. The quote appears on page 260.

77. Harold Kerbo, *Social Stratification and Inequality*, 3rd ed. (New York: McGraw Hill, 1996), p. 348; Gary Solon, "Intergenerational Income Mobility in the United States," *American Economic Review*, 82 (1992): 393–409; Keith Bradsher, "America's Opportunity Gap," *New York Times* (June 4, 1995): E4.

78. Sally Quinn, "C. Z. Guest: The Rich Fight Back," *Post* (May 1, 1977): M-1; Cleveland Amory, *The Proper Bostonians* (New York: Dutton, 1947), p. 347.

79. For insights into the negative aspects of growing up wealthy, see Joanie Bronfman, "The Experience of Inherited Wealth: A Social-Psychological Perspective," Ph.D. Dissertation, Brandeis University, 1987. See also Louis Crosier, ed., *Casualties of Privilege* (Washington, DC: Avocus Publishing, 1991).

80. Susan Ostrander, *Money for Change* (Philadelphia: Temple University Press, 1995). See also Christopher Mogil and Anne Slepian, *We Gave Away a Fortune: Stories of People Who Have Devoted Themselves and Their Wealth to Peace, Justice, and a Healthy Environment* (Philadelphia: New Society Publishers, 1992).

81. These principles of social change are drawn from the work of a number of social psychologists. For a series of articles applying most of them to grassroots organizing, see the special issue of the *Journal of Social Issues*, 52 (1996). See especially Laura Woliver, "Mobilizing and Sustaining Grassroots Dissent," pp. 139–151, and the synthesis of several key points in Anthony Pratkanis and Marlene Turner, "Persuasion and Democracy: Strategies for Increasing Deliberative Participation and Enacting Social Change," pp. 187–205.

   For an inspired and inspiring application of social psychology principles to the way in which Branch Rickey and Jackie Robinson broke the color barrier in major league baseball in 1947, see Anthony Pratkanis and Marlene Turner, "Nine Principles of Successful Affirmative Action: Mr. Branch Rickey and Mr. Jackie Robinson and the Integration of Baseball," *Nine: A Journal of Baseball History and Social Policy Perspectives*, 3 (1994): 36–65. See especially the discussions of the social psychology of nonviolent resistance (pp. 46–50) and redemption (pp. 54–55).

   It should be stressed, however, that none of these authors is attempting to apply these principles at the societal level to which I am extrapolating them. The best social psychologist for large-scale social change remains Martin Luther King, Jr.
82. Tamkins, "Being Special," op. cit., p. 60.
83. Burnham, op. cit., p. 205.
84. Robert Lampman, *The Share of Top Wealth-Holders in National Wealth* (Princeton, NJ: Princeton University Press, 1962), p. 2. For thorough discussions of wealth and income in the past, see Gabriel Kolko, *Wealth and Power and America* (New York: Praeger, 1962); Jonathan Turner and Charles Starnes, *Inequality: Privilege and Poverty in America* (Santa Monica, CA: Goodyear Publishing, 1976).
85. James Smith, "An Estimate of the Income of the Very Rich," *Papers in Quantitative Economics* (Lawrence: University of Kansas Press, 1968); Edward Wolff, *Top Heavy* (New York: Twentieth Century Fund, 1996).
86. Baltzell, *Philadelphia Gentlemen*, op. cit., pp. 36–40.
87. C. Wright Mills, *The Power Elite* (New York: Oxford University Press, 1956), p. 117; Domhoff, *Who Rules America?*, op. cit., p. 47.
88. "The Private 500," *Forbes* (Dec. 2, 1996): 155.
89. Philip Burch, *The Managerial Revolution Reassessed* (Lexington, MA: Heath, 1972), pp. 29–30, 70.
90. Stephen Albrecht and Michael Locker, eds., *CDE Stock Ownership Directory: Fortune 500* (New York: Corporate Data Exchange, 1981).
91. Edward Herman, *Corporate Control, Corporate Power* (New York: Cambridge University Press, 1981), pp. 54–65, Appendix A.
92. Shelby White, "Cradle to Grave: Family Offices Manage Money for the Very Rich," *Barron's* (March 20, 1978): 9.
93. Marvin Dunn, "The Family Office: Coordinating Mechanism of the Ruling Class," in G. William Domhoff, ed., *Power Structure Research* (Beverly Hills, CA: Sage Publications, 1980).
94. "American Financial Moves into the Big Time," *Business Week* (March 3, 1973): 72; Abrecht and Locker, op. cit., p. 208.

95. Roger Lowenstein, *Buffett: The Making of an American Capitalist* (New York: Random House, 1995).

96. Sarah Bartlett, *The Money Machine* (New York: Warner Books, 1991). For accounts of the takeover movement, see Connie Bruck, *The Predators' Ball* (New York: Simon and Schuster, 1988); James B. Stewart, *Den of Thieves* (New York: Simon and Schuster, 1991); and Mary Zey, *Banking on Fraud: Drexel, Junk Bonds, and Buyouts* (New York: Aldine de Gruyter, 1993).

97. Edward S. Herman, *Conflicts of Interest: Commercial Bank Trust Departments* (New York: Twentieth Century Fund, 1975); Herman, *Corporate Control, Corporate Power,* op. cit., chapter 4.

98. Michael Useem, "Corporations and the Corporate Elite," *Annual Review of Sociology,* 6 (1980): 64; Michael Useem and Jerome Karabel, "Pathways to Corporate Management," *American Sociological Review,* 51 (1986): 184–200.

99. Thomas Dye, *Who's Running America?* (Englewood Cliffs, NJ: Prentice-Hall, 1976), pp. 151–152. Dye leaves out the details of his findings in the latest edition (1995) of this book, which is why it is not cited here.

100. Zweigenhaft and Domhoff, *Diversity in the Power Elite,* op. cit.

101. Ibid., chapter 8; Zweigenhaft and Domhoff, *Blacks in the White Establishment?,* op. cit., chapter 7.

102. Useem, "Corporations and the Corporate Elite," op. cit., p. 57.

103. Rosabeth Kanter, *Men and Women of the Corporation* (New York: Basic Books, 1977), p. 49. For a detailed statement of this argument, see Nancy DiTomaso, "Organizational Analysis and Power Structure Research," in *Power Structure Research,* ed. G. William Domhoff (Beverly Hills, CA: Sage Publications, 1980), pp. 255–268.

104. Andrew Hacker, "The Elected and the Anointed: Two American Elites," *American Political Science Review,* 55 (1961): 539–549.

105. Ibid., pp. 541, 544.

106. Capital gains are the profits made from the sale of assets such as stocks, bonds, and real estate. They were taxed at a rate of 39 percent in the years when the top rate on large incomes was well over 50 percent, then cut to 28 percent in 1978 and 20 percent in 1981, but raised to 28 percent in 1986.

107. Useem, "Corporations and the Corporate Elite," pp. 50–51.

108. Ibid., p. 49.

109. Maynard S. Seider, "Corporate Ownership, Control, and Ideology: Support for Behavioral Similarity," *Sociology and Social Research,* 62 (October 1977): 113–128.

110. Coleman and Rainwater, op. cit., p. 148. For the conclusion that "Capital S Society" in the United States includes "probably no more than four-tenths of one percent in large cities, and even a smaller proportion in smaller communities," see Coleman and Neugarten, op. cit., p. 270.

4

The Policy-Formation Network

This chapter explains the ways in which leaders within the corporate community and upper class develop general policies on issues of concern to them. The nonprofit, nonpartisan organizations discussed in this chapter are necessary features of the corporate landscape because common economic interests and social cohesion are not enough in themselves to lead to agreed-upon policies without research, consultation, and deliberation. The issues facing the corporate rich are too complex and the economy is too big for new policies to arise naturally from common interests.

Members of the corporate community and upper class involve themselves in the policy-formation process in four basic ways. First, they finance the organizations at the core of these efforts. Second, they provide a variety of free services, such as legal and accounting help, for some of the organizations in the network. Third, they serve as the directors and trustees of these organizations, setting their general direction and selecting the people who will manage their day-to-day operations. Finally, they take part in the activities of some of the groups in the network.

Although this chapter shows that the corporate rich have a near monopoly on what is considered "respectable" or "legitimate" expertise by the academic community and mass media, this expertise does not go unchallenged. There also exists a small group of think tanks and advocacy groups financed by unions, direct mail appeals, and wealthy liberals. Some of these liberal policy organizations also receive part of their funding from major foundations—to the great annoyance of ultraconservatives in the power elite.

As the annoyances expressed by the ultraconservatives reveal, the policy network is not totally homogeneous. Reflecting differences of opinion within the corporate community, the moderate and ultra-conservative subgroups within the policy-formation network have long-standing disagreements. The ultraconservative organizations are the ones most often identified with "big business" in the eyes of social scientists and the general public. The fact that they are generally nay-sayers who sometimes lose on highly visible issues is another reason for the belief that the corporate community is not the dominant influence in shaping government policy. What is not understood is that those setbacks are usually at the hands of the moderate conservatives within the policy network and the corporate community.

No single factor is the basis for the division into moderate conservatives and ultraconservatives within the corporate community and power elite. There is a tendency for the moderate organizations to be directed by executives from the very largest and most internationally oriented of corporations, but there are numerous exceptions to that generalization. Moreover, there are corporations that support policy organizations within both policy subgroups. Also, there are instances in which some top officers from a corporation are in the moderate camp, and others are in the ultraconservative camp. However, for all their differences, leaders within the two clusters of policy organizations have a tendency to search for compromise policies due to their common membership in the corporate community, their social bonds, and the numerous interlocks among all policy groups. When compromise is not possible, the final resolution of policy conflicts often takes place in legislative struggles in Congress, which are discussed in chapter 7.

Pluralists and state autonomy theorists overlook the policy-formation network, which is another reason why they continue to reject a class-dominance theory. They consistently claim that the corporate rich have no way to develop general policy consensus and therefore function only as a fragmented set of interest groups that lobby the government on narrow issues through trade associations and Washington-based lawyers.

The existence of a policy-formation network that overlaps with the corporate community and upper class also provides the answer to another frequent claim by both pluralists and state autonomy theorists: that independent experts have their own power in the policy and legislative arenas. According to political scientist Hugh Heclo, for example, whose work is widely quoted, these experts form floating "issue networks" on various topics and have a strong influence on policy through them. In a somewhat similar vein, another political scientist, Nelson Polsby, examining the origins of new policy ideas on a variety of issues, concludes that the ideas come from independent experts in think tanks and universities.[1]

Although Heclo and Polsby are accurate in saying that the experts do much of the policy work, they miss the critical point in terms of power because they fail to connect the issue networks and experts to the corporate-financed organizations in the policy network that give them financial support, confer legitimacy on their efforts, and provide the occasions for them to present their ideas to decision makers. That is, any emphasis on the independence of experts in an organizational sense is completely misguided. The experts who have the greatest impact are those who are asked to join the policy network.

Nor are the experts from outside the policy network necessarily independent. In fact, they are often part of the liberal-labor coalition. They are housed in liberal think tanks and hired as consultants by liberal political candidates. As for the many independent experts in the United States, they are most often teaching and doing research at universities; they rarely have any impact on public policy except on highly technical issues in the natural sciences and engineering.

THE POLICY-FORMATION NETWORK

The policy-formation process begins informally in corporate boardrooms, social clubs, and discussion groups, where problems are identified as "issues" to be solved by new policies. It ends in government, where policies are enacted and implemented. In between, however, there is a complex network of people and institutions that play an important role in sharpening the issues and weighing the alternatives. This network has three main components—foundations, think tanks, and policy-discussion groups.

Foundations are tax-free institutions created to give grants to both individuals and nonprofit organizations for activities that range from education, research, and the arts to support for the poor and the upkeep of exotic gardens and old mansions. They are an upper-class adaptation to inheritance and income taxes. They provide a means by which wealthy people and corporations can in effect decide how their tax payments will be spent, for they are based on money that otherwise could go to the government in taxes. From a small beginning at the turn of the twentieth century, they have become a very important factor in shaping developments in higher education and the arts, and they play a significant role in policy formation as well. The most influential of them historically are the Ford Foundation, the Rockefeller Foundation, the Carnegie Corporation, and the Sloan Foundation.

Think tanks are nonprofit organizations that provide settings for experts in various academic disciplines to devote their time to the study of policy alternatives free from the teaching and departmental duties that are part of the daily routine for most members of the academic community. Supported by foundation grants, corporate donations, and government contracts, think tanks are a major source of the new ideas discussed in the policy-formation network.

The policy-discussion organizations are nonpartisan groups that bring together corporate executives, lawyers, academic experts, university administrators, and media specialists to discuss such general problems as foreign aid, tariffs, taxes, and welfare policies. Using discussion groups of varying sizes, these organizations provide informal and off-the-record meeting grounds in which differences of opinion on various issues can be aired and the opinions of specialists can be heard. In addition to their numerous small-group discussions, they encourage general dialogue within the power elite by means of luncheon and dinner speeches, written reports, and position statements in journals and books. Taken as a whole, the several policy-discussion groups are akin to an open forum in which there is a constant debate concerning the major problems of the day and the best solutions to those problems.

The three types of organizations making up the policy-formation network are interlocked with each other and the corporate community in terms of both common directors and funding. The evidence for this conclusion is presented throughout the chapter. Figure 4.1 presents an overview of the network, with linkages expressed in terms of (1) director interlocks, (2) money flows, and (3) the flow of ideas and plans. Anticipating the discussion of how the power elite dominates government, which is presented in chapter 7, the diagram shows some of the ways the "output" of the policy network reaches government.

No one type of organization is more important than the others. It is the network as a whole that shapes policy alternatives, with different organizations playing different roles on different issues. There is, however, one organization in the network, the Business Roundtable, that plays the main role in attempting to influence government on the most important issues relating to economic policy. In so doing, it works closely with the Business Council, the Committee for Economic Development, and the Conference Board.

FOUNDATIONS

Among the nearly 6,300 foundations that exist in the United States, only a few hundred have the money and interest to involve themselves

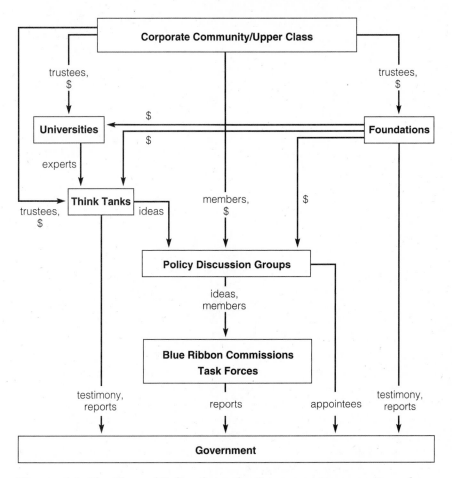

Figure 4.1 The Flow of Policy from the Corporate Community and Upper Class to Government through the Policy-Formation Network

in funding programs that have a bearing on public policy. Foundations are of four basic types:[2]

1. There are several thousand general-purpose foundations created by families to support a wide variety of projects; twenty of them have an endowment of $1 billion or more. Most of the large foundations are controlled by a cross-section of leaders from the upper class and corporate community, but there are several ultraconservative foundations that are tightly controlled by the original donors.

2. There are 862 corporate foundations funded by a major corporation and directed by the officers of that corporation. Their number and importance have increased greatly since the 1970s, especially in donations to education, medical research, environmental protection, and the arts. They also give about 1 to 3 percent of their funds to think tanks and policy groups.

3. There are 272 local community foundations designed to aid charities, voluntary associations, and special projects in their home cities. They receive funds from a variety of sources, including other foundations, wealthy families, and corporations, and they are directed by boards that include both corporate executives and community leaders.

4. Finally, there is a group of 189 foundations that use their money to finance a particular museum, garden project, or artistic exhibit. They are called "operating foundations" and are not of concern in terms of the policy-formation process. These operating foundations are often directed by the women of the upper class, as discussed in chapter 3.

Upper-class and corporate representation on the boards of the large general-purpose foundations most involved in policy-oriented grants has been documented in several studies. In one study of the twelve largest foundations, for example, it was found that half the trustees were members of the upper class. A study of corporate connections into the policy network showed that ten of these twelve foundations had at least one connection to the 201 largest corporations; most had many more than one connection.[3] Table 4.1 lists the assets and the number of corporate connections for the most important moderate-conservative and ultraconservative foundations in the policy network. As the table shows, the moderate foundations are generally larger—especially the Ford Foundation, which is twice the size of the largest ultraconservative foundation.

Foundations often become much more than sources of money that respond to requests for funding. Some foundations set up programs that are thought to be necessary by their trustees or staff. Then they search out appropriate organizations to undertake the project or create special commissions within the foundation itself. A few foundations have become so involved in a specific issue area that they function as a policy-discussion organization on that particular issue. This is especially the case with the Carnegie Corporation and its affiliates in the area of higher education. Their study groups, commissions, and fellowship programs have been central to the history of

Table 4.1 Corporate Connections and Assets of Moderate-Conservative and Ultraconservative Foundations

Moderate-Conservatives		
Name	Corporate Connections	Assets
Carnegie Corporation	29	1.1 billion
Ford Foundation	18	6.6 billion
Sloan Foundation	18	789 million
Rockefeller Foundation	12	2.4 billion
Andrew W. Mellon Foundation	12	2.2 billion
Rockefeller Brothers Fund	7	328 million

Ultraconservatives		
Name	Corporate Connections	Assets
Lynde and Harry Bradley Foundation	5	393 million
Noble Foundation	2	557 million
Sarah Scaife Foundation	0	203 million
Smith Richardson Foundation	0	361 million
Lilly Endowment	0	3.1 billion
John M. Olin Foundation	0	304 million

Source: *Who Knows Who 1997* (Detroit: Gale Research, 1997).

college and university development throughout the twentieth century. For example, the Carnegie Commission on Higher Education of the late 1960s and early 1970s spent $6 million and produced eighty books with policy implications for all aspects of higher education.[4]

Similarly, the Ford Foundation became the equivalent of a policy group on the issue of urban unrest in the 1950s and 1960s. It created a wide range of programs to deal with the problems generated by urban renewal programs and racial tensions resulting from the large black migration from the South into the inner cities of the North. One of these programs, called the Gray Areas Project, became the basis for the War on Poverty declared by the Johnson Administration in 1964 in the face of serious urban unrest.[5] Once the War on Poverty was launched, the Ford Foundation invested tens of millions of dollars in support for minority-group and community action organizations.

Table 4.2 Donations by the Ford Foundation to Minority Groups and to a Civil Liberties Group for Support of Minorities, 1994–1995

American Civil Liberties Union (for race, poverty, and immigration rights projects)	$1,265,000
American Indian Lawyer Training Project	400,000
Asian Pacific American Legal Center of Southern California	150,000
Mexican-American Legal Defense and Education Fund	695,000
NAACP Legal Defense and Education Fund	600,000
NAACP Special Contribution Fund	500,000
National Asian Pacific American Legal Consortium	50,000
National Coalition of Black Voter Participation	275,000
National Congress of American Indians	200,000
National Council of La Raza	3,225,000
National Council of Negro Women	530,000
National Puerto Rican Coalition	350,000
Puerto Rican Legal Defense and Education Fund	500,000
Total	$8,740,000

Source: *Foundation Grants Index*, 1997. See Ford Foundation in the civil rights section.

These investments were seen at the time as a way of encouraging insurgent groups to take a nonviolent and electoral direction in addressing the problems they perceived. But by the 1970s, when the social disruption had subsided, ultraconservatives began to criticize the Ford Foundation for its support for what were called liberal "experiments." The foundation has persisted in this support, however, as can be seen in the list of minority-group and civil liberties organizations in table 4.2 receiving large grants in 1994–1995.

In early 1997, the Ford Foundation renewed its focus on low-income and minority citizens with a five-year program that provides $20 million, including several million to create savings accounts in which a person's own deposits are matched by Ford and other foundations in an effort to stimulate housing purchases and business start-ups. Liberals are skeptical about the program because it seems to acquiesce in a shrinking role for government, and conservatives praise it because it emphasizes private initiative and self-help without government involvement.[6]

The Ford Foundation also has played a major role in creating and sustaining the environmental movement. Its conference on resource management in 1953 and subsequent start-up funding led to the establishment of the first and most prominent environmental think tank, Resources for the Future, which broke new ground by incorporating market economics into thinking about conservation.[7] In the early 1960s the Ford Foundation spent $7 million over a three-year period developing ecology programs at seventeen universities around the country, thereby providing the informational base and personnel infrastructure for efforts to control pesticides and industrial waste products. At the same time, the foundation put large sums into the land-purchase programs of the Nature Conservancy and the Audubon Society and encouraged environmental education and citizen action through grants to municipal conservation commissions and the nationwide Conservation Foundation—the latter founded by the Rockefeller family as a combined think tank and policy-discussion group.[8]

The Ford Foundation aided environmentalists further in 1970 by backing a new environmental law firm under the leadership of corporate lawyers, the National Resources Defense Council, with a grant of $750,000. To aid this new organization and several similar law firms that were soon formed, the foundation set up an advisory committee consisting of four former presidents of the American Bar Association.[9]

Ford's involvement with these and other environmental organizations continued into the late 1990s, but with help from both independent and corporate foundations. In 1994–1995, for example, it gave $600,000 to the National Resources Defense Council, which received grants from 52 other foundations as well. It also gave $78,000 to the Nature Conservancy, which had 128 other grants from foundations for the same time period, including $1 million from the David and Lucille Packard Foundation in California and $500,000 from the ultraconservative Lilly Endowment in Indiana.[10]

Ford's support for low-income minority communities and the environmental movement led to the claim that it had become a "liberal" organization despite its corporate-dominated board of trustees at the time, including the chairman of Ford Motor Company, Henry Ford II. But this seeming liberalism did not extend to support for unionization efforts. In 1967 it entered into the emerging conflict over public employee unions by financing a think tank study that was very negative toward them. In 1970 it granted $450,000 to three associations of government managers—the U.S. Conference of Mayors, the National League of Cities, and the National Association of Counties—to establish the Labor-Management Relations Service, an organization intended to help government managers cope with efforts at union organizing. One year later, this organization set up the National Public Employer Labor Relations Association, aided in good part by Ford and other foundation monies. Publications from these two organizations provided advice on defeating organizing drives and surviving strikes. They suggested "contracting out" public services to private businesses to avoid unions and lower wage costs.[11]

Systematic studies of state laws and the degree to which public employees are unionized in each state suggest that Ford's efforts to help government managers were successful. Less than half of the fifty states allow full collective bargaining for all public employee groups, and nearly all states forbid public employees to strike. The relative strength of the corporate-conservative and liberal-labor coalitions in each state was the main factor in determining the degree to which state employees were successful in their efforts to unionize. Union "density" in the public sector—meaning the percent of public employees who are in unions—rose from 10.8 percent in 1960 to a peak of 40.2 percent in 1976 and has stabilized at 36 percent since that time.[12]

Foundations, then, are an integral part of the policy-formation process both as sources of funds and program initiators. Contrary to the usual perceptions, they are not merely donors of money for charity and value-free academic research. They are in fact extensions of the corporate community in their origins, leadership, and goals.

THINK TANKS

The deepest and most critical thinking within the policy-formation network takes place in various think tanks. New initiatives that survive criticism by experts are brought to the discussion groups for modification and assimilation by corporate leaders. Among the dozens of think tanks, some highly specialized in one or two topics, the most important are the Brookings Institution, the American Enterprise Institute, the Urban Institute, the National Bureau of Economic Research, Resources for the Future, the Rand Corporation, and centers for international studies at MIT, Harvard, and Georgetown. The institutes and centers connected to universities receive much of their funding from foundations; the larger and less specialized independent think tanks receive money from businesses or government research contracts as well.

Three highly visible think tanks—the Brookings Institution, the American Enterprise Institute, and the Heritage Foundation—vie for attention and influence in Washington. The Brookings Institution, the oldest and generally most respected of the three, was founded in 1927 from three institutes, one of which dated from 1916. Virtually all of its early money came from foundations, although by the 1930s it was earning income from a small endowment provided by the Rockefeller Foundation and other sources. The Brookings Institution is sometimes said to be a "liberal" think tank, but that is a misperception generated in good part by ultraconservatives, especially the zealous aide to Nixon—later to become a federal prisoner and then a prison chaplain—who proposed firebombing it in the early 1970s to see if one of its employees had incriminating information on Nixon in his office. The fact that Keynesian economists from Brookings advised the Kennedy and Johnson Administrations also contributed to this stereotype.[13]

In fact, the Brookings Institution always has been in the mainstream or on the right wing. It started out in the center in the 1920s, but its employees opposed most New Deal programs, and it drifted to the right under the influence of a strong-willed president until the 1950s, when a new president changed its direction and it began to receive funding from the Rockefeller and Ford Foundations. Although some of its economists were important advisers to the Democrats in the 1960s, by 1975 these same economists were criticizing government initiatives in ways that later were attributed to the employees of their main rival, the American Enterprise Institute.[14]

The American Enterprise Institute (AEI) was formally created in 1943 as an adjunct to the Chamber of Commerce of the United States, but it had little money and no influence until the early 1970s, when a former Chamber employee began selling the need for a new think tank to corporate executives by exaggerating the liberal inclinations of the Brookings Institution. His efforts received a large boost in 1972 when the Ford Foundation gave him a $300,000 grant, which was viewed as a turning point by the institute's staff because of the legitimacy a Ford grant conferred for future fund-raising. The institute went from a budget of $1.1 million in 1971 to over $10 million in the 1980s.[15]

The AEI's fund-raising efforts also were aided when appointees from the Nixon Administration joined it as honorary fellows, and then former president Gerald Ford became an honorary fellow in 1977. Several prominent economists also were hired. Given this lineup of highly visible conservatives, it is not surprising that the AEI is often given credit for the "right turn" in Washington policy circles in the 1970s, but in fact the institute came to prominence after the turn had begun. Political scientist Joseph Peschek illustrated this point in a close textual analysis of Brookings and AEI recommendations that is too often overlooked by the pundits and commentators who have a large role in shaping people's views of recent history.[16] By the early 1980s, however, the AEI did play a very important role in providing ideas and staff members to the Reagan and Bush Administrations, and it has been central to the policy network ever since.

The Heritage Foundation, created in 1974, is the most recent and famous of the Washington think tanks. It is thought to reflect current wisdom in the corporate community, but it is actually the product of a few highly conservative men of great inherited wealth. The most important of these ultraconservatives are members of the Coors family, owners of the beer company that bears their name.[17] Close behind them is Richard Mellon Scaife, who is discussed in a later section of this chapter.

Unlike the AEI, the Heritage Foundation made no effort to hire established experts or build a record of respectability within the academic or policy communities. Instead, it hired young ideologists who were willing to attack all government programs and portray government officials as bureaucratic empire builders. While this approach didn't endear the Heritage Foundation to its counterparts in Washington, it did lead to staff positions in the Reagan and Bush Administrations, which needed people to carry out their antigovernment objectives.

The relationship of these three think tanks to the corporate community can be seen through their boards of directors. Brookings and the AEI have similar interlock patterns. Twenty-five of the Brookings Institution's thirty-three directors (86 percent) hold fifty corporate directorships at forty-eight corporations; seventeen of AEI's twenty-six directors (65 percent) have forty directorships at thirty-seven corporations. Moreover, there are seven corporations that have directors on the boards of both think tanks: Alcoa, American Presidents Lines, AT&T, Coca-Cola, CSX, Dow Chemical, and Levi Strauss.

The Heritage Foundation, on the other hand, had no directors who were also directors of any corporations included in *Who Knows Who 1997*. One former Heritage director, who died at age 80 in 1997, was a retired director of the company he founded, Loctite, and another is part of the Coors family, but the only current interlocks for the Heritage Foundation are with five ultraconservative foundations that provide much of its funding. The most important of these shared directors, William Simon, president of the Olin Foundation, who made hundreds of millions of dollars in company takeovers after many years on Wall Street, is one of the most vocal leaders in the ultraconservative camp. His Lakeside Talk at the Bohemian Grove in 1993—entitled "Freedom Isn't Everything, It's the Only Thing"—was so unrelentingly hostile toward the recently defeated Bush Administration that it was considered in bad taste by many Bohemians, especially because Bush himself was in the audience.[18]

Several less-known organizations function as a combination of think tank and discussion group in specialized issue-areas. The Population Council, for example, was established in 1952 to fund research and develop policy on population control. Relying at the outset on large personal donations from John D. Rockefeller III as well as grants from the Ford and Rockefeller foundations, it helped to create population research institutes at several carefully selected universities in different regions of the country that would aid in giving respectability to this area of concern. It also held conferences and publicized find-ings to show that population growth was a major problem. Working closely with several other organizations, including the Population Reference Bureau and International Planned Parenthood, it had enor-mous success in the 1960s in popularizing its policy suggestions and having them implemented at both the national and international lev-els, as a detailed case study of population policy demonstrates.[19] The step-by-step fashion in which the population groups proceeded, in-cluding the establishment of research institutes and disseminating information through the mass media before approaching government, provides a classic example of the policy network in action. This suc-cess did not continue, however. The way in which the top leadership in the Catholic Church and the right wing joined forces to stymie the movement after 1974—largely through opposition to abortion, con-traception, and family planning—is a separate case study in itself.[20]

Two organizations, the American Law Institute and the Ameri-can Judicature Society, join with committees of the American Bar Association in dealing with problems within the issue-area of the law. The focus of the American Law Institute is on such general areas as tax law and the penal code. Its goal is to write model acts for state legislatures to consider or to propose revisions in areas of the law through its written documents of restatement and clarification. The Judicature Society, on the other hand, is more specifically focused on the functioning of the court system, proposing methods to improve or streamline the administrative procedures of the judicial process. As one aspect of this interest, it is concerned with the processes by which state and federal judges are selected, and it attempts to influence stan-dards of judicial conduct. For both groups, the leadership comes pri-marily from the same corporate lawyers who also play the dominant role within the American Bar Association.

Although the experts within the think tanks and university insti-tutes relate to other members of the power elite primarily through the policy-formation groups, they are not without their own connections to the corporate community, either as directors or consultants. This point is made most systematically in the work of physicist Charles Schwartz. He found through careful checking of corporate documents that there are many more such connections than are mentioned by these experts in standard biographical sources. Of fifty-five full-time university professors who served on the President's Science Advisory Committee, for example, over half had served as directors of a corpo-ration with annual sales or total assets of more than $100 million. Another 15 percent had served as consultants to these large firms or as directors of smaller companies.[21] Schwartz also looked at the inter-connections of corporations and university experts by studying the boards of 130 of the largest corporations. Just over half (66) of these corporations had university presidents and professors on their boards. More specifically, sixty-eight people from forty-four different universities held eighty-five directorships on these boards.[22]

The extent of the consulting relationship between university experts and corporations is difficult to determine because such information is considered private by both the professors and the corporations. A survey for the Carnegie Commission on Higher Education reported that 17 percent of the professors at major universities had acted as consultants for a national corporation in the two previous years.[23] The fees for such consulting, which can run as high as $1,000 a day, usually add up to between $10,000 and $50,000 a year, but sometimes the payments are quite dramatic. In 1981, for example, it was revealed that AT&T had paid a Yale law professor active in several policy groups a total of $456,000 over a four-year period to help in its defense against a government antitrust suit. Another Yale professor received between $44,000 and $50,000 a year for four years from the same company.[24]

A NOTE ON UNIVERSITIES

In a very general sense, universities are part of the power equation because they educate future leaders and train the experts who work for the think tanks discussed in the previous section. This is especially the case for the handful of prestigious private schools such as Harvard, Yale, Stanford, and the University of Chicago that have very large endowments to support their students and programs. Indeed, as Dye shows, just twenty-five such schools have over 67 percent of all the private endowment funds in the United States.[25] Also, the trustees of the top private universities—and many large state universities for that matter—are disproportionately from the corporate community and upper class, as demonstrated by numerous investigations stretching back to the early twentieth century.[26]

Nevertheless, this book does not include universities as part of the institutional infrastructure of the power elite because only specific institutes within them are directly involved in governance. Furthermore, faculty members at many universities are too diverse in their intellectual and political orientations to be considered part of the power structure unless they are employed by corporations or organizations in the policy-formation network, and a significant minority of them in some departments support the liberal-labor coalition or are leftists of various kinds.[27]

In addition, the institution of tenure, which protects senior faculty members from arbitrary dismissal to encourage academic freedom, gives the faculty some degree of independence from trustees and administrators. The tenure system and other faculty rights are zealously guarded by the nationwide American Association of University Professors and other faculty organizations. Universities that in any way violate the procedures called for by the American Association of University Professors are investigated and censured. The fifty-two currently censured universities listed ranges from small denominational schools to the heavily endowed University of Southern California.[28]

Nor are all students who graduate from high-status universities uniformly destined to join the power elite. A small minority become leading activists in the liberal-labor coalition, sometimes immediately after graduation, sometimes after a career in business. Longtime consumer activist Ralph Nader is a graduate of Princeton University and Harvard Law School, for example. James P. Warburg, who provided much of the money in the early 1960s to start the Institute for Policy Studies, a very liberal to left-wing think tank in Washington, D.C., was a wealthy graduate of Harvard who worked as an investment banker on Wall Street before beginning his journey to liberalism.[29] A prominent pacifist and anti–Vietnam War leader, David Dellinger, the son of a corporate lawyer, called his autobiography *From Yale to Jail*, a title that provides a useful reminder of why universities and their graduates cannot be considered part of the power structure as it actually functions.[30]

Put another way, universities provide an organizational base for both the power elite and its critics. Even though liberals and leftists are in the minority, universities are far more important for them than for the power elite. Indeed, the educational system in general may be the most supportive institutional home of liberalism in the United States, and the only real home for socialists and other leftists. The educational system in general is the basis for two of the largest unions in the liberal-labor coalition, the National Education Association (2,300,000 members) and the American Federation of Teachers (950,000 members by 1998).

THE POLICY-DISCUSSION GROUPS

The first policy-discussion group, the National Civic Federation, was created at the turn of the twentieth century by the big corporations that emerged as leaders in the new nationwide corporate community. The federation's members met with academic experts and union leaders in an effort to solve the intense labor conflict of the era. Although the corporate leaders seemed willing at first to accept unions and collective bargaining in principle, they rejected government enforcement of union rights and tried to restrict unions to the relative handful of skilled trades, thereby excluding industrial workers in factories.

When these efforts at conciliation failed, federation leaders urged corporations to adopt a variety of social and benefit programs—ranging from athletic leagues to educational classes—that would make unions less attractive, a strategy that came to be known as "welfare capitalism."[31]

The National Civic Federation had its greatest success when it led the way in establishing workers' compensation programs as a way to deflect the many lawsuits that injured workers were winning. It also developed the legislation that created the Federal Trade Commission as a government agency to regulate the business practices of corporations. From the point of view of National Civic Federation leaders, regulation was a useful method for dealing with the agitation by reformers and socialists for greater public ownership and control of corporations.[32]

By World War I, the National Civic Federation had outlived its usefulness because its top leaders had accomplished their main goals and no longer wanted to be in a group with labor leaders. After that, the organization was dominated by its staff and a small group of conservative trade union leaders. Its wide-ranging functions were taken over by somewhat more specialized groups. The Council on Foreign Relations, founded in 1921, gradually became the center for discussions of foreign policy for the next fifty years. In the 1970s it was supplemented by other groups—such as the Atlantic Council and the Center for Strategic and International Studies—because it grew to nearly 3,000 members, making it too unwieldy for sustained discussion on some issues. For domestic economic policies, the National Association of Manufacturers (created in 1895), the Chamber of Commerce of the United States (1912), the Conference Board (1916), the Business Council (1933), and the Committee for Economic Development (1942) were the focal points until 1972, when the Business Roundtable arrived on the scene.

The policy groups have several important functions, some inside the power elite, some in relation to society as a whole. These functions provide the answer to the claim by pluralists and state autonomy theorists that corporate leaders are too uninformed and inexperienced on policy matters to have an impact on the government.

1. They provide a setting in which corporate leaders can familiarize themselves with general policy issues by listening to and questioning the experts from think tanks and university research institutes.

2. They provide a forum where conflicts between moderate conservatives and ultraconservatives can be resolved, usually by including experts of both persuasions within the discussion group, along with an occasional liberal on some issues.

3. They provide an informal training ground for new leadership. It is within these organizations that corporate leaders can determine in an informal fashion which of their peers are best suited for service in government and as spokespersons to other groups.

4. They provide an informal recruiting ground for determining which academic experts may be best suited for government service, either as faceless staff aides to the corporate leaders who take government positions, or as high-level appointees in their own right.

In addition to their several functions within the power elite, the policy groups have three functions in relation to the rest of society:

1. These groups legitimate their members as "serious" and "expert" persons capable of government service. This image is created because group members are portrayed as giving of their own time to take part in highly selective organizations that are nonpartisan and nonprofit.

2. They convey the concerns, goals, and expectations of the corporate rich to those young experts and professors who aspire to foundation grants, invitations to work at think tanks, or consultative roles with government agencies.

3. Through such avenues as books, journals, policy statements, press releases, and speakers, these groups influence the climate of opinion in both Washington and the country at large. (This point is developed when the opinion-shaping process is discussed in chapter 5.)

The most extensive study of the relationship of policy-discussion groups to foundations and think tanks was undertaken by sociologist Mary Anna Culleton Colwell, a former executive officer of a small foundation who conducted lengthy interviews with foundation officials as part of her study. Starting with a sample of seventy-seven large foundations, which included the twenty-six with over $100 million in assets at the time, she found twenty that gave over 5 percent of their total grants, or over $200,000, to public policy groups. These twenty foundations were closely connected to thirty-one think tanks and discussion groups.[33]

The density of the network revolving around these core organizations was even greater than any previous studies had led social scientists to expect. Of the 225 trustees who served on the twenty foundations, 124 also served as trustees of 120 other foundations as well. Ten of the twenty foundations had trustee interlocks with eighteen of the thirty-one policy-formation organizations and think tanks. The Rockefeller Foundation had the largest number of trustee interlocks with other foundations (thirty-four), followed by the Sloan Foundation, the Carnegie Corporation, the Ford Foundation, and Rockefeller Brothers Fund. The Rockefeller Foundation also had the largest number of trustee connections to the policy groups it finances (fourteen), followed once again by the Sloan, Carnegie, Ford, and Rockefeller Brothers foundations. Moreover, all five of these foundations tended to be involved with the same policy groups. These foundations, then, are part of the moderate-conservative portion of the network.

Colwell's analysis also showed that a set of policy groups and think tanks identified with ultraconservative programs—the American Enterprise Institute, the American Economic Foundation, the Hoover Institution, the Foundation for Economic Education, and the Freedoms Foundation—were linked to another set of foundations, such as the Lilly Endowment, the Olin Foundation, and the Smith Richardson Foundation. Unlike the large foundations in the moderate part of the network, all of the very conservative foundations are under the direct control of the original donating family. On the basis of tax records and interviews, Colwell believes that many, if not all, of the ultraconservative nonprofit organizations receive a very large percentage of their annual budgets from philanthropic foundations and corporations, a conclusion supported in a study by sociologist Michael Allen. Analyzing the income tax reports of ten ultraconservative think tanks from 1977 to 1986, Allen found that twelve foundations provided half the funding of the American Enterprise Institute and 85 percent or more of the funding for the other prominent ultraconservative groups.[34]

The tremendous impact of a few extremely wealthy ultraconservatives can be seen in the funding career of the aforementioned Richard Mellon Scaife, an heir to a large portion of the famous Mellon oil and banking fortune in Pittsburgh. It is estimated that Scaife has given about $300 million to ultraconservative and New Right groups and causes since the mid-1960s, but he remains worth $800 million. His donations come through both his foundations and his personal income. He also provides large donations to conservative political candidates and the Republican Party. His grants through two foundations to the most visible ultraconservative think tanks in 1994–1995 are listed in table 4.3, along with some of his many grants to ultraconservative and New Right "advocacy" organizations. A similar picture of combined policy and advocacy donations could be drawn for several other extremely wealthy individuals.[35]

A sophisticated network analysis by another sociologist, Val Burris, shows that the ultraconservative groups became more central

Table 4.3 Donations to Selected Ultraconservative Think Tanks and Advocacy Groups in 1994–1995 by Two Richard Mellon Scaife Foundations

Think Tank	Foundation	Funding
American Enterprise Institute	Scaife	465,000
Center for Security Policy	Carthage/Scaife	175,000
Heritage Foundation	Carthage/Scaife	1,438,000
Hoover Institution	Carthage/Scaife	500,000
Hudson Institute	Carthage	160,000
Manhattan Institute	Scaife	175,000
Total		2,913,000

Advocacy Group	Foundation	Funding
Accuracy in Media	Carthage	145,000
Americans for Tax Reform	Carthage	75,000
American Spectator Magazine	Carthage/Scaife	450,000
Center for Popular Culture	Scaife	1,000,000
Defenders of Property Rights	Carthage	100,000
Free Congress Research/ Education Fund	Carthage/Scaife	685,000
Intercollegiate Studies Institute	Carthage/Scaife	675,000
National Association of Scholars	Scaife	300,000
Western Journalism Center	Carthage	100,000
Women's Freedom Network	Carthage	50,000
Total		3,580,000

Source: *Foundation Grants Index*, 1997, under Carthage and Scaife in all subject sections.

to the overall policy network between 1973 and 1990. Using director overlaps for twelve think tanks and policy groups for 1973, 1980, and 1990, he found that the network became much more tightly interlocked (more "dense") between 1973 and 1980 and that the most central discussion groups developed more ties with the ultraconservative think tanks. The density of the network declined slightly in 1990, with some ultraconservative think tanks moving to the periphery again, but the network was still much more dense than it had been in 1973.

Burris also studied the occupational and social backgrounds of those directors in the policy network who sat on two or more think tank or policy-discussion boards. Over 90 percent were corporate

Table 4.4 Centrality Scores and Bohemian Grove Participation for 12 Think Tanks and Policy-Discussion Groups

Organization	Centrality Scores				Bohemian %, 1991
	1973	1980	1990	Total*	
Business Roundtable	.59	.78	.66	2.03	20
Business Council	.59	.61	.72	1.92	26
Conference Board	.59	.64	.57	1.80	6
Committee for Economic Development	.56	.49	.59	1.64	5
Brookings Institution	.41	.56	.42	1.39	6
American Enterprise Institute	.26	.57	.55	1.38	19
Council on Foreign Relations	.32	.44	.62	1.35	8
Trilateral Commission	.34	.41	.20	.95	18
Hoover Institution	.47	.28	.19	.94	37
Chamber of Commerce	.14	.37	.28	.79	0
Heritage Foundation	.00	.28	.04	.32	0
National Association of Manufacturers	.08	.14	.07	.29	4
Average of all groups	.32	.46	.41		

Source: Val Burris, "Elite Policy-Planning Networks in the United States," *Research in Politics and Society*, Vol. 4, 1992, p. 126; Peter Phillips, *A Relative Advantage: Sociology of the San Francisco Bohemian Club*, Ph.D. Dissertation, University of California, Davis, 1994, p. 123.

*The total of the three centrality scores provides a rough way to rank the twelve organizations overall, even though there are some fluctuations from year to year.

executives, mostly from very large corporations. In 1980, nearly half of them were on the board of one of the ten largest commercial banks. About half attended high-status universities as undergraduates, and half were in upper-class social clubs, but only a small percentage came from upper-class families originally.[36] Utilizing Burris's 1990 list of policy directors, Phillips found that 13 percent were members or guests at the Bohemian Grove in 1991.[37] Table 4.4 presents the centrality scores for each organization, along with the percentage of its directors at the Bohemian Grove in 1991.

With the overall nature of the policy network now clearly established, including the centrality of the policy-discussion groups, the next step is to look at some of the policy-discussion groups in more detail and also to see if the findings by Burris hold into the late 1990s.

The Council on Foreign Relations

The Council on Foreign Relations (CFR) is the largest and best-known of the policy organizations. Established by bankers, lawyers, and academicians who were fully cognizant of the larger role the United States would play in world affairs as a result of World War I, the council's importance in the conduct of foreign affairs was well established by the 1930s. Before 1970 the members were primarily financiers, executives, and lawyers, with a strong minority of journalists, academic experts, and government officials. After that time there was an effort to respond to criticism by including a larger number of government officials, especially foreign-service officers, politicians, and aides to congressional committees concerned with foreign policy. By the 1990s the council had nearly 3,000 members, most of whom do little more than receive reports and attend large banquets.

Several studies demonstrate the council's connections to the upper class and corporate community. A sample of 210 New York members showed that 39 percent were listed in the *Social Register*, and a random sampling of the full membership found 33 percent in that directory.[38] In both studies, directors of the council were even more likely than regular members to be part of the upper class. Council overlaps with the corporate community are equally pervasive. Twenty-two percent of the 1969 council membership served on the board of at least one of *Fortune*'s top 500 industrials, for example. In another study, it was found that 125 of 201 large corporations had 293 interlocks with the council. Twenty-three of the very largest banks and corporations had four or more directors who were members.[39]

The full extent of council overlap with the corporate community and government is shown in my study of its entire membership list. My analysis determined that about one of every five members is an officer or director of a business listed in *Poor's Register of Corporations, Directors, and Executives*. Membership was once again found to be greatest for the biggest industrial corporations and banks. Overall, 37 percent of the 500 top industrials had at least one officer or director who was a member, with the figure rising to 70 percent for the top 100 and 92 percent for the top 25. Twenty-one of the top 25 banks had members, as did 16 of the largest 25 insurance companies. However, only the top 10 among utilities, transports, and retails were well represented. For all sectors of the economy, the companies with the most members among their officers and directors were J. P. Morgan Bank (16), Chase Manhattan Bank (15), Citibank (10), and IBM (8).

Table 4.5 Major Companies with One or More Directors Who Are Also Directors of the Council on Foreign Relations

Aluminum Company of America	IBM
Atlantic Richfield	Mobil
AT&T	J. P. Morgan Bank (2)
Bristol-Myers Squibb (2)	New York Times
Boeing	Pepsi-Cola
Chase Manhattan Bank	Prudential Insurance
Chevron	Sara Lee
Chrysler	Time Warner
Disney	Times Mirror (2)
Exxon	Xerox (2)
Federal Express	

Note: CFR directors are also directors of 16 less well known or smaller companies not listed here.

The success of the council's effort to include more government officials is reflected in this study: 250 members were listed in the index of the *Governmental Manual*. About half were politicians and career government officials; the other half were appointees to the government who came from business, law, and the academic community. In addition, another 184 members were serving as unpaid members of federal advisory committees.[40]

Another study of all council members found a considerable number of linkages to foundations. According to a 1994 analysis by the *Foundation Reporter*, a service for those seeking information on where to send grant proposals, 115 CFR members sat on sixty-seven foundation boards.[41] My analysis of major foundation boards in 1996 discovered that the largest overlaps are with the Rockefeller Foundation (seven) and the Carnegie Corporation, Sloan Foundation, and Ford Foundation, each with six trustees who are members of the council.

The CFR remains very closely connected to the corporate community through its board of directors. In 1997, seventeen of its thirty-two directors held forty-three directorships in thirty-seven corporations. The twenty-one of those companies that are best known are listed in table 4.5. Two directors each from Bristol-Myers Squibb, J. P. Morgan Bank, Times-Mirror (publisher of the Los Angeles *Times*), and Xerox are CFR directors.

The council receives its general funding from wealthy individuals, corporations, and subscriptions to its influential periodical *Foreign*

Affairs. For special projects it often relies on major foundations for support. The council conducts an active program of luncheon and dinner speeches at its New York clubhouse, featuring government officials and national leaders from all over the world. It also encourages dialogue and disseminates information through books, pamphlets, and articles in *Foreign Affairs.* The most important aspects of the CFR program, however, are its discussion and study groups. These small gatherings of about fifteen to twenty-five people bring together business executives, government officials, scholars, and military officers for detailed consideration of specific topics in the area of foreign affairs. Discussion groups, which meet about once a month, are charged with exploring problems in a general way, trying to define issues and identify alternatives.

Discussion groups often lead to a study group as the next stage. Study groups revolve around the work of a council research fellow (financed by a foundation grant) or a regular staff member. The group leader and other experts present monthly papers that are discussed and criticized by the rest of the group. The goal of such study groups is a detailed statement of the problem by the scholar leading the discussion. Any book that eventuates from the group is understood to express the views of its academic author—not of the council or the members of the study group—but the books are nonetheless published with the sponsorship of the council, and the names of the people participating in the study group are sometimes listed at the beginning of the book.

One of the state autonomy theorists' only pieces of evidence from the realm of foreign policy, political scientist Stephen Krasner's study of how the "national interest" is defined, is directly refuted by one of the council's most important projects. Krasner claims that the national interest is formulated in the White House and State Department, which he sees as the purest embodiments of the state on issues of foreign policy. He develops case studies from the post–World War II era to support his theory.[42]

But, in fact, the War-Peace Studies of the Council on Foreign Relations, beginning in 1939 with financial support from the Rockefeller Foundation, created the postwar definition of the national interest through a comprehensive set of studies and discussion groups that involved approximately 100 top bankers, lawyers, executives, economists, and military experts in 362 meetings over a five-year period. The academic experts within the study groups met regularly with officials of the State Department and in 1942 became part of the department's new postwar planning process as twice-a-week consultants while at the same time continuing work on the War-Peace project. As all accounts agree, the State Department had little or no planning capability of its own.[43]

Although the study groups sent hundreds of reports to the State Department, the most important one defined the minimum geographical area needed for the American economy to make full utilization of its resources and at the same time maintain harmony with Western Europe and Japan. This geographical area, which came to be known as the "Grand Area," included Latin America, Europe, the colonies of the British Empire, and all of Southeast Asia. Southeast Asia was necessary as a source of raw materials for Great Britain and Japan and as a consumer of Japanese products. The American national interest was then defined in terms of the integration and defense of the Grand Area, which led to plans for the United Nations, the International Monetary Fund, and the World Bank and eventually to the decision to defend Vietnam from a communist takeover at all costs. The many details of the case have been presented elsewhere.[44]

Contrary to Krasner, who believes that the anticommunist dimension of American ideology was the chief factor in defining the country's postwar national interest, there was very little emphasis on communism in the discussion papers and minutes from study group meetings. Nor were Eastern Europe and the area encompassed by the Soviet Union part of the Grand Area. It thus seems more likely that the American planners were prepared to "live and let live" with the Soviet and Chinese communists until they began to support anticapitalist insurgencies in Western Europe, Korea, and Vietnam. This claim is borne out by the good relations that American leaders developed with China in the 1970s.

In other words, the new definition of the national interest created by the War-Peace Studies and adopted by the American government was in good part pragmatic and "economic" in that it concerned the full functioning of the American economic system without having to make any major changes in it. The goal was to avoid both another Great Depression and greater government control of the economy. The acceptance by government leaders of the smallest possible role for the government suggests that the corporate community, through the Council on Foreign Relations, had the dominant role in the process of defining a new national interest for the post–World War II era. Krasner therefore puts too much emphasis on both state autonomy and anticommunist ideology because he overlooks corporate power and the policy-formation network in making his analysis.

Just as in the crisis years of the late 1930s, so too in the late 1960s and early 1970s Council leaders reacted to large-scale international changes by creating several new initiatives, including a new discussion organization, the Trilateral Commission, which had members from Japan and Western Europe as well as the United States. Its goal was to develop closer economic and political cooperation among the industrialized democracies and to neutralize challenges from underdeveloped countries.[45] Although the organization is now written off as a tired old debating society by pluralists and some journalists, a comparison of its original goals with current international relations by scholar-activist Holly Sklar suggests that the international organizational environment in the 1990s looks much like what the Trilateral leaders hoped it would when they ventured forth in 1973. Although the Trilateral Commission is primarily a rallying and coordinating point for the corporate executives and government officials who belong, the important organizations they head in their home countries did play the central role in making the changes that were deemed necessary—a point too quickly forgotten by the critics of those who discuss the Trilateral Commission.[46]

The CFR itself is far too large for its members to issue policy proclamations as a group. Moreover, its usefulness as a neutral discussion ground would be diminished if it tried to do so. For example, its leaders helped to mediate the dispute that broke out in the foreign policy establishment in the 1970s over the nature of the Soviet Union's intentions and the extent of its threat to United States interests. After holding several discussion groups and study groups on the topic, it created a special Commission on U.S.-Soviet Relations in the fall of 1980 that included representatives of both the Soviets-are-expansionists-and-dangerous view and the Soviets-can-be-worked-with view. The discussants had served in all recent administrations—Republican and Democrat—and they were chaired by the editor-in-chief of *Time* magazine. The report that emerged from these discussions was drafted by a specialist in international relations from a major Washington think tank. The thirty-one-page report was distributed free of charge with the aid of a grant from the Ford Foundation and publicized in newspapers and magazines read by members of the power elite.[47]

Time described the commission's recommendations as "tough-minded." The participants agreed that the Soviets were a "vastly more formidable foe" than had been thought a decade earlier and that their intentions were relentlessly hostile to Western interests. The report called for an even bigger defense buildup than either presidential candidate had advocated in the 1980 elections, and that increased buildup did occur.[48] Throughout the 1980s commentators noted that foreign policy experts were once again basically in agreement in their overall view of the world situation. It is likely that the ongoing debate at the council and the report of its commission played a major role in creating this harmony. The fact that none of these rival experts realized how weak the Soviet Union actually was is a separate story that shows the limits on real understanding when it comes to complex world events.

The Council on Foreign Relations continued to have influence on foreign policy issues in the 1990s, although supplemented by the

Atlantic Council and the Center for Strategic and International Studies in Washington. Its board of directors virtually moved into the State Department and other government agencies after Clinton was elected in 1992, a point that is demonstrated in detail in chapter 7.

The Conference Board

The Conference Board is the oldest of the existing policy-discussion groups focused on domestic issues. Called the National Industrial Conference Board when it was founded during World War I, it was originally a more narrowly focused organization, with a primary interest in doing research for the corporate community itself. During the 1930s and 1940s it took a conservative antigovernment stance under the influence of its executive director, who often denounced other policy groups for their alleged desertion of the free enterprise system. Only with the retirement of this director in 1948 and an infusion of new members into the board of directors did the organization move back into the corporate mainstream and begin to assume a role as a major voice of the corporate community. Further changes in the 1960s were symbolized by the shortening of its name to Conference Board and the election of a moderate conservative from the Committee for Economic Development as its president. It has played a central coordinating role since that time.[49]

In addition to establishing discussion groups and publishing of a variety of statistical and survey studies, the Conference Board has been innovative in developing international policy linkages. In 1961, in conjunction with the Stanford Research Institute, a West Coast think tank now known as SRI, the Conference Board sponsored a weeklong International Industrial Conference in San Francisco, bringing together 500 leaders in industry and finance from sixty countries to hear research reports and discuss common problems. The International Industrial Conference has met every four years since that time. Along with the Trilateral Commission and the "sister" committees that the Committee for Economic Development has encouraged in numerous nations, the International Industrial Conference is one of the mainstays in an international policy-discussion network that has existed since the 1950s, well before the more widely publicized Trilateral Commission came along.[50]

The Committee for Economic Development

The Committee for Economic Development (CED) was established in the early 1940s to help plan for the postwar world. The corporate leaders who were instrumental in creating this new study group had two major concerns at the time: (1) There might be another depression after the war; and (2) if business executives did not develop economic programs for the postwar era, other sectors of society might offer ideas that would not be acceptable to the corporate community. The purpose of the committee was to avoid any identification with special-interest pleading for business and to concern itself with the nation as a whole: "The Committee would avoid promoting the special interests of business itself as such and would likewise refrain from speaking for any other special interests. The CED was to be a businessman's organization that would speak in the national interest."[51] It coordinated its early efforts with the War-Peace Studies of the Council on Foreign Relations, working diligently for the acceptance of the International Monetary Fund and World Bank by skeptical conservative Republicans.[52]

With the exception of a strong antiunion stance that is standard for all corporate policy groups, the Committee for Economic Development was the model of a moderate-conservative group from its founding until corporate leaders decided to change its orientation in the mid-1970s. For example, in 1945 it crafted a compromise on legislation drafted by liberals calling for policies that would generate full employment, in the 1960s it called for higher taxes to pay for the Vietnam War, and in the early 1970s it supported modest improvements in government programs for income maintenance and health care.

In its early years, the CED consisted of 200 corporate leaders. Later it added a small number of university presidents. In addition, leading economists and public administration experts serve as advisers and conduct research for the CED; many go on to serve in advisory roles in both Republican and Democratic administrations. Although there is an overlap in membership with the larger Council on Foreign Relations (in 1996, 25 percent of the CED's 257 trustees were in the CFR; four of the CFR's thirty-two directors were CED trustees), the committee has a different mix of members. Unlike the council, it has few bankers and no corporate lawyers, journalists, or academic experts among its trustees.

Like the council, the CED works through study groups that are aided by academic experts. The study groups have considered every conceivable issue—from farm policy to government reorganization to campaign finance laws—but the greatest emphasis is on economic issues of both a domestic and international nature. The most ambitious of its projects have been financed by large foundations, but its general revenues come directly from its corporate members.

Unlike at the CFR, the results of CED study groups are released as official policy statements of the organization. The statements are published in pamphlet form and disseminated widely in business, government, and media circles. They contain footnotes in which trustees register any disagreements they may have with the overall recommendations. These statements are of great value to social scientists for studying the range of policy orientations in the corporate community.

There were major changes in the orientation of the CED between 1974 and 1976 that provide an ideal example of how a new policy direction on the part of leading trustees can bring about shifts within a policy group and quickly end any role for liberal experts.[53] This shift in orientation was related to the general pressure for greater government intervention in the economy due to the inflationary crisis of the period, but the specific triggers were internal to the organization. First, the economist who was president of the CED made the mistake of signing a liberal-labor public statement calling for exploration of small steps toward greater government planning. Second, a CED study group on controlling inflation, advised in part by liberal economists, was moving in the direction of advocating wage and price controls by government.

Conservative trustees from several of the largest companies represented in the CED were extremely upset by what they interpreted as a trend toward greater acceptance of government controls. They reacted on a number of levels. First, several of their companies lowered their financial contributions or threatened to withdraw support altogether. Since large companies make the biggest contribution to the CED budget, these threats were of great concern to the president and his staff.

Second, the chair of the trustees, a senior executive at Exxon, appointed top executive officers from General Motors, Cutler-Hammer, and Itek as a committee to make a study of the internal structure of the organization. One result of this study was the retirement of the president one year earlier than expected. He was replaced by a conservative monetary economist from the Federal Reserve Bank of Minneapolis. The new president immediately wrote to all trustees, asking for their advice on future policy directions and pledging greater responsiveness to the trustees. He also brought in several new staff members, one of whom told me in an interview in 1995 that it was their job to neutralize liberal staff members.

Third, many of the trustees on the Research and Policy Committee that oversees all study groups decided to oppose the report on inflation and price controls. In all, there were fifteen pages of dissents attached to the report, most from a very conservative perspective. Seven trustees voted to reject publication of the statement.

Fourth, the three economists primarily responsible for drafting the report—a university president, a prominent think tank representative, and a CED staff member—were criticized in letters to the CED president and in internal memos for having too much influence in shaping the recommendations. In 1977 the CED leader from Exxon characterized the ill-fated statement as a "poor compromise between the views of trustees and a stubborn chairman and project director."[54]

Fifth, some trustees were personally hostile to the economists who were said to be too liberal. The think tank economist was even accused of being a Communist. In a telephone interview in September 1992—many years after the event—the economist in question told me that until these unpleasant personal confrontations, he had enjoyed participating in CED study groups because of the diversity of views and the open give and take, but that he was not interested in going back after the atmosphere changed.

The dramatic difference between the CED at the beginning and end of the 1970s is demonstrated by business school professor William Frederick in a comparison of policy statements issued in 1971 and 1979. In the first report, the emphasis was on the social responsibility of corporations and the need for corporations to work in partnership with government on social problems. The report at the end of the decade stressed the need to "redefine" the role of government in a "market system." As Frederick concludes, the CED was "now silent" on all the social issues it had addressed before 1974. This change occurred even though 43 percent of the forty members of the Research and Policy Committee in 1979 were on the committee and endorsed the more liberal policy statement in 1971.[55]

The CED's internal critics also claimed that it was ineffective in its attempts to influence the policy climate in Washington and that it overlapped with other policy groups in any case. The new president was instructed to find a new niche for the CED in relation to other organizations, especially the Business Roundtable. Although the outgoing president had produced evidence of the CED's behind-the-scenes effectiveness despite a legal restriction on lobbying due to its tax-exempt status, the success of the Business Roundtable led to a repositioning of the CED by corporate executives who were top officers in both the CED and the Business Roundtable. As one of these officers wrote in a letter to several trustees in the summer of 1978, after a meeting "with a small group of chief executive officers of leading U.S. corporations":

> The meeting was especially helpful in sharpening our sense of CED's special role within the spectrum of major national business-related organizations. The group was encouraged to learn of new efforts by CED to coordinate its work with that of the Business Roundtable, the Conference Board, the American Enterprise

Institute, and others, thus minimizing duplication and overlap. CED can be especially effective, it was felt, in synthesizing the ideas of scholars and converting them into practical principles that can provide guidance for public policy on a selected number of key issues.[56]

None of this upheaval was visible to outside observers, showing once again the importance of historical studies to understand how the policy network functions. The only article mentioning the CED's problems appeared in the *Wall Street Journal* in December 1976. It quoted one trustee, an executive from Mobil Oil, who claimed that "in the early days, the trustees were men who saw a need for some more government intervention, but now some of the trustees believe the intervention has gone far enough." An academic economist who once advised the CED said it had "lost its purpose" and "doesn't have the sense to go out of business."[57] Given the ultraconservative nature of the *Wall Street Journal* leadership, it would have been hard to know what to make out of such charges at the time without extensive interviewing or access to internal documents that usually do not become available to social scientists.

Nor is the fate of the liberal experts at the CED unique. In the late 1940s, for example, the Carnegie Corporation told Harvard University it had to dismiss one of the experts at its Russian Research Institute, H. Stuart Hughes, because he was too liberal. There was no claim that this distinguished son of a former Supreme Court justice was a Socialist or Communist; he simply did not think that American foreign policy toward the Soviet Union made sense. Or, to take another example, John D. Rockefeller III made a speech in 1974 criticizing his staff at the Population Council after Third World representatives chastised the organization at an international conference for an alleged overemphasis on family planning. Rockefeller then passed over his own population specialists in selecting a new president for the council, deeply wounding the feelings of many people who had been loyal to him for decades.[58]

When the fate of the liberal experts in these examples is coupled with the importance of foundation grants and positions in think tanks for experts in general, along with the need for experts to be found "relevant" and useful by corporations and government, there is little reason to believe that experts are free to say and recommend whatever they wish. To the contrary, they work within the constraints of what is acceptable to the corporate leaders who finance and direct the organizations of the policy-formation network. What is acceptable can vary from time to time, depending on the circumstances, but that does not mean there are no constraints. It is likely that most experts who want to advance their careers and feel effective in their work understand this point extremely well.

The Business Council

The Business Council is a unique organization in the policy-formation network because of its close formal contact with government. It was created during the 1930s as a quasi-governmental advisory group and still holds regular consultative meetings with government officials even though it became an independent organization in 1962. Since the 1960s, most of its private meetings with government officials have been held in the relaxed and friendly atmosphere of the Homestead Hotel in Hot Springs, Virginia, sixty miles from Washington. During the meetings, council members hear speeches by government officials, conduct panels on issues of the day, receive reports from their staff, and talk informally with each other and the government officials in attendance. Business sessions are alternated with social events, including golf tournaments, tennis matches, and banquet-style dinners for members, guests, and wives. The expenses for the meetings, reports, and social events are paid by the corporate leaders.[59]

The members are, with few exceptions, the chairs or presidents of the largest corporations in the country. The centrality of the Business Council within the corporate community can be seen in my tabulation of all the directorships listed by the 154 Business Council members in one of the biannual editions of *Who's Who in America*. This self-report information showed that they held 730 directorships in 435 banks and corporations, as well as 49 foundation trusteeships in 36 different foundations and 125 trusteeships with 84 universities. The 435 corporations were at the heart of the corporate community; 176 of them were among the 800 largest corporations at that juncture. The companies most heavily represented were Chase Manhattan Bank (eleven directors), J. P. Morgan Bank (ten directors), General Electric (ten directors), General Motors (nine directors), and Metropolitan Life (nine directors).[60]

Business Council members were part of other policy groups as well; forty-nine were trustees of the Committee for Economic Development and forty-two were members of the Council on Foreign Relations. They also were in numerous social clubs. Not surprisingly, then, an analysis of membership overlaps among thirty social clubs and policy groups using the mathematics of matrix algebra determined that the Business Council had the highest centrality score in the matrix. As shown in table 4.6, it was rivaled only by the Committee for Economic Development, but the study did not include the Business Roundtable, which was only in its infancy at the time.[61]

Table 4.6 The 21 Most Central Policy Groups and Clubs
Among 30 Groups

Organization	Centrality Score
Business Council	.95
Committee for Economic Development	.91
Conference Board	.83
Links Club	.80
Advertising Council	.73
Council on Foreign Relations	.68
Pacific Union Club	.67
Chicago Club	.65
Brookings Institution	.65
American Assembly	.65
Bohemian Club	.62
Century Association	.48
California Club	.46
Foundation for American Agriculture	.45
Detroit Club	.44
National Planning Association	.36
Eagle Lake Club	.33
National Municipal League	.33
Somerset Club	.32
Rancheros Visitadores Club	.26
National Association of Manufacturers	.25

Source: G. William Domhoff, "Social Clubs, Policy-Planning Groups, and Corporations: A Network Study," *The Insurgent Sociologist*, Vol. 5, No. 3, p. 178. Used with
permission of the publisher.

The Business Roundtable

As the earlier cited network analysis by Burris shows, the Business
Roundtable joined the Business Council at the heart of both the corporate community and the policy-formation network and now has the
most powerful role. Its seventy-nine directors for 1997 had 206 directorships with 134 corporations, 32 of which were in the top 50 in size
and 19 of which were among the 28 with the most connections to other
companies. Table 4.7 presents the 17 companies with three or four
director interlocks with the Business Roundtable.

Table 4.7 Companies with Three or Four Interlocks with
the Business Roundtable

Three	Four
Abbott Laboratories	CSX
Amoco	J. P. Morgan Bank
AT&T	Mobil Oil
Bristol-Myers Squibb	Procter & Gamble
Caterpillar	
Chase Manhattan Bank	
Cummins Engine	
Dayton Hudson	
Georgia Pacific	
IBM	
Minnesota Mining & Manufacturing	
Phelps Dodge	
USX	

Thirty-six of the seventy-nine Business Roundtable directors were in the Business Council as well. The Roundtable's interlocks with other policy groups and with think tanks are presented in figure 4.2. The seven interlocks with the National Association of Manufacturers—one of the most conservative policy groups of the past—suggests that the NAM is now a more moderate organization than it has been at any time in the twentieth century, although its adamant opposition to unions remains unchanged (and is shared by the Business Roundtable).

In effect, the Business Roundtable is the lobbying extension of the Business Council. Whereas the Business Council prefers to remain in the background and talk informally with members of the executive branch, the Business Roundtable has an activist profile. It sends its leaders to lobby members of Congress as readily as it meets privately with the president and cabinet leaders. Indeed, it was formed because corporate leaders came to the conclusion that the Business Council was not effective enough in pressing the corporate viewpoint on government. There was also a fear that the corporate community was relying too heavily on specific trade associations and hired lobbyists in approaching Congress. The founders of the Business Roundtable hoped that direct lobbying of legislators by chief executives would have more impact.[62]

Figure 4.2 The Network around the Business Roundtable.
Source: Updated from Val Burris, "Elite Policy-Planning Networks in the United States," *Research in Politics and Society*, Vol. 4, 1992, p. 124.

Irving S. Shapiro, at one time chair of both DuPont Corporation and the Business Roundtable, explained the difference between the Business Roundtable and the Business Council as follows:

> The Roundtable is only for chief executive officers. Once I'm through with that I am out. There's a counterpart to the Roundtable that you may not be familiar with, and that's the Business Council, and that you stay involved with. It is not an advocacy organization. It simply deals with public issues. The Roundtable was created to have an advocacy organization. It wasn't created by the Business Council, but by the same people. I am a member of the Council and will stay with that. People who are retired stay with it the rest of their lives if they choose to.[63]

The 150 companies in the Business Roundtable pay from $10,000 to $35,000 per year in dues, depending on their size. This provides a budget of over $3 million a year. Decisions on where the Roundtable will direct its efforts are determined by a policy committee that meets every two months to discuss current policy issues, create task forces to examine selected issues, and review position papers. The policy committee ignores problems in any one industry and concentrates instead on issues that have a broad impact on business. The organization is designed so that task force members utilize the resources of their own companies and the information developed in other parts of the policy network.

The Business Roundtable began its activist efforts by coordinating a successful lobbying campaign against a consumer-labor proposal for a new governmental Agency for Consumer Advocacy in the mid-1970s.[64] It created the Clean Air Working Group that battled an environmental-labor National Clean Air Coalition to a standstill from 1980 to 1990 on proposed tightening of the Clean Air Act, agreeing to amendments only after several standards were relaxed or delayed and a plan to trade pollution credits in market-like fashion was accepted by environmentalists.[65] According to detailed work by sociologist Michael Dreiling, it organized the grassroots pressure and forceful lobbying for the corporate community's victory in 1994 on NAFTA (the North American Free Trade Agreement), a proposal to lower tariff barriers that was strongly resisted by organized labor and many of its liberal allies.[66]

If the last few years are any indication, then the Business Roundtable has given an even greater focus to the policy-formation network than it has in the past. A class-domination theory would therefore predict that no legislation affecting the corporate community can pass Congress in the future if it does not have at least the tacit approval of the Business Roundtable.

THE LIBERAL-LABOR POLICY NETWORK

As noted at the outset of the chapter, there is also a small liberal-labor policy network. Its members suggest new ideas and perspectives to liberal political organizations, unions, and the government in an attempt to challenge the power elite. They also issue detailed critiques of proposals put forward by organizations in the corporate policy-formation network, receiving wide media coverage in many instances. Because the organizations in this network are small in comparison to the corporate-backed organizations, they also serve as advocacy groups. That is, there is less division of labor than there is in the corporate network.

Some organizations in the liberal-labor network are supported by donations from labor unions, but the sums are seldom more than a few hundred thousand dollars per year except in the case of the Economic Policy Institute, which receives a little over $1 million a year from union sources. (Grants by unions are not catalogued in any one source because they come from individual unions as well as AFL-CIO headquarters, so I have not been able to assemble specific figures on the overall amount of union contributions.) Whether or not liberal policy organizations receive support from unions, they are funded primarily by grants from a small number of liberal foundations and by grants for specific projects from a few mainstream foundations, especially Ford, Rockefeller, and Carnegie.

Even with grants from the mainstream foundations, and backing from labor unions, the liberal-labor policy organizations do not come close to matching the budgets of their moderately conservative and ultraconservative opponents. Most liberal groups have budgets of from $1 million to $5 million a year, less than one-third of the figures for the Brookings Institution ($22 million), the American Enterprise Institute ($15 million), and the Heritage Foundation ($28.5 million).[67] As one manager from a liberal policy group told me in a telephone interview in June 1997, "Even with the foundation grants, we are still fighting with bows and arrows."

Although the liberal-labor coalition has existed since the 1930s, and people known as "reformers" go back to the Progressive Era, most of its current organizations were created more recently. The founding dates, estimated budgets, and major foundation supporters for 1994–1995 for three of the most visible liberal policy groups, the Economic Policy Institute, the Institute for Policy Studies, and the Center on Budget and Policy Priorities, are presented in table 4.8.

As briefly noted in the first chapter, the liberal-labor coalition has excellent media connections, in part because some of its members are prominent journalists. It therefore has the ability to obtain wide coverage for stories critical of policy proposals by its rivals. This media visibility is further enhanced by claims about liberal-labor power in ultraconservative fund-raising pitches. The successes and failures of the liberal-labor policy advocates are examined as part of a discussion of important legislative initiatives in chapter 7.

CONCLUSION

This chapter has filled out the concept of a power elite as the leadership group of the corporate rich by adding policy advisers into the equation. As briefly explained in chapter 1, the power elite is composed of members of the upper class who have taken on leadership roles in the corporate community and the policy network, along with high-level employees in corporations and policy-network organizations. More formally, it now can be stated that the power elite consists of those people who serve as directors or trustees in profit and nonprofit institutions controlled by the corporate rich through stock

Table 4.8 Founding Dates, Estimated Budgets, and Top Foundation Supporters in 1994–1995 for Three Liberal-Labor Policy Groups

	Economic Policy Institute	Institute for Policy Studies	Center on Budget and Policy Priorities
Founding Date	1986	1963	1981
Estimated Budget	1,500,000–2,500,000	2,000,000–3,000,000	1,500,000–2,500,000
Mainstream Foundation Support			
Ford	229,000	130,000	900,000
Rockefeller	53,000	0	450,000
Carnegie	25,000	0	150,000
Liberal Foundation Support			
Arca	140,000	64,000	0
Cummings	75,000	20,000	76,000
MacArthur	50,000	99,000	0
Corporate Foundation Support			
Chrysler	25,000	0	0
McDonnell Douglas*	0	0	12,000
Metropolitan Life	75,000	0	0
Conservative Foundation Support			
Smith Richardson†	0	0	300,000

Sources: *Public Interest Profiles* (Washington, DC: Congressional Quarterly, Inc., 1993 and 1996); *Foundation Grants Index 1997.*

*Also gave $10,000 to the American Enterprise Institute, $15,000 to the Brookings Institution, and $20,000 to the Heritage Foundation.

†Also gave $60,000 to the American Enterprise Institute and $200,000 to the Manhattan Institute.

ownership, financial support, or involvement on the board of directors. This definition includes the top-level employees who are asked
to join the board of the organization that employs them.

In theory, the corporate community, the upper class, and the
policy-formation network from which this power elite is drawn can be
imagined in terms of the three intersecting circles presented in chapter 1, figure 1.1. A person can be a member of one of the three, or two
of the three, or all three. There can be upper-class people who are only
socialites, corporate leaders who are neither upper class nor involved
in policy formation, and policy experts who are neither upper class
nor members of the corporate community.

As a practical matter, however, the interrelations among these
three sectors are even closer than the image of three intersecting
circles would indicate. Most male members of the upper class between 45 and 65 are, in fact, part of the corporate community as
major stock owners, financiers, active investors, corporate lawyers,
officers of privately held companies, or titled executives, even if they
are not directors in top corporations. Also, a great many members of
the policy network become involved in the corporate community as
consultants and advisers even if they do not rise to the level of corporate directors. In other words, the corporate community becomes the
common sector that encompasses most older males within the three
overlapping circles.

Although this chapter provides evidence for the existence of a
network of policy-forming organizations that are extensions of the
corporate community in their financing and leadership, it does not
claim there is a completely unified power elite policy outlook. Instead,
it shows that the upper class and corporate community have created
a complex and only partially coordinated set of institutions and organizations that often disagree among themselves about what policies
are most compatible with the primary objectives of the corporate
community. Nonetheless, the weight of the emphasis has to be on the
considerable similarity in viewpoint among institutions that range
from moderately conservative to highly conservative in their policy
suggestions and that have in their two contending camps a near monopoly of nongovernmental expertise and research support. Even
though they are not able to agree completely among themselves, they
have accomplished a more important task: They have been able to
marginalize the few experts with a more liberal point of view.

The findings on how the policy-formation network employs experts are a direct refutation of the view of pluralists and state autonomy
theorists when they claim that advisers are an independent power
source in the United States. Issue networks are in fact rooted in the
money and settings provided by the policy network. The think tanks

are financed by corporations and foundations, and they develop their ideas and position papers for the policy discussion groups in which their employees often serve as paid consultants.

As the changes at the Committee for Economic Development in the mid-1970s indicate, the independence of experts can be curtailed in a variety of ways. For any expert who wants to be funded and invited to policy discussions, it would be foolhardy to voice opinions that are outside the boundaries set by the policy preferences expressed by corporate directors. This claim does not fit with the subjective experience of the experts themselves, who bitterly resent any suggestion that they are subject to group norms, but it is supported by the kind of case studies that is endorsed by such experts when they are done on other people.

The central role of the policy-formation network also refutes the claim by state autonomy theorists that there is considerable expertise lodged inside the federal government. To the contrary, the government has relatively little expertise of its own on the major power issues in the United States. This was even more true for the eras that the state autonomy theorists emphasize in their case studies, the Progressive Era and the New Deal. Historical case studies show that corporate experts created the Federal Trade Commission, the Bureau of the Budget (the forerunner of the Office of Management and Budget in the White House), the Securities and Exchange Commission, the Agricultural Adjustment Administration, and the Social Security Act. The last two of these innovations are discussed in chapter 7, but for the most part readers must refer to the original studies for the detailed presentation of the evidence.[68]

This chapter thus provides evidence for another form of power exercised by the corporate community and upper class through the power elite—expertise. Expert power is an important complement to the economic power and status deference discussed in the two previous chapters. Since government officials with only small policy-planning staffs must often turn to foundations, policy groups, and think tanks if they are to have new ideas for dealing with emerging problems, it is once again a form of power that can be exercised without any necessary direct involvement in government.

Although economic power, status deference, and expertise are formidable quite independent of any involvement in government, they are not enough to sustain the corporate rich as a dominant class without influencing government directly. Because the government is the main avenue through which some redistribution of the country's wealth and income could be brought about in a democratic way, it is the institution within which the liberal-labor coalition and its policy network press for new rights and benefits. Moreover, it can pass laws that help or hinder profit making, and it can collect taxes and deploy expenditures in ways that either stimulate or discourage economic growth. Also, it is the place in the social system that legitimates new policies through the actions of elected officials.

Given the great stakes involved, there is too much uncertainty in the relationship between the corporate rich and the government for the power elite to rely solely on economic power and a near monopoly on expertise to ensure that its interests are realized.[69] To paraphrase the business executive quoted at the end of chapter 2, it may be true that the power elite has so much structural power that it need not involve itself in the details of governance, but no corporate leaders want to take the risk of finding out. It follows, therefore, that there should be evidence of power elite involvement in government if the corporate rich are a dominant class. Before such evidence is presented, however, it is necessary to consider the influence of public opinion and elections on actions by government, for they are the primary reasons that pluralists so strongly deny that there is a dominant class and power elite in the United States.

NOTES

1. Hugh Heclo, "Issue Networks and the Executive Establishment," in *The New American Political System*, ed. Anthony King (Washington, DC: American Enterprise Institute, 1978); Nelson Polsby, *Political Innovation in America* (New Haven, CT: Yale University Press, 1984).
2. For factual information on the four types of foundations, see the introductory pages to the *Foundation Directory, 1996*, available at any library reference desk.
3. G. William Domhoff, *Who Rules America?* (Englewood Cliffs, NJ: Prentice-Hall, 1967), p. 65; Harold Salzman and G. William Domhoff, "Nonprofit Organizations and the Corporate Community," *Social Science History*, 7 (1983): 208–211.
4. Merle Curti and Roderick Nash, *Philanthropy in the Shaping of American Higher Education* (New Brunswick, NJ: Rutgers University Press, 1965); Frank Darknell, "The Carnegie Council for Policy Studies in Higher Education: A New Policy Group for the Ruling Class," *Insurgent Sociologist* (Spring 1975); Frank Darknell, "The Carnegie Philanthropy and Private Corporate Influence on Higher Education," in *Philanthropy and Cultural Imperialism*, ed. Robert F. Arnove (Boston: Hall, 1980); David E. Weischadle, "The Carnegie Corporation and the Shaping of American Educational Policy," in *Philanthropy and Cultural Imperialism*, ed. Robert F. Arnove (Boston: Hall, 1980); Ellen Lagemann, *The Politics of Knowledge* (Middletown, CT: Wesleyan University Press, 1989).
5. Paul Ylvisaker, *Oral History* (Ford Foundation Archives), p. 23; Leonard Silk and Mark Silk, *The American Establishment* (New York: Basic Books, 1980), chapter 4; Daniel Moynihan, *Maximum Feasible Misunderstanding*

(New York: Free Press, 1969); Alice O'Connor, "Community Action, Urban Reform and the Fight Against Poverty: The Ford Foundation's Gray Areas Program," *Journal of Urban History*, 22 (1996): 586–626.

6. Judith Miller, "Foundation to Announce New Structure and Grants," *New York Times* (April 24, 1997): A16.

7. Irvine Alpert and Ann Markusen, "Think Tanks and Capitalist Policy," in *Power Structure Research*, ed. G. William Domhoff (Beverly Hills: Sage Publications, 1980).

8. Marshall Robinson, "The Ford Foundation: Sowing the Seeds of a Revolution," *Environment*, 35 (1993): 10–20.

9. Ibid.

10. *Foundation Grants Index, 1997* (Washington, DC: The Foundation Center, 1997) under Ford Foundation in the environmental section and under the environmental organizations in the recipients section.

11. Berkeley Miller and William Canak, "There Should Be No Blanket Guarantee: Employers' Reactions to Public Employee Unionism, 1965–1975," *Journal of Collective Negotiations in the Public Sector*, 24 (1995): 29. For a full account of the mixture of indifference and hostility that most foundations have shown toward the labor movement, see Richard Magat, "Organized Labor and Philanthropic Foundations: Partners or Strangers?," *Nonprofit and Voluntary Sector Quarterly*, 23 (1994): 353–370.

12. Berkeley Miller and William Canak, "Laws as a Cause and Consequence of Public Employee Unionism," *Industrial Relations Research Association Series* (1995): 346–357.

13. Charles Saunders, *The Brookings Institution: A Fifty-Year History* (Washington, DC: The Brookings Institution, 1966); G. William Domhoff, *The Higher Circles* (New York: Random House, 1970), pp. 182–184. For the discussion of firebombing the Brookings Institution, see J. Anthony Lukas, *Nightmare: The Underside of the Nixon Years* (New York: Viking Press, 1976), pp. 97–98, and Fred Emery, *Watergate* (New York: Random House, 1994), pp. 26, 48.

14. Joseph Peschek, *Policy-Planning Organizations* (Philadelphia: Temple University Press, 1987), chapter 5.

15. James A. Smith, *The Idea Brokers* (New York: Free Press, 1991), p. 264.

16. Peschek, op. cit., chapter 5.

17. Russ Bellant, *The Coors Connection* (Boston: South End Press, 1991).

18. Peter Phillips, "A Relative Advantage: Sociology of the San Francisco Bohemian Club," Ph.D. Dissertation, University of California, Davis, 1994, p. 106.

19. Phyllis T. Piotrow, *World Population Crisis: The United States Response* (New York: Praeger, 1973); William Barclay, Joseph Enright, and Reid T. Reynolds, "Population Control in the Third World," *NACLA Newsletter* (December 1970).

20. Steve Askin, *A New Rite: Conservative Catholic Organizations and Their Allies* (Washington, DC: Catholics for a Free Choice, 1994); Dallas Blanchard, *The Anti-Abortion Movement and the Rise of the Religious Right* (New York: Twayne Publishers, 1994); Karen O'Connor, *No Neutral Ground?* (Boulder, CO: Westview Press, 1996); Kristin Luker, *Abortion*

and the Politics of Motherhood (Berkeley: University of California Press, 1984), chapter 6.

21. Charles Schwartz, "The Corporate Connection," *Bulletin of the Atomic Scientist* (October 1975).

22. Charles Schwartz, "Academics in Government and Industry" (Paper, Department of Physics, University of California at Berkeley, 1975), p. 25.

23. Ibid.

24. Robert Walters, "Academics on AT&T's Payroll" (Syndicated Column, Newspaper Enterprise Associates, New York, June 22, 1981).

25. Thomas Dye, *Who's Running America?*, 6th ed. (Englewood Cliffs, NJ: Prentice-Hall, 1995), p. 145.

26. Clyde Barrow, *Universities and the Capitalist State* (Madison: University of Wisconsin Press, 1990), especially chapter 2, for a synthesis of all relevant information on the corporate community and foundations in relation to higher education.

27. Seymour Lipset, *Political Man* (New York: Doubleday, 1960), chapter 12; Seymour Lipset, "The Academic Mind at the Top," *Public Opinion Quarterly*, 46 (1982): 143–168.

28. "Academic Freedom and Tenure: University of Southern California," *Academe* (November/December 1995): 40–49; "Censured Administrations," *Academe* (May/June 1997): 85.

29. James P. Warburg, *The Long Road Home: The Autobiography of a Maverick* (New York: Doubleday, 1964); Smith, op. cit., p. 161.

30. David Dellinger, *From Yale to Jail: The Life Story of a Moral Dissenter* (New York: Pantheon Books, 1993).

31. James Weinstein, *The Corporate Ideal in the Liberal State* (Boston: Beacon Press, 1968); Domhoff, *The Higher Circles*, op. cit., pp. 163–170, 196–201.

32. Weinstein, op. cit., chapter 3; Domhoff, *The Higher Circles*, op. cit., pp. 201–206; Gabriel Kolko, *The Triumph of Conservatism* (New York: Free Press, 1963).

33. Mary Anna Culleton Colwell, "The Foundation Connection: Links among Foundations and Recipient Organizations," in *Philanthropy and Cultural Imperialism*, ed. Robert F. Arnove (Boston: Hall, 1980), pp. 418–419; Mary Anna Culleton Colwell, *Private Foundations and Public Policy* (New York: Garland, 1993).

34. Michael Allen, "Elite Social Movement Organizations and the State: The Rise of the Conservative Policy-Planning Network," *Research in Politics and Society*, 4 (1992): 87–109.

35. Karen Rothmyer, "Citizen Scaife," *Columbia Journalism Review*, 20 (July/August 1981): 41–51; Phil Kuntz, "Citizen Scaife," *Wall Street Journal* (October 12, 1995): 1; Joe Conason, "The Starr in Richard Scaife's Eyes," *Washington Post* (March 16, 1997): C4. For an overview of ultraconservative donors and foundations, see *Buying a Movement: Right-Wing Foundations and American Politics* (Washington, DC: People for the American Way, 1996).

36. Val Burris, "Elite Policy-Planning Networks in the United States," *Research in Politics and Society*, 4 (1992): 113–134. For a similar study using a smaller sample, see Stanley Eitzen, Maureen Jung, and Dean Purdy,

"Organizational Linkages among the Inner Group of the Capitalist Class," *Sociological Focus*, 15 (1982): 179–189.

37. Phillips, op. cit., p. 123.

38. Domhoff, *Who Rules America?*, op. cit., p. 72; Lawrence Shoup and William Minter, *Imperial Brain Trust* (New York: Monthly Review Press, 1977), p. 87.

39. Harold Salzman and G. William Domhoff, "The Corporate Community and Government: Do They Interlock?," in *Power Structure Research*, ed. G. William Domhoff (Beverly Hills: Sage Publications, 1980), p. 235.

40. G. William Domhoff, *Who Rules America Now?* (New York: Simon and Schuster, 1983), p. 86.

41. Bohdan Romaniuk, ed., *Foundation Reporter*, 25th ed. (Detroit: Taft Group, 1995).

42. Stephen Krasner, *Defending the National Interest* (Princeton, NJ: Princeton University Press, 1978). For a detailed empirical refutation of Krasner's claims, see G. William Domhoff, *The Power Elite and the State* (Hawthorne, NY: Aldine de Gruyter, 1990), chapter 5.

43. Lawrence Shoup, "Shaping the National Interest: The Council on Foreign Relations, the Department of State, and the Origins of the Postwar World," Ph.D. Dissertation, Northwestern University, 1974, for a detailed account and full bibliography of sources.

44. Shoup and Minter, op. cit.; Shoup, op. cit.; Domhoff, *The Power Elite and the State*, op. cit., chapter 5; Michael Wala, *The Council on Foreign Relations and American Foreign Policy in the Early Cold War* (Providence, RI: Berghahn Books, 1994). For a sophisticated quantitative study of trade patterns among 102 countries in 1990 that shows the persistence of the "Grand Area," see Tie-ting Su and Dan Clawson, "Trade Networks, Trade Blocs, and Hegemonic Conflict," *Sociological Inquiry*, 64 (1994): 369–390.

45. Lawrence Shoup, *The Carter Presidency and Beyond* (Palo Alto, CA: Ramparts Press, 1980); Holly Sklar, ed., *Trilateralism* (Boston: South End Press, 1980).

46. Holly Sklar, "Brave New World Order," in Cynthia Peters, ed., *Collateral Damage: The "New World Order" at Home and Abroad* (Boston: South End Press, 1992), pp. 22–28; Holly Sklar, "Trilateralism: Elite Planning Pays Off" (paper presented to the meetings of the American Sociological Association, New York, August 19, 1996).

47. *The Soviet Challenge: A Policy Framework for the 1980s* (New York: Council on Foreign Relations, 1981).

48. "Tough Response: Meeting the Soviet Threat," *Time* (May 25, 1981); "Foreign Affairs Council Advocates Arms Increase," *New York Times* (May 4, 1981): 10. For the arms buildup in the 1980s, see Daniel Wirls, *Build-up: The Politics of Defense in the Reagan Era* (Ithaca, NY: Cornell University Press, 1992).

49. David Eakins, "The Development of Corporate Liberal Policy Research in the United States, 1885–1965," Ph.D. Dissertation, University of Wisconsin, 1966, chapter 5.

50. Eugene Pasymowski and Carl Gilbert, "Bilderberg: The Cold War Internationale," *Congressional Record*, 117 (September 15, 1971), pp. 32051–32060.

51. Eakins, op. cit., p. 346.
52. Domhoff, *The Power Elite and the State*, op. cit., chapter 6, for a case study of how CFR and CED leaders created the International Monetary Fund and World Bank.
53. The following case study is based on a series of interviews I conducted with retired CED trustees and employees in 1990, 1992, and 1995, along with documents provided to me on the condition of complete confidentiality.
54. Document in my confidential files.
55. William Frederick, "Free Market vs. Social Responsibility: Decision Time at the CED," *California Management Review*, 23 (1981): 20–28.
56. Document in my confidential files.
57. "Rehabilitation Project: Once-Mighty CED Panel of Executives Seeks a Revival, Offers Advice to Carter," *Wall Street Journal* (December 17, 1976): 38.
58. Charles O'Connell, "Social Structure and Science: Soviet Studies at Harvard," Ph.D. Dissertation, University of California, Los Angeles, 1989; Oscar Harkavy, *Curbing Population Growth* (New York: Plenum, 1995), p. 186. For histories of the service of social scientists to the corporate community, see Loren Baritz, *The Servants of Power* (Middletown, CT: Wesleyan University Press, 1960), and Edward Silva and Sheila Slaughter, *Serving Power: The Making of the Academic Social Science Expert* (Westport, CT: Greenwood Press, 1984).
59. Craig Kubey, "Notes on a Meeting of the Business Council," *Insurgent Sociologist*, 3 (1973): 48–55; Kim McQuaid, *Big Business and Presidential Power from FDR to Reagan* (New York: Morrow, 1982).
60. G. William Domhoff, *The Bohemian Grove and Other Retreats* (New York: Harper and Row, 1974), pp. 107–109.
61. G. William Domhoff, "Social Clubs, Policy-Planning Groups and Corporations: A Network Study," *The Insurgent Sociologist*, vol. 5, no. 3 (1975): 173–184.
62. "Business Roundtable: Big Corporation Bastion," *Congressional Quarterly* (November 23, 1974); Peter Slavin, "The Business Roundtable: New Lobbying Arm of Big Business," *Business and Society Review* (Winter 1975–1976); Philip H. Burch, Jr., "The Business Roundtable: Its Make-up and External Ties," *Research in Political Economy*, vol. 14 (1981); Mark Green and Andrew Buschbaum, *The Corporate Lobbies: Political Profiles of the Business Roundtable and the Chamber of Commerce* (Washington, DC: Public Citizen, 1980). For the best account of the origins of the Business Roundtable, see James Gross, *Broken Promise: The Subversion of U.S. Labor Relations Policy, 1947–1994* (Philadelphia: Temple University Press, 1995), chapters 11–13.
63. Richard L. Zweigenhaft, interview with Irving Shapiro, February 23, 1981.
64. Green and Buschbaum, op. cit.
65. George Gonzalez, "Capitalism and the Environment: An Analysis of U.S. Environmental Policy via Competing Theories of the State," Ph.D. Dissertation, University of Southern California, 1998, chapter 4.
66. Michael Dreiling, "Forging Solidarity in the Struggle over the North American Foreign Trade Agreement: Strategy and Action for Labor, Nature,

and Capital," Ph.D. Dissertation, University of Michigan, 1997, chapters 4 and 5; Michael Dreiling, "Corporate Political Action in Defense of NAFTA" (paper presented at the annual meetings of the Pacific Sociological Association, April 17–20, 1997, San Diego).

67. Smith, op. cit., Appendix; *Buying a Movement*, op. cit., p. 8.

68. On the Federal Trade Commission, see Kolko, op. cit., and Weinstein, op. cit. On the Bureau of the Budget, see Eakins, op. cit. For the Securities and Exchange Commission, see Ralph De Bedts, *The New Deal's SEC* (New York: Columbia University Press, 1964), and Michael Parrish, *Securities Regulation and the New Deal* (New Haven, CT: Yale University Press, 1970). For the Agricultural Adjustment Administration and the Social Security Act, see G. William Domhoff, *State Autonomy or Class Domination?* (Hawthorne, NY: Aldine de Gruyter, 1996), chapters 3 and 5. For a study of new government agencies that downplays or ignores the role of corporate leaders and policy-formation experts, see Stephen Skowronek, *Building a New American State* (New York: Cambridge University Press, 1982). Skowronek is frequently cited by state autonomy theorists, but he is not on solid empirical ground.

69. For the first application of the uncertainty argument in the context of power structure studies, see Nancy DiTomaso, "Organizational Analysis and Power Structure Research," in *Power Structure Research*, ed. G. William Domhoff (Beverly Hills: Sage Publications, 1980). For an elaboration, with empirical examples for the United States, see G. William Domhoff, *The Power Elite and the State*, op. cit., pp. 20–24.

5

The Role of Public Opinion

The goal of this chapter is to show that public opinion has little or no influence on presidential actions or congressional legislation except as a constraint in times of unpopular wars or domestic social upheaval. The chapter thereby sets the stage for demonstrating, in the next two chapters, how the power elite dominates the two major political parties and the federal government. (The possible influence of public opinion on elections is considered in the next chapter.)

The idea that public opinion has little or no influence on major policies is in direct opposition to the stance taken by public-opinion pluralists, who reject any notion of a power elite precisely because of the independent power they attribute to public opinion. According to sociologist Paul Burstein, for example, there is "considerable evidence that elected officials respond to public opinion."[1] This evidence, which consists primarily of correlations between public opinion and public policy, is dealt with throughout this chapter.

On some issues, contrary to Burstein's view, the opinions of the majority have differed from those of elected officials for many generations without any effect on public policy. This is possible because people's beliefs do not lead them into opposition or disruption if they have stable roles to fulfill in the society and see no clear path to social change. Routine involvement in a compelling and often enjoyable daily round of activities, the most central of which concern work and family, is a more important factor in social stability and acquiescence in power elite policies than public opinion. Also, what happens in the economy and in government has more impact on how people act than what is said in the opinion-shaping process and the mass media.[2]

To the degree that something as general and nebulous as public opinion can be known in a country with 3.5 million square miles and over 260 million people, it is largely through public opinion surveys. Such surveys, however, present only a rough idea of what people generally think because the results are highly sensitive to a number of factors, especially the order of questions and the way they are worded. Polls probably produce their best results on an issue of greatest moment to politicians: how people are likely to vote in an upcoming election. Polls may even create the impression of public opinion on questions in which none actually exists, a likelihood discussed in the final section of the chapter.

Setting aside the weaknesses of polling for the moment, the results of several decades of such surveys present a seeming paradox. On the one hand, the answers to questions repeated over the years on issues on which people have direct experience suggest that public opinion is rational and sensible within the time constraints on people's lives and the quality of the information presented to them. For example, more people accept the idea of women working outside the home as they see more women in the workplace. More white people came to have positive opinions concerning African-Americans as they learned more about the Civil Rights Movement.[3] In addition, as social psychologist William Gamson concludes on the basis of his content analysis of discussions in focus groups made up of average citizens: "(a) people are not so passive, (b) people are not so dumb, and (c) people negotiate with media messages in complicated ways that vary from issue to issue."[4]

On the other hand, polls asking about the structure of the government, the stands taken by elected officials, or the respondents' views on specific issues being considered in Congress suggest that most people pay little attention to politics, have a limited understanding of the options being considered, and hold no well-developed opinions on impending legislation even when it has received much attention in the media.[5] These findings lead me to wonder whether public opinion exists in any meaningful way on most legislative issues, let alone has much influence on public policy.

From the point of view of a class-domination perspective, there are three questions:

1. Does the power elite have the capacity to shape public opinion on issues of concern to it? If it does, then any correlation between public opinion and public policy on these issues may be due to the efforts of the power elite,

making such a correlation less impressive as evidence for the public-opinion pluralists.

2. To the degree that public opinion on some issues is independent of the shaping efforts of the power elite, what is the evidence that those opinions have an impact? If independent opinions have no impact, then they do not contradict a class-domination argument even though they show the limit of the power elite's ability to shape opinion.

3. Are there issues on which the power elite makes little or no effort to shape public opinion? If so, then the influence of public opinion in the resolution of these issues is irrelevant to a class-domination theory even though such issues might be said to show a certain kind of pluralism, perhaps to be called a "cultural" or "religious" pluralism, depending on what issues fit into the category.

The exploration of these three questions in this chapter begins with an analysis of the general way in which the power elite operates in the area of public opinion. It describes an opinion-shaping network that has at its center some of the same foundations and policy discussion groups found in the policy network, but supplemented by two very important additions—public relations firms and the public affairs departments of large corporations. Then the chapter moves to a consideration of how this opinion-shaping network operates in different issue-areas, and how successful it has been. The chapter shows that the power elite has been very successful in shaping public opinion on issues in which people have little or no direct experience, such as foreign policy and defense spending. On domestic economic issues, in which people have direct experience, there is evidence that they maintain their independent opinions in the face of strong efforts by the power elite to change them, but there is also reason to believe that such opinions are generally ignored in the legislative process. On social issues like abortion and gun control, in which the most important organizations in the opinion-shaping network make no effort to influence public opinion, there is a battle between liberals and New Rightists that receives a large amount of attention in the mass media. On these issues, public opinion seems to have some influence.

THE OPINION-SHAPING PROCESS

Many of the foundations, policy-planning groups, and think tanks in the policy-formation network also operate as part of the opinion-shaping process. In this process, however, they are joined by two other

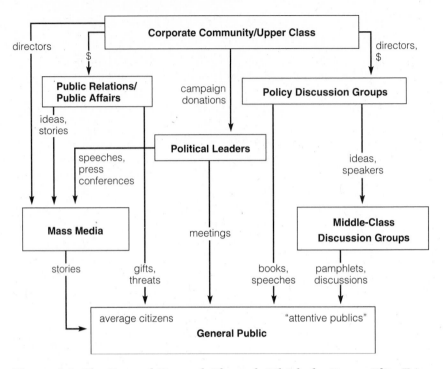

Figure 5.1 The General Network Through Which the Power Elite Tries to Shape Public Opinion

very weighty forces—large public relations firms and the public affairs departments of the major corporations—both of which have large staffs and the ability to complement their efforts with financial donations to target groups by the corporate foundations (discussed in the previous chapter). These core organizations are connected to a large dissemination network that includes local advertising agencies, corporate-financed advertising councils, special committees to influence single issues, and the mass media. In contrast to the policy-formation process, in which a relatively small number of organizations do most of the work, there are hundreds of organizations within the opinion-shaping process that specialize in public relations and education on virtually every issue. Thus, at its point of direct contact with the general public, the opinion-molding process is extremely diverse and diffuse. A general picture of the opinion-shaping network is provided in figure 5.1.

One of the most important goals of the opinion-shaping network is to influence public schools, churches, and voluntary associations.

To that end, organizations within the network have developed numerous links to these institutions, offering them movies, television programs, books, pamphlets, speakers, advice, and financial support. However, the schools, churches, and voluntary associations are not part of the network. Rather, they are independent settings within which the power elite must constantly contend with spokespersons from the liberal-labor coalition. To assume otherwise would be to overlook the social and occupational affiliations of the members as well as the diversity of opinion that often exists in these institutions of the middle and lower levels of the social hierarchy.

To prevent the development of attitudes and opinions that might interfere with the acceptance of policies created in the policy-formation process, leaders within the opinion-molding process attempt to build on and reinforce the underlying principles of the American belief system. Academically speaking, these underlying principles are called laissez-faire liberalism, and they have their roots in the work of several European philosophers and the American Founding Fathers. These principles emphasize individualism, free enterprise, competition, equality of opportunity, and a minimal reliance on government in carrying out the affairs of society. Slowly articulated during the centuries-long rise of the capitalist system in Europe, they arrived in America in nearly finished form and had no serious rivals in a small new nation that did not have a feudal past or an established church.[6]

Although this individualistic ideology remains pervasive, it is an independent factor in shaping the opinions and behaviors of Americans only because rival power groups like the liberal-labor coalition have not been strong enough to create alternative organizations to challenge its acceptance from a more communal or cooperative viewpoint. American cultural beliefs that seem timeless are in fact sustained by the organizations created and funded by the power elite. Such beliefs, in other words, are "institutionalized," made into taken-for-granted habits and customs and constantly reinforced by how organizations function. Popularly speaking, these unchallenged values are known to most citizens as plain "Americanism." They are seen as part of human nature or the product of good common sense. If Americans can be convinced that some policy or action is justified in terms of this emotion-laden and unquestioned body of beliefs, they are more likely to accept it. Thus, the organizations that make up the opinion-shaping network strive to become the arbitrators of which policies and opinions are in keeping with good Americanism, and which are "un-American."

The efforts of the opinion-shaping network sometimes reach a more subtle level as well. Even though many people do not accept the overt messages in its ads, speeches, and booklets, they often accept the implicit message that their problems lie in their own personal inadequacies. An individualistic ideology, with its strong emphasis on personal effort and responsibility, not only rewards the successful but blames the victims. Educational failure and other phenomena that are best understood in terms of the ways in which a class system operates to encourage some and discourage others are turned into reproaches of the victims for their alleged failure to correct personal defects and take advantage of the opportunities offered to them.[7]

Using in-depth interviews with employed people in Boston, sociologists Richard Sennett and Jonathan Cobb provide a social-psychological account of how an individualistic ideology leaves many working people with a paralyzing self-blame for their alleged failures, even though they know the social system is not fair to them:

> Workingmen intellectually reject the idea that endless opportunity exists for the competent. And yet, the institutions of class force them to apply the idea to themselves: If I don't escape being part of the woodwork, it's because I didn't develop my powers enough. Thus, talk about how arbitrary a class society's reward system is will be greeted with general agreement—with the proviso that in my own case I should have made more of myself.[8]

Sennett and Cobb then suggest that this self-blame is intimately related to questions of social change. Self-blame is important in understanding the reluctant acquiescence of wage earners in an unjust system:

> Once that proviso [that in my own case I should have made more of myself] is added, challenging class institutions becomes saddled with the agonizing question, Who am I to make the challenge? To speak of American workers as having been "bought off" by the system or adopting the same conservative values as middle-class suburban managers and professionals is to miss all the complexity of their silence and to have no way of accounting for the intensity of pent-up feeling that pours out when working people do challenge higher authority.[9]

The system is not fair, but that's the way things are: The average American seems to have a radical critique and a conservative agenda, and the result is a grumbling acceptance of the status quo. When people conclude that they in some sense deserve their subordinate position in the power structure, there is in effect a social-psychological interaction taking place between the dominant class and the subordinated underclasses, reinforcing a sense of superiority in members of the power elite and a sense of inferiority in average working people.

This social-psychological relationship complements the economic and political relationships that are created by the class structure and class conflict.[10]

Public Relations/Public Affairs

Public relations is a multibillion-dollar industry created by the corporate rich in the 1920s for the sole purpose of shaping opinion in their interest. The largest firm, Burson-Marsteller, with sixty-three offices in thirty-two countries and clients ranging from General Electric to Philip Morris to the National Restaurant Association to several foreign governments, had billings of $192 million in 1994. Most public relations firms are in turn owned by even larger advertising companies. Burson-Marsteller, for example, is owned by Young & Rubicam, which had revenues of $7.5 billion in the same year.[11]

Since public relations often operates through the mass media, it is not too surprising that one-third of its 150,000 practitioners are former journalists and that about half of current journalism school graduates go into one form of public relations or another. Still, public relations as it is practiced today involves far more than attempting to influence the mass media. Burson-Marsteller created the National Smokers Alliance in the early 1990s for the tobacco industry, sending its paid canvassers into bars to find members and potential activists. The second largest PR firm, Shandwick, helped plan Earth Day in 1995; its client list includes Procter & Gamble, Monsanto Chemicals, and the Western Livestock Producers Alliance. There is even a public relations firm, National Grassroots and Communications, that specializes in creating local organizations to oppose neighborhood activists.[12]

Public relations experts put their contacts to work trying to keep corporate critics from appearing in the media. One company keeps files on journalists for possible use in questioning their credibility. Public relations experts use their skills to monitor the activities of groups critical of specific industries, meaning everyone from animal rights groups opposed to corporations that use animals in testing their products to antilogging groups to vegetarian groups that oppose the eating of meat (a threat to meat industry sales). Some of the actions taken against these groups, which include infiltration of meetings and copying materials in files, add up to spying.[13]

Public affairs, on the other hand, is a generally more benign form of public relations practiced by departments within large corporations, in which the emphasis is on polishing the image of corporations rather than criticizing journalists and opposition groups. Public affairs is staffed by women and minorities more frequently than other corporate departments to provide the company with a human face more reflective of the larger community. In one large corporation, the employees in public affairs referred to their workplace as the "velvet ghetto" because the job is a pleasant one with an excellent salary and expense account, but one that rarely leads to positions at the top of the corporation.[14]

The first task of employees in public affairs departments is to gather newspaper stories and radio and TV transcripts to monitor what is being said about their own corporation at the local level. They then try to counter any negative commentary by placing favorable stories in local newspapers and giving speeches to local organizations. At a more general level, they join with members of other public affairs departments to take part in an effort to shape public opinion in the interests of corporations in general. In the words of sociologist Jerome Himmelstein, who interviewed public affairs officers at large corporations, the general goal of public affairs personnel is "looking good and doing good."[15]

The efforts of the public affairs departments are in good measure based on the financial gifts they are able to provide to middle-class charitable and civic organizations through the corporation's foundation. Such gifts reached $6.1 billion in 1994, 33 percent of which went to education, 25 percent to health and charitable services, 12 percent to civic and community affairs, and 11 percent to culture and the arts.[16] The emphasis on improving the image of the corporation and cultivating good will is seen most directly in the fact that it is tobacco companies and corporations with bad environmental reputations that give the most money to sporting events, the arts, and the Public Broadcasting System.[17]

From the point of view of ultraconservatives, some of these donations are to liberal groups that are in opposition to the corporate system. The American Cancer Association and the American Heart Association, for example, are both rated as very liberal groups by the ultraconservative Capital Research Center because they advocate the use of government research and spending to find cures for cancer and heart disease. So too are all minority and environmental groups due to their call for some kinds of protective legislation.[18] From the perspective of moderate conservatives, however, the donations provide evidence to the general public of corporate responsibility and good citizenship. Table 5.1 presents donations by corporate foundations to leading minority and environmental groups for the early 1990s.

Despite considerable public criticism from the ultraconservatives for how corporate foundations allocate a small percentage of their funds, no changes have been ordered by chief executive officers. According to Himmelstein's interviews, the managers of the corporate foundations label the criticisms by the Capital Research Center as "ridiculous," "pretty bizarre," and "nonsense."[19] From a power per-

Table 5.1 Support for Minority Groups and Environmental Groups by Corporate Foundations in Three Separate Years

	Minority Groups			
Organization	1991	1993	1994	Total for Organization
Urban League	$3,139,898	2,855,664	2,845,704	8,841,266
NAACP*	1,587,255	1,535,401	1,511,383	4,634,039
MALDEF†	493,900	471,500	506,000	1,471,400
National Council of La Raza	427,010	426,500	416,000	1,269,510
NAACP Legal Defense Fund	236,600	230,600	132,950	600,150
Puerto Rican Legal Defense Fund	35,500	56,000	26,000	117,500
Yearly Total	5,920,163	5,575,665	5,438,037	$16,933,865

	Environmental Groups			
Organization	1991	1993	1994	Total for Organization
Nature Conservancy	$1,221,177	1,873,213	2,534,652	5,629,042
World Wildlife Fund	229,070	1,200,445	206,095	1,635,610
Resources for the Future	340,500	346,000	292,500	979,000
National Park Foundation	453,225	263,826	157,500	874,551
Audubon Society	301,857	194,932	163,498	660,287
Yearly Total	2,545,829	3,878,416	3,354,245	$9,778,490

Source: *Patterns of Corporate Philanthropy* (Washington, DC: Capital Research Center), 1994, p. 10; 1996, p. 8; 1997, p. 8.

* National Association for the Advancement of Colored People.

† Mexican American Legal Defense Fund.

spective, it is almost amusing that the ultraconservatives do not want corporations to spend even a few percent of their foundation budgets trying to create good relations with health advocates, minorities, and environmentalists, on the principle that it is difficult to bite the hand that feeds you, but their strong antigovernment ideology encompasses every aspect of their thinking.

Table 5.2 Top 5 National Nonprofit Groups in Links Created by 273 Interlocking Corporate Directors from 100 Largest Industrials

Organization	Industrial Interlocks
United Way (national and local)	37
Boys and Girls Clubs of America	14
Boy Scouts of America	14
Junior Achievement	9
World Wildlife Fund	6

Source: J. Allen Whitt and Gwen Moore, "Network Ties Between National Charities and Large Corporations." Paper presented at Sunbelt Social Network Conference, San Diego, February, 1997.

In the case of the most important charitable groups and civic associations, such as the United Way or the Boy Scouts and Girl Scouts, directors and executives from the top corporations may agree to serve on the boards of directors as well as give financial support. They thereby join with women of the upper class in bringing the perspective of the corporate rich to some of the organizations that serve the largest numbers of middle-level Americans. Table 5.2 presents the number of directorships at major voluntary associations held by 273 interlocking directors from the 100 largest industrial corporations.

The Advertising Council

Although it is not feasible to discuss very many of the small organizations that attempt to shape public opinion, the Advertising Council provides a good example of how they operate. In effect, it attempts to sell the free enterprise system through public-interest advertising in a wide range of venues. The overall effectiveness of the organization can be questioned, but its efforts are highly revealing.

The Advertising Council, often called the Ad Council, began its institutional life as the War Advertising Council during World War II as a means to support the war effort through advertising in the mass media. Its work was judged so successful in promoting a positive image for the corporate community that it was continued in the postwar period as an agency to support the Red Cross, United Way, conservation, population control, and other campaigns that its corporate-dominated boards and advisory committees believed to be in the public interest. Although it has an annual budget of only a few million dollars, the council nonetheless places well over $500 million worth of free advertising each year through radio, television, magazines, newspapers, billboards, and public transportation. It claimed in 1991 that it had placed $64 billion of free advertising in its first 50 years.[20] After the council leaders decide on which campaigns to endorse, the specifics of the program are given to one or another Madison Avenue advertising agency, which does the work without charge.

Most council campaigns seem relatively innocuous and in a public interest that nobody would dispute. Its best-known figures for many years, Smokey the Bear and Crime Dog McGruff, were created for the campaigns against forest fires and urban crime. However, as media analyst Glenn Hirsch demonstrated in a detailed study of these campaigns, many have a strong slant in favor of corporations. The council's environmental ads, for example, suggest that "people start pollution, people can stop it," thereby putting the responsibility on individuals rather than on a system of production that allows corporations to avoid the costs of disposing of their waste products by dumping them into the air or water. A special subcommittee of the council's Industry Advisory Committee gave very explicit instructions about how this particular ad campaign should be formulated: "The committee emphasized that the [advertisements] should stress that each of us must be made to recognize that each of us contributes to pollution, and therefore everyone bears the responsibility."[21] Thus, the Keep America Beautiful campaign is geared to show corporate concern about the environment while at the same time deflecting growing criticism of the corporate role in pollution by falling back on the individualism of the American creed.

The council also tries to help restore order in times of crisis. Between 1965 and 1971 there was an unprecedented 95 percent growth in expenditures by the mass media in support of council campaigns, and most of this effort was directed at ghetto unrest. One set of commercial messages in 1965 urged people to "Put Your Racial Problems on the Table—Keep Them Off the Streets." In 1970 the council assembled over 100 notables from business, labor, sports, and politics to demonstrate racial harmony by joining together to sing "Let the Sun Shine" from a hit musical of the era, *Hair.* In a more sober vein, the council ran a "crisis series," which urged businesspeople to give jobs to ghetto blacks. The same type of special campaign was undertaken in 1992 in the wake of rioting and deaths in Los Angeles, but without the singing chorus.[22]

As noted at the outset of this section, the effectiveness of such campaigns is open to question. It is not clear that they have a direct influence on very many opinions. Studies by social scientists suggest that advertising campaigns of a propagandistic nature work best "when used to reinforce an already existing notion or to establish a logical or emotional connection between a new idea and a social norm."[23] But even when an ad campaign can be judged a failure in this limited role, it has filled a vacuum that might have been used by a competing group. This is especially the case with television, in which the council is able to capture more than 80 percent of the public-service advertising time that television networks provide. Thus, Hirsch concludes his assessment of the effectiveness of the Advertising Council by stressing both its direct and indirect effects: "Its commercials reinforce and channel existing values, while simultaneously preventing groups with a different ideology from presenting their interpretation of events."[24]

The Advertising Council is in some ways unique because of its prominence, massive resources, and wide range of concerns. In its major activities, however, it is typical of a wide variety of opinion-shaping organizations that operate in specific areas—from labor relations, in which the National Right to Work Committee battles union organizers, to something as far removed as the arts, in which the Business Committee for the Arts encourages the artistic endeavors of low-income children as a way to boost the morale of those trapped in the inner city. Such organizations do three things:

1. They provide think-tank forums where academics, journalists, and other cultural experts can brainstorm with corporate leaders about the problems of shaping public opinion.
2. They help to create a more sophisticated corporate consciousness through forums, booklets, speeches, and awards.
3. They disseminate their version of the national interest and good Americanism to the general public on issues of concern to the power elite.

It is now time to see how the power elite tries to shape public opinion in different issue-areas.

SHAPING OPINION ON FOREIGN POLICY

The opinion-shaping network achieves its clearest expression and greatest success in the area of foreign policy, where most people have little information and are predisposed to agree with top leaders out of patriotism and a fear of whatever is strange or foreign. Political scientists Benjamin Page and Robert Y. Shapiro, authors of the most comprehensive case for the rationality of public opinion, concede foreign policy to the power elite when they write that "especially in the realm of foreign policy, where information can be centrally controlled, it seems especially likely that public opinion is often led."

They say that this leading is done by "public officials and other influential groups and individuals through complex processes involving
objective events, official accounts and media reports of events, and
interpretations by politicians, commentators, and experts."[25] Because
so few people take an interest in foreign policy issues, the most important efforts in opinion shaping are aimed toward a small stratum of
highly interested and concerned citizens with college backgrounds.

The central organizations in the shaping of opinion on foreign
policy are the Council on Foreign Relations and the Foreign Policy
Association (FPA). Although the council does very little to influence
public opinion directly, it publishes *Foreign Affairs*, the most prestigious journal in the field, and occasionally prints pamphlets on major
issues that can be used by other discussion groups. For local leaders,
the council sponsors Committees on Foreign Relations in over thirty-
five cities, which meet about once a month, or when a special digni-
tary visits, to hear speakers. The aim of this program is to provide
local leaders with the information and legitimacy in the area of foreign affairs that make it possible for them to function as community
opinion leaders.

The most important organization involved in shaping upper-
middle-class public opinion on foreign affairs is the FPA, based in
New York. In 1996, one-third of its seventy-six-person governing
council were also members of the Council on Foreign Relations. Although the association does some research, its primary focus is on
molding opinion outside the power elite, a division of labor with the
CFR that is well understood within foreign-policy circles. As long ago
as the 1930s a council director explained that the FPA had "breadth
of influence," whereas the CFR had "depth"; he went on to say that
"anyone with the slightest experience in such matters knows that you
must have policy-making individuals and groups working closely in
a government" as well as "the support of the electorate," made possible
in part by organizations that function "as channel-ways of expression."
More bluntly, a retired president of the council explained to historian
Lawrence Shoup that the CFR and its Committees on Foreign Relations
attempt to reach top-level leaders, whereas the Foreign Policy Association attracted the "League of Women Voters type."[26]

The association's major effort is an intensive program to provide
literature and create discussion groups in middle-class organizations
and on college campuses. Its general activities are backed by several
dozen private and corporate foundations. In 1996 it received $100,000
from both the Freeman Foundation and the Merrill Lynch Foundation, $75,000 from the Starr Foundation, and $30,000 each from
Bankers Trust, Exxon, J. P. Morgan Bank, Joseph E. Seagram & Sons,
Texaco, and Volvo North America.

The FPA's most important activity since 1954 has been a "Great Decisions" discussion program that now reaches 300,000 participants in forty-seven states. A color map of the world was provided to each participant in 1996 thanks to a grant from the New York Times Company Foundation. A grant from the Carnegie Corporation made it possible to strengthen the volunteer network and increase the diversity of the participants. The program is coordinated with a Public Broadcasting System series on Great Decisions that is funded by four foundations.[27]

The CFR and the FPA, in turn, are linked to other opinion-molding organizations influential in foreign affairs. Perhaps the most important of them is the United Nations Association, which attempts to build support for American involvement in that organization. Another is the American Assembly, which sponsors discussion groups around the country on a variety of issues, not all of them concerning foreign policy.

The established organizations are supplemented when the need arises by special committees to publicize specific issues. The biggest effort of this type was the Committee for the Marshall Plan, formed in 1947 to combat isolationist sentiment at a time when the power elite believed it was necessary to provide massive foreign aid to Western Europe in order to restore the economy and stave off social unrest that might be exploited by the Soviet Union. This successful effort is of particular interest because it shows that the corporate PR campaigns of the 1980s and 1990s on key legislation were nothing new. Chaired by a former secretary of state who had been a member of the Council on Foreign Relations since the 1920s, it enlisted two labor leaders to join with five CFR members on its seven-member executive committee. Working with $150,000 in private contributions (about $1.5 million in 1997 dollars), the committee ran an all-out promotional campaign:

> Regional committees were promptly organized, the cooperation of national organizations enlisted, and relevant publications given wide circulation. The committee promoted broad news and editorial coverage in metropolitan newspapers, set up a speaker's bureau, and employed a news agency which arranged for press releases, a special map service for small town and country newspapers, and national and local radio broadcasts.[28]

In addition to its media efforts, the committee circulated petitions in every congressional district, then sent the results to the elected representatives. It also created an office in Washington to lobby Congress and to help prepare supportive testimony for appearances before congressional committees.[29]

Although the efforts of the foreign-policy groups are significant, the major influences on foreign-policy opinions are the actions of the president and top foreign-policy officials. Public opinion polls conducted before and after critical events in the Vietnam War still provide the most dramatic examples of this point. Before the bombing of Hanoi and Haiphong began in late spring 1966, the public was split fifty-fifty, but when asked in July 1966 if "the Administration is more right or more wrong in bombing Hanoi and Haiphong," 85 percent were in favor. Conversely, 51 percent of those polled in March 1968 opposed a halt to the bombing, but when asked one month later if they approved or disapproved of a decision by President Lyndon B. Johnson to stop the bombing, only 26 percent disagreed with the president. Sixty-four percent agreed and 10 percent had no opinion. College-educated adults and people in younger age groups were most likely to show this change in opinion shortly after a presidential initiative.[30]

Even on foreign policy, however, there are limits to the ability to shape public opinion. Opposition to both the Korean and Vietnam Wars grew consistently as the number of American casualties mounted.[31] Demonstrations and teach-ins at universities in the mid-1960s helped consolidate a large minority against the Vietnam War by 1967. Then a surprise countrywide attack by the Viet Cong, including the temporary occupation of the American embassy, solidified public opinion against the war, which in turn convinced President Johnson's advisory group from the Council on Foreign Relations that escalating the ground war was no longer worth the disruption and discontent it was causing on the home front. Indeed, the communist threat in Southeast Asia was seen as less dangerous by 1967 for several reasons, including the public split between the Soviet Union and China and the massacre of several hundred thousand communists by the Indonesian government, but the growing opposition within the United States was the final straw in leading to the abandonment of the ground war and the beginning of peace talks.[32]

TRYING TO SHAPE OPINION ON ECONOMIC POLICIES

Attempts to shape public opinion on domestic economic issues such as unemployment, in which people feel directly involved and have their own experiences to rely on, are far more difficult than in the area of foreign policy. This is especially the case when there is no threat of a menacing external enemy to bind people together in common economic sacrifice.

Corporate leaders find the generally liberal opinions held by a majority of people on economic issues to be very annoying and potentially troublesome. They blame these liberal opinions in part on a lack of economic understanding. They label this alleged lack of understanding "economic illiteracy," a term that implies that people have no right to their opinions because of their educational deficiencies. They claim these negative attitudes would change if people had the facts about the functioning of corporations and the economy, and they have spent tens of millions of dollars trying to present the facts as they see them. An analysis of one of the many ways the power elite attempts to shape economic understanding also provides an example of how the opinion-shaping network reaches into the school system on an issue of concern to it.

The central organization in the field of economic education is the National Council on Economic Education (NCEE). Founded in 1949 by leaders within the Committee for Economic Development, the NCEE received much of its early funding from the Ford Foundation. Most of its financial support now comes from corporations and corporate foundations: in the 1990s, its biggest backers included the Ameritech Foundation, with a four-year grant of $486,000, the Securities Industry Foundation for Economic Education, and the AT&T Foundation.

The NCEE's twenty-nine-person board reflects the fact that it is part of the opinion-shaping network. For example, it includes Harold Burson, the founder of Burson-Marsteller; vice presidents from Ameritech and General Mills; the chief economist from AT&T; a vice president from the American Farm Bureau Federation's insurance companies; and four university professors. The board is unusual in also including two leaders from the AFL-CIO, one the director of education, the other the director of public policy.

The NCEE attempts to influence economic understanding by means of books, pamphlets, videos, and press releases, but its most important effort is focused on elementary and high schools through its EconomicsAmerica program. This program provides schools with the curriculum plans and materials designed to introduce basic economic ideas at each grade level. To prepare teachers to carry out the curriculum, the NCEE has created a network of state councils and 260 university centers to coordinate the training of teachers in the nation's colleges and universities. The NCEE claims:

> Each year the network trains about 120,000 teachers serving 8 million students. More than 2,600 school districts, teaching about 40 percent of the nation's students, conduct comprehensive programs in economic education with assistance from the network.[33]

As this brief overview shows, the NCEE's program begins in corporate boardrooms and foundation offices, flows through affiliated councils and university centers, and ends up in teacher-training programs and public school curricula. In that regard, it is an ideal example of the several steps and organizations that are usually involved in attempts to shape public opinion on any domestic issue. And yet, despite all this effort, the level of "economic illiteracy," according to polls taken for the corporations, remained as high in the 1990s as it was in the 1940s. The average American receives a score of 39 percent; college graduates average 51 percent.[34] This inability to engineer wholehearted consent to the views of the power elite on economics reveals the limits of the opinion-shaping process in general. These limits are in good part created by the work experiences and general observations of average citizens, which lead them to be skeptical about many corporate claims. Moreover, the alternative analyses advocated by trade unionists, liberals, and socialists also have a counteracting influence.

Although the power elite is unable to alter the liberal views held by a majority of Americans on a wide range of economic issues, this does not mean the liberal opinions have any influence. To the contrary, much evidence suggests that the majority's opinion is often ignored. This point is made most clearly by the "right turn" taken by the Carter and Reagan Administrations from 1978 to 1983 despite strong evidence that the public remained liberal on the issues in contention. As Page and Shapiro summarize, "Throughout that period the public consistently favored more spending on the environment, education, medical care, the cities, and other matters, and it never accepted the full Reagan agenda of "deregulation."[35] Political scientist Howard Gold's even more detailed analysis of survey data relating to the alleged rightward shift in public opinion revealed little support for the claim except on issues of crime. He concludes that "beginning in the mid-1970s, Democratic and Republican politicians embraced conservatism," but "the American electorate, however, did not."[36]

SOCIAL ISSUES

There are several highly charged issues that receive great attention in the mass media and figure prominently in political campaigns: abortion, affirmative action, busing, the death penalty, gun control, school prayer, pornography, and protection against discrimination for gays and lesbians. Despite the time and energy that goes into these issues, they are not ones that are of concern to the power elite. There is no power elite position on any of them. Some individuals within the power elite may care passionately about one or more of them, but these issues are not the subject of discussion at the policy groups or of position papers from the mainstream think tanks.

Nevertheless, these issues are often front and center in battles between the corporate-conservative and liberal-labor coalitions because liberals seek changes on all of them and the New Right resists such changes. Although committed members of the New Right are deeply concerned with one or more of these issues, they are seen by conservatives in the power elite as "cross-cutting" issues that may be useful as "wedges" in trying to defeat liberal-labor candidates in the electoral arena. Social issues are thought to be helpful to conservatives because voters who agree with the liberal-labor coalition on economic issues often disagree with it on one or more social issues, providing an opportunity for the corporate-conservative coalition to win their allegiance. Although a majority of Americans were liberal or tolerant on most of these issues by the 1980s, conservatives stress them because they hope to gain support from just a few percent of the most emotional opponents who might otherwise vote Democratic. In that sense, the social issues are often part of the corporate-conservative electoral strategy even though they are not issues of substantive concern to the power elite.[37]

The importance of these "wedge issues" for conservatives is seen most clearly in the case of reactions to the civil and voting rights won by African-Americans and their liberal allies in the mid-1960s. The resentments generated in many Southern whites by these gains for African-Americans were used by Republican presidential candidate Barry Goldwater in 1964 to capture the previously pro-Democratic Deep South states of South Carolina, Georgia, Alabama, and Mississippi—the only states he won besides his home state of Arizona. The Democratic governor of Alabama, George Wallace, drew on the same resentments to win 13.5 percent of the vote nationwide in his third-party presidential race in 1968. In 1972 Richard Nixon captured alienated white Democrats for the Republicans at the presidential level, especially in the South, paving the way for the Reagan-Bush era from 1980 to 1992. "The Party of Lincoln," the party that opposed slavery in the Civil War era, became the party of white Americans. From the 1970s on, first busing and then affirmative action were used as wedge issues by the Republicans, usually joined by abortion, school prayer, and gun control. It is not likely that these issues won very many new voters for the Republicans outside the South, but they did help to move many Southern whites out of the Democratic Party. They also attracted new party activists and new campaign donors, and they may have frightened liberal and moderate Democrats into taking more cautious stances.[38]

THE ROLE OF THE MASS MEDIA

The mass media—newspapers, magazines, radio, and most especially television—are a major source of information for most Americans.

Some critics claim that the media therefore have a means to shape public opinion that is at least somewhat independent of the power elite.

The mass media have a complex relationship to the upper class and corporate community. On the one hand, they are lucrative business enterprises, owned by members of the upper class and directed by members of the corporate community, with extensive connections to other large corporations. Moreover, the three major television networks—ABC, NBC, and CBS—are owned by even larger corporations: Capital Cities owns ABC, General Electric owns NBC, and the Disney Corporation owns CBS.[39] Evidence presented later in this section, however, casts doubt on the idea that these companies have any large effect on public opinion.

There is also an increasing concentration in newspaper ownership, but big newspapers and newspaper chains are not monoliths. A range of opinions appears in them, including critical ones. Using survey responses from 409 journalists at 223 newspapers, journalism professor David Demers found that their reporters and editors report high levels of autonomy and job satisfaction. He also discovered through a content analysis of two editions of 198 of these newspapers that large newspapers and newspaper chains are more likely than small local newspapers to publish editorials and letters that deal with local issues or are critical of mainstream groups and institutions.[40]

The relationship between media executives and the rest of the corporate community is sometimes strained because corporate leaders place part of the blame on journalists for any negative opinions held by the general public about business. This rift seemed especially large in the 1970s, leading the corporations and foundations to fund conferences and journalism programs to develop new relationships. The corporations also began to run their own analyses as advertisements on the opinion pages in major newspapers and in liberal weeklies and reviews, thereby presenting their viewpoints in their own words on a wide variety of issues. Since that time, they have spent several hundred millions of dollars a year on such "advocacy advertising."[41]

But it is not only corporate executives who are critical of the media. Many leftist and ultraconservative commentators have their own criticisms. The leftists say that the media reflect the corporate point of view, do not link their occasional exposés of illegal corporate activities to the underlying structure of the socioeconomic system, treat new political parties as curiosities, uncritically report government claims, and receive much of their content from events staged by politicians and corporations expressly for media coverage. Moreover, smaller newspapers often print editorials and commentaries sent to them by business trade associations, and many articles and opinion pieces in major newspapers are written by members of the policy-formation network or are greatly influenced by those public relations specialists who spend much of their time cultivating close relationships with the media.[42] None of these criticisms demonstrate independent media power, however. They demonstrate the power of business, government, and the policy-formation network.

Ultraconservatives and New Rightists have a different criticism. They believe reporters insert liberal biases into their coverage of events at the expense of the owners and directors. Dye accepts much of the ultraconservative analysis, calling newscasters and commentators a "liberal establishment" that "has established itself as equal in power to the nation's corporate and governmental leadership" due to the fact that "television is the major source of information for the vast majority of Americans."[43] He believes that top media employees have a "liberal, reformist" agenda that they further by focusing on scandal, abuse, and corruption, but that their plans have in part backfired by creating cynicism and disaffection.[44]

Much of the ultraconservative critique is based on a poorly done survey in the 1980s. That survey, widely employed by corporations and ultraconservative advocacy groups to attack journalists as deeply biased, used simplistic questions and drew false conclusions that went far beyond the faulty data. For example, the researchers said journalists are in favor of "income redistribution" on the basis of a question asking if the government should work to substantially reduce the income gap between the rich and the poor. As sociologist Herbert Gans points out in a scathing critique of the many weaknesses of this study, the journalists' replies could as easily imply a desire for compensatory education, full employment, or better health care. Furthermore, their small sample was not properly characterized as to the actual level of these "elite" journalists in their organizations, and they were compared only with conservative business executives and an unidentified sample of "middle Americans," not with other professionals or Americans in general, whom they more closely resemble. Claims were made about students at the Columbia Journalism School on the basis of twenty-eight replies.[45]

Still, the fact remains that there are some differences between corporate leaders and media professionals on specific issues, as shown in more carefully constructed opinion surveys of top leaders from business, labor, media, and minority group organizations. These studies show that newspaper and broadcast journalists tend to be more liberal on foreign policy and domestic issues than corporate and conservative leaders, although not as liberal as the representatives of minority groups and liberal organizations. On questions of environment the media professionals hold much the same liberal views as people from labor, minority, and liberal organizations. But the important point is that studies of newsrooms by Gans and other social scientists discovered that journalists' "personal political beliefs are irrelevant, or virtually so, to the way they covered the news."[46] They are trained to present both sides of the story and to develop a skepticism about all advocates, and are required to interview and quote independent sources.

Further contradicting the claims by ultraconservatives, the evidence shows that what appears in the media is most importantly shaped by forces outside of it. Political scientist John Zaller, for example, concludes that the media is "to a considerable degree dependent on subject matter specialists, including government officials among others, in framing and reporting the news" and that people's opinions on complex issues are shaped by these specialists.[47] When the experts differ, there is polarization in public opinion. When the experts agree, or dissident experts are not included, there is unanimity in public opinion.

Based on these findings, Zaller emphasizes that it is necessary to understand "the politics of expert communities as they relate to the generation and diffusion of knowledge claims, policy recommendations, and general frames of reference."[48] Although the expert communities Zaller has in mind are scientific ones, this is also where the policy-formation network comes into the picture in relation to the mass media. It supplies the experts, including the corporate executives who have been legitimated as general leaders on the basis of their longtime involvement in policy discussion groups. The media's dependence on government leaders and outside experts as sources for its stories greatly constrains any tendency that liberals in the media might have to further their personal views. This is seen in the case of defense spending, in which Zaller concludes that public opinion moves "in tandem" with "shifts in media coverage."[49] Since it is unlikely that liberals inside or outside the media advocated the vast increases in defense spending from 1978 to 1985 to which Zaller is referring, this finding supports his claim that government officials and experts are the main influences on media content on most issues of political importance.

Studies of media content reveal that there is a great emphasis on bad news and sensationalism, with a special emphasis on crime and disasters. Contrary to Dye's opinion, it is unlikely that such stories appear because of a liberal bias. They are an overwhelming aspect of news coverage, especially local news, because they are believed to attract audiences. Moreover, these same studies suggest that crime stories have the largest impact on public opinion of any type of news item. The more television news that people watch, the more likely they are to overestimate the actual amount of crime, support more money for crime prevention, and favor the death penalty.[50] None of these outcomes could be claimed as fulfillment of a liberal agenda.

When the whole range of studies on media concentration, media influence, and the socialization of journalists is taken into consideration, it seems unlikely that the media are directly responsible for very much independent shaping of people's opinions on issues that have to do with power in America. For the most part, the media reflect the biases of those with access to them—corporate leaders, government officials, and policy experts. The liberal exposés that sometimes scuttle specific corrupt deals or sink notable politicians are few and far between. Media can amplify the message of the powerful and marginalize the concerns of the less powerful, but I do not think they are a central element in the power equation. In the case of radio and television, they are primarily a form of entertainment. Thus, there is no evidence for Dye's claim that broadcast journalists are as important as corporate and government officials.

None of this denies that the media can be useful to those who can buy access to them. There is no doubt that advertising can sell products, but that is evidence for the power of the corporations that design and pay for the ads. There is also evidence that political ads— especially negative ones—can help candidates win elections, but that demonstrates only the power of campaign finance for hiring consultants and purchasing airtime, not any independent media power. There is also evidence that fundamentalist ministers who purchase airtime to deliver apocalyptic warnings can raise large sums of money in small donations from viewers, but once again, that is not what is meant by media power.

Whatever emphasis the reader may decide to put on the influence of the mass media, the important point here is that none of my claims for a class-dominance theory rely in any way on the mass media. Thus, pluralists cannot dismiss my theory on the basis of an alleged overemphasis on the mass media. The mass media reach more people than any other outlet for the pamphlets, speeches, and infomercials created by the opinion-forming network, but the people they reach are those who matter the least from the point of view of the opinion molders, and the message they provide can be ambiguous and confusing.

THE ROLE OF POLLS

So far in this chapter, public opinion polling has been accepted at face value as a neutral way to gain useful information for the social sciences. But polls also have another dimension: They can be used in policy conflicts by political leaders and advocacy groups. Contradicting those pluralists who claim that politicians try to be responsive to public opinion, interviews with former congressional and White House aides by Robert Y. Shapiro and Lawrence Jacobs suggest that information about public opinion is used to decide how to present and package the vote the elected official intends to make.[51] Also, polls are sometimes constructed so that their results can be used to shape public opinion when they are reported to the public via the media. This is done by using loaded terms or political labels. In a study asking the public about a law that did not really exist, for example, public opinion differed by 15 to 20 percentage points, depending on whether it was alleged to be of interest to Democratic or Republican leaders. Poll results also change depending on the choices included in the question. In a poll of the general public in early 1997, it was found that a majority favored an amendment to the Constitution to balance the federal budget if cutbacks in Social Security were not mentioned, but that a majority opposed such an amendment if they were asked whether they favored it even if it meant a cut in Social Security.[52]

Thus, poll results are usually suspect when the poll is conducted by an advocacy group. The most notorious offender in this regard is the National Federation of Independent Business, the ultraconservative lobbying group (discussed in chapter 2) that claims it is the voice of small business in general. Its poll results have been criticized repeatedly by social scientists. It also came under criticism for suppressing survey results that did not support its claims about the viewpoints of small business on government-supported health care.[53]

Some of the questions used to demonstrate "economic illiteracy" by the National Council on Economic Education also show an ideological bias. For example, its test asks what "the best measure of the economy's performance is," then counts as incorrect "the unemployment rate" and the "consumer price index," even though both are excellent measures from the average person's point of view. The correct answer is supposedly "gross domestic product," the money value of all goods and services produced within the country.[54]

Polls also can be used to suggest that a "public opinion" exists on issues in which there is none. This does not mean people do not have general opinions, but that they often "make it up as they go along" when responding to specific questions about policy preferences. If questions about affirmative action or oil drilling are framed in one way, they yield one answer, but framed in another way they yield a different answer, especially for those without knowledge or firm opinions.[55] It therefore becomes relatively easy for advocacy groups to obtain whatever results they wish when they conduct a survey.

Results such as these suggest that the alleged public opinion on an issue is often a myth based on the results of polls reported in newspapers, giving the numbers a far greater legitimacy than they deserve.

In those cases, the "public opinion" reported by the media is only another weapon in the battle between the liberal-labor and corporate-conservative coalitions. Although there is a sensible public opinion on many general issues of great import to the average American, there are some aspects of public opinion that seem to be as superficial, chaotic, and contrived as Zaller's summary of the literature on specific issue-areas suggests.

THE ENFORCEMENT OF PUBLIC OPINION

There are limits to the tolerance within the power elite for opposition to public policies it favors, although these limits vary from era to era and are never fully clear until they are tested. There thus may be personal costs for people who move outside the general consensus. The attempt to enforce the limits on dissent are carried out in a variety of ways that begin with exclusion from events or dismissal from jobs. Those who disagree with the consensus are sometimes criticized in the media or branded as "extremists" or "un-Americans." Such punishments are relatively minor for those who are extremely committed to their viewpoint, but social psychology experiments on conformity and field studies of social movements both suggest that most people are very uncomfortable when they are in any way excluded or criticized by their peers. Similar studies show that most people also find it very hard to be in disagreement with authority figures.[56]

The use of scorn, isolation, and other sanctions is seen most directly in the treatment of "whistle-blowers"—employees of corporations or government agencies who expose wrongdoing by their superiors. Contrary to the impression that they are rewarded as good citizens for stepping forward, they are treated as pariahs, relieved of their responsibilities by higher authority figures in the organization, and shunned by peers. Friends are afraid to associate with them. Their lives are often turned upside down. Many regret that they took the action they did, even though they thought it was the honest or moral course to take.[57]

Those who become prominent public critics of some aspect of conventional wisdom receive similar harsh treatment unless they can be isolated as oddball characters. Their motives are questioned and stories appearing in the media about their lives attempt to demonstrate they are acting from irrational psychological motives. When consumer activist Ralph Nader dared to testify before Congress in 1966 about the defects in one of the small cars manufactured by General Motors, to take the most famous example, the company hired a private detective agency to try to find personal gossip about him that could be used to discredit his testimony. The efforts by the detective agency included a series of harassing telephone calls and pick-up attempts by women. At first General Motors denied any involvement, then claimed that the investigation concerned Nader's possible connection to false car insurance claims. Later the company apologized even while denying any harassment, but then the detective agency admitted that it had been hired to "get something somewhere on this guy . . . get him out of their hair . . . shut him up." There was no personal wrongdoing to be discovered, the company was heavily criticized in the media, and Nader collected damages when his lawsuit was settled out of court.[58] As noted in the discussion of public relations firms, there are examples of such firms spying on several different types of anticorporate groups. There is also evidence of attempts at disruption and intimidation. The tactics used against the opponents of lumber, chemical, and meat companies have been especially harsh.[59]

Government officials also have resorted to severe sanctions in an attempt to shape public opinion. The government not only spied on Martin Luther King, Jr., and many other civil rights activists, but planted false information and issued false threats in order to disrupt their efforts. Such actions serve as a reminder that attempts to change opinions and laws can have serious negative consequences. Government violence and other extralegal methods are seldom or never used on dissenters in times of domestic calm, but they have been employed in times of social upheaval when members of the power elite serving within the government felt it necessary to do so.[60]

CONCLUSION

This chapter shows quite conclusively that "public opinion" does not have the routine importance that public-opinion pluralists attribute to it. It is shaped on foreign and defense issues and ignored on domestic economic issues. It is irrelevant in a substantive sense to the power elite on social issues. Although the general opinions people hold are rational and reasonable within their time constraints and the quality of the information available, it is unlikely that any focused public opinion exists on most of the complicated legislative issues of concern to the power elite.

At the same time, there are some situations in which public opinion may have an impact—particularly on issues where there is a strong social movement or social disruption. That is, public opinion may help to set limits on power elite actions even though it does not have the general effects accorded to it by public-opinion pluralists.

The overall picture, then, is one that provides a large amount of latitude for the power elite and little support for the public-opinion version of pluralism. But the chapter is incomplete in one important respect: It has not considered the possible effect of public opinion on the electoral process. Perhaps political candidates must take heed of public opinion in order to be elected, which is the point most emphasized by both types of pluralists. This possibility is considered as one aspect of the next chapter.

NOTES

1. Paul Burstein, "Might the Public Influence Public Policy? Two Views," p. 13 (paper presented at the annual meetings of the American Sociological Association, New York, August 16–20, 1996). For the claim that politicians are sensitive to very small changes in public opinion, with their responses in turn supporting new opinion trends, see James A. Stimson, Michael B. MacKuen, and Robert S. Erikson, "Dynamic Representation," *American Political Science Review,* 89 (September 1995): 543–564.
2. For an excellent argument against an overemphasis on public opinion in explaining the stability of power structures, see Michael Mann, "The Ideology of Intellectuals and Other People in the Development of Capitalism," in *Stress and Contradiction in Modern Capitalism,* ed. Leon N. Lindberg, et al. (Lexington, MA: Lexington Books, 1975). For arguments on the compelling nature of everyday life for most people, making them unlikely to join political movements unless their routines are disrupted, see John R. Logan and Harvey Molotch, *Urban Fortunes* (Berkeley: University of California Press, 1987), and Richard Flacks, *Making History: The Radical Tradition in American Life* (New York: Columbia University Press, 1988).
3. Benjamin Page and Robert Y. Shapiro, *The Rational Public* (Chicago: University of Chicago Press, 1992).
4. William Gamson, *Talking Politics* (New York: Columbia University Press, 1992), p. 4.
5. John Zaller, *The Nature and Origins of Mass Opinion* (New York: Cambridge University Press, 1992).
6. Louis Hartz, *The Liberal Tradition in America* (New York: Harcourt, 1955); Seymour M. Lipset, *The First New Nation* (New York: Basic Books, 1963); Francis X. Sutton, *The American Business Creed* (Cambridge, MA: Harvard University Press, 1956).
7. Robert Lane, *Political Ideology* (New York: Free Press, 1962); William Ryan, *Blaming the Victim* (New York: Random House, 1971).
8. Richard Sennett and Jonathan Cobb, *The Hidden Injuries of Class* (New York: Random House, 1971), pp. 250–251.
9. Ibid., p. 251.
10. Richard L. Zweigenhaft and G. William Domhoff, *Blacks in the White Establishment? A Study of Race and Class in America* (New Haven, CT: Yale University Press, 1991), pp. 159–166.
11. John Stauber and Sheldon Rampton, *Toxic Sludge Is Good for You: Lies, Damn Lies, and the Public Relations Industry* (Monroe, ME: Common Courage Press, 1995), pp. 207–208. For the history of public relations, see Kenneth Henry, *Defenders and Shapers of the Corporate Image* (New

Haven, CT: College & University Press, 1972); Richard Tedlow, *Keeping the Corporate Image* (Greenwich, CT: JAI Press, 1979); Stuart Ewen, *PR!: A Social History of Spin* (New York: Basic Books, 1996).

12. Stauber and Rampton, op. cit., pp. 29–31, 79, 91, 135–136.

13. Ibid., chapter 5.

14. Beth Ghiloni, "The Velvet Ghetto: Women, Power, and the Corporation," in *The Power Elite and Organizations*, eds. G. William Domhoff and Thomas Dye (Beverly Hills, CA: Sage Publications, 1987); Sharon Collins, *Black Corporate Executives* (Philadelphia: Temple University Press, 1997).

15. Jerome Himmelstein, *Looking Good and Doing Good* (Bloomington: Indiana University Press, 1997).

16. Ibid., p. 151 n. 2.

17. M. David Ermann, "The Operative Goals of Corporate Philanthropy: Contributions to the Public Broadcasting Service, 1972–1976," *Social Problems*, 25 (1978): 504–514. For somewhat more benign views, see Ronald Burt, "Corporate Philanthropy As a Cooptive Relation," *Social Forces*, 62 (1983): 419–449, and Joseph Galaskiewicz and Ronald Burt, "Interorganizational Contagion in Corporate Philanthropy," *Administrative Science Quarterly*, 36 (1991): 88–105.

18. Austin Fulk, *Patterns of Corporate Philanthropy: Funding Enemies, Forsaking Friends* (Washington, DC: Capital Research Center, 1997).

19. Himmelstein, op. cit., p. 117.

20. Warren Berger, "Ad Council: A Grand Idea That Worked" (Special Advertising Section: The Advertising Council, 50 Years of Public Service), *Advertising Age* (Nov. 11, 1991): A2–A5; "50-Year Pin," *Broadcasting* (Dec. 9, 1991): 74; Stuart Elliott, "Advertising Council," *New York Times* (Jan. 16, 1992): C4.

21. Glenn Hirsch, "Only You Can Prevent Ideological Hegemony: The Advertising Council and Its Place in the American Power Structure," *Insurgent Sociologist*, 5 (1975): 69.

22. Ibid., pp. 76–77; Warren Berger, "Council Acts in Urban Crisis to Stir Action, Understanding," *Advertising Age* (Nov. 11, 1991): A13; Marcy Magiera, "Ad Council Targets Racism in Wake of L.A. Rioting," *Advertising Age* (May 11, 1992): 1–20.

23. Hirsch, op. cit., p. 78.

24. Ibid., p. 79. For a similar argument from a different theoretical perspective, see Peter M. Hall, "A Symbolic Interactionist Analysis of Politics," *Sociological Inquiry*, 42 (1972): 35–75.

25. Page and Shapiro, op. cit., p. 205.

26. Lawrence Shoup and William Minter, *Imperial Brain Trust* (New York: Monthly Review Press, 1977), pp. 31, 71.

27. *Annual Report 1996* (New York: Foreign Policy Association, 1997).

28. Harry B. Price, *The Marshall Plan and Its Meaning* (Ithaca, NY: Cornell University Press, 1955), p. 56.

29. Michael Wala, *The Council on Foreign Relations and American Foreign Policy in the Early Cold War* (Providence, RI: Berghahn Books, 1994), chapter 7, for excellent behind-the-scenes detail on the "managing" of public opinion on this issue.

30. John E. Mueller, *War, Presidents and Public Opinion* (New York: Wiley, 1973), pp. 70 and 72ff, tables 4.2 and 4.3.
31. Ibid. The influence of rising casualties on public opinion is the major finding of Mueller's book.
32. Shoup and Minter, op. cit., chapter 6; Samuel Huntington, "A Policy Adviser's Response on Vietnam," *Washington Post* (Feb. 1, 1977): A17; Mueller, op. cit.
33. National Council on Economic Education, *EconomicsAmerica: Directory, 1996–1997*, p. i.
34. Dave Kansas, "Economic Illiteracy Abounds in U.S., New Survey Shows," *Wall Street Journal* (Sept. 11, 1992): A11. For an in-depth analysis, see Karl Kraeplin, "The American Upper Class and the Problem of Legitimacy: The Joint Council on Economic Education," *Insurgent Sociologist* (Winter 1979). For corporate influence in classrooms beyond the teaching of economics, see *Captive Kids: A Report on Commercial Pressures on Kids at School* (Washington, DC: Consumers Union, 1995), and Deborah Stead, "Corporations, Classrooms, and Commercialism," *New York Times*, Education Life Section (Jan. 5, 1997): 30–47.
35. Page and Shapiro, op. cit., p. 117. For an excellent earlier statement of this argument, see Thomas Ferguson and Joel Rogers, *Right Turn* (New York: Hill and Wang, 1986).
36. Howard Gold, *Hollow Mandates: American Public Opinion and the Conservative Shift* (Boulder, CO: Westview Press, 1992), p. 145. The work cited in this and the previous footnote contradicts the claims by Stimson, MacKuen, and Erikson (op. cit., in the first footnote of this chapter) about the responsiveness of politicians to public opinion. Since all four studies focus on the same time period, 1975–1985, I think the differences are due to the emphasis on small changes in the Stimson, MacKuen, and Erikson model. These small changes are accentuated by their quantitative treatment of the survey data.
37. Jerome Himmelstein, *To the Right* (Berkeley: University of California Press, 1989), chapters 3 and 4.
38. Edward Carmines and James Stimson, *Issue Evolution: Race and the Transformation of American Politics* (Princeton, NJ: Princeton University Pres, 1980); Dan T. Carter, *The Politics of Rage: George Wallace, the Origins of the New Conservatism, and the Transformation of American Politics* (New York: Simon & Schuster, 1995). For doubts on the effects of social issues on voters outside the South, see Himmelstein, *To the Right*, op. cit., and Warren E. Miller and J. Merrill Shanks, *The New American Voter* (Cambridge: Harvard University Press, 1996).
39. Ben Bagdikian, *The Media Monopoly*, 4th ed. (Boston: Beacon Press, 1992); Mark Miller and Janine Biden, "The National Entertainment State," *The Nation* (June 3, 1996): 23–27; Peter Dreier, "The Position of the Press in the U.S. Power Structure," *Social Problems*, 29 (1982): 298–310.
40. David Pearce Demers, *The Menace of the Corporate Newspaper: Fact or Fiction?* (Ames: Iowa State University Press, 1996), p. 302.
41. Peter Dreier, "Capitalists vs. the Media," *Media, Culture, and Society* (April 1982). Corporate anger with the media declined in the late 1980s and 1990s.

42. For example, see Noam Chomsky and Edward Herman, *Manufacturing Consent: The Political Economy of the Mass Media* (New York: Pantheon, 1988). On PR influence, see Alicia Mundy, "Is the Press Any Match for Powerhouse PR?," *Columbia Journalism Review*, 31 (1992): 27–35.

43. Thomas Dye, *Who's Running America?*, 6th ed. (Englewood Cliffs, NJ: Prentice-Hall, 1995), p. 108.

44. Ibid., p. 120.

45. Herbert Gans, "Are U.S. Journalists Dangerously Liberal?," *Columbia Journalism Review* (November/December 1985): 29–33. The work in question is by S. Robert Lichter and Stanley Rothman, "Media and Business Elites," *Public Opinion* (October/November 1981), and Linda Lichter, S. Robert Lichter, and Stanley Rothman, "The Once and Future Journalists," *Washington Journalism Review* (December 1982). The findings later appeared in their book, *The Media Elite* (Bethesda, MD: Adler & Adler, 1986).

46. Gans, op. cit., p. 32. For evidence on Gans's point, see Gaye Tuchman, *Making News* (New York: Free Press, 1978); Herbert Gans, *Deciding What's News* (New York: Pantheon, 1979); and Michael Schudson, *The Power of News* (Cambridge: Harvard University Press, 1995).

47. Zaller, op. cit., p. 319.

48. Ibid., Appendix.

49. Ibid., p. 15.

50. George Gerbner, "The Hidden Side of Television Violence," in *Invisible Crises: What Conglomerate Control of Media Means for America and the World*, eds. George Gerbner, Hamid Mowlana, and Herbert Schiller (Boulder, CO: Westview Press, 1996).

51. Lawrence R. Jacobs and Robert Y. Shapiro, "The Myth of Pandering and Public Opinion during President Clinton's First Term" (unpublished report, Barnard-Columbia Center for Urban Policy, Columbia University, January 17, 1997); Lawrence R. Jacobs and Robert Y. Shapiro, "Debunking the Pandering Politician Myth," *The Public Perspective* (April/May 1997): 3–5. For archival and interview evidence on presidential manipulation of poll questions and the way results are presented, especially in the Nixon administration, see Lawrence Jacobs and Robert Y. Shapiro, "Presidential Manipulation of Polls and Public Opinion," *Political Science Quarterly*, 110 (1995): 519–539.

52. David Rosenbaum, "Deficit: Public Enemy No. 1, It's Not," *New York Times* (Feb. 16, 1997): D1. For a telling demonstration that people will pretend they have an opinion on a legislative issue made up by the pollster, and vary their support considerably depending on whether Democrats or Republicans supposedly favor the phantom legislation, see Richard Morin, "What Informed Opinion? A Survey Trick Points Out the Hazards Facing Those Who Take the Nation's Pulse," *Washington Post Weekly Edition* (April 10–16, 1995): 36.

53. Richard Hamilton, *Restraining Myths* (New York: Wiley, 1975), pp. 249–256. G. William Domhoff, "Who Killed Health Care Reform in Congress, Small Business or Rich Conservatives, and Why Did They Do It?" (paper presented at the annual meetings of the American Sociological Association, Washington, DC, August 21, 1995).

54. Jonathan Marshall, "Council Setting Standards for Stamping Out Economic Illiteracy," *San Francisco Chronicle* (Jan. 6, 1997): E1.
55. Zaller, op. cit., chapter 5.
56. For the classic studies on social conformity, see Solomon Asch, *Social Psychology* (Englewood Cliffs, NJ: Prentice-Hall, 1952). For recent studies on conformity, see Elliot Aronson, *The Social Animal*, 6th ed. (New York: W. H. Freeman & Co., 1992), chapter 2. For a summary of field studies making this point about conformity, see Laura R. Woliver, "Mobilizing and Sustaining Grassroots Dissent," *Journal of Social Issues*, vol. 52, no. 1 (1996): 139–151. For the classic study of deference to authority, see Stanley Milgram, *Obedience to Authority* (New York: Harper and Row, 1974). For recent experimental work, see once again Aronson, *The Social Animal*, chapter 2, and for field studies on this issue see once again Woliver, "Mobilizing and Sustaining Grassroots Dissent."
57. Ralph Nader, Peter Petkas, and Kate Blackwell, *Whistle Blowing* (New York: Grossman, 1972). For evidence of the difficulties faced by whistleblowers, see Joyce Rothschild, "Whistleblowing as Occupational Deviance and Dilemma" (paper presented at the annual meeting of the American Sociological Association, 1992); Joyce Rothschild, "The Right to Express Dissent as Necessary for Organizational Democracy: The Case of Whistleblowers" (paper presented at the annual meeting of the International Sociological Association, 1994).
58. "Ralph Nader," in *Current Biography* (New York: H. H. Wilson, 1968), p. 280.
59. Stauber and Rampton, op. cit., chapter 5 and pp. 140–142. For the most recent and credible account of opposition to environmentalists, see Jacqueline Vaughn Switzer, *Green Backlash: The History and Politics of Environmental Opposition in the U.S.* (Boulder, CO: Lynne Rienne Publishers, 1997).
60. James K. Davis, *Spying on America* (New York: Praeger, 1992).

6

Parties and Elections

The right to vote and the existence of two rival political parties provide pluralists with their main arguments against a class-domination theory for the United States. Drawing on an analogy with an idealized market economy, they liken voters to consumers and the electoral process to the marketplace. People's votes supposedly can influence parties to offer their favorite policies in the same way that their consumer purchases influence businesses to offer their favorite products. Competition between the two parties thereby leads inexorably to citizen control. The eighteenth-century economist Adam Smith's famous "invisible hand" metaphor is applied to politics.[1] In other words, self-interested behavior by business owners and politicians leads to the best possible public outcome.

According to this theory, the fear of losing office keeps politicians responsive to voters. "In a competitive two-party situation such as exists in American presidential politics," write political scientists Nelson Polsby and Aaron Wildavsky, "the lively possibility of change provides an effective incentive for political leaders to remain in touch with followers."[2] They contrast their view with what they claim unfairly to be the power-elite perspective: "A cynical view would hold that the United States was ruled by a power elite—a small group outside the democratic process."[3] The inaccurate portrayal of the power-elite position is in the phrase "outside the democratic process." If there is anything to a power-elite analysis of the United States, it is in its ability to show how the power elite operates within—not outside—the democratic process, including the two-party system, as this chapter demonstrates.

There is, first of all, evidence that the premises underlying the pluralist model of how the parties operate are incorrect. The assumption that politicians will adopt the views of the majority in order to be elected is contradicted by the fact that most politicians do not subscribe to the very liberal views on economic issues that are held by a majority of the electorate. Sixty-five to 72 percent of Americans, for example, say in polls that the federal government should "see to it that everyone who wants to work can find a job," but few candidates in either major party have tried to develop employment programs.[4] Nor does a party always put forth the candidate most likely to win. There are several historical examples in which party leaders have preferred candidates who shared their views rather than ones who seemed to be more popular with the electorate. Wealthy Democratic leaders in the Midwest in the late nineteenth century opposed the candidacies of populist Democrats with very liberal economic programs. More recently, Democratic leaders rejected antiwar candidate Eugene McCarthy at the Democratic National Convention in 1968 even though many polls suggested he would do much better against former vice president Richard M. Nixon or New York governor Nelson Rockefeller than would Vice President Hubert Humphrey, the candidate who eventually lost.[5]

Second, there is evidence that the parties sometimes collude rather than compete. This is especially the case when an "unacceptable" candidate wins the nomination in one or the other party. In 1972, for example, Southern and labor Democrats openly or tacitly supported Nixon against the party's candidate, George McGovern. To reciprocate this support, "more than a hundred Republican candidates for seats held by Southern and labor-backed Democrats were simply written off by White House strategists."[6] Such collusion is even more likely if both parties share a common policy or ideological preference, as they often do. Leaders of both parties, for example, opted for cutbacks in Social Security in the early 1980s, even though 80 to 90 percent of the citizenry opposed cuts.[7]

Contrary to the pluralist claim, then, there is no *a priori* theoretical reason to believe that political parties and their candidates must reflect the policy preferences of the majority of the voters. Candidates and parties are relatively free to say one thing and do another. Once in office, the president and other elected officials have the ability to interpret their mandate just about any way they wish. Lyndon B. Johnson's landslide victory in 1964 was based in part on his professions of a less "warlike" policy for Southeast Asia than Barry Goldwater seemed to have, but he and his party escalated the war soon after his victory. In 1980, polls showed that Ronald Reagan's victory reflected in part the dissatisfaction with unemployment on the part of the traditional Democratic voters who defected to him, along with their belief that he would stimulate the economy and leave their "safety net" intact. But his administration claimed its success as a mandate for conservative economic policies and proceeded to increase unemployment and cut social welfare programs.[8]

It even may be that a two-party system discourages policy discussion and political education rather than encourages these activities, contrary to the pluralist analogy with the free market. The need for a majority vote when the stakes are high, such as during the presidential election, may lead to campaigns in which the issues are buried by both political parties in an attempt to gain the allegiance of centrist voters. Virtually every account of a presidential election since at least 1968 concludes that the campaign was one of image building and issue avoiding, with both candidates asking voters to trust them on the basis of their personal qualities. Meanwhile, both parties concentrated on the personal defects, weaknesses, and indiscretions of the other candidate.

Also, there is reason to believe that a two-party system actually discourages voting because those in a minority of even 49 percent receive nothing for their efforts. In countries where geographical districts have been replaced by a system in which a party's representation in the legislature is determined by its percentage of the overall national vote, called "proportional representation," voting has increased considerably.[9] Perhaps the major conclusion to be drawn about the political consequences of the two-party system is not that it allows citizens to express their policy preferences, but that it creates a situation in which there is very little relationship between politics and policy. Such a system creates a set of circumstances in which the parties may or may not reflect citizen preferences in the way in which pluralists claim. The question thus becomes: How and when do elections matter in terms of the policy preferences of ordinary voters? This is a far cry from the certitudes about the impossibility of class dominance in a two-party system that are espoused by pluralists.

The picture becomes even cloudier when the exclusion of African-Americans from voting booths in most Southern states until 1965 is factored into the equation. This exclusion provided wealthy white Southerners with a virtual veto power over public policy at the national level because of the seniority they could accumulate in Congress and made it all but impossible for the Democratic Party to distinguish itself from the Republicans in the eyes of many voters. Before considering this problem, however, it is necessary to explain why there have been only two major political parties in the United States for all but a few years since the adoption of the Constitution in 1789.

WHY TWO PARTIES?

In some democratic countries, there are three or more substantial political parties with clearly defined programs that are understood by voters, who therefore are able to vote on the basis of policy preferences if they so desire. In Canada, for example, the Conservative and Liberal Parties that until recently received the great majority of the votes had to contend with a leftist party with a program slightly more liberal than that advocated by the liberal-labor coalition in the United States. This party, called the New Democratic Party, received 15 to 20 percent of the vote in the 1970s and 1980s due to strong support from trade unionists. Its vote rose even higher in 1990, then fell even lower in 1993, but its problems are not due to the nature of the electoral system.[10]

In sharp contrast, there have been only two major parties for most of American history. The only exceptions were a brief one-party era from about 1812 to 1828, after the Federalist Party collapsed, and a few years in the 1850s, when the conflict over extending slavery into Western territories led to the breakup of the Whig Party (the party that, roughly speaking, replaced the Federalist Party). Even the Republican Party that developed in the 1850s does not really qualify as a third party because it replaced the Whigs in the space of just one or two elections.

But why have there been only two major parties despite the country's tumultuous history of regional, religious, and class rivalries? Two fundamental features of American government lead to a two-party system. The first is the selection of senators and representatives from states and districts in elections that require only a plurality, not a majority. Such an arrangement is called a "single-member district plurality system," and it has led to two-party systems in 90 percent of the 109 countries included in an exhaustive comparative study of party systems. The exceptions tended to be in countries where a third party had some strength in a single region for ethnic or religious reasons. The second reason for the American two-party system is relatively unique in the world—the election of a president. The election of a president is, in effect, a strong version of the single-member district plurality system, with the nation serving as the only district. It strengthens the pull toward two parties that is present in any single-member district system and makes third parties even more unlikely and smaller than in countries that do not elect a president.[11]

The fact that only one person can win the presidency or be elected from a given state or district—which seems trivial and is taken for granted by most Americans—leads to a two-party system by creating a series of "winner-take-all" elections in which a vote for a third-party candidate of the right or left is in effect a vote for the voter's least-favored candidate on the other side of the political spectrum. Because a vote for a third candidate is a vote for "your worst enemy," the most sensible strategy for those who want to avoid this fate is to join the largest possible preelection coalition, even if numerous policy preferences must be abandoned or compromised. The inevitable result is two coalitional parties that attempt to blur their differences in order to win the voters in the middle.

By way of contrast, the parliamentary system that exists in most democratic countries, including Canada, makes possible three or more parties. Because a prime minister is selected by the legislature from among its members after the election, there is less pressure toward two preelectoral coalitions, thus making the existence of three issue-oriented parties possible or for a new third party to grow over the period of several elections. Even more parties are likely to exist if the parliament is elected by proportional representation. According to sociologist Seymour Martin Lipset, every country that uses proportional representation has four or more parties in its legislature.[12] Thus, comparative studies of the relationship between electoral rules and the number of political parties suggest how candidate selection in the United States came to be conducted through a two-party system despite the existence of class, regional, and ethnic conflicts that have led to three or more parties in other countries. On the basis of these studies, Lipset suggests the following relationship between electoral systems and party systems:

> If enough cases existed for analysis, the following rank-order correlation might be found between electoral systems and the number of political parties: presidential system with single-member districts and one plurality election—two parties; parliamentary system with single-member districts and one plurality election—tendency to two parties; parliamentary system with single-member districts and alternative ballot or run-off (second) election—tendency to many parties; proportional representation—many parties.[13]

Although the American system of presidential elections and single-member congressional districts generates a strong tendency toward a two-party system, it was not designed with this fact in mind. The Founding Fathers tried to create a system of checks and balances that would keep power within bounds—including the potential power of an aroused and organized majority of farmers and artisans—and they largely succeeded. However, the creation of a two-party system was not among their plans. Indeed, the Founding Fathers disliked the idea of parties, which they condemned as "factions" that were highly divisive. Parties are a major unintended consequence of their deliberations, and it was not until the 1830s and 1840s that a new generation of political leaders finally accommodated themselves to the idea that the two-party system was not disruptive of rule by the wealthy few.[14]

Within the context of these electoral rules, third parties face many additional barriers and handicaps. For example, Republicans and Democrats have joined together in each state to make it difficult for third parties to gain access to the ballot by requiring them to collect signatures in order to be listed. Also, third parties receive less financial support from individual donors and little or no press coverage. But it is a mistake to focus on the barriers and handicaps in explaining the failure of third parties. Their real problems are created by the way in which the governmental and electoral systems are organized.

Perot's Reform Party

The major third party of the 1990s, H. Ross Perot's Reform Party, might seem at first glance to contradict this analysis. After all, Perot received an amazing 19 percent of the vote in the 1992 presidential race and nearly 9 percent in 1996. But his success is atypical and easily explained.

First, his party was unique among third parties in that it was the top-down creation of a single billionaire—one of the twenty-five richest people in the United States in 1996. In 1992 he spent a cool $72 million of his own money to put his party on the ballot and buy television advertising.

Second, and equally important, the Reform Party had more success than the usual third party because it was positioned between the two major parties. Thus, it was not as big a threat to the Democrats as it would have been if it had been to their left, nor to the Republicans if it had been to their right. As a centrist party it was more likely to draw from both parties, and that is what seemed to happen in both 1992 and 1996, according to exit polls and a very careful analysis of the 1992 campaign by two leading experts on voting behavior.[15]

Third, the Reform Party is not really a party. It is an independent candidacy by Perot and is therefore likely to disappear when he steps aside. He and his "party" are best understood as evidence for the power of money in American politics.

WHEN AND HOW DO ELECTIONS MATTER?

Even though the existence of elections does not support a pluralist analysis, they have an important role, and the potential to play an even larger role in the future. They matter in several important ways.

First, elections provide a mechanism for rival segments of a dominant class to resolve disputes in a peaceful way. Historically, this was their first function in both Europe and America, when only white male property holders could vote. Not until elections were well established were they seen as a way to engage more of the population in governance. In the case of the United States, wider participation was resisted by many members of the dominant class and only grudgingly accepted as it became clear in the 1830s and 1840s that parties could be a useful way to bind citizens to the country.

This does not mean, however, that all disputes among class segments could be resolved through elections. In fact, as sociologists John Higley and Michael Burton argue, democratic systems and the regular, peaceful, and binding electoral contests they involve did not emerge in any European country until the rival "elites," as they call the contending forces, had settled their major differences in a "pact" or "settlement," usually after years of violence or in the face of extreme political crisis.[16] In the United States, the equivalent of these "elite pacts" was the Constitution, which dealt with several issues that rival colonial leaders said were not negotiable. Most importantly, Northern wealthholders had to make several concessions to the Southern slave owners to win their agreement to the new constitution. Even in this example, the limited nature of elections and the importance of elite pacts is shown by the American Civil War. The slaveholders decided to secede from the union and risk war rather than see their way of life gradually eroded by an inability to expand slavery westward. They were not prepared to abide by election results and legislative majorities on an issue involving "their" labor force.

In the wake of stable elite pacts, elections gradually come to have a second function. They allow ordinary citizens to help determine which segment of the dominant class will play the lead role in government. In essence, different occupational and ethnic groups become part of rival upper-class coalitions that contend for office on a wide range of appeals, some issue-based, some not. Ordinary voters are thus often able to eliminate those they perceive as extremists.

Third, as part of rival electoral coalitions, average citizens in many countries have an influence on economic and social issues. This is best seen in those European countries where social democrats have won a majority and created social insurance systems for unemployment, disability, health, and old age that are far more extensive than

American programs. As chapter 7 demonstrates, this electoral function has been highly limited in the United States.

Fourth, and finally, elections matter as a way to introduce new policies in times of social disruption caused by extreme domestic problems. In the nineteenth and early twentieth centuries, this role was often fulfilled by third parties that appeared suddenly on the scene, such as the new parties of the 1840s and 1850s that first advocated the abolition of slavery. By the second decade of the twentieth century, the main electoral arena for new ideas became the primary elections of the two major parties. Primary elections developed gradually in the late nineteenth and early twentieth centuries due to the efforts of reformers who believed that the electoral rules (discussed earlier in this chapter) made it unlikely that very much of importance could be accomplished by a third party.[17]

In 1903 Wisconsin became the first state to pass a law calling for statewide primaries, but it was North Dakota where they first had a dramatic impact due to an innovative approach developed by a one-time wheat farmer who also had been an organizer for the local Socialist Party. It was his idea to run candidates in the primaries of both major parties on a very specific program that ignored all ideological labels. The platform of the organization he formed, called the Nonpartisan League to emphasize its effort to work through the primaries of both parties, advocated state-owned grain elevators, a state-owned bank, government crop insurance against destructive rainstorms, public housing for farmworkers, and other policies that would make the farmers of North Dakota and other nearby states less dependent on railroads and grain companies, which were viewed as highly exploitative.

Despite high emotion and much opposition from business leaders and mainstream politicians, the Nonpartisan League swept to power in North Dakota in 1916 and instituted much of its program. The Bank of North Dakota, which focuses on credit for farmers and low-income rural residents, is still the only one of its kind in the United States. Even though the Nonpartisan League has been gone for many decades and is almost completely forgotten, it had a large impact throughout the Midwestern farming states in its day. As the historian who studied it most closely concludes: "Not only was it to control for some years the government in one state, elect state officials and legislators in a number of midwestern and western states, and send several of its representatives to the Congress—its impact was to help shape the destinies of a dozen states and the political philosophies of an important segment of the nation's voters."[18] Perhaps its greatest impact outside of North Dakota was in neighboring Minnesota, where its efforts led to the transformation of the moribund Democratic Party into the Democratic-Farmer-Labor Party that still exists today and often sends liberals to Congress.

The first major insurgency in Democratic presidential primaries came in 1952 from a Tennessee senator who advocated integration and opposed the influence of organized crime in several urban Democratic Party political organizations in the North. Although he won several primaries and fared well in polls, too many convention votes were controlled by party leaders for him to receive the nomination.[19] By the 1960s ultraconservatives were using Republican primaries to spread their ideas and recruit activists, and antiwar liberals were using Democratic Party primaries to allow Democrats to register their dissatisfaction with the Vietnam War. Both groups had a strong impact on their parties. Primaries are now taken for granted as the way to select presidential candidates for both parties.[20]

Perhaps even more dramatically, socialists have entered Democratic primaries and demonstrated to mainstream party leaders and government officials that there was more support for left-wing economic programs than was generally realized. In 1934, for example, in the midst of the Great Depression, the most famous socialist of his day, the prolific author Upton Sinclair, switched his party registration from Socialist to Democrat and won the California primary for governor with 51 percent of the vote in a field of seven candidates. He lost the general election with 37 percent of the vote, but the party was liberalized for years thereafter because young liberal and socialist activists had run for other offices as part of Sinclair's campaign to End Poverty in California (EPIC). Moderates in the California Democratic and Republican Parties then worked together to contain liberals until ultraconservatives were able to win Republican primaries and general elections in the post–World War II era.[21]

So elections can and do matter. They allow for a limited amount of input by citizens who are not wealthy, and they provide an opening for critics of the social system to present their ideas. In the United States, however, elections have yielded far fewer successes for the liberal-labor coalition than might be expected on the basis of social-democratic victories in most Western democracies. Even the narrowness of a two-party system does not entirely explain this situation, for it is not clear why the liberal-labor coalition could not triumph in one of the two parties.

Republicans and Democrats

Two contrasting images predominate in most discussions of the Republican and Democratic Parties. One says there is not a "dime's worth of difference between them," which reflects the need to appeal to the centrist voters in a two-party system. The other says that the Republicans represent big business and the Democrats the liberal-labor coalition. Both images are incorrect in several important respects, but the primary emphasis of this section is on why the Democrats must be understood for most of their long history as the party of the Southern segment of the dominant class, not as the party of liberals and unions. However, Southern white control of the Democratic Party has declined in the past thirty years because the Voting Rights Act of 1965 made it possible for African-American voters to use party primaries to force the most racially conservative white political leaders into the Republican Party. What the party becomes in the future depends on a number of unknowns, including the creativity of the programs and leaders that emerge in the liberal-labor coalition.

Although the Constitutional Convention of 1787 settled the major issues between the Northern and Southern rich—at least until the 1850s—it did not take long for political parties to develop. From the day in 1791 when wealthy Virginia plantation owners made contact with landowners in upstate New York to create what was to become the first incarnation of the Democratic Party, the two parties have represented rival segments of the dominant class. For the most part, the Democrats were originally the party of agrarian wealth, especially in the South, and the Republicans the party of bankers, merchants, and rising industrialists.*

As with all generalizations, this one needs some qualification. The Democratic-Republican Party, as it was first known, also found many of its adherents in the North among merchants and bankers of Irish origins, who disliked the English-origin leaders in the Federalist Party for historical reasons. Also, religious dissenters and Protestants of low-status denominations often favored the Democratic-Republicans over the "high church" Federalist Party. These kinds of differences persist to the present: In terms of social status, the Federalist-Whig-Republican Party has been the party of the secure and established, and the Democrats the party of those who were in the out-group on some dimension. Such a characterization even fits the long-standing slaveholders who controlled the party in its early years, for they were agrarians in an industrializing society, slaveholders in a land of free labor. They were on the defensive, and they knew it.[22]

---

*The South is defined for purposes of this book as the following thirteen states: Alabama, Arkansas, Florida, Georgia, Louisiana, Kentucky, Mississippi, North Carolina, Oklahoma, South Carolina, Tennessee, Texas, Virginia. Although there is no standard definition of "the South," this one has been used by many social scientists since at least the 1930s.

Following the Civil War, the Democratic Party became even more completely the instrument of the Southern segment of the dominant class because all white Southerners moved into that party as the best strategy to maximize their impact in Washington and at the same time force the Southern populists to accept marginalization within the Democratic Party or start a third party.[23] Meanwhile, white Southerners gained new allies in the North with the arrival of millions of ethnic Catholic and Jewish immigrants after 1870 who were often treated badly and scorned by the Protestant majority. When some of these new immigrants grew wealthy in the first half of the twentieth century, they became major financial backers of urban Democratic organizations (called "machines" in their day). Contrary to liberal and ultraconservative protestations, the liberal-labor coalition that developed within the party in the late 1930s was no match for the well-established Southern rich and their wealthy urban ethnic allies.[24]

Still, the liberal-labor coalition did begin to elect about 100 Democrats to the House starting in the 1930s, when they joined with roughly 100 Southern Democrats and 50 "machine Democrats" to form a strong Democratic majority in all but a few sessions of Congress before 1994. By 1938, however, the Southern Democrats and Northern Republicans had formed a conservative voting bloc that stopped the liberal Democrats from passing legislation concerning union rights, civil rights, and the regulation of business, even when the liberals could convince some machine Democrats to support them. The fact that Democrats dominated Congress for several decades is therefore in many ways irrelevant from a class-domination perspective. The important point is that a strong conservative majority has been elected to Congress—except in the mid-1930s and mid-1960s, times of great social turmoil—and the majority always has voted together on the issues that relate to class conflict (with two exceptions to be explained later in the book).[25]

There is, of course, far more to the story of the Democratic Party, some of which is told in the remainder of this chapter and the next two chapters, but enough has been said for now to explain why it is a mistake to think of that party as the instrument of the liberal-labor coalition. More generally, it is now possible to state why the liberal-labor coalition does not have a party of its own, as it does in most democratic countries: The electoral rules leading to a two-party system and the dominance of the Democrats by wealthy Southern whites left the liberal-labor coalition with no good options, at least until the 1990s. It cannot form a third party without assuring the election of even more Republicans, but it has been unable to win control of the Democratic Party because it has not been able to create liberal black-white voting coalitions in the South.

WHY LOCAL ELECTIONS ARE DIFFERENT

Perhaps some readers at this point are recalling from their own experience that local elections in many cities do not conform to the two-party pattern, but are instead nonpartisan in nature (i.e., without parties). The reasons for this and other differences from county, state, and national levels are well worth considering because they show that electoral rules—and even the structure of government itself—are subject to change by outside forces. In this case they were changed as part of electoral battles between local growth coalitions and ordinary citizens in the years between 1870 and 1920. The end result was a defeat for average voters in a majority of cities, which made American politics even more atypical among Western democracies and rendered the Democratic Party even less useful as an organizational base for labor unions and their liberal allies.

When American cities were small and relatively homogeneous, and not everyone could vote, they were easily dominated by the local well-to-do. In the second half of the nineteenth century, as the country urbanized and new immigrants poured into the cities to become industrial workers, the situation changed dramatically. Ethnic-based political machines, usually affiliated with the Democratic Party, came to dominate many city governments. In the early twentieth century, these machine Democrats were sometimes joined by members of the Socialist Party formed in 1900. In 1912, the high point of Socialist electoral success, the party elected 1,200 members in 340 cities across the country, including 79 mayors in 24 different states. There were also 20 Socialists in nine different state legislatures, with Wisconsin (7), Kansas (3), and Illinois (3) heading the list.[26]

The local growth coalitions were deeply upset by these defeats. They claimed ethnic machines were raising taxes, appointing their supporters to government jobs, and giving lucrative government contracts to their friends. Even when the established growth coalitions could reach an accommodation with the machines by joining them as financial supporters—as they very frequently did—they also worked to undercut them through a series of "reforms" and "good government" strategies that gradually took shape over a thirty-year period. Although the reforms were presented as efforts to eliminate corruption, reduce costs, and improve efficiency, they in fact made it more difficult for Democrats and Socialists to hold on to elected positions. These reforms and their effects are as follows:

1. *Off-year elections*. It was argued that local elections should not be held in the same year as national elections because city issues are different, but what this reform did was to break the many

policy connections between local and national levels while at the same time reducing voter turnout for local elections, thereby favoring conservative candidates.

2. *Nonpartisan elections*. It was claimed that parties should not play a role at the local level because the citizens of a community have common interests that should not be overshadowed by partisan politics. This reform made it necessary for candidates to increase their name recognition because voters could no longer rely on labels like "Democrat" or "Socialist" to identify those candidates with whom they sympathized.

3. *Citywide elections*. It was argued that city districts (wards) did not have the same usefulness they do at the congressional level because the problems facing members of a city council involve the city as a whole and not separate neighborhoods. The net effect of this reform was to make it more difficult for neighborhood leaders—whether Democrats, Socialists, or ethnic and racial minorities—to hold their seats on city councils because they did not have the money and name recognition to win citywide elections.

4. *Elimination of salaries for city council members*. It was argued that serving on a city council should be a civic service done in a volunteer fashion in order to eliminate corruption and self-serving motives for seeking office. The effect of this reform was to make it more difficult for average-income people to serve on city councils because they could not afford to do so.

5. *Creation of a city-manager form of government*. It was claimed that a city is like a corporation and the city council like a corporate board of directors, so the city council should set general policy and then turn the management of the city over to a trained professional called a "city manager." By requiring the votes of five of the seven council members, the proposed model charters for city-manager governments made it difficult to replace city managers. The effect of this reform was to increase the power of upper-middle-class professionals who were natural allies of the growth coalitions through training in special university programs (financed by several large foundations) and later work experience.

Most of these reforms, along with civil service protection for government employees and competitive bidding on government contracts, were packaged and publicized by a national-level policy-planning organization, the National Municipal League. Formed in 1894 by 150 city developers, lawyers, political scientists, and urban planners from twenty-one cities in thirteen states, the organization embodied many years of experimenting with reform efforts in various cities. It did not have many successes beyond civil-service protection and competitive bidding until the early 1900s, when the city-manager idea reached its final form. After that point, its successes were sudden and dramatic. Riding a call for unity between the two major parties in the face of large gains by Socialists in 1908 and 1912, it then capitalized on the fear and patriotism created by World War I, branding the Socialists as antiwar traitors, disrupting their meetings, and removing their newspapers from the U.S. mail. By 1919, the reformers had been able to implement their model charter in 130 cities and could claim partial successes in many more.[27]

The reform movement continued to make gains in the next several decades. A large-scale survey conducted in 1991 revealed that 75 percent of American cities have nonpartisan elections, making that reform the most successful in the entire array. Over 90 percent of cities west of the Rocky Mountains used nonpartisan elections, but only 12 percent in the states of New York, New Jersey, and Pennsylvania did so, reflecting the entrenched nature of machine politics in areas with a long political history. In addition, 59 percent of cities used citywide ("at-large") elections, compared to only 12 percent that relied exclusively on the old ward system. The other 29 percent used a combination of citywide and ward representation. Finally, 52 percent of cities had adopted either the council-manager or commission form of government recommended by the reformers, abandoning the election of a "strong" mayor who presided over the city council and had responsibility for city employees. Most of the resistance to council-manager government came from large cities with strong Democratic Party organizations.[28]

Despite the partial failures in big cities, the goals of the good-government movement were achieved. The direct connections between local and national government were obscured, making it possible for leaders of the growth coalition to sound plausible when they claimed their goal at the local level was to create jobs, while at the same time opposing any legislation at the national level that actually might help create more jobs. Most importantly, the local branches of the two major parties were eliminated in half of all American cities, removing city councils as a training ground for liberal-labor candidates and making it harder to create a comprehensive liberal-labor program.

None of this came as a surprise to the leaders of the reform movement. They clearly wanted to reclaim cities for what they thought of as the "better class" of citizens. Some of them openly questioned the right of ordinary citizens to vote at the local level, claiming that those who did not own property should not be able to raise taxes on property holders. As a noted historian and reform advocate of the nineteenth century, Francis Parkman, put it in 1878, "indiscriminate suffrage" was putting an "ignorant proletariat" in seats of power.[29] Nor is it speculation to say that the various reforms reduced voter turnout. A quantitative study comparing cities that had adopted one, two, or three of the basic reforms showed that each of the reforms reduced voter turnout.[30]

Moreover, the electoral results were there for all to see. From a point before World War I when thousands of blue-collar and lower white-collar workers were serving on city councils, by the 1940s there were very few such people being elected. Businesspeople, often legitimated for office by service on well-publicized committees of the local Chamber of Commerce, were the overwhelming presence on most city councils. They were also the most frequent appointees to the non-elected boards and commissions that mattered most to the local growth coalitions: planning and zoning commissions, off-street parking authorities, water boards, and other local entities concerned with municipal infrastructure or retail sales.[31]

At the same time, a municipal policy-formation network was developed to complement the National Municipal League. It began with bureaus of municipal research funded by wealthy citizens and foundations, then was supplemented by associations for city managers, county officials, and planners. In the 1930s the organizations were brought together in Chicago with money from various Rockefeller foundations so they could interface with experts at the University of Chicago. Many of these organizations moved to Washington in the 1960s to become part of an "urban lobby" as the importance of federal spending and rule-making increased.[32]

The net result of the local reforms and the national-level policy network is that there are very few cities where the growth coalition does not dominate city government through success in the electoral arena and advice from the policy network. The results from studies of local power structures from the 1950s to 1970s were so strikingly similar that most social scientists lost interest in doing them.[33] The few exceptions were in unique university towns like Santa Cruz, California, where the votes and other resources of students, faculty, and alumni led to an alternative power group that defeated the growth coalition on every major initiative after the 26th Amendment gave the vote to 18-year-olds in 1971; in suburban and retirement cities for the well-to-do; and in small towns and urban neighborhoods where an environmental justice movement—often led by women and minorities—was able to resist the creation of chemical dumps and waste treatment plants.[34]

One of the few studies claiming pluralism at the local level—an examination of New Haven, Connecticut, by Dahl, Polsby, and Raymond

Wolfinger—received wide acclaim and many prizes when it appeared in 1961 and was frequently put forward as evidence for the pluralistic nature of power in the United States in general.[35] But that study turned out to be flawed, as shown by subsequent research in the archives of Yale University, the Chamber of Commerce, and key city planners. The local growth coalition and Yale University, contrary to the original research team's conclusions, were in fact the guiding force in the urban renewal program that was the centerpiece of the study. Even the emphasis on local politicians as extraordinary public entrepreneurs in bringing federal money to New Haven was incorrect. Connecticut in general received more money per capita than any other state, reflecting recent hurricane damage and the efforts of one of the state's Republican senators, an investment banker and Yale trustee who served as head of the Senate committee that oversaw the urban renewal program. Moreover, political scientist Heywood Sanders later discovered in federal archives that every city in the country that applied for money actually received it, so no special credit can go to any local politicians or planners for "winning" a grant.[36]

The success of the growth coalitions, despite challenges by neighborhoods and environmentalists, demonstrates that power is not only a matter of economic resources and the deployment of expertise. It is also a matter of having electoral and governmental structures that can be dominated by the use of such resources. When the changing circumstances of the nineteenth century revealed that the existing governmental structures could not be dominated in the traditional ways, it became necessary for place entrepreneurs to create new ones that could be insulated from the Democratic and Socialist Parties. It took the National Municipal League and its predecessors thirty years to develop a comprehensive plan, and several more years to implement it, but the historical record and power structure studies since the 1920s show that the reformers managed to realize a great many of their goals in all but a few large cities.

THE CRITICAL IMPORTANCE OF CAMPAIGN FINANCE

In a system in which policy preferences become blurred for the structural and historical reasons explained in earlier sections of this chapter, the emphasis on the personality and image of the individual candidate becomes very great. In fact, personalities often become more important than policies, even though there is good reason from voting studies to believe that many voters are more concerned about policies that affect their everyday well-being than they are about personalities.[37] This tendency to reduce politics to a personality contest has been increased somewhat with the rise of the mass media—in particular television—but it has existed far longer than is understood by the many columnists and pundits who lament the "recent" decline of political parties.

Because the candidate-selection process in the American two-party system is relatively individualistic, and therefore dependent on name recognition and personal image, it can be in good part dominated by members of the power elite through the simple and direct means of large campaign contributions. Serving as both big donors and fund-raisers, the same people who direct corporations and take part in policy groups play a central role in the careers of most politicians who advance beyond the local level in states of any size and consequence. "Recruitment of elective elites," concludes political scientist Walter D. Burnham, "remains closely associated, especially for the most important offices in the larger states, with the candidates' wealth or access to large campaign contributions."[38]

The roles of wealthy donor and fund-raiser are crucial in the nomination phase of the process. This was the conclusion of one of the earliest systematic studies of campaign finance, which saw money as the choke point in the electoral process:

> The necessity for obtaining essential election funds has its most profound importance in the choosing of candidates. The monies can usually be assured, and often can be withheld, by the relatively small corps of political specialists whose job it is to raise money. As a consequence, money probably has its greatest impact on the choice of public officials in the shadow land of our politics where it is decided who will be a candidate for a party's nomination and who will not be. There are many things that make an effective candidate, but there is a *choke point* [my italics] in our politics where vital fiscal encouragement can be extended or withheld.[39]

This insight, based on research conducted in the 1950s, is supported by the evidence from every decade since that time. In fact, the increased use of polling, focus groups, television commercials, computerized mailings, and political consultants has made campaigning even more expensive, especially in party primaries. "Because of its ability to buy the kinds of services that produce name recognition and exposition of positions," writes campaign finance analyst Herbert E. Alexander, "money wields its greatest influence on campaigns during the prenomination period."[40]

The money for political campaigns is provided by a relative handful of people. In 1996, for example, only 4 percent made a contribution of any size at any level of government, and only .25 percent gave $200 or more. The .25 percent who gave $200 or more provided

80 percent of all political money. As might be expected, most of the big donors are wealthy business executives and lawyers. Combining donations to individual candidates and to political action committees (explained in the next paragraph), a study of campaign finance for 1994 estimated that total corporate contributions were $289 million compared to $42 million from organized labor, a ratio of 6.9 to 1.[41]

Several reforms in campaign finance laws during the 1970s restricted the size of donations by large contributors at the national level, but those reforms did not diminish the influence of the corporate community. If anything, they increased it quite inadvertently. Before 1975, a handful of owners and executives would give tens or hundreds of thousands of dollars to candidates of interest to them. Now they organize luncheons and dinners at which all of their colleagues and friends are asked to give a few thousand dollars each to specific candidates and party finance committees. Corporate leaders also form what are called political action committees (PACs), which are simply committees set up to provide donations to candidates, political parties, and other PACs. Coporations can ask their shareholders and executives to give up to $5,000 each year to a PAC, which means in effect that wealthy donors are able to give twice—once directly to the individual, once through a PAC. Business associations, professional societies, and unions also organize PACs.

The largest PAC donors for 1994 are listed in table 6.1. Over half of these top PACs are maintained by unions. This is an impressive showing for the unions, but the fact remains that corporate PACs gave a total of $131 million in 1994—$67 million to the Democrats, $64 million to the Republicans—whereas union PACs gave only $42 million—$40 million to Democrats and $2 million to Republicans. Moreover, very few union members give individual contributions, which is why the corporate rich outspent unions by such a great amount in 1994.[42]

A detailed analysis by sociologists Alan Neustadtl, Denise Scott, and Dan Clawson of PAC donation patterns provides strong evidence that the differences between the corporate-conservative and liberal-labor coalitions are present in the electoral process. They found that corporate and conservative PACs usually supported one set of candidates, and liberal and labor PACs a different set.[43] Other studies of PAC donations by these researchers show that corporate PACs almost never oppose each other. They may not all give to the same candidate, but they seldom give to two different candidates in the same race. This evidence based on clustering techniques has been supplemented by their interviews with PAC executives, which revealed that there is indeed a large amount of coordination among corporate PACs. Furthermore, their studies reveal that when corporate PACs support a

Table 6.1 The 50 Largest PAC Contributors to the 1994 Elections

Rank	Contributor	Total	% to Democrats	% to Republicans
1	United Parcel Service	$2,661,515	51	49
2	American Medical Association	2,547,956	42	58
3	Teamsters Union	2,542,203	97	3
4	American Federation of State/County/ Municipal Employees	2,529,827	98	2
5	National Education Association	2,271,938	98	1
6	United Auto Workers	2,165,390	99	1
7	Association of Trial Lawyers of America	2,161,535	94	6
8	National Association of Realtors	1,853,578	54	46
9	National Rifle Association	1,853,538	22	78
10	National Auto Dealers Association	1,822,570	30	70
11	American Institute of CPAs	1,739,520	50	50
12	Machinists/Aerospace Workers	1,717,881	99	1
13	International Brotherhood of Electrical Workers	1,663,975	98	1
14	American Bankers Association	1,507,860	46	54
15	Marine Engineers Union	1,487,481	72	28
16	Carpenters Union	1,474,400	96	3
17	Laborers Union	1,473,684	95	4
18	Food & Commercial Workers Union	1,456,139	98	2
19	National Association of Letter Carriers	1,444,410	93	7
20	AT&T	1,372,007	59	41
21	National Association of Life Underwriters	1,346,340	48	52

Table 6.1 *(continued)*

Rank	Contributor	Total	% to Democrats	% to Republicans
22	National Association of Home Builders	1,336,699	36	64
23	American Federation of Teachers	1,294,190	99	1
24	National Beer Wholesalers Association	1,248,724	23	77
25	United Transportation Union	1,236,855	95	4
26	AFL-CIO	1,225,127	98	2
27	American Dental Association	1,191,997	52	48
28	Communications Workers of America	1,095,173	99	0
29	American Nurses Association	1,085,008	91	8
30	American Hospital Association	1,073,513	66	34
31	United Steelworkers	1,040,262	99	0
32	Airline Pilots Association	1,014,286	85	15
33	National Association Retired Federal Employees	996,500	89	10
34	RJR Nabisco	933,425	46	54
35	Service Employees International Union	896,694	98	2
36	American Academy of Ophthalmology	877,155	60	40
37	MBNA Corp (banking company)	868,055	7	93
38	League of Conservation Voters	840,805	95	4
39	Federal Express Corp	835,950	69	31
40	Plumbers/Pipefitters Union	828,110	96	4
41	Sheet Metal Workers Union	781,300	98	1

42	National Committee for an Effective Congress	780,499	100	0
43	Associated Milk Producers	779,231	76	24
44	Philip Morris	771,591	59	41
45	Americans for Free International Trade	770,700	23	77
46	American Postal Workers Union	751,185	96	4
47	General Motors	747,572	60	40
48	Seafarers International Union	745,894	90	10
49	BellSouth Corp	730,346	50	50
50	Associated General Contractors	714,047	19	81

Source: *Open Secrets* (Washington, DC: Common Cause, 1995), p. 28.

Note: Percentages do not total to 100% in all cases due to rounding errors.

Democrat it is usually (1) because the Democrat is a moderate or conservative, and most often from the South or a rural area; (2) to maintain access to a Democrat who sits on a congressional committee that is important to the corporation; or (3) as a favor to another corporation that wants to maintain access to the Democrat.[44]

The restrictions on the size of individual donations—and on direct donations from corporate revenues—were in effect lifted in 1979 when the Federal Election Commission ruled that unrestricted donations to state parties for "party building" were permissible as long as the money was not used to support a particular candidate by name. In practice, this distinction boils down to the fact that the party's candidate cannot be named even though his or her opponent can be named (and pilloried). This "soft money," as it came to be known, gradually reached the level of $89 million in 1992, then jumped to $263.5 million in 1996. In 1996, 92 percent of soft money came from business leaders and their corporations, 5 percent from organized labor, and 3 percent from other sources.[45] Table 6.2 lists the biggest soft money donors for 1996. Once again, unions are represented at the top levels even though they are outspent overall.

The large amount of money spent in campaigns is a source of great concern to liberal reformers, who try to use the issue to win more voters to their causes. As part of their reform package, some of

Table 6.2 The 50 Largest Soft Money Contributors to the 1996 Elections

Rank	Contributor	Total	% to Democrats	% to Republicans
1	Philip Morris	$3,017,036	16.5	83.5
2	Joseph E. Seagram & Sons	1,938,845	65.1	34.9
3	RJR Nabisco	1,442,931	17.7	82.3
4	Walt Disney	1,359,500	78.2	21.8
5	Atlantic Richfield	1,250,843	38.9	61.1
6	American Federation of State/County/ Municipal Employees	1,134,962	100.0	0.0
7	Communications Workers of America	1,130,300	100.0	0.0
8	AT&T	974,524	43.3	56.7
9	Federal Express	973,525	60.9	39.1
10	MCI Telecommunications	964,514	63.0	37.0
11	Association of Trial Lawyers of America	803,400	75.5	24.5
12	Lazard Freres & Co	787,600	79.3	20.7
13	Revlon Group	763,250	81.7	18.3
14	Anheuser-Busch	761,057	52.7	47.3
15	Eli Lilly & Co	746,835	32.1	67.9
16	Food & Commercial Workers Union	727,550	100.0	0.0
17	Time Warner	726,250	55.2	44.8
18	Chevron Corp	702,306	25.1	74.9
19	Archer-Daniels-Midland	700,000	42.1	57.9
20	Enron Corp	686,900	20.7	79.3
21	US Tobacco Co	674,965	17.5	82.5
22	News Corp	674,700	3.0	97.0
23	NYNEX Corp	651,602	36.9	63.1
24	Textron Inc	648,000	42.4	57.6
25	American Financial Corp	645,000	17.8	82.2

26	Goldman, Sachs & Co	644,685	84.1	15.9
27	Brown & Williamson Tobacco	642,500	1.2	98.8
28	Laborers Union	634,588	98.8	1.2
29	Loral Corp	632,000	95.2	4.8
30	Integrated Health Services	609,000	94.3	5.7
31	Northwest Airlines	584,445	56.0	44.0
32	Entergy Corp	581,975	50.9	49.1
33	Blue Cross & Blue Shield	577,688	24.2	75.8
34	WMX Technologies	576,500	32.5	67.5
35	Paine Webber	560,750	27.8	72.2
36	Bristol-Myers Squibb	552,400	20.7	79.3
37	Bank of America	546,789	35.3	64.7
38	Travelers Groups Inc	539,944	36.9	63.1
39	Tele-Communications Inc	533,950	24.3	75.7
40	Tobacco Institute	530,839	20.0	80.0
41	DreamWorks SKG	530,000	100.0	0.0
42	Milberg, Weiss (law firm)	530,000	100.0	0.0
43	Coca-Cola Co	519,740	31.2	68.8
44	Pfizer	511,895	19.6	80.4
45	Glaxo Wellcome Inc	510,000	9.1	90.9
46	General Motors	503,325	15.3	84.7
47	Public Securities Association	494,102	39.4	60.6
48	American Federation of Teachers	486,668	100.0	0.0
49	Occidental Petroleum	486,350	53.6	46.4
50	Flo-Sun Inc	478,000	42.8	57.2

Source: Web Site, Center for Responsive Politics, June 1997.

Note: Five cases in which reporting errors may have been made are replaced with organizations 51 through 55 on the original list.

them call for the abolition of PACs, but that makes their allies in organized labor very uneasy. Although labor is greatly outspent by business in most elections, union leaders believe that the little influence they have would be dissipated if they were not allowed to accumulate a war chest and then make donations to a few favored candidates. Similarly, several successful campaigns by women have been at least in part due to the collection of funds by feminist PACs, so women activists are also wary of new restrictions on how money is raised.

If past experience is any indication, then the unintended effects of any campaign finance reforms that eliminate PACs or limit individual donations to candidates are likely to favor the corporate rich unless there is public financing of all campaigns, which is highly unlikely. Limits on donations or spending probably would have the following effects:

(1) There might be more millionaire and multimillionaire candidates because the Supreme Court ruled in 1976 that it is unconstitutional to keep people from spending their own money on their campaigns, on the grounds that any limitations would interfere with their right of free speech.

(2) There would be greater importance for groups that can stage events for which potential candidates could receive payment for speeches. If, for example, a potential candidate could receive hundreds of thousands of dollars for speeches to corporations and trade associations—which is already a common occurrence—then she or he would have more personal money to spend on campaigns.

(3) There would be greater importance for groups that have the money to run independent support campaigns for a candidate, which cannot be restricted (on the grounds of free speech) as long as the groups do not coordinate their efforts with the candidate. This means greater power for groups that are unaccountable to either the candidate or the electorate. Corporations and trade associations probably would be the main beneficiaries, but organized labor could run such campaigns as well. In fact, the AFL-CIO spent $35 million in this fashion to support the Democratic Party in 1996.[46]

Given the problems of creating effective campaign finance reforms that are both constitutional and acceptable to a congressional majority, it seems likely that large donations will remain an essential part of the electoral system, and that means a continuing role for members of the corporate community and the upper class. Generally speaking, Republican candidates outspend Democrats by anywhere from 2:1 to 6:1 on individual and PAC contributions, but the important point from a class-domination view is that both sides are dependent on wealthy donors. Republican domination holds for soft money as well. In 1996, the Republicans raised $141.2 million in soft money, the Democrats $122.3 million. Republican donations came primarily from corporations and wealthy individuals; Democratic donations came from organized labor, corporations, and wealthy individuals.[47]

In short, campaign donations from members of the corporate community and upper class are a central element in determining who enters politics with any hope of winning a nomination. Campaign money is not the only element in the political process, as studies of high-spending losers reveal, but it is an essential one given the nature of the two-party system and the need for name recognition. It is the need for a large amount of start-up money—to travel around the district or the country, to send out large mailings, to schedule radio and television time in advance—that gives members of the power elite a very direct role in the process right from the beginning and thereby provides them with personal access to politicians of both parties. Even if they do not tie specific strings to their monies—as they often do not—they are able to ensure a hearing for their views and to work against those candidates whom they do not consider sensible and approachable.[48]

OTHER FINANCIAL SUPPORT FOR CANDIDATES

As important as money is in the electoral process, there are numerous other methods besides campaign donations by which members of the corporate community can give support to politicians. One of the most direct is to give them corporate stock or to purchase property from them at a price well above the market value. In 1966, for example, just this kind of favor was done for a future president, Ronald Reagan, shortly after he became governor of California. Twentieth-Century-Fox purchased several hundred acres of his land adjacent to its large outdoor set in Malibu for nearly $2 million, triple its assessed market value and thirty times what he had paid for it in 1952. The land was never utilized and later was sold to the state. This transaction—along with $20,000-an-appearance speeches to business and conservative groups—gave Reagan the financial security to devote full time to his political career. In another example, the Republican presidential candidate in 1996, Senator Robert Dole of Kansas, earned $800,000 speaking to business groups while he was a senator, a road to wealth that is now barred for Senate members.[49]

A very direct method of benefiting the many politicians who are lawyers is to hire them or their law firms as legal consultants or to provide them with routine legal business. Corporations can be especially helpful to lawyer-politicians when they are between offices. The chair of *Encyclopedia Britannica*, a campaign fund-raiser for Democratic presidential candidate Adlai E. Stevenson throughout the 1950s, hired Stevenson as a director and consultant between 1952 and 1964. Then he did the same thing for former vice president and Democratic presidential hopeful Hubert Humphrey between 1968 and 1970.[50] Similarly, the chair of Pepsico retained former vice president and future Republican president Richard M. Nixon as the company's lawyer after 1963 and thereafter paid for every trip Nixon made overseas in the next two years. This made it possible for Nixon to remain in the political limelight as a foreign-policy expert.[51]

Other methods are used to support nonlawyers when they are out of office. Jack Kemp, a member of Congress for 18 years and the Republican's vice presidential candidate in 1996, receives $136,000 a year as a Fellow of the Heritage Foundation. In addition, he earned more than a million dollars lecturing to business groups from 1992 through 1995, and he receives $100,000 a year as a director of six corporations while he works toward the Republican presidential nomination in the year 2000.[52]

THE RESULTS OF THE CANDIDATE-SELECTION PROCESS

What kinds of elected officials emerge from a political process that puts such great attention on campaign finance and media recognition? The answer emerges from numerous studies. First, politicians are from the top 10 to 15 percent of the occupational and income ladders, especially those who hold the highest elective offices. Only a minority are from the upper class or corporate community, but in a majority of cases elected officials share in common a business and legal background with members of the upper class.[53]

Second, a great many elected officials in the United States are lawyers. In 1996, for example, 53 percent of the senators and 40 percent of the representatives were lawyers, and the percentages are even higher for earlier times and in most state legislatures. Twenty-seven of the first forty-one American presidents were lawyers.[54] The large percentage of lawyers in the American political system is highly atypical when compared with other countries, where only 10 to 30 percent of legislators have a legal background. Insight into this overrepresentation is provided by comparing the United States with a deviant case at the other extreme, Denmark, where only 2 percent of legislators are lawyers. The class-based nature of Danish politics since the late nineteenth century—and the fact that political careers are not pathways to judicial appointments—is thought to discourage lawyer participation in that country. The Danish situation thus suggests that the marginalization of class issues by the two main American political parties—combined with the intimate involvement of the parties in the judicial system—creates a climate for strong lawyer involvement in the political system.[55]

Whatever the reasons for their involvement, lawyers are the occupational grouping that by training and career needs is the ideal go-between and compromiser. They have the skills to balance the relationship between the corporate community that finances them on the one hand and the citizens who vote for them on the other. They are the supreme "pragmatists" in a nation that prides itself on a pragmatic and can-do ideology. They have an ability to be dispassionate about the issues and to discuss them in legalistic ways that are often impressive and disarming to the uninitiated. They have been socialized to be discreet, and they can claim the cloak of lawyer-client privilege when questioned about work for their clients that seems to overlap their political activities. In network analysis terms, they are the "brokers" who link two separate networks—namely, the corporate-conservative and liberal-labor coalitions.

Whether elected officials are lawyers or not, the third general result of the candidate-selection process is a large number of very ambitious people who are eager to "go along to get along," in the famous advice of Texas Democrat Sam Rayburn, Speaker of the House from 1940 to 1961, when the Democrats were in the majority. To understand the behavior of a politician, concludes political scientist Joseph A. Schlesinger, "it is more important to know what he wants to be than how he got to where he is now."[56] This ambition, whether it be for wealth or higher office, makes politicians especially available to those who can help them realize their goals. Such people are often members of the corporate community or upper class who have money to contribute and connections to other districts, states, or regions where striving candidates need new friends. Thus, even the most liberal or ultraconservative of politicians may develop a new circle of moderate supporters as they move from the local to the congressional to the presidential level, gradually becoming more and more involved with leading figures within the power elite.

The fourth generalization about successful political candidates is that they are either conservative or silent on the highly emotional social issues. Basically, very few candidates can win if their views on such issues fall outside the limits that have been set by the actions and television advertising of the New Right. As long as 75 percent of the people say they believe in the death penalty, for example, and a significant minority of fervent single-issue voters oppose strict gun control laws, it is unlikely that anyone who openly challenges these beliefs can be elected to any office except in a few liberal districts and cities. Here, then, is an instance in which public opinion has a direct effect on the

Table 6.3 Potential Strength of the Conservative Voting Bloc in the House and Senate in Selected Years Between 1933 and 1980

	% Potential Conservative Voting Bloc	
Year	*House*	*Senate*
1933	54	64
1935	51	53
1937	47	44
1939	66	51
1949	67	71
1959	60	59
1965	55	54
1975	54	56
1977	54	57
1980	57	60

Source: Mack C. Shelley II, *The Permanent Majority: The Conservative Coalition in the United States* (Montgomery, AL: University of Alabama Press, 1983), pp. 140–143.

behavior of candidates and elected officials, even though it is also true that most voters make their voting decisions based on their party identification and degree of satisfaction with the state of the economy.[57]

The fifth general finding, alluded to earlier in the chapter, is that the majority of elected officials at the national level are part of the conservative voting bloc. This point is demonstrated most readily in table 6.3, which lists the percentage of House and Senate members who were potential members of this bloc in selected years from 1933 to 1980. The only years the figures dropped below 50 percent were 1937 and 1938 in the wake of President Roosevelt's landslide victory in 1936. During that rare two-year period, the long-standing rule of selecting committee chairs on the basis of their number of years on the committee (the seniority system), along with several other procedural devices, kept the liberal-labor coalition at bay. In the mid-1960s the liberal-labor coalition and centrists almost equaled the conservatives in voting strength, but the important civil rights laws of that period were nonetheless due to support from Northern Republicans in the face of domestic turmoil.

The conservative voting bloc became somewhat less important in the 1980s and 1990s as Republicans replaced Southern Democrats in both the House and Senate. Even so, conservative Southern Democrats were essential to Reagan's large tax cuts in 1981 and to stopping spending initiatives and defense cuts in the first Clinton Administration. As late as 1996, with the Republicans in control of both houses of Congress, and conservative Southern Democrats accounting for less than thirty votes, the conservative voting coalition formed on 11.7 percent of the congressional votes and was successful 98.9 percent of the time. It had fifty-one victories and no defeats in the House, thirty-seven victories and one defeat in the Senate. The Southern Democratic votes were essential to thirty-three of the fifty-one victories in the House and nineteen of the thirty-seven victories in the Senate, offsetting defections by the handful of moderate Republicans from the Northeast who are still in office despite ultraconservative challenges in primaries and a drift to the Democrats by centrist Northeastern voters.[58]

The Log Cabin Myth

Since at least the 1830s, according to careful biographical research by historian Edward Pessen, presidential candidates have tended to claim they are from far more humble financial circumstances than is actually the case. Their claims are usually taken at face value in the mass media and textbooks. Pessen calls this tendency the "log cabin myth" because of the several nineteenth-century presidents who falsely claimed to have lived in log cabins at one time or another. This myth is the political equivalent of the Horatio Alger story in the realm of business. Contrary to the myth, most of the presidents were wealthy or connected to wealth by the time they became president. George Washington was one of the richest men of his day, partly through inheritance, partly through marriage. Andrew Jackson, allegedly of humble circumstances but raised in a well-to-do slave-holding family because his father died before he was born, became even more wealthy as an adult. He "dealt in slaves, made hundreds of thousands of dollars and accumulated hundreds of thousands of valuable acres in land speculation, owned racehorses and racetracks, bought cotton gins, distilleries, and plantations, was a successful merchant, and married extremely well."[59] Abraham Lincoln was a corporate lawyer for railroads and married into a wealthy Kentucky family.

Few twentieth-century presidents have been from outside the very wealthiest circles. Theodore Roosevelt, William H. Taft, Franklin D. Roosevelt, John F. Kennedy, and George Bush were from upper-class backgrounds. Herbert Hoover, Jimmy Carter, and Ronald Reagan were millionaires before they became deeply involved in national politics. Lyndon B. Johnson was a millionaire several times over through his wife's land dealings and his use of political leverage to gain a lucrative television license in Austin, Texas. Even Richard M. Nixon, whose father ran a small store, was a rich man when he finally attained the presidency in 1968, after earning high salaries as a corporate lawyer between 1963 and 1968.

Bill Clinton: The Prototypical Politician

Bill Clinton, elected president in 1992 and 1996, is the ideal example of an American politician on every dimension that has been discussed in this chapter. First, he is a frequent user of the "log cabin" myth, claiming that he is just a poor boy from little Hope, Arkansas, born of a widowed mother. But Clinton left Hope, where he lived in comfortable circumstances with his grandparents, by the age of 6 when his mother married Roger Clinton, whose family owned a car dealership in the nearby tourist town of Hot Springs. He grew up playing golf at the local country club and drove a Buick convertible, taking it to college with him when he entered Georgetown University in Washington, D.C. His mother sent him money throughout his years in college.

Clinton's ambition for political office manifested itself by the time he was 16. He had his eyes set on the presidency by his early 20s and always calibrated his behavior with that goal in mind. He was a glad-hander who befriended everyone and kept a name-and-address file that had grown to thousands of listings by 1978, when he was elected governor of his native state. He was careful in his opinions. Contrary to claims by his ultraconservative critics, he took virtually no part in the antiwar movement in the 1960s. His ambition took precedence over his policy preferences.

Clinton is also a typical American politician in that he has a law degree, but it was clear to his classmates at Yale University that he never intended to practice law. He simply knew that a law degree was the best union card for a political candidate. While at Yale he spent more time working for political campaigns than he did studying.

Clinton's political success is first and foremost based on his ability to gain the enthusiastic support of people who believe in him, or who believe he has the ability to rise to higher office and take them with him as appointees. Many people find him charismatic or charming, and he is a good listener who makes people feel he cares about them. Building on this kind of base, which is an essential starting point for most politicians who succeed, he gained the financial backing of the wealthiest people in his state because of his party loyalty and pragmatic approach. Throughout the 1980s he cultivated large donors outside Arkansas in preparation for his bid for the presidency.

During his first presidential campaign, Clinton cleverly defused the social issues that often foil Democrats. He pointedly distanced himself from civil rights leader Jesse Jackson while quietly befriending local African-American leaders in the South. He went to church regularly and was often photographed holding a Bible. He returned to Arkansas during the 1992 primary campaign for a state execution in order to highlight his support for the death penalty, which he had opposed in his college years. He made it clear that he was not an opponent of gun owners by going duck hunting.[60]

Once in the White House, Clinton showed he had no great commitment to any particular issue, another typical trait of most successful political leaders in the United States. On the other hand, he showed the ability to build coalitions, create compromises, and accept defeat on specific legislation. He is successful because he is able to accommodate the corporate rich on their key issues, say and do what is necessary to win elections, and develop legislative packages that can win majorities in Congress. While such qualities are always lamented by the commentators of the day, it is compromises and symbolic gestures that maintain the social system.

WHO REPRESENTS AMERICA?

Studies of the social backgrounds and occupations of members of Congress have consistently shown that they come from the highest levels of society and are involved in the business and legal communities. A study of the Congress for 1972, for example, found that 66 percent of the senators and 74 percent of the representatives came from the 10 percent of families with business or professional occupations and that virtually all of the senators and representatives were themselves professional people or former business executives. Twenty percent of the senators and 5 percent of a sample of representatives were members of the upper class. Only 5 percent of the senators had been farmers or ranchers; none had been blue-collar workers. Three percent of the representatives had been farmers or ranchers, and 3 percent had union backgrounds. A comparison of these findings with a study of the Senate in the mid-1950s and the House in the early 1940s showed that there had been very little change over that time span, except for a decrease in the number of farmers and a slight increase in the number of professionals and business executives.[61]

The stringent financial disclosure laws adopted by Congress in the mid-1970s in the aftermath of Watergate and other scandals provided detailed information on the wealth and income of senators and representatives for 1978, but changes in the law since that time make the annual wealth and income reports less useful because each type of ownership and income is reported separately and the size categories are very general. In 1978, the highest point on the ownership scale was "over $5 million" in the Senate and "over $250,000" in the House.

Even so, it was clear that nineteen members of the Senate were millionaires that year, ten from the Republican side and nine from the Democratic. It was possible that another thirteen or fourteen were also millionaires, but the general categories did not permit accurate assessment in their cases.[62]

The less complete information on House members for 1978 was still revealing in that one-third of House members had outside jobs, many in real estate or as bank directors, and 460 had income from stock or rent from real estate. At least 30 representatives were millionaires, and nearly 100 had outside incomes of $20,000 or more. The conclusions drawn by the editors of *Congressional Quarterly* from this information are similar to those reached by the authors of earlier studies: "With few exceptions, members of Congress were successful lawyers or businessmen before coming to Washington. Most members kept and expanded their lucrative financial investments after election to Congress."[63]

Although there are no systematic studies of the social and occupational backgrounds of members of Congress since the late 1970s—partly because the information available is less exact, partly because most social scientists assume that little has changed since the earlier studies—it seems likely that those who took office in the 1990s are even richer than previous members of Congress. For example, a review of the disclosure forms for 1994 by one journalist suggested that at least twenty-eight members of the Senate and fifty members of the House were millionaires, with many other likely millionaires in both houses.[64] A study of the occupational backgrounds of members of the new Congress for 1997 showed that the number of business executives, bankers, and realtors in the House had risen to 204, surpassing the number of lawyers for the first time, who fell to 172. Fifty-eight of the businesspeople are Democrats, 146 are Republicans; the lawyers are split about evenly between the two parties. In the Senate there are now 41 members in the business/banker/realtor category and 53 lawyers. Ten of the 41 businesspeople are Democrats, 31 are Republicans, and the lawyers are once again evenly balanced between the two parties. There is one former union official in the House, and none in the Senate.[65]

As pluralists are quick to point out, most of the members of Congress—whether businesspeople or not—are from the middle and upper-middle classes, not the upper class. But that misses the point when it comes to the political arena: A majority of them are part of the corporate-conservative coalition on foreign policy and economic issues, which is why they receive enough financial support from the corporate rich to survive party primaries and run viable campaigns in the general election. Those business-oriented members who are

Table 6.4 The Demographics of the Progressive Caucus in Comparison to All Democrats and Republicans in the House, 1997–1998

	Progressive Caucus	Democrats	Republicans
% female	23.6	17.0	7.0
% non-Anglo minority[1]	50.9	25.7	2.2
% African-American	38.2	17.5	0.4
% Latino	10.9	7.3	1.3
% Asian-American	1.8	1.0	0.4

Source: My calculations from the *Congressional Yellow Book* (Washington, DC: Leadership Directories, Inc., 1997).

[1]The phrase "non-Anglo minority" is used instead of "non-white minority" because most Latinos are Caucasians. The percentages for African-Americans, Latinos, and Asian-Americans do not equal the "% non-Anglo minority" due to rounding errors.

Republicans are sometimes highly conservative on social issues, whereas the businesspeople who are Democrats are likely to vote with the liberals on feminist and civil rights issues.

In terms of electoral evidence for pluralism, the Progressive Caucus created in the House in 1997 is of much greater interest than class backgrounds. It consists of fifty-five members with voting rights and three nonvoting delegates from the District of Columbia, Puerto Rico, and American Samoa. The existence of the caucus symbolizes the willingness of 12.6 percent of House members to allow voters to identify them with the concerns of organized labor and liberal causes. Generally speaking, the fifty-five caucus members with voting rights in the House are very different from the rest of the House in terms of their social backgrounds. As table 6.4 shows, women and minorities are more prevalent in the caucus than among Democrats in general or Republicans. Using the ratings by both the AFL-CIO and the liberal Americans for Democratic Action, I estimate that another fifty Democrats in the House are almost as liberal as members of the Progressive Caucus, as defined by an average liberal rating of 80 percent over a two-year period from the two organizations. This means that about 50 percent of the Democrats in the House are sympathetic to the liberal-labor coalition, which translates to 25 percent of all House members. Using the same rating system, I found that 25 to 30 percent of Senate members also can be identified as liberals.[66]

As the existence of a Progressive Caucus and the percentage of liberals in the House and Senate indicate, the corporate-conservative coalition is not completely successful, despite its numerous financial advantages. In the sense of diversity, this is evidence for pluralism, but the problem with adopting a pluralist theory on the basis of these figures is that there are not enough liberals for them to have a significant impact by themselves.

Still, the minority of liberals in Congress is not the whole story when it comes to possible liberal-labor success because independence may be exercised by politicians who are supported by and feel sympathetic toward the corporate rich, at least under some conditions and on a few issues. Thus, there is the possibility of disagreement between a majority of elected officials and the power elite over specific issues. As noted at the end of chapters 2 and 4, there is too much uncertainty and potential volatility in the workings of government for the power elite to leave anything to chance. This means that members of the power elite need to influence government directly. The next chapter demonstrates how the power elite goes beyond the candidate-selection process to involve itself in matters of government and public policy.

CONCLUSION

Contrary to both public-opinion and interest-group pluralists, this chapter shows that American political parties and elections do not necessarily lead to a significant role for voters in shaping public policy. Candidates are relatively free to say one thing in campaigns and vote as they please in Congress, except on highly charged social issues of little moment to the power elite. This is because of the restrictive nature of a two-party system and the legacy of 300 years of slavery and segregation in the South, which together have made it impossible to create a nationwide liberal-labor organizational base in the political arena.

When the governmental system and the history of the South are given their due, it is not hard to see why the two political parties have been controlled by different segments of the dominant class rather than rival social classes. Politics can be dominated by money and personal image because the parties do not develop distinctive programs. Money would count for a lot less in a system with programmatic political parties, as the experience in many European countries shows. Within the American context, issues become so blurred and the possibility of passing liberal legislation so unlikely that many voters do not have any incentive to develop an economically based voting perspective, instead voting on the basis of racial and ethnic resentments or religious identification. Many citizens, especially those with low incomes, do not even bother to vote.

Despite the corporate-conservative dominance of parties and elections, the liberal-labor coalition is able to elect representatives to both the House and Senate and bring its legislation before Congress. Furthermore, legislation it favors is sometimes passed, and legislation it opposes is sometimes blocked. The explanation for these successes, which at first glance may seem to contradict much of what has been said in this and the preceding chapter, is presented as part of the next chapter.

NOTES

1. Anthony Downs, *An Economic Theory of Democracy* (New York: Harper and Row, 1957), is considered one of the classic statements of this tradition, but the same basic idea appears in many introductory textbooks in political science. See, for example, Everett C. Ladd, *The American Polity*, 3d ed. (New York: W. W. Norton and Co., 1989), pp. 490–491; and John Bibby, *Governing by Consent* (Washington, DC: Congressional Quarterly, 1992), pp. 163, 176–177, 179.
2. Nelson Polsby and Aaron Wildavsky, *Presidential Politics*, 9th ed. (Chatham, NJ: Chatham House Publishers, 1996), p. 315.
3. Ibid., pp. 274, 314.
4. Richard Hamilton, *Class and Politics in the United States* (New York: Wiley, 1972), chapter 1, brings together all the arguments and evidence against the unexamined assumptions of those who believe the two-party system is of necessity responsive to voter performance. For recent evidence on the disjuncture between public opinion and political responsiveness on economic issues, see Benjamin Page and Robert Y. Shapiro, *The Rational Public* (Chicago: University of Chicago Press, 1992). The figures on public support for a greater government effort to expand job opportunities can be found on page 121 of their book.
5. Horace Samuel Merrill, *Bourbon Democracy of the Middle West: 1865–1896* (Baton Rouge: Louisiana State University Press, 1953). On the McCarthy campaign, see Richard Stout, *People* (New York: Harper & Row, 1970); George Rising, *Clean for Gene: Eugene McCarthy's 1968 Presidential Campaign* (New York: Praeger, 1997); Jules Witcover, *The Year the Dream Died* (New York: Warner Books, 1997).
6. Walter D. Burnham, "American Politics in the 1970s," in *The American Party Systems*, eds. William N. Chambers and Walter D. Burnham (New York: Oxford University Press, 1975), pp. 321–322.
7. Page and Shapiro, op. cit., pp. 119–120.
8. Walter D. Burnham, "The 1980 Earthquake: Realignment, Reaction, or What?," in *The Hidden Election*, eds. Thomas Ferguson and Joel Rogers (New York: Pantheon, 1981).
9. Seymour Martin Lipset, *The First New Nation* (New York: Basic Books, 1963), p. 336.

Politicians lie? no - alone they cannot implement their campaign promises - 3 branches of gov't provide checks + balances

10. Ron Verzuh, "New Democratic Party Wins Big in Canada," *Utne Reader*, 49 (Jan.–Feb. 1992): 32; Reza Nakhaie, "Class and Voting Consistency in Canada," *Canadian Journal of Sociology*, 17 (1992): 275–299; Doug Saunders and Carl Wilson, "The Collapse of Canada's NDP," *Nation*, 18 (Nov. 29, 1993): 660–664; Peter Dreier, "Canada: A Kinder, Gentler Nation," *Social Policy*, 23 (1992): 6–19.

11. Steven Rosenstone, Roy Behr, and Edward Lazarus, *Third Parties in America*, 2d ed. (Princeton, NJ: Princeton University Press, 1996).

Technically speaking, the president in the United States is selected by the electoral college, where each state has a number of electors equal to the size of its congressional delegation. They cast their ballots for the candidate who wins in their state. The focus on the electoral votes in each state forces the candidates to concentrate on winning a plurality in as many states as possible, not simply on winning the most votes in the nation overall. This system creates a further disadvantage for third parties.

12. Lipset, op. cit., p. 336.

13. Ibid. For the first full presentation of this argument in relation to the United States, see E. E. Schattschneider, *Party Government* (New York: Holt, 1942).

14. Richard Hofstader, *The Idea of a Party System* (Berkeley: University of California Press, 1969).

15. Warren Miller and J. Merrill Shanks, *The New American Voter* (Cambridge: Harvard University Press, 1996), chapter 16.

16. John Higley and Michael Burton, "The Elite Variable in Democratic Transitions and Breakdowns," *American Sociological Review*, 54 (1989): 17–32.

17. Charles Merriam, "Nominating Systems," *The Annals of the American Academy of Political and Social Science*, 56 (March 1923); Allen Lovejoy, *La Follette and the Establishment of the Direct Primary in Wisconsin, 1890–1904* (New Haven, CT: Yale University Press, 1941).

18. Robert Morlan, *Political Prairie Fire* (Minneapolis: University of Minnesota Press, 1955).

19. Joseph Gorman, *Kefauver: A Political Biography* (New York: Oxford University Press, 1971); Charles Fontenay, *Estes Kefauver* (Knoxville: University of Tennessee Press, 1980).

20. Jerome Himmelstein, *To the Right* (Berkeley: University of California Press, 1989); Rising, op. cit., on McCarthy's use of Democratic Party primaries.

21. Greg Mitchell, *The Campaign of the Century* (New York: Random House, 1992).

22. G. William Domhoff, *The Power Elite and the State* (Hawthorne, NY: Aldine de Gruyter, 1990), chapter 9, for a theoretical account of the history of the Democratic Party and relevant references. For a recent excellent account of the Democratic Party as "the party of peripheral regions and disaffected minorities," see William G. Mayer, *The Divided Democrats* (Boulder, CO: Westview Press, 1996), pp. 98ff.

23. C. Vann Woodward, *Reunion and Reaction: The Compromise of 1877 and the End of Reconstruction*, 2d ed. (New York: Doubleday, 1956).

24. Richard Bolling, *Power in the House* (New York: Dutton, 1968); David Potter, *The South and the Concurrent Majority* (Baton Rouge: Louisiana

State University Press, 1972); G. William Domhoff, *Fat Cats and Democrats* (Englewood Cliffs, NJ: Prentice-Hall, 1972), chapters 3 and 4. For the most recent and detailed demonstration of his point, based on original research in budgetary archives, see Michael K. Brown, *Divergent Fates: Race and Class in the American Welfare State, 1935–1985* (Ithaca, NY: Cornell University Press, 1998).

25. James Patterson, *Congressional Conservatism and the New Deal* (Lexington: University of Kentucky Press, 1967); Mack Shelley II, *The Permanent Majority* (Tuscaloosa: University of Alabama Press, 1983); Domhoff, *The Power Elite and the State*, op. cit., pp. 240–242; David Brady and Charles Bullock, "Is There a Conservative Coalition in the House?," *Journal of Politics*, 42 (1980): 549–559. Brady and Bullock argue convincingly that the "conservative coalition" should be called a "conservative voting bloc" because it is really a voting alliance based on shared policy objectives and a common ideology. Their term has been adopted in this book. Brady and Bullock stress that the coalition emerged to oppose organized labor (p. 550). For the conclusion that "the coalition of northern Republicans and southern Dixicrats was an important fact of American political life as early as the 1880s," see Kenneth Stampp, *The Era of Reconstruction, 1865–1877* (New York: Alfred A. Knopf, 1965), p. 214.

26. James Weinstein, *The Decline of Socialism in America, 1912–1925* (New York: Monthly Review Press, 1967), pp. 93–118.

27. James Weinstein, "Organized Business and the Commission and Manager Movements," *Journal of Southern History*, 28 (1962): 166–182; Samuel Hays, "The Politics of Reform in the Progressive Era," *Pacific Northwest Review*, 55 (1964): 157–169; Martin Schleisl, *The Politics of Efficiency* (Berkeley: University of California Press, 1979).

28. Tari Renner and Victor DeSantis, "Contemporary Patterns and Trends in Municipal Government Structures," *The Municipal Year Book 1993* (Washington, DC: International City Managers Association, 1994).

29. Schleisl, op. cit., p. 6.

30. Robert Alford and Eugene Lee, "Voting Turnout in American Cities," *American Political Science Review*, 62 (1968): 796–813.

31. John R. Logan and Harvey Molatch, *Urban Fortunes* (Berkeley: University of California Press, 1987), chapter 3.

32. G. William Domhoff, *Who Really Rules? New Haven and Community Power Re-Examined* (New Brunswick, NJ: Transaction Books, 1978), pp. 160–171; Alasdair Roberts, "Demonstrating Neutrality: The Rockefeller Philanthropies and the Evolution of Public Administration," *Public Administration Review*, 54 (1994): 221–228.

33. Domhoff, *Who Really Rules?*, op. cit., chapter 5, and G. William Domhoff, *Who Rules America Now?* (New York: Simon & Schuster, 1983), chapter 6, for a summary and analysis of all of these studies.

34. Richard Gendron, "The Fault Lines of Power: Post-Earthquake Development in a Progressive City," Ph.D. Dissertation, University of California, Santa Cruz, 1998; Andrew Szasz, *EcoPopulism* (Minneapolis: University of Minnesota Press, 1994); Hal Aronson, "Constructing Racism into a

Resource: A Portrait and Analysis of the Environmental Justice Movement," Ph.D. Dissertation, University of California, Santa Cruz, 1997.

35. Robert Dahl, *Who Governs?* (New Haven, CT: Yale University Press, 1961); Raymond Wolfinger, *The Politics of Progress* (Englewood Cliffs, NJ: Prentice-Hall, 1974).

36. Domhoff, *Who Really Rules?*, op. cit., chapters 1–3; Domhoff, *Who Rules America Now?*, op. cit., pp. 163–166, 184–196; Heywood Sanders, personal communication, July 16, 1996.

37. Miller and Shanks, op. cit.

38. Burnham, "American Politics in the 1970s," op. cit., p. 277.

39. Alexander Heard, *The Costs of Democracy* (New York: Doubleday, 1962), p. 34.

40. Herbert E. Alexander, *Financing Politics* (Washington, DC: Congressional Quarterly Press, 1976), p. 44.

41. David Donnelly, Janice Fine, and Ellen S. Miller, "Going Public," *Boston Review* (April/May 1997): 1; Larry Makinson and Joshua Goldstein, *Open Secrets: The Encyclopedia of Congressional Money and Politics* (Washington, DC: Congressional Quarterly Press, 1996), p. 26.

42. Makinson and Goldstein, op. cit., p. 24.

43. Alan Neustadtl, Denise Scott, and Dan Clawson, "Class Struggle in Campaign Finance? Political Action Committee Contributions in the 1984 Elections," *Sociological Forum*, 6 (1991): 219–238.

44. Alan Neustadtl and Dan Clawson, "Corporate Political Groupings: Does Ideology Unify Business Political Behavior?," *American Sociological Review*, 53 (1988): 172–190; Dan Clawson, Alan Neustadtl, and James Bearden, "The Logic of Business Unity: Corporate Contributions in the 1980s," *Sociological Quarterly*, 51 (1986): 797–811; and Dan Clawson, Alan Neustadtl, and Denise Scott, *Money Talks* (New York: Basic Books, 1992). For similar results, see Val Burris, "The Political Partisanship of American Business: A Study of Corporate Political Action Committees," *American Sociological Review*, 52 (1987): 732–744; and Val Burris and James Salt, "The Politics of Capitalist Class Segments," *Social Problems*, 37 (1990): 341–359.

45. "'Soft Money' Donations Almost 3 Times '92 Total," *San Francisco Chronicle* (Feb. 17, 1997): A7.

46. Peter Donohue, "The AFL-CIO's $35 Million Campaign Put Labor on the Political Map, But Did It Get Working People Politically Involved?," *In These Times* (Dec. 9, 1996): 24–25. For a good set of articles arguing the pros and cons of campaign finance reform, see "The Pull of Money," *Boston Review* (April/May 1997). The articles are available in reprint form for $1 from *Boston Review*, Box E53-407, MIT, Cambridge, MA 02139.

47. "'Soft Money' Donations," op. cit.

48. I believe it is a mistake to assume that all large campaign donations are motivated by a desire for economic favors, as the main writers on the topic for leftist periodicals like *The Nation* and *Mother Jones* usually do. In fact, many donations by wealthy liberals are motivated by a concern for civil liberties and other liberal values, especially those given by religious, ethnic, and racial minorities of wealth. For a demonstration of the

importance of noneconomic factors in shaping donations during the New Deal, see Michael Webber and G. William Domhoff, "Myth and Reality in Business Support for Democrats and Republicans in the 1936 Presidential Election," *American Political Science Review*, 90 (1996): 824–833. For similar evidence for the 1960s through 1980s, see my *The Power Elite and the State*, op. cit., pp. 247–254.

49. Nicholas M. Horrock, "Reagan Resists Financial Disclosure," *New York Times* (August 13, 1976): A-10; "Ronald Reagan Up Close," *Newsweek* (July 21, 1980): 39; Phil Kuntz, "Dole Has Ably Used the Lucrative Perks Those in Congress Get," *Wall Street Journal* (Oct. 10, 1996): 1.

50. Sidney Hyman, *The Lives of William Benton* (Chicago: University of Chicago Press, 1969), pp. 262, 274, 512, 572; "Humphrey to Join Britannica Board of Directors," *New York Times* (January 9, 1969): 34.

51. Paul Hoffman, *Lions in the Street* (New York: Saturday Review Press, 1973), p. 106.

52. Douglas Frantz, "Influential Group Brought into Campaign by Kemp," *New York Times* (Sept. 1, 1996): 15.

53. Donald R. Matthews, *The Social Background of Political Decision-Makers* (New York: Doubleday, 1954); Suzanne Keller, *Beyond the Ruling Class* (New York: Random House, 1963), pp. 310ff; Richard Zweigenhaft, "Who Represents America?," *Insurgent Sociologist*, 5 (1975): 119–130.

54. Heinz Eulau and John D. Sprague, *Lawyers in Politics* (Indianapolis: Bobbs-Merrill, 1964), pp. 11–12. For a comprehensive overview up to 1994, see Mark Miller, *The High Priests of American Politics* (Knoxville: University of Tennessee Press, 1995).

55. Morgens D. Pederson, "Lawyers in Politics: The Danish Folketing and United States Legislatures," in *Comparative Legislative Behavior*, eds. Samuel C. Patterson and John C. Wahlke (New York: Wiley, 1972). The fact that class issues are marginalized in American politics does not mean there is no class voting. To the contrary, voting along class lines remains as strong in the 1990s as it was in any other period, as shown by new analyses based on advances in statistical methodology. The main difference is that professionals and white-collar workers have moved into the Democratic Party and the self-employed have tended to cluster in the Republicans. For these and other findings on class voting, see Jeff Manza, Michael Hout, and Clem Brooks, "Class Voting in Capitalist Democracies Since World War II," *Annual Review of Sociology*, 21 (1995): 137–162; Michael Hout, Clem Brooks, and Jeff Manza, "The Democratic Class Struggle in the United States, 1948–1992," *American Sociological Review*, 60 (1995): 805–828; and Clem Brooks and Jeff Manza, "The Social and Ideological Bases of Middle-Class Political Realignment in the United States, 1972–1992," *American Sociological Review*, 62 (1997): 191–208. It is also important to report that religious affiliation has a higher correlation with voting behavior than social class.

56. Joseph A. Schlesinger, *Ambition and Politics* (Chicago: Rand McNally, 1966), p. 5. See also Alan Ehrenhalt, *The United States of Ambition* (New York: Random House, 1991).

57. Miller and Shanks, op. cit.

58. "Will the Rise of 'Blue Dogs' Revive Partisan Right?," *Congressional Quarterly*, 54 (Dec. 21, 1996): 3436–3438.
59. Edward Pessen, *The Log Cabin Myth* (New Haven, CT: Yale University Press, 1984), p. 81.
60. This account of Clinton's political life is drawn from David Maraniss, *First in His Class* (New York: Simon & Schuster, 1995); Martin Walker, *The President We Deserve* (New York: Crown Publishers, 1996); and Roger Morris, *Partners in Power* (New York: Holt, 1996).
61. Zweigenhaft, op. cit.
62. "Outside Earnings Swell Wealth of Congress," *Congressional Quarterly* (September 1, 1979).
63. Ibid., p. 1823.
64. Glenn R. Simpson, "Of the Rich, By the Rich, For the Rich: Are Congress's Millionaires Turning Our Democracy into a Plutocracy?" *Washington Post*, 117 (April 17, 1994): C4.
65. "Lawyers Take a Back Seat in the 105th Congress," *Congressional Quarterly*, 55 (January 4, 1997): 27–30.
66. Joel Bleifuss, "Whose Party Is It?," *In These Times* (Feb. 3, 1997): 12–14. Thanks to Karen Dolan at the Institute for Policy Studies for providing the list of members as of June 1997.

7

How the Power Elite Dominates Government

This chapter shows how the power elite builds on the ideas developed in the policy-formation process and its success in the electoral arena to dominate the federal government. Lobbyists from corporations, law firms, and trade associations play a key role in shaping government on narrow issues of concern to specific corporations or business sectors, but their importance should not be overestimated because a majority of those elected to Congress are predisposed to agree with them. The corporate community and the policy-formation network supply top-level governmental appointees and new policy directions on major issues.

Once again, as seen in the battles for public opinion and electoral success, the power elite faces opposition from a minority of elected officials and their supporters in labor unions and liberal advocacy groups. These opponents are sometimes successful in blocking ultra-conservative initiatives, but most of the victories for the liberal-labor coalition are the result of support from moderate conservatives.

The chapter begins with a discussion of the role and importance of the state as a central institution in large-scale societies. It then considers claims by Dye and state autonomy theorists that are based on the large size of the federal government. It next discusses numerous legislative issues at the interest-group and policy-formation levels, showing that the corporate-conservative coalition never loses when it is united. The liberal-labor coalition has had its greatest successes when the moderate conservatives agree with it in situations of extreme social disruption.

There is only one major issue that does not fit these generalizations—the National Labor Relations Act of 1935, which gave most workers the right to join unions and enter into collective bargaining with their employers. The act was vehemently opposed by virtually every major corporation in the United States. In a context of dramatic strikes in 1934 and ongoing union organizing, the liberal-labor coalition succeeded because the legislation excluded the agricultural, seasonal, and domestic workers so important at the time in the South.

The chapter ends with highly critical commentaries on pluralism, state autonomy theory, and institutional elitism.

THE ROLE OF GOVERNMENTS

Governments are potentially autonomous because they have a unique function: territorial regulation. They set up and guard boundaries, and then regulate the flow of people, money, and goods in and out of the area for which they have responsibility. They also have regulatory functions within a territory, such as settling disputes through the judicial system, and setting the rules that shape the economic marketplace.[1]

Neither business, the military, nor churches are organized in such a way that they could provide these necessary functions. The military sometimes steps in—or forces its way in—when a government is weak or collapsing, but it has a difficult time carrying out routine regulatory functions for very long. Nor can competing businesses regulate themselves. There is always some business that will try to improve its market share or profits by adulterating products, reducing wages, or telling half-truths. As most economists and other social scientists agree, a business system could not survive without some degree of market regulation. Contrary to claims about markets being free, they are historically constructed institutions dependent on governmentally sanctioned enforcement of property and contract rights.[2] Governments are also essential in creating money, setting interest rates, and shaping the credit system. Although the United States tried to function without a central bank for much of the nineteenth century, the problems created by a privately controlled money system were so great that bankers worked together to create the governmental central bank known as the Federal Reserve System in 1912.[3]

Nor is the state any less important in the context of a globalizing economy. If anything, it is even more important because it has to enforce rules concerning patents, intellectual property, quality of merchandise, and much else in an unregulated international arena. The international economy simply could not function without the agreements on monetary policy and tariffs that the governments of the United

States, Japan, Canada, and Western Europe negotiate through the International Monetary Fund, World Trade Organization, and other international agencies. For the American corporate rich, domination of the state also remains essential in a globalizing economy because the laws encouraging free trade and favoring American corporations that move production overseas could be easily changed. Tax breaks to offset taxes paid overseas could be eliminated, for example, or laws could be passed stipulating that goods could not enter the United States from countries that ban unions and use government force to suppress wages. The global economy is not an autonomous system that is independent of the most powerful national governments.

IS THE FEDERAL GOVERNMENT
TOO BIG AND GROWING BIGGER?

Most people seem to believe that the American government is too big and growing even bigger. This belief derives from (1) budget figures in the hundreds of billions that seem astronomical from the point of view of individuals earning a few tens of thousands of dollars each year; (2) headlines decrying budget increases; (3) publicity about the large federal debt; and (4) constant ultraconservative criticisms of big government. Dye reinforces this perception when he writes that government expenditures increased from 8 percent of the gross national product (a measure of the size of the economy) early in the nineteenth century to nearly 35 percent in the early 1990s.[4]

The size of government is an important issue for Dye and state autonomy theorists because they use its size and growth as indicators of power. Dye concludes that "governmental power may be even more concentrated than corporate power in America" and claims that "one indicator of its growing concentration is the increasing proportion of the gross national product produced by government."[5] State autonomy theorists assume in a similar fashion that a growing budget and an increasing number of employees are two indicators of the power of any agency or department within government.[6]

But Dye and the state autonomy theorists are wrong on three counts. First, the size of a government does not necessarily indicate how it is controlled. The government could grow and still be controlled by a power elite. There are no substitutes for the four power indicators. Second, the growth of government since at least the 1960s has been at the state and local levels, which does not fit with the image of an independently powerful government that aggrandizes more resources to itself. Federal expenditures as a percentage of gross domestic product (the total money value of the goods and services

Table 7.1 Government Growth at Federal and State/Local Levels

	Expenditures as % of Gross Domestic Product		Civilian Employees (in thousands)		Employees per 1,000 U.S. Population	
	Federal	State/Local	Federal	State/Local	Federal	State/Local
1962	18.9	6.3	2,510	6,549	13.5	35.1
1972	19.5	8.4	2,865	10,649	13.6	50.7
1982	22.4	9.2	2,825	13,098	12.2	56.4
1992	21.6	10.3	3,083	15,675	12.1	61.4
1996	20.3	10.3	2,847	16,669	10.7	62.8

Source: *The Budget for Fiscal Year 1998, Historical Tables* (Washington, DC: U.S. Government Printing Office, 1997), tables 15.5 and 17.5.

produced in the country, used since 1991 instead of gross national product to measure the size of the economy) have been stable since the 1950s, and the number of federal civilian employees declined in the 1990s, both in absolute numbers and as a percentage of the nation's total population. The exact figures for selected years from 1962 to 1996 are presented in table 7.1. Even worse for Dye's argument, most of this growth at the state and local levels has been in teachers, university professors, social welfare workers, and police personnel.

Third, as the most detailed and sophisticated study of federal government budgets revealed, budgets actually declined from 1950 to 1977 by 8.8 percent as a percentage of gross domestic product when various biasing factors such as inflation are taken into account. This decline is all the more impressive—and contradictory to the claim by Dye—in the context of the large increases in the size of government budgets in Canada and other comparable countries.[7]

To the degree that the federal government seems large, it is because of the expenditures it makes in just three categories: (1) defense; (2) interest payments on the national debt; and (3) human resources, a category that includes expenditures for education, health, income security, social security, veterans benefits, and welfare. As table 7.2 shows, these three categories accounted for 70 percent of budget expenditures in 1940 and for 85 to 93.9 percent from 1952 to 1996.

Because such a large percentage of the federal budget goes to weapons contractors, interest payments, and support payments for individuals and families, the number of government employees provides a more useful indicator regarding the size of specific departments and agencies. The main finding that emerges from a comparison of

Table 7.2 Categories of Government Spending by Percent

	% for Defense	% for Interest on Debt	% for Human Resources	Other
1940	17.5	9.5	43.7	29.3
1952	68.1	6.9	17.4	7.6
1962	49.0	6.4	29.6	15.0
1972	34.5	6.7	46.5	12.3
1982	24.8	11.4	52.1	11.7
1992	21.6	14.4	55.9	8.1
1996	17.0	15.5	61.4	6.1

Source: *The Budget for Fiscal Year 1998, Historical Tables* (Washington, DC: U.S. Government Printing Office, 1997), Table 3.1.

departments is that the Department of Defense dwarfs all others, employing over half of all federal employees when military personnel are included. When only civilian employees are counted, it was still three to seven times bigger than its nearest rivals in 1996, a fact that Dye obscures when he writes that "there are nearly three million civilian employees of the federal government, compared to only one and a half million people in the armed forces."[8] Not coincidentally, the second largest department is Veterans Affairs, which arguably could be included in the military budget as a cost of fighting wars because a large number of VA employees are hospital and medical personnel. The full picture since 1962 for military personnel and the five largest departments of the executive branch is presented in table 7.3.

These findings contradict any claim that self-aggrandizing government officials are expanding their departments and the federal government in general. If that view were correct, there should not be declining federal budgets as a percentage of gross domestic product and smaller staffs in most federal bureaucracies. Class-dominance theory, on the other hand, expects government departments and budgets to expand or contract as a function of external needs and demands. This is in fact what happens according to the earlier-cited longitudinal study of federal budgets from 1950 to 1977. There was no evidence that the "selfish interests" of public officials led to the expansion of the federal budget, whether in defense spending, government purchases of civilian goods and services, or support payments like Social Security: "It appears that the relative cost of providing government goods and services has grown not because of the self-serving behavior of government employees, but instead because of the basic

Table 7.3 Total Federal Government Employment (in Millions) and Percent in Various Categories for Selected Years

Year	Total Federal Employ- ment	% for Military	% for Defense (civilian employ- ees)	% for Veterans Adminis- tration	% for Treasury	% for Agri- culture	% for Health/ Human Services
1962	5,354	53.0	20.0	3.3	1.6	2.1	1.4
1972	5,225	45.6	21.2	3.5	2.0	2.3	2.2
1982	4,972	43.2	19.9	4.7	2.4	2.4	3.1
1992	4,931	37.5	19.3	5.3	3.3	2.6	2.8
1996	4,354	34.6	17.6	5.8	3.4	2.5	3.0

Source: *The Budget for Fiscal Year 1998, Historical Tables* (Washington, DC: U.S. Government Printing Office, 1997), table 17.5.

character of government goods and services."[9] Buttressing this conclusion, a study focused exclusively on the military budget found that it rose and fell as a function of wars or the perception of external threat by the president and his foreign policy advisers.[10]

In short, it is not true that the federal government is "big" when compared to its size either in the recent past or to the size of government in other countries. It did grow somewhat in the face of large-scale unemployment and unrest during the Great Depression, and even more in response to World War II, but it has been surprisingly stable since the 1950s, and the end of the Cold War in 1990–1991 precipitated a decline in the number of military and civilian personnel in the Department of Defense. The main growth in recent decades has been in the benefit payments sent to the growing number of retirees and to those who cannot afford the rising costs of modern high-technology health care. But expenditures for war, the elderly, and health care at the national level, and for teachers, social workers, and police at the local level, do not add up to "big government" or evidence for state autonomy.

The claims by Dye and the state autonomy theorists are also refuted by the movement at all levels of government toward "privatization," which generally means turning over the provision of public services to private businesses by selling government facilities or awarding government contracts. It also can include contracts with private organizations to operate government-owned buildings and parks. Privatization is supposed to increase efficiency and cut costs because the companies operate on "market" principles, but any cost reductions are usually due to the fact that private organizations can pay lower salaries and benefits than the unionized governmental departments and reduce the quantity and quality of the services provided.[11] It is in effect another form of "outsourcing" that increases the power of the corporate community at the expense of the liberal-labor coalition.

The movement toward privatization has gone furthest at the state and local levels, where waste management, janitorial services, data processing, vehicle maintenance, and health services are increasingly provided by private companies. State governments have always hired private contractors to build roads, and now they are turning to private companies to provide prisons as well. A voucher system in which the government pays the costs for students who enroll in schools of their own choice is a form of privatization.

There are also aspects of the federal government that are privatized or in the process of being privatized. The list starts with the longstanding practice of awarding defense contracts to private companies for new airplanes and weapons systems. The need for expertise and information on many critical issues also is privatized through a system of contracts with private consultants, many of whom are housed in think tanks (discussed in chapter 4). More recently, there have been efforts to privatize three traditional government services: welfare, in which several companies are eager for contracts to manage benefit payments; Medicare, in which private health maintenance organizations (HMOs) and private hospitals want to replace public clinics and hospitals; and Social Security, in which stockbrokers want to handle retirement investments for individuals.

Those who talk of "big government" and the growth of government budgets seldom enter privatization into their calculations, but it has far more implications for power analysts than the size of government budgets because the real issue is which groups and organizations have control over government budgets.

APPOINTEES TO GOVERNMENT

The first way to test a class-dominance view of the federal government is to study the social and occupational backgrounds of the people who are appointed to manage the major departments of the executive branch, such as state, treasury, defense, and justice. If pluralists are correct, these appointees should come from a wide range of interest groups. If the state autonomy theorists are correct, they should be disproportionately former elected officials or longtime government employees. If the class-dominance view is correct, they should come disproportionately from the upper class, the corporate community, and the policy-formation network.

There have been numerous studies over the years of major governmental appointees under both Republican and Democratic administrations, usually focusing on the top appointees in the departments that are represented in the president's cabinet. These studies are unanimous in their conclusion that most top appointees in both Republican and Democratic administrations are corporate executives and corporate lawyers—and hence members of the power elite. Moreover, they are often part of the policy-formation network as well, supporting the claim in chapter 4 that the networks play a central role in preparing members of the power elite for government service.

In the most quantitative study of the factors leading to appointments, Useem showed that corporate executives from large companies who had two or more outside directorships were four times more likely to serve in a federal government advisory position than executives from smaller companies with no directorships, and that participation in at least one policy group increased the chances of an appointment for the big corporate interlockers by a factor of 1.7. In a subsequent interview study, he learned that chief executive officers often mentioned participation in a policy group as a qualification for an appointment to government.[12]

Reflecting the different coalitions that make up the two parties, there are some differences between the second-level and third-level appointees in Republican and Democratic administrations. Republicans frequently appoint ultraconservatives to agencies that are thoroughly disliked by the appointee, such as the Environmental Protection Agency, the Occupational Safety and Health Administration, the National Highway Traffic Safety Administration, and the Office of Civil Rights. Democrats, on the other hand, often place liberals in the same agencies, creating a dramatic contrast when a Democratic administration replaces a Republican one.

To the degree that there is any disagreement with these conclusions, there are two reasons. First, the pluralists and Dye put all lawyers in a "professional" or "civic" category separate from business, even if they are corporate lawyers and sit on corporate boards. Such an approach leads Dye to say that there is relatively little corporate representation in the Clinton Administration, a claim that is refuted later in this section.[13] Second, the pluralists and state autonomy theorists put policy experts in a "professional" category and classify them as independent of business, ignoring any corporate directorships or affiliations within the policy-formation network.[14]

Two historical studies of cabinet appointees from the founding of the country through the Carter Administration provide relevant background information. Detailed studies of the top appointees in the Kennedy, Reagan, and Clinton Administrations provide comparisons between Democrats and Republicans that bring the information forward to 1996.

The most ambitious historical study, a three-volume work by Philip Burch that covers cabinet officers, diplomats, and Supreme Court justices from 1780 to 1980, found that (1) 96 percent of the cabinet and diplomatic appointees from 1780 to 1861 were members of the economic elite (defined as the top few percent of wealthholders), with a predominance of landowners, merchants, and lawyers; (2) from 1862 to 1933, the figure was 84 percent, with an increasing number of financiers and corporate lawyers; and (3) from 1934 to 1980, the overall percentage was 64, but with only 47 percent during the New Deal period.[15] In a more detailed study, sociologist Beth Mintz looked at the percentage of members from the "social elite" and "business elite" for the 205 individuals who served in presidential cabinets between 1897 and 1972. She found that 60 percent were members of the upper class and 78 percent members of the corporate community. There were no differences in the overall percentages for Democrats and Republicans or for the years before and after 1933.[16]

The way in which presidents rely on corporate leaders and experts from the policy groups in making appointments to government can be seen very dramatically in the contrasting cases of John F. Kennedy, Ronald Reagan, and Bill Clinton. After winning an election in 1960 based on promises of a "new frontier" and the image of an urbane liberalism, President-elect Kennedy called in Republican Robert Lovett, a Wall Street investment banker who was a former member of the Committee for Economic Development and the Council on Foreign Relations as well as a former secretary of defense. Kennedy wished to have Lovett's advice on possible appointments to the new administration. Lovett soon became, according to historian and Kennedy aide Arthur M. Schlesinger, Jr., the "chief agent" between Kennedy and the "American Establishment." Schlesinger defined this establishment as consisting primarily of financiers and corporate lawyers who were an "arsenal of talent which had so long furnished a steady supply of always orthodox and often able people to Democratic as well as Republican administrations."[17] Lovett seemed to be an unusual adviser for a president-elect who had promised to "get the country moving again," but Kennedy said he needed experienced experts to run the government:

> He had spent the last five years, he said ruefully, running for office, and he did not know any real public officials, people to run a government, serious men. The only ones he knew, he admitted, were politicians, and if this seemed a denigration of his own kind, it was not altogether displeasing to the older man. Politicians did need men to serve, to run the government. The implication was

obvious. Politicians could run Pennsylvania and Ohio, and if they could not run Chicago, they could at least deliver it. But could politicians run the world? What did they know about the Germans, the French, the Chinese? He needed experts for that, and now he was summoning them.[18]

Kennedy first asked Lovett if he would be interested in serving as the secretary of state, defense, or treasury, but he gracefully declined for reasons of health. When talk then turned to possible people for these positions, Lovett named several. Among them were Dean Rusk, president of the Rockefeller Foundation and a member of the Council on Foreign Relations; Robert McNamara, president of the Ford Motor Company; and C. Douglas Dillon, head of the investment banking firm of Dillon, Read and a member of the Council on Foreign Relations. Kennedy solicited other names, and there was intense lobbying for some of the candidates, but in the end there was general consensus around Rusk for secretary of state, McNamara for secretary of defense, and Dillon for secretary of the treasury.

Many other members of the Kennedy Administration came from the policy-formation groups. In particular, they were members of the policy network who had taken part in a special set of commissions and panels sponsored by the Rockefeller Brothers Fund in the late 1950s. These panels, whose deliberations were published as a book entitled *Prospect for America*, were designed to assess the prospects for the United States in the 1960s on such issues as foreign policy, national security, education, and the domestic economy. Among the eighty-three men who served on one or more of these panels and lived into the 1960s, twenty-six later served in the Kennedy Administration. Most were consultants or advisers, but the list also included the secretary of state, the undersecretary of state, two assistant secretaries of state, and four other State Department appointees.[19]

Ronald Reagan came to the presidency in 1980 with a promise to do something about all the problems that allegedly were being caused by the federal government. However, as a conservative he would accomplish this feat by removing the liberal establishment figures who supposedly had caused them. Edward Meese III, who went on to serve as one of Reagan's most important White House advisers, told *Business Week* that "you will see people who have never served in Washington before and who can make a significant change in the course of government. It's like bringing a new management team to turn around a failing business."[20]

Nonetheless, Reagan's first secretary of state was a former army officer, Alexander Haig, who had served as an aide to the secretary of defense in the 1960s and to President Nixon in the 1970s. He was president of United Technologies and a director of Chase Manhattan Bank, Crown Cork & Seal, Texas Instruments, and ConAgra, as well as being a member of the Council on Foreign Relations. Reagan's second appointment to that position, George Schultz, was president of the Bechtel Corporation, one of the largest construction firms in the world, and a director of J. P. Morgan Bank. He also was a director of the Council on Foreign Relations, a former adviser to the Committee for Economic Development, and a former secretary of both labor and the treasury in the Nixon Administration.

The secretary of defense, Caspar Weinberger, was a corporate lawyer from San Francisco who had served in three different positions in Washington between 1970 and 1975. He was a vice president and general counsel of the Bechtel Corporation, a director of Pepsico and Quaker Oats, and a member of the Trilateral Commission. As for the secretary of the treasury, Donald T. Regan, he was the chief executive officer of Merrill, Lynch, a trustee of the Committee for Economic Development, a member of the policy committee of the Business Roundtable, and a member of the Council on Foreign Relations.

The rest of the Reagan Administration also consisted of members of the corporate community who had previous government experience or visibility in the policy-formation network. To the consternation of the ultraconservatives, there were many other appointees in addition to Haig, Shultz, and Regan who were members of the Council on Foreign Relations. They included the director of the CIA, the secretary of commerce, the special trade adviser, the deputy secretary of defense, and eight top-level appointments at the State Department. According to one cataloguing of over ninety advisers, consultants, and members of the Reagan Administration in early 1981, thirty-one were members of the Council on Foreign Relations, twenty-five were associated with the American Enterprise Institute, thirteen were affiliated with the Center for Strategic and International Studies, and twelve were participants in the Trilateral Commission.[21]

The Clinton Administration drew just as heavily from the corporate community and policy network as its predecessors. Dye stresses the legal backgrounds and governmental experience of the Clinton appointees, and the administration itself emphasized that it had a greater number of women and minorities than past administrations, but the appointees were first and foremost wealthy people with many corporate and policy network connections.[22] Warren Christopher, the first secretary of state, was a director of Lockheed Martin, Southern California Edison, and First Interstate Bancorp, a trustee of the Carnegie Corporation, a recent vice-chair of the Council on Foreign Relations, and officially a corporate lawyer. The second secretary of state, Madeleine Albright, is from a Czechoslovakian diplomatic family, had married into wealth in the United States, and was a director of the Atlantic Council.

The first secretary of the treasury, Lloyd Bentsen, inherited millions from his rancher father and founded his own insurance company in Texas before becoming a senator and then secretary of the treasury. He was succeeded by Robert Rubin, a codirector of the Wall Street investment banking firm of Goldman, Sachs and a trustee of the Carnegie Corporation, with a net worth between $50 and $100 million and an income of $26 million in 1992. The first director of the CIA, R. James Woolsey, a corporate lawyer, was a director of Martin Marietta, a large defense contractor; the second, John Deutch, a professor and administrator at MIT, was a director of Citicorp, Perkins-Elmer, and CMS Energy.

The first secretary of agriculture, Michael Espy, is an African-American from the Mississippi Delta and a former member of Congress, but his grandfather and father were major landowners and business owners. The first secretary of commerce, Ronald Brown, also an African-American, came from a family that managed a hotel in Harlem; at the time of his appointment he was a lawyer with one of the leading corporate firms in Washington, which paid him $580,000 in 1992 even though he spent most of his time as chair of the Democratic Party. The secretary of energy, Hazel O'Leary, is both African-American and female, but she is also the daughter of two physicians and was the executive vice president of Northern States Power, a utility company in Minnesota.

The first secretary of housing and urban development, Henry Cisneros, is a Mexican-American who had been mayor of San Antonio, but at the time of his appointment he was the chair of an investment firm, the head of an air charter company, and a trustee of the Rockefeller Foundation. The least-connected major figure in the cabinet, Janet Reno, the attorney general, is the daughter of journalists in Florida and had been a state attorney in Miami.

Clinton's White House team also is tightly connected with the corporate world. His first White House chief of staff was the president of a large natural gas company in Arkansas. The legislative liaison to Congress had been the president of the Washington office of one of the biggest public relations firms in the world, Hill and Knowlton; he earned $154,943 from the firm in 1992 and another $287,377 from a Washington lobbying firm, Timmons and Co., headed by a top Republican adviser. The head of the Office of Management and Budget, a woman, sat on the boards of Union Carbide and Unisys and was a Fellow of the Brookings Institution.

The administration drew many of its key members from a small group of current or recent directors on the board of the Council on

Foreign Relations. In addition to Warren Christopher, a Council director from 1982 to 1991, three other Council directors held top positions in the State Department at one point or another: Clifton Wharton, Jr., a well-to-do African-American who sat on the board of Ford Motors; Strobe Talbott, the son of an upper-class investment banker and Clinton's close friend since their years at Oxford University as Rhodes Scholars; and Peter Tarnoff, president of the council at the time of his appointment. Clinton's third secretary of defense, William S. Cohen, was a council director at the time of his appointment, as was Donna Shalala, the chancellor of the University of Wisconsin and a trustee of the Committee for Economic Development, the Brookings Institution, and the liberal Children's Defense Fund, who became secretary of health and human services. Other CFR directors who served in the Clinton Administration at one point or another were the White House special counsel, the director of the Office of Management and Budget, and the head of the Federal Reserve Board. A list of council directors and members with important positions in the two Clinton Administrations is presented in table 7.4.

Clinton also made liberal and nonwealthy appointments, but they tended to be in secondary positions from a power point of view. Robert Reich, a friend from their days as Rhodes Scholars together, and a liberal, was the secretary of labor in the first Clinton Administration but had little impact on major policies. The African-Americans who served as secretary of veterans affairs, Jesse Brown (1993–), as secretary of transportation, Rodney Slater (1997–), and as secretary of labor, Alexis Herman (1997–), are not from well-to-do-backgrounds or high-status universities. Ellen Haas, a consumer advocate and a longtime critic of the Department of Agriculture, was put in charge of nutrition and consumer affairs in that department. Carol Bellamy, head of the Peace Corps, is the daughter of a telephone installer and nurse, served in the Peace Corps in Guatemala in the 1960s, and worked as a waitress to put herself through law school. Such examples are few and far between in policy-making positions of concern to the power elite.

The general picture that emerges from this information is that the highest levels of the executive branch—especially in the State, Defense, and Treasury Departments—are interlocked constantly with the corporate community through the movement of executives and lawyers in and out of government. Although the same person is not in government and corporate positions at the same time, there is enough continuity for the relationship to be described as one of "revolving interlocks." Corporate leaders resign from their numerous directorships to serve in government for two or three years, then return to the corporate community. This system gives corporate officials temporary

Table 7.4 Clinton Appointees Who Were Directors or Members of the Council on Foreign Relations Before Their Appointments

Name	Dates CFR Director	Government Position
Warren Christopher	1982–1991	Secretary of state (1993–1996)
William S. Cohen	1989–1996	Secretary of defense (1997–)
Lloyd Cutler	1977–1979	Special counsel to president (1994–1995)
Alan Greenspan	1982–1988	Chair, Federal Reserve Board (1993–)
Alice Rivlin	1989–1992	Deputy director (1993–1994), Director (1995–1996), Office of Management and Budget
Donna Shalala	1992–1993	Secretary of health and human services (1993–)
Strobe Talbott	1988–1992	Deputy secretary of state (1995–)
Peter Tarnoff	1986–1992	Undersecretary of state for political affairs (1995–)
Clifton Wharton, Jr.	1983–1992	Deputy secretary of state (1993–1994)

Members	
Name	Government Position
Madeleine Albright	U.S. representative to the United Nations (1993–1996); secretary of state (1997–)
Roger Altman	Deputy secretary of treasury (1993–1995)
Les Aspin	Secretary of defense (1993–1994)
Bruce Babbitt	Secretary of interior (1993–)
Reginald Bartholomew	Undersecretary of state for international security affairs (1993–1995); ambassador to Italy (1996–)
Samuel Berger	Deputy assistant to the president for national security affairs (1993–1996); assistant to the president for national security affairs (1997–)
Henry Cisneros	Secretary of housing and urban development (1993–)
Lynn Davis	Undersecretary of state for arms control and international security affairs (1994–)

John Deutch	Deputy secretary of defense (1994–1995); director, CIA (1995–1996)
Jeffrey Garten	Undersecretary of commerce for international affairs (1994–1995)
Arnold Kanter	Undersecretary of state for political affairs (1993–1996)
W. Anthony Lake	Assistant to the president for national security affairs (1993–1996)
Franklin Raines	Director, Office of Management and Budget (1997–)
Walter Slocombe	Undersecretary of defense for policy (1995–)
Joan Spero	Undersecretary of state for economic and agricultural affairs (1996–)
Lawrence Summers	Undersecretary of treasury for international affairs (1993–)
Laura Tyson	Chair, Council of Economic Advisers (1993–1996)
John P. White	Deputy secretary of defense (1995–)
Thomas S. Williamson, Jr.	Solicitor, Department of Labor (1993–)
Timothy Wirth	Undersecretary of state for global affairs (1995–)
Frank Wisner	Undersecretary of defense for policy (1993–1995); ambassador to India (1996–)
R. James Woolsey	Director, CIA (1993–1995)
Robert Zoellick	Undersecretary of state for economic and agricultural affairs (1993–1996)

independence from the narrow concerns of their own companies and allows them to perform the more general roles they have learned in the policy-discussion groups. However, it does not give them the time or inclination to become fully independent of the corporate community or to develop a perspective that includes the interests of other classes and groups.[23] In terms of the "Who sits?" indicator of power, then, it is clear that the power elite is the predominant voice in the top-level appointive positions in the executive branch.

It is now time to turn to the decisional indicator of power by studying who wins and loses on (1) the narrow issues that are handled at the interest-group level and (2) the more general issues that relate to work within the policy-formation network (explained in chapter 4).

The boundary between the two levels of issues is not a hard and fast one—and some issues, such as environmental ones, often overlap—but the distinction is a useful one for sorting out most policy conflicts. It also guards against making too much out of minor defeats for business interest groups when they are trying to gain tax breaks and other favors, especially when those defeats are due to protestations by other business groups.

THE INTEREST GROUP PROCESS

The interest group process consists of the means by which specific corporations and business sectors gain the favors, tax breaks, regulatory rulings, and other governmental assistance they need to realize their narrow and short-run interests. The process is based on the efforts of people who do what is called lobbying. Lobbying is carried out by people with a wide range of experiences: experts who used to serve on congressional staffs or in regulatory agencies, employees of trade associations, corporate executives whose explicit function is government liaison, and an assortment of public relations specialists, former politicians, and lawyers. The process is based on personal contact, but its most important ingredients are the information and financial support that the lobbyists have to offer.

Political scientists who study the impact of interest groups on government have abandoned an emphasis by their predecessors on "pressure" as an old-fashioned way to think about lobbying. They rightly note that more often than not the legislators and regulators already agree with the interest-group lobbyists who have access to them. They therefore put their greatest emphasis on the useful information about substantive issues, political ramifications, and voter sentiment that lobbyists can provide.

Thirty years ago, there seemed to be a consensus among political scientists that interest groups were able to shape the part of government of concern to them. It was assumed they did so by entering into tight alliances with the relevant congressional oversight committee and the corresponding agency in the executive branch, creating what were sometimes called "iron triangles." Within this framework, any pluralism in the general power structure was due to the influence that ordinary citizens have on the presidency and Supreme Court, especially through the political parties. In the words of political scientist Grant McConnell:

> Fortunately, not all of American politics is based upon this
> array of small constituencies. The party system, the Presidency
> and the national government as a whole represent opposing

tendencies. To a very great degree, policies serving the values of liberty and equality are the achievements of these institutions. Public values generally must depend upon the creation of a national constituency.[24]

Just as these conclusions started to be accepted, making it possible for class-domination theorists to turn their attention to the policy-formation network and the political parties, the social activists of the 1960s that modeled themselves on the Civil Rights Movement began to flourish. The antiwar and feminist movements were the most prominent and visible, but the new form of liberalism called the "public interest movement" was just as important in the long run in terms of government legislation. It focused on consumer and environmental issues. It also challenged corporations to be responsible citizens, thereby generating a concern with "corporate responsibility."

According to a new generation of interest-group pluralists, the growth of the public interest movement broke the iron triangles and reopened the interest-group process to ordinary citizens. The alleged victories by the public interest activists—with the aid of several large foundations, especially the Ford Foundation—led to new forms of business regulation and the growth of government in general. Then special interest groups on the right, such as the National Rifle Association, began to exert influence. Finally, the story continues, the corporate community began to mobilize. Corporations by the hundreds opened offices in Washington, invested more money in lobbying and campaign finance, and created the Business Roundtable. Trade associations from around the country moved their headquarters to Washington.[25]

As the insurgent interest groups were developing, changes were taking place in Congress that are seen by interest-group pluralists as further evidence for their views. In particular, the Democratic Congress elected in 1974 in the wake of Nixon's resignation seemed to be poised to make major changes. The Democratic Caucus adopted a new rule whereby its members would elect congressional committee chairs rather than letting them be determined only by seniority. In the Senate, the number of votes needed to halt a filibuster was lowered from 67 to 60, making it harder for a small minority to stop new legislation.

Leaders in the corporate community were indeed concerned. Rising inflation due to agricultural shortages and sudden large increases in crude oil prices by the small oil-producing nations, revelations about corporate bribes to officials overseas, detailed information about large secret campaign donations by corporate lobbyists, and the Watergate scandal itself had an unsettling effect. For example, one of the most senior corporate lobbyists of the day, who had come to Washington as a Procter & Gamble executive in the Eisenhower Administration, predicted that business was in for the worst trouble it had seen since the New Deal. In a widely circulated and quoted speech given to the Chamber of Commerce, he called on executives to redouble their efforts in Congress and urge President Ford to veto the impending liberal legislation.[26]

Despite these corporate concerns, the pluralist recounting of this era depends on the human tendency to rearrange memories, glorify the golden past, and focus on the present. The revised version of pluralism is false because (1) the corporate community was active and dominant in the early 1960s; (2) the corporate community did not lose nearly as often as the pluralists claim; and (3) the real problems for the power elite were the Civil Rights Movement, urban riots, and the antiwar movement, which had to be accommodated or pacified before the corporate leaders could turn their attention to the consumer and environmental issues emphasized by the pluralists. Indeed, a strong grassroots antinuclear movement helped put an end to the nuclear power industry, and the environmental movement forced a tightening of pollution controls, but for the most part the power elite was able to modify or defeat the legislation it opposed. This point can be demonstrated through an analysis of the laws passed since 1965 that are most often offered by pluralists as evidence for their claims.

The Consumer Movement

The new consumer movement developed out of the activism of the civil rights and antiwar movements of the 1960s. Inspired in good part by the efforts of Ralph Nader, the movement led to the passage of many new consumer protection laws between 1967 and 1974. When Jimmy Carter became president in 1976, he appointed the leader of the Consumer Federation of America as an undersecretary of agriculture and the head of Nader's congressional watchdog group as the chair of the National Highway Traffic Safety Administration. In addition, a respected academic researcher was put in charge of the Occupational Safety and Health Administration, and a Senate staff member who had helped to draft many of the new consumer safety laws became chair of the Federal Trade Commission.

According to political scientist David Vogel, the successes of the consumer movement are evidence for pluralism, but his claim is off the mark because the relevant business groups either agreed with the legislation or forced modifications to make it acceptable to them. As Vogel himself recounts, there was no business opposition to any of the consumer protection legislation of the 1960s except for the automobile industry's objections to the National Traffic and Motor Vehicle

Safety Act, an effort to force them to make safer cars. Vogel agrees that the effects of the various consumer acts were "rather modest," but then calls them defeats for business because the increased regulation, however minor, allegedly indicated "that the relative political influence of business had begun to erode."[27]

The profound weakness of the consumer movement was exposed in 1975 and 1977 when it could not win enactment for its mild proposal for an Agency for Consumer Advocacy. The envisioned agency would not have had any power to enforce laws or issue regulations, but only to gather information and help consumer groups "in proceedings before federal agencies and in judicial reviews of agency actions."[28] Nevertheless, the Business Roundtable and other corporate organizations strongly opposed the idea through the Roundtable's Consumer Issues Working Group. Although the act passed both houses of Congress in 1975, a final version was not sent to the White House because President Ford said he would veto it. Two years later, despite support from the newly elected Democratic president, Jimmy Carter, the House rejected the bill.[29]

The movement also failed in all its efforts to legislate greater corporate responsibility. Congress refused to consider the idea of federal charters for corporations, leaving them free to continue to incorporate in states with very weak laws governing corporations. Nor did whistle-blowers within corporations receive any protection, leaving them at great risk for being disloyal to their employers. Plans to increase shareholder rights and strengthen the laws on corporate crime were rejected. The flurry of new initiatives at the Federal Trade Commission led to a strong reaction by Congress when it was inundated by complaints from the car dealers, funeral directors, and other business groups that felt put upon and harassed. Every reform was lost. In the early 1980s the ultraconservatives tried to abolish the commission entirely, but it was saved with the help of corporate moderates who believe it has some uses.[30]

Surveying the successes and failures of the consumer movement from the vantage point of the 1990s, political scientists Ardith Maney and Loree Bykerk conclude that the new interest-group pluralists are wrong to claim that the "new" regulation starting in the 1970s is different from earlier forms of regulation even though it usually covers a wider array of industries. They also find no evidence for the purely theoretical claim by conservative free-market economists that the regulation of business is due to the efforts of "empire-building" government "bureaucrats." Most generally, they conclude that business is the dominant force in the interest-group community despite the increase in nonbusiness interest groups in the 1970s.[31]

The Giant Killers

After a term as the activist chair of the Federal Trade Commission from 1977 to 1980, Michael Pertschuk wrote a book celebrating the "giant killers" who have won victories as lobbyists for the liberal-labor coalition. But none of these successes is support for pluralism. For example, he extols the liberal lobby that led to the extension of the Voting Rights Act in 1982 but then reports that there was no lobbying opposition, and that moderate Republicans agreed that legislative oversight in Southern states was needed in the face of evidence of continuing discrimination there.[32] He then explains how a liberal arms-control coalition defeated the Reagan Administration's proposal in 1984 to build an additional 100 MX missiles but also says the coalition included what he calls "respectable" members of the defense community, such as former secretaries of defense, directors of the CIA, and retired army generals who once had held leadership roles in nuclear defense. He says these defense leaders were essential in reassuring lawmakers that the MX missiles were not necessary.[33]

Pertschuk also coauthored a book explaining how the liberal-labor coalition was successful in blocking the nomination of Robert J. Bork to the Supreme Court in 1987. The AFL-CIO, civil rights groups, and women's groups formed a large and vigorous coalition to claim that Bork was an ideological extremist, as evidenced by assertions in his many speeches, articles, and court briefs. Bork argued, for example, that courts had no right to rule on the issues of civil rights and abortion. Ultraconservative groups were unable to counter this liberal-labor pressure, and Bork was rejected in the Senate by a 58 to 42 vote. But this was not a defeat for the power elite. Corporations were silent on the issue. Some moderate civic groups opposed him. The centrist Federation of Business and Professional Women's Clubs was open in its opposition. He also was opposed by some of the most distinguished conservative law professors in the country as well as by a great many centrist law professors. Several members of the American Bar Association's Committee on the Federal Judiciary opposed the nomination. In other words, the liberal-labor coalition could not have won in the Senate without the support of centrists, moderate Republicans, and conservative law professors.[34]

The National Rifle Association

Many pluralists point to the success of the National Rifle Association (NRA) in fighting gun control laws as evidence for the power of narrow interest groups. But the NRA is not doing battle with the power elite in thwarting the will of the majority on this issue. In fact, it is part of the corporate-conservative coalition and gains much of its support through its appeal to antigovernment sentiment, alleging a Second Amendment right to bear arms that has been rejected by every federal court and a special committee of the American Bar Association. It receives significant financial support from gun manufacturers, especially through their ads in NRA publications and their payments for display space at NRA meetings. One investigator concludes that the NRA "has evolved into the unofficial trade association for the firearm's industry."[35] Thus, the success of the NRA is consistent with a class-domination theory. The NRA is not part of the power elite, but it is not opposed by the power elite either.

Four Policy Domains

A research team of pluralists in sociology and political science conducted a detailed empirical study in the 1980s of four "policy domains": agriculture, energy, health, and labor. Their data consisted of a wide range of interview and questionnaire responses from the individuals and groups they thought to be influential in each policy domain. The study found that there was no cohesive overall group in any of the four domains. To the contrary, they found that business organizations were in one camp and liberal and labor organizations in the other. This was especially the case on labor issues, which should come as no surprise to readers at this point. Sometimes government agencies were part of the issue network, especially in agriculture. The authors believe that their findings contradict what they understand to be the "power elite" thesis. To make the contrast between their findings and a class-dominance theory more dramatic, they entitled their book *The Hollow Core* to highlight the absence of a cohesive power group.[36]

In fact, their findings are almost exactly what would be expected in terms of the argument in this book. No class-dominance theorist has claimed that there should be united "issue networks" or even uses the concept. Nor are the authors accurate in claiming that their findings contradict the observation by C. Wright Mills that corporate lawyers and investment bankers play an integrative role within the power elite. Mills said that such people moved between the corporate community and government, not between the corporations and the liberal-labor coalition.[37] (The one thin reed these pluralists can point to on this issue is the discovery in a reputational study by sociologist Gwen Moore that a few labor leaders were part of a national circle of leaders, but Moore did not claim that this acquaintance and discussion network was equivalent to the power elite.[38])

The authors asked their respondents how successful they were on the five issues of most concern to them in the time period under study. Although conservatives claimed to be successful more often than liberals, liberals felt they were successful on some issues.[39] The authors then make two important points:

1. The issues that are disputed in Congress are a very narrow range of all possible issues, which is evidence for the success of the power elite in protecting their past victories. They are the issues that have not been kept off the agenda. Indeed, a reading of the issues in their study suggests that most of them are very limited in scope.[40]

2. Liberals must be winning on some issues, or they wouldn't continue their efforts. That is, the ongoing functioning of a democratic system means by definition that power is not completely controlled at the top.[41]

The pluralist team reports one other finding that supports a class-dominance view. When it comes to policy-making in most domains, they say, there is no distinct boundary between interest groups and government. Moreover, they report that 80 percent of executive department officials above the middle levels had worked for an interest group in the private sector in the past. The researchers therefore conclude that the claims of state autonomy theory are not tenable for the United States.[42]

Despite its claims to thoroughness, this pluralist team never traces the development of any policy position into the policy-formation network. Various business organizations are listed without comment or any sense of ordering, and with no indication that the Business Roundtable coordinates the business response on any issue of importance to the corporate community.

In conclusion, there is no case study at the interest-group level that successfully challenges a class-domination theory. Victories by one business group are often at the expense of another. Victories by organizations like the National Rifle Association over the liberal-labor coalition are not relevant. The successes of liberal nonbusiness interest groups and unions are few and far between.

THE POLICY-FORMATION PROCESS

General policy-making on issues of concern to the corporate community as a whole is in good part the culmination of work done in the policy network explained in chapter 4, but the differences between moderate conservatives and ultraconservatives often lead to conflicts over some new policies within the executive branch and the legislative process, and the proposals put forward by the liberal-labor coalition—through pamphlets, books, and well-timed media releases—must be countered as well.

The policy recommendations developed in the policy-formation groups reach government in a variety of ways. On the most general level, their reports, news releases, and interviews are read by elected officials and their staffs, if not in their original forms, then as they are summarized in the *Washington Post, New York Times,* and *Wall Street Journal.* Members of the policy organizations also testify before congressional committees and subcommittees that are writing legislation or preparing budget proposals. For example, I found that in one year alone, 1980, 134 of 206 Committee for Economic Development trustees (65 percent) testified at least once before Congress on issues ranging from oil prices to tax cuts to cutting regulatory red tape. Not all of this testimony related directly to CED projects, but all of it related to issues of concern to the corporate community. In several instances the testimony was written by CED staff members; three of these staff members also presented their own testimony for the CED.

Impressive as these numerous appearances before legislative committees are, the most important contacts with government are more direct and formal. First, people from the policy-formation network are often members of the many unpaid committees that advise specific departments of the executive branch on general policies. Second, they are prominent on the presidential commissions that have been appointed with regularity since World War II to make recommendations on a wide range of issues from foreign policy to highway construction. Of fifteen commissions dealing with aspects of foreign and military policy, for example, twelve were headed by members of the Council on Foreign Relations, two others by trustees of the Committee for Economic Development. Of five commissions concerned with problems of government reorganization and federal salaries, four were chaired by trustees of the Committee for Economic Development.[43]

Third, corporate leaders have personal contact with both appointed and elected officials as members of the two policy organizations with the most access to government, the Business Council and the Business Roundtable. Fourth, they serve as informal advisers to the president in times of foreign policy crisis. Finally, as shown in an earlier section of this chapter, they are appointed to government positions with a frequency far beyond what would be expected if all groups had an equal chance, putting them in a position to endorse the policy suggestions brought to them by their colleagues and former employees in the policy-formation network.

For the most part, the positions taken by moderate conservatives determine the outcome of policy battles. If they do not wish to see any change, they side with their ultraconservative counterparts in the power elite to defeat any programs suggested by liberals or labor. There have been only a few instances in the twentieth century when the conservative voting bloc did not unite to block liberal-labor legislation through an outright majority, maneuvering within key congressional committees, or resort to a filibuster.

If the moderate conservatives favor policy changes, they seek the backing of liberal-labor elected officials for a program developed in moderate think tanks or policy-discussion groups, or even modify a plan advocated by liberals. They are especially likely to take this course in times of extreme social disruption like the 1930s and 1960s. This is because they have preferred an accommodation with insurgent forces rather than the police repression and imprisonment that are a likely consequence of the ultraconservative call for "law and order." The only exception to this generalization is the National Labor Relations Act of 1935. The moderate conservatives opposed this legislation as vehemently as they could, but it passed anyhow for reasons that are explained in the next section of this chapter. The alliance of moderate conservatives with the liberal-labor coalition on a few issues under exceptional circumstances does not mean that the ultraconservatives are easily defeated. Due to their great strength in Congress, they are often able to delay or modify the proposals they oppose.

These general conclusions based on a wide range of case studies can now be demonstrated by looking first at two recent policy conflicts, and then at classic pieces of legislation that are alleged to demonstrate pluralism or state autonomy.

The Environmental Movement

Pluralists claim that the rise of an environmental movement is evidence for pluralism in the United States. Here they are on somewhat firmer ground for a change because there was business opposition to some of the environmental legislation that was passed, particularly by the automobile, oil, and chemical industries. But there is much less substance than meets the eye.

To begin with, many of the environmental groups that are said to be in opposition to the corporate community are in fact long-standing organizations of the policy-formation network. They were in place long before the environmental movement rose to prominence in the late 1960s, as shown in chapter 4. As also shown in chapter 4, several are among the top recipients of funds from family and corporate foundations. The importance of foundations to the environmental movement is well understood by the pluralist Vogel. However, he does not see this funding as evidence for a class-dominance theory because he wrongly believes the foundations are separate from the corporate community.[44]

Moreover, many of the early environmental protection laws were not opposed by business. The most critical environmental law, which created the Environmental Protection Agency in 1970, was a product of organizations in the policy-formation network. It was only later that corporate executives began to complain about the alleged burdens and costs of environmental regulation, which always proved to be far, far lower than they claimed. Aside from the automobile and oil companies, most corporations moved into compliance once they were given (1) sufficient time to recover the costs on their old equipment and (2) tax breaks to purchase new equipment. As the head of the Business Roundtable's working group on clean air explained after passage of amendments to the Clean Air Act in 1990, most businesses see pollution laws as a "cost of doing business."[45] Today, the most vocal complaints about environmental laws come from ultraconservatives who oppose any government regulation on principle, or believe that the issue can be used to defeat liberal-labor candidates in elections.

The history of the Clean Air Act demonstrates many of these points. There was no opposition to its earliest version, in 1963, which called merely for further study. In fact, much of the backing for it came from the efforts of the centimillionaire Mellon family and its corporations to clean up the air in their headquarters city of Pittsburgh.[46] Nor did the somewhat stronger Clean Air Act of 1970 lead to an outcry by corporate leaders, some of whom openly admitted their preference for environmentalism to the antiwar movement.

The renewal of the act in 1977 led to the first major battles because the automobile companies insisted that they did not have the technology to meet the high standards of the law. In their successful effort to win a postponement, they claimed that the industry would have to shut down, leading to the rare situation in which a union—the autoworkers union in this case—lobbied Congress on the same side as the manufacturers. It is an example of the kind of coalition pluralists use to question a class-domination theory, but it was in effect coerced by the threat of job losses. Some environmentalists were disappointed by the postponement given to the car makers, but others pointed out that higher standards in the future had been gained as part of the trade-off.[47]

The arguments over amendments to the Clean Air Act in the 1980s took place between the Business Roundtable's Clean Air Working Group and the National Clean Air Coalition, a liberal-labor lobby that included all environmental groups, most trade unions, and many other liberal groups. The Roundtable group won the day by forcing delays in new legislation until its opponents agreed to a new way of regulation using market principles. It also insisted on the standards acceptable to oil, coal, and automobile companies. Once the moderate environmentalists from the policy network accepted these principles— to the great dismay of liberal environmentalists—the legislation moved forward.[48]

Environmentalists have had great success in sensitizing public opinion on environmental issues. They have been able to create watchdog groups whose reports receive considerable attention in the mass media. They have developed new ideas and technologies for controlling pollution that have been accepted by the corporate community. But they have not been able to pass any legislation that is opposed by the Business Roundtable. The environmental movement as a whole is more marginal in a power sense than its public reputation would suggest, and many of its successes are the result of compromises fashioned by the old-line environmental groups that are in fact part of the policy-formation network.

The Anatomy of a Recent Liberal Victory

The Family and Medical Leave Act of 1993 allows both male and female employees of companies with fifty or more employees to take up to 12 weeks of unpaid leave a year for child care or family illness. The bill was opposed by business groups when it was first introduced in 1986, so it is sometimes considered a liberal-labor victory. But how was passage possible?

The bill passed because the aspects most opposed by business groups were compromised. The original bill called for 18 weeks of unpaid leave for childbirth or adoption and 26 weeks of unpaid medical leave for employees in companies with fifteen or more workers. The 18 and 26 weeks were reduced to 12, and the minimum number of employees to qualify a company was raised from fifteen to fifty. Leave could be denied to those who were defined as "key" employees. The number of work hours before leave could be granted was raised. The penalties for noncompliance were reduced. In the end, the act covered only a few more employees in large corporations than already had this option, and the fact that the leaves were unpaid meant that relatively few workers could afford to take advantage of the provisions.[49]

HISTORICAL CASE STUDIES

This section presents brief analyses of five pieces of legislation that are often said to contradict a class-domination theory. In every instance, however, the case study on which this conclusion rests can be shown to be inadequate in the depth of its analysis. Furthermore, in each case the legislation passed because of support from moderate conservatives in the power elite. In some instances this support was due to strong social disruption caused by economic upheaval or a social movement, but that is not the same thing as voluntary groups contacting elected officials in the manner said to be common by pluralist theorists.

It is not possible to present a complete analysis of any of these cases within the confines of this book. Only the broad outlines of the legislation and the key turning points in its passage can be analyzed without taxing the patience of readers. The main goal is to show in a clear and direct fashion that the pluralist case is far weaker and far more contested than the impression given in mainstream textbooks in sociology and political science, which read as if there were no critiques or new information on the alleged evidence for pluralism. The necessary details for those who want to see more can be found in the sources in the accompanying footnotes.

Social Legislation in the Progressive Era

Reformers proposed several different pieces of social legislation between 1900 and 1912, some for the benefit of all workers, some especially for women. The proposals for all workers included (1) worker's compensation for those injured on the job, (2) unemployment insurance, (3) old-age pensions, and (4) government health insurance. The proposals especially for women were (1) maximum working hours, (2) minimum wages, and (3) and giving counties the right to provide income maintenance to widowed mothers (called "mother's pensions" at the time). Worker's compensation was the only one of the four general proposals to pass. Maximum hours and the possibility of granting mother's pensions were legislated for women, but not minimum wages.

This pattern of successes and failures is presented as evidence against a class-dominance view by sociologist Theda Skocpol in a book that emphasizes both the autonomy of government and the ability of interest groups to influence legislation if they are organized in a way that is compatible with the structure of the state. In her view, women's reform groups were ideally organized in relation to the "shape and contour" of the American state. The groups she has in mind are the National Congress of Mothers (now known as the PTA), the General Federation of Women's Clubs, and the National Consumers League.[50]

When the successful and unsuccessful efforts are compared with the stances taken by organized business, organized labor, and various reform groups, the main point that emerges is that business leaders were the decisive factor. They organized and led the successful campaign for worker's compensation because they were losing too many injury-related lawsuits in the courts, and they opposed the three general proposals (sponsored in varying degrees by reformers and union leaders) that failed. In the case of the legislation for women, business leaders were vigorously opposed to minimum wages, which failed, and indifferent to the two proposals that passed.

Maximum hours for women were not opposed by the corporate community because they did not impose any costs. More women could be hired if necessary without extra costs because there were no benefit payments that had to be made for each worker. Moreover, there were ways that the laws could be evaded, such as not counting time spent in cleaning or shutting down machinery. In this context, a coalition of women's groups, aided by male reformers who wanted working women to spend more time at home with their children, was able to pass such legislation in forty-one states between 1874 and 1920, with most of the successes coming between 1910 and 1920.[51]

As for mother's pensions, they were not of great concern to business leaders because they were intended for only a small percentage of the population and would have no effect on employment patterns. Moreover, the laws simply made it possible for counties to provide such pensions if they wished to, so the legislation was unlikely to add to the tax burden. In fact, very few counties took advantage of this legislation in the many states where it was passed, and the payments were very low when they were made.[52]

The failure of the movement for a minimum wage for women is of special interest as support for a class-domination theory because the upper-class women's groups were silent on the issue, meaning in effect that they were siding with their fathers, husbands, and brothers on a proposal that would have raised wage costs for business. The burden of the campaign therefore fell to one reformist organization, the National Consumers League, which was led by both women and men, contrary to Skocpol's emphasis. The campaign also had the support of local labor leaders, who saw minimum wages for women as a possible starting point for minimum wages for men.

Given this clear lineup of the power elite of the day against reformers and labor leaders, it supports a class-dominance view that the legislation passed in only fifteen states between 1912 and 1923, most of them Western ones with little industry at the time, and two states soon repealed those laws. In one of the few industrial states where such legislation passed, Massachusetts, it had very little impact because minimum wages were set industry by industry by a commission sensitive to business pressures, and the only penalty for violations was the publication of the names of violators.[53]

In short, there is no aspect of the social legislation of the Progressive Era that challenges a class-dominance view, and much that raises questions about interest-group power or state autonomy.

The Origin of Farm Subsidies

In 1933, with prices for cotton, hogs, and other major farm products sinking to all-time lows in the face of huge surpluses and declining consumer purchasing power, Congress quickly enacted a program that provided plantation owners and farmers with direct cash payments in exchange for taking some of their land out of production. These payments came to be known as farm subsidies, and they remained in existence until 1996. As already shown in chapter 2 (table 2.6), a large percentage of the money in the early 1990s went to a small number of large-scale farmers; this was also the case in the 1930s, except then much of the money also went to insurance companies that had come to own many farms when the owners defaulted on their mortgage payments.[54]

According to Skocpol and political scientist Kenneth Finegold, the program for farm subsidies was created by agricultural economists within the Department of Agriculture, which they claim is evidence for state autonomy theory. They assert that no farm groups played a significant role in creating the program, and that state officials ran the program.[55] They are wrong on all counts. The idea for the program was introduced into the policy-formation network by the president of a foundation controlled by the wealthiest industrial family of the era, the Rockefellers, owners of several large oil companies as well as many other forms of wealth. The idea was analyzed and amended by agricultural economists serving on the Agricultural Committee of the Social Sciences Research Council, a fledgling think tank that received over 90 percent of its funding from various Rockefeller foundations. Archival records show that the agricultural economist most responsible for writing up the program and demonstrating its feasibility was in regular correspondence with the Rockefeller employee who introduced him to the idea.[56]

The new farm subsidy plan was brought to the attention of business and farm leaders by another agricultural economist who worked with the Social Science Research Council. In so doing, he had the support of the president of the American Farm Bureau Federation in Montana and the Agricultural Committee of the nationwide Chamber of Commerce, where he served as a member. This economist not only sold the program to business leaders, who liked it because it dealt with farm surpluses in a way that did not interfere with their other policy preferences, but made significant changes in how the program would be administered, showing the kind of independence that is emphasized by pluralists and state autonomy theorists. He also incorporated important suggestions from a leading Boston businessman who was also a Chamber of Commerce official, showing the kind of interchange between experts and corporate leaders that is typical of the policy-formation network in action. Through a contact created by the Rockefeller employee who started the whole process, the agricultural economist then met with an adviser of presidential candidate Franklin D. Roosevelt during the 1932 campaign, and Roosevelt adopted the program.[57]

At first, organized farm groups showed little interest in the program, as Skocpol and Finegold point out. They still liked a plan of their own that would lead to the disposal of surplus crops in overseas markets at bargain prices, but that plan was heartily disliked by corporate leaders and most Republicans in Congress. The farm leaders' initial lack of interest in the new plan does not mean they were without influence, however. In fact, the newly elected president and Congress were unwilling to enact the program without their support. As the farm leaders were thinking about the issue and making adjustments in the plan, Southern plantation owners made their support for the program clear to President Roosevelt and Southern Democrats in Congress. They did so in the context of growing concern over falling cotton prices, which had been more stable up to 1932 than for most farm crops despite the fact the Depression had begun in 1929.[58] After leaders from the Farm Bureau made their final changes and Southern plantation owners signaled their support, the legislation sailed through Congress, and the Agricultural Adjustment Administration set up as a result was managed at the top by farm leaders and business executives, including several key officials from the South.[59]

Contrary to Skocpol and Finegold's view, then, agricultural experts in the federal government had very little to do with the origins of the farm subsidy program, although one of them did help to put the finishing touches on the overall package. Instead, it came from the corporate community and the policy-formation network. Nor did state officials run the program. There is no evidence for either state autonomy theory or pluralism in the farm subsidy program.

The Origins of Social Security

The Social Security Act of 1935 created what is perhaps the most popular and successful program ever developed by the federal government. According to state autonomy theorists, it is the product of experts, social workers, and elected officials, with little or no input from business leaders.[60] This view is completely wrong, as recent research in newly opened historical archives has revealed. In fact, large corporations began in the 1920s to be concerned about what to do with workers when they grew too old to be productive. They first developed the idea of private pension plans, but most of them were willing to accept government pensions in the context of the Great Depression, when it was hoped that pensions would have the added benefit of helping to stabilize the social system.

The main work on the program was done by experts from a private organization called Industrial Relations Counselors, Inc., which had been founded in 1921 by John D. Rockefeller, Jr., to search for ways to deal with labor unrest and avoid unionization. The organization was closely linked to both the family's main oil companies (today no longer controlled by the family) and charitable foundations. These Rockefeller experts worked with other experts and some business leaders through committees of the Social Science Research Council, the think tank mentioned in the previous case study.[61]

Many of these committee members, including three employees from Industrial Relations Counselors, Inc., were appointed to President Roosevelt's Social Security task force. It is generally agreed by historians and social scientists that the plans for old-age pensions were brought to Congress almost exactly as the Industrial Relations Counselors experts had written them.[62] In the case of the other major aspect of the bill, unemployment insurance, there were disagreements between the IRC experts, who wanted a nationwide plan, and experts from the University of Wisconsin, who wanted a state-level plan. Although the Wisconsin plan was sent to Congress, the issue is whether this was a victory for Wisconsin experts or anticipation of Southern Democratic resistance to a nationwide plan because it would undercut their control of their low-wage black labor force.

The legislation that went before Congress had the backing of several major industrialists of the time, who were serving on an advisory commission. These supporters included the chief executive officers of Standard Oil of New Jersey, General Electric, and Filene's Department Store of Boston, all prominent figures in the policy-formation network. Even so, the proposal for old-age pensions met resistance from the Southern Democrats because they thought it would be helpful to black workers. They therefore modified it so that states could set their own pension levels and determine eligibility.[63] The Southern Democrats accepted the unemployment plan much as it had been written because it gave so much discretion to individual states. The entire legislation then passed by a large margin.

From a class-domination point of view, the legislative conflict was between Northern corporate moderates and Southern plantation conservatives. For the state autonomy theorists, the argument was between rival experts, although one state autonomy theorist did write that "the extraordinary political leverage of southern representatives in Congress, out of proportion to the population and economic might of their states, was a factor that could never be neglected as FDR [the president] and the CES [his planning committee] formulated the bill."[64]

The following information supports the class-dominance argument on the old-age pension aspect of the legislation:

1. The experts who wrote it were direct employees of one of the most powerful upper-class families of the day, the Rockefellers, who kept these experts on their payroll even while they were serving in government so they would not have to draw government salaries.
2. Several top executives supported the plan.
3. The level of benefits was tied to salary level, thus preserving the values established in the labor market.
4. There were no government contributions from general taxes, an exclusion that business leaders insisted on.
5. There were both employer and employee contributions to old-age pensions, which business leaders insisted on.

The following arguments support the class-domination view on the importance of the Southern Democrats in forcing Roosevelt and his cabinet leaders to favor a state-level unemployment insurance program:

1. The expert from Wisconsin who oversaw the development of the overall legislation wrote in letters to friends and family that he was worried about Southern opposition to the program. He wrote to one person that Southern congressmen "feared that someone in Washington would dictate how much of a pension they should pay to the Negroes."[65]
2. According to a young corporate lawyer from an upper-class background who had a major role in writing the actual legislation, Southern Democrats were its major opponent.[66]
3. To the surprise and dismay of staff experts, the plan Roosevelt put forward had virtually no federal standards for unemployment compensation. Tax and benefit levels were entirely at the discretion of the states. Since the reformers from Wisconsin believed in setting minimum standards, it follows that these reformers were not the main concern if states were given a free hand to set their own standards.[67]

The way in which the Social Security Act was formulated in the policy-formation network and then amended in Congress reinforces several general points made throughout this book. First, it shows that the federal government had very little expertise of its own. Second, it shows the great power of the Southern segment of the dominant class in Congress. Third, the large role of the Southern rich in the Democratic party on issues of economic importance shows the limits that the two-party system placed on the liberal-labor coalition as long as African-Americans could not vote in the South, a point that has been demonstrated in detail for the years 1936 to 1964 by historian Alan Brinkley and political scientist Michael K. Brown.[68]

The Employment Act of 1946

The Employment Act of 1946 is one of the first pieces of legislation to be studied in great detail by a political scientist, and it is often claimed as evidence for pluralism even though the author's concern was simply to examine all aspects of the legislative process on a single bill.[69] The study is of special interest in the context of this book because it shows how members of the liberal-labor coalition who worked within the federal government, known as "New Dealers" at the time, were able to develop and put forward a bold economic plan. Their plan would have allowed the federal government to invest in the economy if there was not enough private investment to provide full employment. That is, it was a direct attack on the "privileged position of business" discussed at the end of chapter 2 as a "structural power" of the corporate rich.

Contrary to what might be expected from the structural perspective, the plan had to be fought vigorously by the corporate-conservative coalition, which in the end had enough votes from the conservative voting bloc in the House to win easily. But the setback for the liberal-labor coalition is not the issue here; the very fact that such legislation was proposed shows the weakness of any argument based on the assumption that current economic arrangements are immutable. If the liberal-labor coalition had had enough votes, the American economy might have looked very different from the way it does today.

At a more mundane level, the case study also reveals very clearly the differences between the moderate conservatives and ultraconservatives within the corporate-conservative coalition. Once the liberal-labor proposal was amended to the point at which it might be useful to moderate conservatives, they added a provision of their own and then joined with the liberal-labor coalition to pass the legislation.

The program that began its career as the "Full" Employment Act was the product of numerous liberal experts inside government who had been influenced by the thinking of John Maynard Keynes, the English economist who broke with orthodoxy in the face of the Great Depression and called for deficit spending by the government as the best way to increase consumer spending and restore economic growth. Their bill called for a careful government analysis of exactly how much business investment was needed to ensure full employment, and then for government investment in useful public infrastructure and social programs to make up for any shortfall in private investment. Eventually, the government could invest in its own utility companies, where it already had the precedent of the government-owned Tennessee Valley Authority (TVA), and in other companies as well. The liberals who wrote the bill knew that it had very little chance of passage in its original form, but they hoped it would generate widespread debate and accomplish a few of their goals.

The senator who introduced the bill quickly agreed to several amendments in order to move it out of committee, and it suffered more amendments on the Senate floor—to the great disappointment of its most liberal authors—but it did pass with its emphasis on full employment and government spending intact. The automatic mandate to spend in the face of high unemployment had been removed, however, as had any implication that the government would make any investments of its own.[70]

Despite the support in the Senate, the bill was soundly defeated by the conservative voting bloc in the House, which has been the story for most liberal legislation ever since. However, leaders within the Committee for Economic Development thought that some of the bill's provisions should be salvaged. They acted partly to ensure that the government had some capacity to deal with economic depressions, partly to convince Great Britain and other European countries that the new international economic order proposed by the planners at the Council on Foreign Relations—the "Grand Area" plan, discussed in chapter 4—would not be pulled into a worldwide depression by any lingering downturn in the American economy. In other words, the "business Keynesians" at the CED were convinced that pump-priming might be necessary on occasion to avoid another Great Depression.[71]

Armed with this analysis, the CED leaders went to a conservative Southern Democrat from Mississippi to suggest several amendments to what was by then called only the Employment Act. Specifically, CED leaders thought it would be useful to have an independent government commission that would prepare an annual report on the state of the economy and then submit that report to a new Joint Committee on the Economic Report made up of members from both the House and Senate. Shortly thereafter, the legislation was passed.[72]

Although the bill as passed by the House and Senate was almost exactly what the moderate conservatives called for, the liberal-labor coalition was able to influence its final form when it arrived in the conference committee appointed to iron out small differences between the Senate and House versions. In particular, they succeeded in making the new Council of Economic Advisers a part of the president's office rather than an independent commission. More generally, they ensured that the bill made the president responsible in principle for the overall functioning of the economy, although later events showed that this principle was not often carried out in practice.[73]

Strikingly, the final bill also has implications concerning the relationship between the policy-formation network and the government. This is due to the inclusion of a specific mandate for the Council of Economic Advisers and the Joint Committee on the Economic Report to utilize the work of "private research agencies."[74] The Brookings Institution and other think tanks thereby assumed a more formal standing. The act thus ended up helping to ensure that what little planning there was to be in the United States would take place outside the government in organizations closely related to the corporate community in terms of their financing and top-level governance.

The success of this arrangement can be seen very clearly in the career backgrounds of the people appointed to the Council of Economic Advisers. Eleven of the first thirteen chairs had worked for a policy-discussion group or think tank. Six had been advisers to the CED, six had an affiliation with the National Bureau of Economic Research, four were associated with the Brookings Institution, and three had an affiliation with the American Enterprise Institute. Half of the regular (nonchair) members of the three-person Council of Economic Advisers were members of the policy-formation network. The integration of the policy network and the government on economic issues through this agency is best summarized in its overall relationship with the Committee for Economic Development. In all, half of the people appointed to the Council of Economic Advisers were consultants to the CED either before or after their government appointments.[75]

As the overlap of the policy network and the Council of Economic Advisers shows, the story of the Employment Act of 1946 contradicts both pluralism and state autonomy theory. The key actors in bringing about its passage were moderate conservatives from the corporate community, and the end result was a further integration of the policy-formation network and the government. The policy groups and think tanks are strictly private in terms of citizen access, but they are part of the government in terms of some of their financing and to the degree that government agencies must rely on them for information and expert personnel. The corporate-conservative coalition had to defend the right of business to control all economic investments, but the end result was a strengthening of its position in terms of keeping a close rein on government.

The Trade Expansion Act of 1962

The most frequently cited evidence for pluralism comes from a study concerning a conflict over the lowering of tariffs that went on for several years before it ended with the passage of the Trade Expansion Act in 1962. Although the study, conducted by Raymond Bauer, Ithiel de Sola Pool, and Lewis Dexter, was concerned primarily with communication patterns among corporate leaders, lobbyists, elected officials, and the general public—and not directly with power—it is nonetheless used by pluralists because it presents a picture of inept businesspeople, general confusion, misunderstandings, and haphazard lawmaking.[76] Pluralist sociologist James Q. Wilson, for example, calls it "indisputably the best single study of business-government relations in postwar America," then quotes the authors' portrait of hapless corporate lobbyists: "The lobbies were on the whole poorly financed, ill-managed, out of contact with Congress, and at best only marginally effective in supporting tendencies and measures which already had behind them considerable impetus from other sources."[77]

This picture may or may not be accurate when it comes to the lobbyists, but the corporate leaders involved in the issue were anything but inept and disorganized, and Congress was not much more than the proverbial rubber stamp when it came to the resolution of the issue. The argument dragged on for several years because it involved differences between large corporate exporters on the one hand, who wanted lower tariffs, and textile and chemical manufacturers on the other, who feared competition from low-cost foreign imports. Once the two warring factions reached a compromise, the new legislation passed immediately. The lack of any serious involvement in the negotiations on the part of legislators is in stark contradiction to pluralist claims.

The drive for lower tariffs was initiated in the 1950s by the same corporate leaders and policy planners at the Council on Foreign Relations and Committee for Economic Development who formulated the Grand Area strategy as part of the War-Peace Studies (discussed in chapter 4). They were resisted in Congress by ultraconservative Republicans and the nationalist manufacturing segment of the corporate community that existed at the time. The low-tariff advocates would have won with ease except that Southern Democrats had abandoned their long-standing preferences for low tariffs. They made this change for the simple reason that the textile manufacturing industry gradually had moved from New England into the South over the previous two or three decades in search of low-wage, nonunion labor.

The textile industry's trade association expended considerable energy convincing its business colleagues in the South that lower tariffs would be ruinous for the industry. As part of its effort, it urged all corporate leaders in the South to lobby Congress against lower tariffs. As the authors of the study under scrutiny agree, this effort was organized and efficient, and almost overnight the vaunted free-trade philosophy of Southern Democrats—allegedly based on the deepest of principles—went out the window. In fact, there are few examples of an industry changing the stance of political representatives so quickly.[78]

In this context, the Committee for Economic Development once again came into the picture, this time as the main advocate for lower tariffs, publishing several statements on the issue. As part of these efforts, a lawyer/banker who served as president of the Philadelphia National Bank, one of the largest banks at the time, emerged as the CED's spokesperson on tariffs. He worked on several reports and held personal meetings with representatives of the textile and chemical industries. In 1961, after John F. Kennedy became president, this lawyer/banker was named as the Special White House Adviser on Free Trade. Bauer et al. make note of his appointment, but they do not connect him to the CED and his previous work on trade.[79] It is this lack of sociological context that causes the authors to see nothing but chaos.

Apparently unknown to Bauer et al., sociologist Floyd Hunter had published the details of these CED negotiations in an interview study released several years before. Unfortunately, the book reporting Hunter's results was criticized by pluralists because several of its chapters were based on the reputational method, so his findings were ignored. If Bauer et al. had read his study, they would have learned that CED leaders, American textile manufacturers, and Japanese textile manufacturers were in constant dialogue. Furthermore, the CED leaders had brokered an agreement by which the Japanese would "voluntarily" limit their exports of textiles to the United States, which was a key factor in the textile industry's ultimate willingness to accept new legislation. This private agreement preserved the general policy stance of free trade while at the same time responding to the concerns of the textile industry.[80]

Once appointed to the White House staff in 1961, CED's lawyer/banker met privately with top executives from the chemical industry while one of his aides carried out final negotiations with leaders from the textile industry. Congress then immediately passed the legislation. As the authors conclude: "It was the indirect effect of the administration's approach to and conversion of the textile industry lobby and to numerous other businessmen that indirectly affected Congress."[81] Although they miss the role of the CED when they talk about "the administration's approach," at least their conclusion shows the complete lack of independence on the part of Congress.

In other words, the avowed "protectionists" in Congress simply abandoned their opposition once there was an agreement among business leaders that satisfied chemical and textile manufacturers. The real battle was between what were then rival segments of the dominant class. A case study constantly cited by pluralists as evidence for their theory actually boils down to a clash within the corporate community that is resolved when Congress quickly ratifies the agreement between class segments.

There is, however, one element of pluralism in the story. The bill also included a provision for "adjustment assistance" for those workers who were hurt by import competition. This provision was advocated by unions and opposed by the CED, but President Kennedy and his aides insisted on it. Even here, there were limits to what was accomplished because it was very hard for workers to qualify for assistance. Moreover, funds for the program were cut back in the 1980s and then eliminated entirely in 1996 as part of the attempt to balance the budget.[82]

THE GREAT EXCEPTION: LABOR POLICY IN THE 1930s

So far, this chapter has stressed the importance of (1) the conservative voting bloc in defeating the liberal-labor coalition on class-based issues and (2) the alliance of moderate conservatives with the liberal-labor coalition against ultraconservatives in times of social unrest. There is, however, a third possible alliance, one between Northern and Southern Democrats. This alliance passed the most liberal piece of labor legislation of the twentieth century, the National Labor Relations Act of 1935, which created the National Labor Relations Board (NLRB) to oversee unionization and the process of collective bargaining.

In the years between 1932 and 1994, Northern and Southern Democrats often voted together on nonclass issues that increased government spending on programs that benefited their major constituencies. The Northern Democrats, for example, voted for agricultural subsidies desired by Southern agribusinesses, and the Southern Democrats reciprocated by supporting the spending programs favored by urban growth coalitions and unions.[83] But they never voted together on legislation concerning business regulation or unions. On such issues Southern Democrats usually were in complete agreement with Northern Republicans, thereby forming the conservative voting bloc (discussed in chapter 6).

The disagreement between the Southern Democrats and Northern Republicans over collective bargaining legislation in 1935 was the first of only two occasions when they did not support each other on a labor issue. The second came in 1964 when the Northern Republicans joined with liberal Democrats to end a lengthy filibuster in the Senate by Southern Democrats and then pass civil rights legislation in the face of major social disruptions in the South, including bombings of black homes and churches in Birmingham, Alabama. In that instance the power elite was confronted with the potential for ongoing social turmoil in inner cities across the nation and decided to move in an accommodating direction to bring the South more in line with practices in the rest of the country.[84] In 1934–1935, by contrast, social disruption was coming from industrial workers, socialists, and communists in the North, and the Southern Democrats broke rank with the Republicans.

Two intertwined factors are usually invoked in explaining the success of the National Labor Relations Act. First, Northern voters reacted to the Great Depression by electing liberal Democrats to Congress in 1932 and 1934 to replace conservative Republicans. Second, the organizing efforts by unions outside the South put pressure on Congress to act. This explanation supports pluralist theory because it adds up to a liberal-labor victory over the corporate community.

Although I see liberal electoral success and union organizing as necessary conditions for passage of pro-union legislation, I do not believe they are sufficient because they do not take into account two other critical factors in the power equation of the 1930s: control of Congress by Southern Democrats through the seniority system and other procedural rules, and President Franklin Roosevelt's unwillingness to do anything that would alienate his Democratic Party allies from the South. The pivotal question, therefore, is why Southern Democrats did not weaken or block the National Labor Relations Act. The answer is found in the fact that liberal Democrats excluded agricultural, seasonal, and domestic workers from the protections of the act. Since such workers were the heart of the Southern workforce at the time, this meant that the Southern segment of the dominant class was exempted from the legislation and therefore did not oppose it. The exclusion of agricultural workers also made it easier for the Progressive Republicans from the predominantly agrarian states of the Midwest and Great Plains to support the legislation, leaving the employers of Northern industrial labor almost completely isolated. As a perceptive observer from the 1930s wrote,

> Most of our social legislation, in fact, has been enacted as a result of a political "deal" between organized labor and the farm groups.

The basis of this deal has always been: we, the farm representatives, will not object to this legislation, if you, the representatives of organized labor, will agree to exempt agricultural employees.[85]

This bargain was fully understood at the time. When the leader of the Socialist Party wrote the main sponsor of the National Labor Relations Act asking why agricultural workers had been excluded from the bill, the senator wrote back as follows:

I am very regretful of this, because I should like to see agricultural workers given the protection of my bill, and would welcome any activity that might include them. They have been excluded only because I thought it would be better to pass the bill for the benefit of industrial workers than not to pass it at all, and that inclusion of agricultural workers would lessen the likelihood of passage so much as not to be desirable.[86]

This stance was affirmed many years later by the staff member in charge of writing the legislation when he explained why the liberal secretary of agriculture also favored the exclusion of farm labor: "He was entirely beholden to the chairmen of the agricultural committees in the Senate and House, who were all big Southern landholders. . . ."[87] The importance of excluding agricultural labor to assure the passage of this legislation is further demonstrated by recalling what happened when the Social Security Act was considered by Congress in the same year: It was greatly modified to satisfy the Southerners.

Support for this analysis can be found in events that unfolded after the legislation passed. Due to disruptive sit-down strikes throughout the North in 1937, along with attempts to create integrated industrial unions in some parts of the South, the Southern Democrats turned against the act, doing everything they could to undermine it throughout the years leading up to World War II.[88] When Republicans gained control of Congress for a two-year period after the war, the Southerners joined with them in passing conservative changes in the act that had severe consequences for the union movement. After the liberal-labor coalition worked very hard to restore a Democratic Congress and elect a Democratic president in 1948, it argued that the Democrats should remove the conservative amendments because of the large liberal-labor contribution to their victory. But the Southern Democrats would not agree:

Although President Truman dutifully supported revision of Taft-Hartley, even under Democratic control Congress remained in conservative hands. Southern Democrats, almost uniformly hostile to the labor movement, dominated key congressional committees. While the tally sheets of labor lobbyists showed that most Democratic senators and congressmen from northern, eastern, and blue-collar districts loyally supported labor's goals, they also revealed that labor simply could not muster the strength to gain significant revision of the law.[89]

Nor has the union movement had any legislative victories on organizing issues since that time. It lost to the conservative voting bloc on reform efforts in 1961, 1967, and 1977. Then it was defeated in 1978 by a filibuster in the Senate in its attempt to make even larger changes in the law.[90] In effect, then, the history of labor legislation since 1935 is as follows: The liberal-labor coalition conceded to government the right to regulate methods of union organizing in exchange for governmentally protected rights, then had those rights taken away gradually by a series of court decisions, NLRB rulings, and legislative amendments.[91] It was able to take advantage of what turned out to be a temporary disagreement between Northern and Southern employers in a time of crisis but could not defeat a united power elite after World War II even when Democrats were in power. This is not a record that can be claimed by pluralists for their theory. It is not tyranny, but it is not pluralism either.

Although the passage of the National Labor Relations Act was unexpected at the time, and has provided rival theorists with an interesting explanatory challenge ever since, I do not want to leave the impression that it was the reason for the surge in union membership that began in 1937 with the sit-down strikes. In fact, Roosevelt's re-election in 1936 and the election of liberal Democratic governors in big industrial states like Pennsylvania and Michigan were far more important to union success. This is because these elected officials refused to send federal troops or state police to arrest workers when they took over factories. Their refusal to honor repeated requests from corporate leaders for armed intervention marked the first time in American history that government force was not used to break a major strike, making it possible for union organizers to triumph in the automobile, rubber, and other heavy industries. Just a year later, however, state police in Ohio, Indiana, and Illinois helped owners defeat strikers who were trying to organize the steel industry. At that point the union movement was stalled until the need for management-labor cooperation during World War II made its revival possible.[92]

Once unions were established, the National Labor Relations Board assumed the administrative role in the regulation of class conflict that had been envisioned for it by the congressional majority in 1935. For purposes of this book, however, the act is of interest because of the challenge it poses for a class-domination theory.

BUT BUSINESS LEADERS FEEL POWERLESS

Despite the strong "Who sits?" and "Who wins?" evidence that the power elite has great power in relation to the federal government, many corporate leaders feel that they are relatively powerless in the face of government. To hear them tell it, Congress is more responsive to organized labor, environmentalists, and consumers than it is to them. They also claim to be harassed by willful and arrogant bureaucrats who encroach upon the rightful preserves of the private sector, sapping them of their confidence and making them hesitant to invest their capital.

These feelings have been documented most vividly in a book by David Vogel and Leonard Silk, a business columnist for the *New York Times*. They were permitted to observe a series of meetings at the Conference Board in which the social responsibilities of business were being discussed. The men at these meetings were convinced that everybody but them was listened to by government officials, who were viewed as responsive to the immediate preferences of the majority of citizens. "The have-nots are gaining steadily more political power to distribute the wealth downward," complained one executive. "The masses have turned to a larger government."[93]

Some even wondered whether democracy and capitalism are compatible. "Can we still afford one man, one vote? We are tumbling on the brink," said one. "One man, one vote has undermined the power of business in all capitalist countries since World War II," announced another. "The loss of the rural vote weakens conservatives."[94] However, Silk and Vogel concluded that businesspeople in America are unlikely to go so far as to be fascists—even with their antidemocratic bias—because they are so antigovernment:

> Even with their elitist, anti-populist, and even anti-democratic
> bias, however, few American businessmen can fairly be regarded
> as "fascist," if by that term one means a believer in a political
> system in which there is a combination of private ownership and
> a powerful, dictatorial government that imposes major restrictions
> on economic, political, social and religious freedoms. Basically,
> the anti-governmental mind set of the great majority of American
> businessmen has immunized them against the virus of fascism.[95]

The fear business leaders express of the democratic majority leads them to view recessions as a saving grace, for recessions help to keep the expectations of workers in check. Workers who fear for their jobs are less likely to demand higher wages or government social programs. For example, different corporate executives made the following comments:

This recession will bring about the healthy respect for economic values that the Depression did.

People need to recognize that a job is the most important thing they can have. We should use this recession to get the public to better understand how our economic system works. Social goals are OK, provided the public is aware of their costs.

It would be better if the recession were allowed to weaken more than it will, so that we would have a sense of sobriety.[96]

The negative feelings these business leaders have toward government are not a new development in the corporate community. A study of businesspeople's views in the nineteenth century found that they believed political leaders to be "stupid" and "empty" people who went into politics only to earn a living. As for the ordinary voters, they were "brutal, selfish and ignorant."[97] A comment written by a businessman in 1886 could have been made at the Conference Board meetings just discussed: "In this good, democratic country where every man is allowed to vote, the intelligence and the property of the country is at the mercy of the ignorant, idle and vicious." The attitudes held by nineteenth-century business leaders undercut the claim by Vogel and Silk that business hostility toward government stems largely from the growth of government programs during the New Deal.[98]

The emotional expressions of businesspeople, or anyone else, about their power or lack of it cannot be taken seriously as power indicators. To do so, as Mills wrote, is to "confuse psychological uneasiness with the facts of power and policy," which are in the realm of sociology, economics, and politics.[99] But it is nonetheless important to understand why corporate leaders complain about a government they dominate. There are several intertwined reasons.

First, complaining about government is a useful political strategy. It puts government officials on the defensive and forces them to keep proving that they are friendly to business. Political scientist Grant McConnell made this point as follows:

Whether the issue is understood explicitly, intuitively, or not at all, denunciations serve to establish and maintain the subservience of government units to the business constituencies to which they are actually held responsible. Attacks upon government in general place continuing pressure on governmental officers to accommodate their activities to the groups from which support is most reliable.[100]

Still, it seems surprising that business executives would feel the need to resort to this tactic. This is especially the case given the evidence that bureaucrats who in any way speak out or criticize their elected or appointed superiors are removed from their positions, left with no duties, or otherwise punished in a dramatic and public way that is a clear lesson to other civil servants.[101] Silk and Vogel suggest that part of the explanation might be found in the fact that so few civil servants are part of the upper class and corporate networks. They quote economist Edward S. Mason on the contrast between Western Europe and the United States on this point:

> It is clear to the most obtuse observer that there is a much more distant relationship between business and government in the United States than, say, in Britain, or France or the Netherlands. A British businessman can say, "some of my best friends are civil servants," and really mean it. This would be rare in the United States.[102]

In Western Europe, the government officials whom American business leaders vilify with the hostile label "bureaucrats" are part of the same social networks as the business leaders due to common class background and common schooling. But such is not the case in the United States, where the antigovernment ideology tends to restrain members of the upper class from lifetime government careers except in the State Department. Because middle-class people who are not part of the in-group network are employed in the bureaucracies, the different method of domination that McConnell describes is necessary. It means that "tough-talking" members of the corporate community have to come into government as top-level appointees in order to "ride herd" on the "bureaucrats" in Washington. In other words, lack of social contact in a situation of uncertainty explains some of the hostile feelings toward bureaucrats whose great power exists more in imagination than in reality.

There also seems to be an ideological level to the corporate stance toward government. In a perceptive discussion of why corporate leaders "distrust their state," Vogel explains their attitude in terms of their fear of the populist, democratic ideology that underlies American government. Since power is in theory in the hands of all the people, there is always the possibility that some day "the people," in the sense of the majority, will make the government into the pluralist democracy it is supposed to be.[103] In the American historical context, the great power of the dominant class is illegitimate, and the existence of such power is therefore vigorously denied. Another political scientist, James Prothro, studying business views during the 1920s, when everyone agrees it dominated the federal government, found the same mistrust of government. He reached conclusions similar to those of Vogel, conclusions that show once again that the hostility expressed by businesspeople is not a response to "big government": "The conspicuous anti-governmental orientation of business organizations is itself an incident of the more basic fear that popular control will, through the device of universal suffrage, come to dominate the governmental process."[104]

The most likely reason for this fear of popular control is revealed by the power elite's unending battle with unions, as described throughout this book. It is an issue like no other in evoking angry rhetoric and near-perfect unity among corporate leaders. It also has generated more violence than any other issue except civil rights for African-Americans. The power elite's unusually strong reaction to any government help for unions supports the hypothesis that the corporate community, the growth coalitions, and small businesses are all antigovernment because they fear government as the only institution that could tighten labor markets, thereby changing the functioning of the system to some extent and reducing the power of employers. It is also noteworthy that this fear is even greater in the South, where Southern property owners have twice experienced the intervention of the federal government in their dealings with their primary labor force, African-Americans, first in the Civil War, which freed the slaves, then in the Civil Rights Movement, when federal troops were stationed in Southern cities at different times to deal with the tension and turmoil brought on by white resistance to the end of segregation.

The federal government can influence labor markets in five basic ways:

1. The government can hire unemployed workers to do necessary work relating to parks, schools, roadways, and the environment. Such government programs were a great success during the New Deal when unemployment reached 25 percent and social disruption seemed imminent, but the programs were quickly shut down at the insistence of business leaders when order was restored and the economy began to improve.[105]

2. It can support the right to organize unions and bargain collectively, as described in the previous section. This kind of government initiative is opposed even more strongly than government employment because it gives workers a sustained organizational base for moving into the political arena.

3. Although the corporate rich see the value of Social Security, disability insurance, and even unemployment insurance, they worry that politicians might allow these programs to become too generous. Rolling back the growth of these programs, which occurred in the turmoil of the 1960s and 1970s, was a primary goal of the Reagan Administration in order to reduce inflation and make corporations more profitable—and it largely succeeded.[106]

4. The government can tighten labor markets by limiting immigration. The immigration of low-wage labor has been essential to the corporate community throughout American history. Immigration also has been the route to freedom and a better life for tens of millions of people from all over the world, so it is now a highly emotional issue deeply intertwined with people's image of the country. It is therefore not easily seen or discussed as a labor-market issue, which means that employers are likely to have an unending supply of new workers to loosen labor markets. When conservative Republicans began to think about passing anti-immigration legislation in the mid-1990s, as called for in their campaign rhetoric, they were met with a barrage of employer opposition—particularly from leaders in agribusiness—and quickly retreated.

5. The government can reduce unemployment and tighten labor markets by lowering interest rates through the operations of the Federal Reserve System. This fact has been made obvious to a large percentage of the public by the way in which the Federal Reserve increases unemployment by increasing the interest rates whenever the unemployment rate dips too low. Although the issue is cast in terms of "inflation," in fact the economics of inflation are often the politics of labor markets. That is, the use of high interest rates to cut inflation is possible primarily because of the decline of organized labor and the weakness of the liberal-labor coalition since the 1970s.

Given the many ways the government could tighten labor markets, and thereby reduce profits and increase the economic power of American workers, it is understandable that the power elite would be fearful of the government it dominates. Although government is essential to the power elite for the many reasons outlined at the beginning of the chapter, it also could be used to further the aims of the liberal-labor coalition, as it has been in many Western European countries, where business leaders did not have as much power at crucial historical moments in labor history because of the independent power exerted by landed aristocrats and government officials.[107]

CONCLUSION

This chapter has demonstrated the power elite's wide-ranging access to government through the interest-group and policy-formation processes, as well as through its ability to influence appointments to major government positions. When coupled with the several different kinds of power discussed in earlier chapters, this access and involvement add up to power elite domination of the federal government.

By *domination,* as stated in the first chapter, social scientists mean the ability of a class or group to set the terms under which other classes or groups within a social system must operate. By this definition, domination does not mean control on each and every issue, and it does not rest solely on involvement in government. Influence over government is only the final and most visible aspect of power elite domination, which has its roots in the class structure, the corporate control of the investment function, and the operation of the policy-formation network. If government officials did not have to wait for corporate leaders to decide where and when they will invest, and if government officials were not further limited by the general public's acceptance of policy recommendations from the policy-formation network, then power elite involvement in elections and government would count for a lot less than they do under present conditions.

Domination by the power elite does not negate the reality of continuing conflict over government policies, but few conflicts, it has been shown, involve challenges to the rules that create privileges for the upper class and domination by the power elite. Most of the numerous battles within the interest-group process, for example, are only over specific spoils and favors; they often involve disagreements among competing business interests.

Similarly, conflicts within the policy-making process of government often involve differences between the moderate conservative and ultraconservative segments of the dominant class. At other times they involve issues in which the needs of the corporate community as a whole come into conflict with the needs of specific industries, which is what happens to some extent on tariff policies and also on some environmental legislation. In neither case does the nature of the conflict call into question the domination of government by the power elite.

The chapter shows that there is no evidence from within the governmental arena for the rival theories considered in this book. Contrary to what pluralists claim, there is not a single case study on any issue of any significance that shows a liberal-labor victory over a united corporate-conservative coalition, which is strong evidence for a class-domination theory on the "Who wins?" power indicator. The classic case studies frequently cited by pluralists have been shown to be gravely deficient as evidence for their views. Most of these studies reveal either conflicts among rival groups within the power elite or situations in which the moderate conservatives have decided for their own reasons to side with the liberal-labor coalition. Nor are recent pluralist studies such as *The Hollow Core* any better than the classics.

They state the power elite theory incorrectly, and therefore unfairly; they use methods of doubtful utility, remain on the surface of issues, and still end up with findings that are more in keeping with the thesis of this book than pluralism.

As for state autonomy theory, it is highly deficient when applied to the United States. State autonomy is possible only when a state is unified and relatively impermeable to the employees and representatives of private organizations. But the American government is neither. It is a fragmented government that is completely open to outside agents and is therefore vulnerable to domination through the electoral process (explained in chapter 6) and through the appointments from the corporate community and policy-formation network documented in this chapter.

Ignoring the backgrounds of government officials, state autonomy theorists make the implicit assumption that "roles" overpower all other factors in shaping people's decision-making practices while in government. There is, however, no evidence for such an assumption except for extremely hierarchical and regimented aspects of government like the military. In the military, training and roles matter more than background, but the military is a lifetime career for officers who have gone through rigorous initiations, not a relatively short sojourn in a government agency, as is the case for most American government officials.

The movement between the private sector and government on the part of members of the power elite creates a system of "revolving interlocks" in which a person is first part of one sector and then part of the other for a short time. This system is another factor in blurring the line between the power elite and the state. Aside from military officers and diplomats in the foreign service, there are few top-level government officials who have long careers in government. The career employees, constantly criticized as allegedly imperious "bureaucrats," are not the decision makers.

Dye's version of institutional elitism fares no better in the governmental arena than it does in relation to the corporate community, corporate lawyers, and the mass media. It has been found wanting in its claims about the role of self-interested bureaucrats in causing the growth of government budgets and in its characterization of the Clinton Administration as one with relatively little corporate presence.

More generally, it now can be concluded that all four indicators of power introduced in chapter 1 point to the corporate rich and their power elite as the dominant organizational structure in American society. First, the wealth and income distributions are skewed in their favor more than in any other industrialized democracy. They are clearly the most powerful group in American society in terms of "Who benefits?" Second, the appointees to government come over-whelmingly from the corporate community and its associated policy-formation network. Thus, the power elite is clearly the most powerful in terms of "Who sits?"

Third, the power elite wins far more often than it loses on policy issues resolved in the federal government. Thus, it is the most powerful in terms of "Who wins?" Finally, as shown in reputational studies in the 1950s and 1970s (that were not discussed in this book, but were foot-noted), corporate leaders are the most powerful group in terms of "Who shines?" By the usual rules of evidence in a social science investigation using multiple indicators, the owners and managers of large income-producing properties are the dominant class in the United States.

Still, as noted at the end of the first chapter, power structures are not immutable. Societies change and power structures evolve or crumble from time to unpredictable time, especially in the face of challenge. When it is added that the liberal-labor coalition persists in the face of its numerous defeats, and that free speech and free elec-tions are not at risk, there remains the possibility that class domina-tion could be replaced by a greater sharing of power in the future. The next chapter therefore looks at the future of American politics in terms of those factors that could lead to changes in the power struc-ture over the next 10 to 20 years.

NOTES

1. For the best contemporary theorizing on the state, see Michael Mann, "The Autonomous Power of the State: Its Origins, Mechanisms and Re-sults," *Archives of European Sociology*, 25 (1984): 185–213; and Michael Mann, *The Sources of Social Power*, vol. 2 (New York: Cambridge University Press, 1993), chapter 3. For the state autonomy view, see Theda Skocpol, *States and Social Revolution* (New York: Cambridge University Press, 1979); and Theda Skocpol, *Protecting Soldiers and Mothers* (Cambridge: Harvard University Press, 1992), pp. 41–44. For a fine overview of recent theories of the state, see Clyde Barrow, *Critical Theories of the State* (Madison: University of Wisconsin Press, 1993). For a telling cri-tique of state autonomy theory, see Rhonda F. Levine, "A Marxist Analy-sis of the State: Has It Withered Away?," *The Wisconsin Sociologist*, 30 (1993): 65–74. For an insightful analysis of American myths about the alleged negative effects of the government on the economy, see Fred Block, *The Vampire State* (New York: The New Press, 1996).
2. Roger Friedland and A. F. Robertson, eds., *Beyond the Marketplace* (New York: Aldine de Gruyter, 1990). Robert Kuttner, *Everything for Sale: The Virtues and Limits of Markets* (New York: Alfred A. Knopf, 1997).

3. James Livingston, *Origins of the Federal Reserve System* (Ithaca, NY: Cornell University Press, 1986); William Greider, *Secrets of the Temple* (New York: Simon & Schuster, 1987).

4. Thomas Dye, *Who's Running America?*, 6th ed. (Englewood Cliffs, NJ: Prentice-Hall, 1995), p. 57.

5. Ibid., p. 107.

6. Kenneth Finegold and Theda Skocpol, *State and Party in America's New Deal* (Madison: University of Wisconsin Press, 1995), pp. 52–53.

7. William Berry and David Lowery, *Understanding United States Government Growth* (New York: Praeger, 1987). The authors point out that previous studies of government expenditures have been flawed by (1) the failure to distinguish real growth from inflationary growth, which turns out to greatly distort results; and (2) the failure to "disaggregate" overall federal expenditures into (a) transfer payments like Social Security and unemployment insurance; (b) the purchase of civilian goods and services; and (c) defense spending. They also point out that the "lion's share" of the increase in government spending has been in what they call "cost growth," meaning that the government cannot switch to machinery in the face of higher wage levels, as many private businesses can, because its services are labor intensive (i.e., require people to do them). The government therefore has to pay higher wages for about the same number of employees, while the private sector can decrease its number of employees and thereby reduce its labor costs.

8. Dye, op. cit., p. 105.

9. Berry and Lowery, op. cit., p. 183.

10. Ted Goertzel, "Militarism As a Sociological Problem," *Research in Political Sociology,* 1 (1985): 119–139.

11. Edward Herman, "Privatization," *Dollars and Sense* (March/April 1997): 10–13.

12. Michael Useem, "Which Business Leaders Help Govern?," in *Power Structure Research*, ed. G. William Domhoff (Beverly Hills: Sage Publications, 1980); Michael Useem, *The Inner Circle* (New York: Oxford University Press, 1984).

13. Dye, op. cit., pp. 84, 88.

14. For example, see David T. Stanley, Dean E. Mann, and James W. Doig, *Men Who Govern* (Washington, DC: Brookings Institution, 1967); Kenneth Prewitt and William McAllister, "Change in the American Executive Elite—1930–1970," in *Elite Recruitment in Democratic Politics*, ed. Heinz Eulau and Moshe M. Chaudnowski (New York: Halstead Press, 1976).

15. Philip Burch, *Elites in American History*, 3 vols. (New York: Holmes & Meier, 1980, 1981). While these volumes are highly useful for social background information and as a contribution to evidence for class dominance on the basis of the "Who sits?" indicator of power, they are flawed by the attempt to analyze decisions strictly on the basis of socioeconomic backgrounds and therefore are ignored by pluralists. It is one thing to study social backgrounds as an indicator of power, quite another to do case studies of decisions, which require a different type of information.

16. Beth Mintz, "The President's Cabinet, 1897–1972: A Contribution to the Power Structure Debate," *Insurgent Sociologist*, 5 (1975): 131–148. For a related study with similar findings, see Peter Freitag, "The Cabinet and Big Business: A Study of Interlocks," *Social Problems*, 23 (1975): 137–152.

17. Arthur M. Schlesinger, Jr., *A Thousand Days* (Boston: Houghton Mifflin, 1965), pp. 128–129.

18. David Halberstam, *The Best and the Brightest* (New York: Random House, 1972), p. 4.

19. Mark Johnson, "The Consensus Seekers: How the Power Elite Shape National Policy," Masters Thesis, University of California at Santa Barbara, 1978.

20. "Putting His Philosophy to Work Fast," *Business Week* (November 17, 1980): 155.

21. Holly Sklar and Robert Lawrence, *Who's Who in the Reagan Administration* (Boston: South End Press, 1981).

22. Dye, op. cit., p. 88.

23. Harold Salzman and G. William Domhoff, "The Corporate Community and Government: Do They Interlock?," in *Power Structure Research*, ed. G. William Domhoff (Beverly Hills, CA: Sage Publications, 1980); G. Calvin MacKenzie, ed., *The In-and-Outers* (Baltimore: Johns Hopkins University Press, 1987).

24. Grant McConnell, *Private Power and American Democracy* (New York: Alfred A. Knopf, 1966), p. 8.

25. For examples of this new version of pluralism, see Jeffrey Berry, *The Interest Group Society* (Boston: Little, Brown, 1984); David Vogel, *Fluctuating Fortunes* (New York: Basic Books, 1989); and John Wright, *Interest Groups and Congress* (Boston: Allyn & Bacon, 1996). For a fine book on interest groups by two political scientists who doubt these new claims, see Kay Schlozman and John Tierney, *Organized Interests and American Democracy* (New York: Harper & Row, 1986).

26. Vogel, op. cit., p. 194.

27. Ibid., p. 53.

28. Ardith Maney and Loree Bykerk, *Consumer Politics* (Westport, CT: Greenwood Press, 1994), p. 153.

29. G. William Domhoff, *The Power Elite and the State* (Hawthorne, NY: Aldine de Gruyter, 1990), p. 269; Vogel, op. cit., p. 149.

30. Michael Pertschuk, *Revolt Against Regulation* (Berkeley: University of California Press, 1982).

31. Maney and Bykerk, op. cit., p. 104.

32. Michael Pertschuk, *Giant Killers* (New York: Norton, 1986), chapter 6.

33. Ibid., pp. 182, 205–206.

34. Michael Pertschuk and Wendy Schaetzel, *The People Rising* (New York: Thunder's Mouth Press, 1989).

35. Josh Sugarman, *National Rifle Association: Money, Firepower, and Fear* (Washington, DC: National Press Books, 1992), p. 87. For a full account of all aspects of the controversy over gun control, see Robert Spitzer, *The Politics of Gun Control* (Chatham, NJ: Chatham House Publishers, 1995).

36. John Heinz, Edward Laumann, Robert Nelson, and Robert Salisbury, *The Hollow Core* (Cambridge: Harvard University Press, 1993), p. xvi.

37. Ibid., p. 299; C. Wright Mills, *The Power Elite* (New York: Oxford University Press, 1956), p. 289.

38. Heinz, et al., op. cit., p. 263. Gwen Moore, "The Structure of a National Elite Network," *American Sociological Review*, 44 (1979): 673–691.

39. Heinz, et al., op. cit., p. 350. Actually, the data are very weak on this issue. In ninety-four instances in which the authors have success/failure judgments from two people in the same organization, "the assessments of success differ substantially." In short, this is a situation in which interview responses are not useful. The authors do not have a good measure of success, and hence no real way to talk about power.

40. Ibid., pp. 351, 409–410.

41. Ibid., p. 359.

42. Ibid., pp. 221, 396.

43. Thomas R. Wolanin, *Presidential Advisory Commissions* (Madison: University of Wisconsin, 1975). For two informative case studies on specific commissions, see Morton H. Halperin, "The Gaither Commission and the Policy Process," *World Politics* (April 1961); Ushaa Mahanjani, "Kennedy and the Strategy of Aid: The Clay Report and After," *Western Political Quarterly* (September 1965).

44. Vogel, op. cit., p. 104.

45. Keith Schneider, "How Clean Air Became Part of the Bottom Line," *New York Times* (Oct. 28, 1990): D4. For evidence that the compliance costs for the Clean Air Act are four to eight times below what the utility industry estimated, see Eban Goodstein and Hart Hodges, "Polluted Data: Overestimating Environmental Costs," *The American Prospect*, 35 (1997): 68. On eleven other environmental regulations, estimated cost exceeded the actual cost by a factor of at least two in all but one instance.

46. Charles O. Jones, *Clean Air* (Pittsburgh: University of Pittsburgh Press, 1975).

47. For details on the Clean Air Act from the 1960s to 1990s, see Gary Bryner, *Blue Skies, Green Politics*, 2d ed. (Washington, DC: Congressional Quarterly Press, 1995). For an excellent analysis of the 1990 version, see George Gonzalez, "Capitalism and the Environment: An Analysis of U.S. Environmental Policy via Competing Theories of the State," Ph.D. Dissertation, University of Southern California, 1997, chapter 4.

48. Mark Dowie, *Losing Ground* (Cambridge: MIT Press, 1995).

49. Paul Taylor, "Study of Firms Finds Parental Leave Impact Light," *Washington Post* (May 23, 1991): A9.

50. Theda Skocpol, *Protecting Soldiers and Mothers*, op. cit.

51. G. William Domhoff, *State Autonomy or Class Dominance?* (Hawthorne, NY: Aldine de Gruyter, 1996), pp. 244–245; Holly McCammon, "The Politics of Protection: State Minimum Wage and Maximum Hours Laws for Women in the United States, 1870–1930," *Sociological Quarterly*, 36 (1995): 217–249.

52. Domhoff, *State Autonomy or Class Dominance?*, op. cit., pp. 246–247.

53. Alice Kessler-Harris, *Out to Work* (New York: Oxford University Press, 1982), p. 196.
54. Pete Daniel, *Breaking the Land* (Urbana: University of Illinois Press, 1985), pp. 170–173.
55. Finegold and Skocpol, op. cit.
56. Domhoff, *State Autonomy or Class Dominance?*, op. cit., pp. 59–69. Chapter 3 of this book is an empirical refutation of the claims by Skocpol and Finegold.
57. Ibid., p. 65.
58. Theodore Saloutos, *Farmer Movements in the South* (Berkeley: University of California Press, 1960), pp. 160, 254, 259, 274, 277–278, 281.
59. Theodore Saloutos, *The American Farmer and the New Deal* (Ames: Iowa State University Press, 1982), chapter 5.
60. Ann Orloff, *The Politics of Pensions* (Madison: University of Wisconsin Press, 1993).
61. Domhoff, *State Autonomy or Class Dominance?*, op. cit., pp. 128–149. Chapter 5 of this book is a detailed empirical analysis of the origins of the Social Security Act based on new archival sources not used for this purpose before.
62. Edwin Witte, *The Development of the Social Security Act* (Madison: University of Wisconsin Press, 1963), pp. 15–16, 29–30; J. Douglas Brown, *An American Philosophy of Social Security* (Princeton: Princeton University Press, 1972), pp. 20–22.
63. Jill Quadagno, *The Transformation of Old Age Security* (Chicago: University of Chicago Press, 1988), chapter 6.
64. Orloff, op. cit., p. 289.
65. Theron Schlabach, *Edwin E. Witte: Cautious Reformer* (Madison: State Historical Society of Wisconsin, 1969), pp. 146–148.
66. Thomas Eliot, *Recollections of the New Deal* (Boston: Northeastern University Press, 1992), p. 88.
67. Witte, op. cit., p. 125; Schlabach, op. cit., p. 115; Domhoff, *State Autonomy or Class Dominance?*, op. cit., p. 173.
68. Alan Brinkley, *The End of Reform* (New York: Alfred A. Knopf, 1995). Michael K. Brown, *Divergent Fates: Class and Race in the American Welfare State, 1935–1985* (Ithaca, NY: Cornell University Press, 1998).
69. Stephen Bailey, *Congress Makes a Law* (New York: Columbia University Press, 1950).
70. Ibid., p. 122.
71. Robert Collins, *The Business Response to Keynes, 1929–1964* (New York: Columbia University Press, 1981), chapter 4. For a detailed analysis of this case, see my *The Power Elite and the State*, op. cit., chaper 6.
72. Collins, op. cit., chapter 4.
73. Bailey, op. cit., pp. 226–227; Bertram Gross, *The Legislative Struggle* (New York: McGraw-Hill, 1953), pp. 178–179. Gross played a major role in drafting this legislation and in coordinating the liberal-labor coalition for the bill's sponsor, Senator James Murray of Montana.
74. Bailey, op. cit., pp. 231–232.

75. G. William Domhoff, "Where Do Government Experts Come From?," in *The Power Elites and Organizations* (Beverly Hills, CA: Sage Publications, 1987).
76. Raymond Bauer, Ithiel de Sola Pool, and Lewis Dexter, *American Business and Public Policy* (Chicago: Aldine-Atherton, 1963).
77. James Q. Wilson, "The Corporation As a Political Actor," in *The American Corporation Today*, ed. Carl Kaysen (New York: Oxford University Press, 1996), p. 426. The quotation in Bauer, et al., op. cit., is on page 324.
78. Bauer, et al., op. cit., p. 359. For a detailed critique of this case study, see my *The Power Elite and the State*, op. cit., chapter 8.
79. Bauer, et al., op. cit., p. 74.
80. Floyd Hunter, *Top Leadership, USA* (Chapel Hill: University of North Carolina Press, 1959), chapter 10.
81. Bauer, et al., op. cit., p. 422.
82. Ibid., pp. 43–44.
83. Domhoff, *The Power Elite and the State*, op. cit., pp. 240–241. This argument is based on the following sources: David Mayhew, *Party Loyalty among Congressmen* (Cambridge: Harvard University Press, 1966); Aage Clausen, *How Congressmen Decide* (New York: St. Martin's Press, 1973); Barbara Sinclair, *Congressional Realignment, 1925–1978* (Austin: University of Texas Press, 1982); and Mack Shelley II, *The Permanent Majority* (Tuscaloosa: University of Alabama Press, 1983).
84. On the origins of the Civil Rights Movement in New Deal agricultural legislation and the subsequent urbanization of the black population, see Frances Piven and Richard Cloward, *Poor People's Movements* (New York: Random House, 1977), chapter 4; and Jack Bloom, *Class, Race, and the Civil Rights Movement* (Bloomington: Indiana University Press, 1987). On the basis of the movement in African-American churches and the ability to disrupt business as usual, see Aldon Morris, *The Origins of the Civil Rights Movement* (New York: Free Press, 1984). For the overall political framework, see Doug McAdam, *Political Process and the Development of Black Insurgency, 1930–1970* (Chicago: University of Chicago Press, 1982).
85. Cary McWilliams, *Ill Fares the Land* (Boston: Little Brown, 1942), p. 356.
86. Domhoff, *The Power Elite and the State*, op. cit., p. 98. Chapter 4 of this book provides a detailed history of the development of the concept of collective bargaining from the 1890s to the 1930s.
87. Kenneth Casebeer, "Holder of the Pen: An Interview with Leon Keyserling on Drafting the Wagner Act," *University of Miami Law Review*, 42 (1987): 334.
88. James A. Gross, *The Reshaping of the National Labor Relations Board* (Albany: State University of New York Press, 1981); Domhoff, *The Power Elite and the State*, op. cit., pp. 101–102.
89. Robert Zieger, *American Workers, American Unions, 1920–1985* (Baltimore: Johns Hopkins University Press, 1986), p. 119.
90. James Gross, *Broken Promise: The Subversion of U.S. Labor Relations Policy, 1947–1994* (Philadelphia: Temple University Press, 1995).

91. For the importance of various legal changes in limiting the effectiveness of union organizing, see Holly McCammon, "Legal Limits on Labor Militancy: U.S. Labor Law and the Right to Strike since the New Deal," *Social Problems*, 37 (1990): 206–229; Holly McCammon, "From Repressive Intervention to Integrative Prevention: The U.S. State's Legal Management of Labor Militancy, 1881–1978," *Social Forces*, 71 (1993): 569–601; and Holly McCammon, "Disorganizing and Reorganizing Conflict: Outcomes of the State's Legal Regulation of the Strike Since the Wagner Act," *Social Forces*, 72 (1994): 1011–1049.

92. For the importance of Democratic victories in the 1936 elections in shaping the outcome of unionization efforts of 1937 and 1938, see Irving Bernstein, *The Turbulent Years* (Boston: Houghton Mifflin, 1970); and Sidney Fine, *Sitdown: The General Motors Strike of 1936–1937* (Ann Arbor: University of Michigan Press, 1965).

    For a critique of the Marxist literature on unionization in the 1930s for ignoring or downplaying the crucial role of state officials, see Marxist historian James Weinstein, *Ambiguous Legacy: The Left in American Politics* (New York: Franklin Watts, 1975), pp. 80–81.

    For an analysis of the failures of the union movement after 1937, see Michael Goldfield, *The Decline of Organized Labor in the United States* (Chicago: University of Chicago Press, 1987), and Michael Goldfield, "Race and Labor Organization in the United States," *Monthly Review*, 49 (1997): 80–97.

93. Leonard Silk and David Vogel, *Ethics and Profits* (New York: Simon & Schuster, 1976), p. 50.

94. Ibid., p. 75.

95. Ibid., p. 197.

96. Ibid., p. 64.

97. Ibid., p. 193.

98. Ibid., pp. 194, 201.

99. Mills, op. cit., p. 244.

100. McConnell, op. cit., p. 294.

101. For evidence that those who disagree with their appointed supervisors are dealt with summarily, see Ralph Nader, Peter J. Petkas, and Kate Blackwell, *Whistle Blowing* (New York: Grossman, 1972).

102. Silk and Vogel, op. cit., p. 199.

103. David Vogel, "Why Businessmen Distrust Their State: The Political Consciousness of American Corporate Executives," *British Journal of Political Science*, 8 (1978): 45–78.

104. James W. Prothro, *The Dollar Decade* (Baton Rouge: Louisiana State University Press, 1954), as quoted in Silk and Vogel, *Ethics and Profits*, op. cit., p. 194.

105. Nancy Rose, *Put to Work: Relief Programs in the Great Depression* (New York: Monthly Review Press, 1994).

106. Frances Piven and Richard Cloward, *The New Class War* (New York: Random House, 1982). For the role of the social disruption created by the Civil Rights Movement and the anti–Vietnam War movement in

delaying this corporate counterattack, see Domhoff, *The Power Elite and the State,* op. cit., chapter 10.

107. For a major contribution to understanding why the American labor movement is so weak compared to those of most democratic capitalist countries, see Kim Voss, *The Making of American Exceptionalism: The Knights of Labor and Class Formation in the Nineteenth Century* (Ithaca, NY: Cornell University Press, 1993). Voss uses comparative history to show that the American labor movement was much like its counterparts in England and France until the 1870s but then failed due to greater employer success in pressuring government officials to discredit and disrupt the union movement. On the other hand, the employers in France and England could not destroy unions because the landed aristocrats and state officials—who held the preponderance of power at the time— would not let them. Employers therefore had to work out compromises with their workers.

By contrast, there was no landed aristocracy in the United States and the government was relatively small and weak. When it is added that the American working class was divided into black and white, North and South, and unable to develop its own political party due to the factors leading to a two-party system, it is understandable that the union movement is smaller and less politically important in the United States than in Western Europe.

Landlord power in late nineteenth-century European governments often has been overlooked due to the claims by Marx and Engels in their journalistic writings that capitalists already were the predominant power in those countries. For a synthesis of all recent historiography showing that capitalists had very little power in the countries that Marx and Engels were analyzing, see Richard Hamilton, *The Bourgeois Epoch: Marx and Engels on Britain, France, and Germany* (Chapel Hill: University of North Carolina Press, 1991). For one excellent history, see Arno Mayer, *The Persistence of the Old Regime* (New York: Pantheon, 1981).

8

The Future of American Politics

American politics is not likely to produce any big surprises in the next few years, which is hardly a daring forecast. The power elite has the economic and political resources to continue its domination of the federal government through campaign finance, lobbying, and policy recommendations, and most people are likely to accept the current arrangements as long as they can make their lives work. The New Right may make gains on some aspects of its social agenda, and the Republican Party may win more congressional seats from Southern states and make more cuts in the federal government. Members of the liberal-labor coalition are likely to remain isolated on major legislative issues concerning foreign trade, the defense budget, social welfare, and union rights, but they may be able to hold back the New Right on some issues relating to civil rights and abortion rights. For the most part, though, it's business as usual.

There have been, however, several major recent social and political changes that could provide the basis for a modest challenge to the power elite as the twenty-first century begins. These changes and what they might portend are the subject of this chapter. They are (1) the collapse of the Soviet Union and the end of the Cold War, (2) the revitalization of the labor movement, (3) the greater willingness to consider coalitional politics on the part of movements organized around gender and civil rights issues, and (4) the continuing transformation of Southern politics, making a nationwide liberal-labor takeover of the Democratic Party possible for the first time in American history.

The emphasis in the previous paragraph is on "modest challenge" because of the relatively small differences among the United States and those industrial democracies where the working classes are not constrained by a two-party system, racial and ethnic conflict, and a history of slavery. Such countries have less income inequality and better social benefit programs, but they do not differ very much in their power structures. In the case of Western European democracies, at least some of their greater social justice may be due to the fact that they were under the wing of the United States during the Cold War. On the one hand, the capitalists in these countries and in the United States had to tolerate greater levels of equality to stave off what was then seen as a very serious challenge from communism. On the other hand, the massive amount of economic, political, and military aid provided to Western European countries by the United States gave their governments some degree of autonomy from their own capitalists, making it possible for government leaders to react positively to demands for better social programs by social democrats. A movement for social change in the United States would not have these advantages.

THE COLLAPSE OF THE SOVIET UNION

The sudden and unexpected collapse of the Soviet Union in 1991 was a momentous historical event with many ramifications for both the American and international power structures—not all of which are likely to be apparent for many years to come. In the short run, it is clear that the end of the Soviet Union has left the United States as far and away the most powerful country in the world, with no serious rivals in the economic, political, or military realms despite all the hand-wringing about "decline" by public officials, journalists, and some historians. From a power point of view, such concerns on the part of public officials are the psychological by-products of the burdens of dealing with day-to-day problems and should not be taken at face value. It is, of course, difficult to deal with terrorist bombings or the unexpected deaths of American troops in small countries, but this is not the stuff of long-term power relations.

For all the outcry and worry over the rise of Japan and Germany, the United States is without doubt the largest, most populous, and richest industrial democracy in the world. As shown in table 8.1, Japan and Germany together are only 56 percent as large as the United States in gross domestic product, and they are smaller in other ways as well. Even adding in France and Great Britain creates a foursome that is only 87 percent as large as the U.S. economy. The concerns expressed by American policy makers and commentators are an example of a gross overreaction by a superpower to the slightest of challenges.

Table 8.1 The Size of the United States Compared to Other Major Countries on Economic, Military, and Other Factors

Country	GDP[1] (in trillions)	GDP per Person (in thousands)	Defense Spending (in billions)	Population (in millions)	Area (sq. miles)
United States	6,935.7	26,640	270.6	265.6	3,536,278
Japan	2,527.4 (36%)[2]	20,200	50.2	125.5	145,850
Germany	1,344.6 (20%)	16,580	29.1	83.5	137,828
France	1,080.1 (16%)	18,670	35.9	58.0	210,026
United Kingdom	1,045.2 (15%)	17,980	34.9	58.5	94,251

Source: *World Almanac and Book of Facts 1997*, pp. 134, 764, 767, 787, 829, 831.

[1]GDP = gross domestic product.

[2]% of U.S. GDP.

The most likely result of this unrivaled power is that the American foreign policy establishment will intervene militarily anywhere in the world that it chooses, a possibility that did not exist when there was a Soviet Union to rattle its nuclear weapons or provide military aid to American enemies, as it did in Vietnam, Iraq, Syria, Libya, North Korea, Cuba, and many other places. Whether such intervention will be seen as necessary by American leaders is a separate question. It may be that the United States will be challenged far less often now that there is no Soviet Union to provide both military aid and the hope of an alternative social model to insurgents in newly industrializing countries.

A second possible result of the collapse of the Soviet Union is that the power elite may be less likely to support dictatorial governments when they face internal opposition. In the past, the United States came to the aid of such dictatorships out of fear that communist forces would take over the leadership of the opposition and then move the country into the Soviet camp. With that threat removed, there is less political need for aiding dictators, and hence more possibility for democracy. There are, however, economic reasons for ignoring dictators as long as possible because more democracy would mean the possibility of more trade unions and higher wages, and hence less incentive for corporations in the United States, Europe, and Japan to move their production facilities to Third World countries.

The end of the Soviet Union has had very different effects in different parts of the world. In some areas it has led to a decline in tensions and a willingness to compromise because one side no longer has the support of the Soviet Union. In other parts of the world it has meant increased ethnic, racial, or religious tensions because rival power groups have stirred up age-old antagonisms. Within the United States, the direct effects have been relatively minor so far. However, the collapse may have played a role in the 1992 elections. If the Soviet Union had still existed as a military threat to the United States, it seems less likely that voters would have focused exclusively on the economy or allowed a Vietnam War "draft dodger" to become the president.

The collapse of the Soviet Union has had one certain impact on the political situation in the United States. It has removed the overwhelming outside enemy that was an important rallying point for both ultraconservatives and the New Right. Their leaders are worried about what will replace anticommunism in attracting voters who might be tempted to vote for centrists and liberals on other grounds. Their attempt to portray China as a threat is difficult to believe given China's lack of air power and its eagerness to attract American corporations. Their attacks on humanism, homosexuality, and pornography as potential substitutes have been limited in their success; sometimes they even produced a backlash. It seems likely that the new appeal will concern the alleged "collectivist" tendencies of liberalism, but it is not clear that such a concept can replace communism as a scare word, especially when "liberalism" is not tied to any foreign enemy and does not challenge the general usefulness of the market system.

The death of the Soviet Union, when combined with China's turn to a market economy, may also mean the end of the Marxist-Leninist parties in the United States that defined themselves primarily in terms of their stances toward those two large communist countries—pro-Soviet communist parties, anti-Soviet Trotskyist parties, and pro-China Maoist parties. In the case of the Communist Party, it was more than pro-Soviet, as its critics always alleged and as newly opened archives in Moscow show. It was heavily subsidized by the Soviet Union, changed its policies on a moment's notice and without consulting its members when the Soviets so requested, and even carried on extensive spying for the Soviet Union. Although the Communists and other Marxist-Leninist parties usually had no more than a few hundred or a few thousand members at any given moment once the Communist Party fell apart in the late 1950s—and had far less impact than ultraconservatives and New Rightists claim—they did consume the energies of many activists, often in battles among themselves. They also ham-

pered the efforts of social democrats and liberals by casting asper-
sions on their sincerity and even disrupting their meetings on occasion.
A fragmented leftist movement at war with itself has little chance of
attracting many activists who stay around for very long.[1]

The collapse of the Soviet Union and the use of the market in
China are also likely to have a profound effect on the goals of future
left-wing movements because both are directly related to the failures
of a centrally planned economy in comparison to a market system.
Although the Soviet Union was a brutal and repressive dictatorship
with no political freedom, I do not believe it disintegrated for that
reason. In fact, its political and military institutions were still powerful when Gorbachev began to make economic reforms. The collapse
was due to the failure of the economy, which was falling further and
further behind the West. The failure of the economy in turn undermined Marxist theory as a source of hope and meaning, which led to
cynicism, despair, and massive morale problems for both the ruling
party and the general population.

The reasons for the failure of the centrally planned economy are
several, but they first of all relate to the sociological insight that large-
scale bureaucracies tend to develop deficiencies because power ac-
crues at the top. Then corruption ensues, such as placing friends and
relatives of questionable competence in positions of responsibility,
withholding important information from rival agencies, and skim-
ming off resources for the personal benefit of the top officials—all of
which add to morale problems and create large economic inefficiencies.
Even more important, the range and depth of information needed to
run a complex consumer economy is too great for any planning bureaucracy. Ironically, recent economic research suggests that market
economies suffer far more distortions, inefficiencies, and failures due
to a lack of full information than most American social scientists realized, making a mixture of government regulation and markets necessary, but in general markets are highly useful because they rely on
many different people with small pieces of information to take small
and limited actions.[2]

The failure of planning bureaucracies means that socialism is
now even less likely to be seen by Americans as a viable alternative to
capitalism. If leftists would come to the same conclusion, then their
programs for realizing egalitarian values would be more likely to include the useful aspects of the current market system, which would
narrow the distance between leftists and liberals, making a more cohesive movement possible. Arguments between leftists and liberals
would then concern the best ways to bring about "economic democracy" and greater social justice within a mixed system of government
regulation and economic competition.[3]

Moreover, rethinking by leftists may go beyond the problems of a planned economy to include the failures of Marxist-Leninist parties as well. As even friendly critics have pointed out, there may be serious flaws in the Marxist view of politics and freedom. According to revolutionary Marxists, parliamentary freedoms are only "bourgeois freedoms," meaning they are freedoms for capitalists, not for workers. Drawing a very different analogy between markets and politics than the benign pluralist one discussed at the start of chapter 6, some Marxists claim that both the market and representative democracy mask control by a few owners and state managers. This long-standing idea is expressed as follows by one of the most visible Marxist theorists of the past twenty-five years:

> In Marxist theory, the "liberal democratic state" is still another capitalist weapon in the class struggle. This is so because the democratic form of the state conceals undemocratic contents. Democracy in the parliamentary shell hides its absence in the state bureaucratic kernel; parliamentary freedom is regarded as the political counterpart of the freedom in the marketplace, and the hierarchical bureaucracy as the counterpart of the capitalist division of labor in the factory.[4]

For revolutionary Marxists, the solution to this alleged problem is "direct democracy"—meaning small face-to-face groups in which the people themselves, not elected representatives, make decisions. This is in fact the meaning of the term *soviet*. But experience shows that such groups come to be controlled by the members of the Communist Party within them. They become creatures of the tightly controlled Marxist-Leninist parties that champion them.

The influence of Marxist theory on socialist politics in general enters the picture at this point. In my view, the Marxists' belief that Marx and Engels are right in predicting the inevitable failure of capitalism and its necessary replacement by socialism often breeds a form of paternalistic thinking that can become very manipulative in the context of a call for direct democracy at the expense of parliamentary representation. Because Marxian theory claims that the market system is inherently flawed and bourgeois freedoms illusory, I think some Marxists also come to believe that it is justifiable to use whatever methods are necessary in order to rid the world of capitalism and usher in socialism. That is, they believe that the ends (socialism) justify whatever means are necessary because capitalism is so intolerable. But it seems unlikely to me that inflexible theories and undemocratic methods can lead to democracy and freedom.[5]

CHANGES IN THE LABOR MOVEMENT

Although this book has emphasized the alliance between the labor movement and liberals, there are often tensions and differences between them. This was especially true between 1965 and 1980, when elements in the labor movement often opposed the major goals of liberals. In the case of the Civil Rights Movement, to take the most prominent example, the rank and file white males in the building trade and craft unions were often less than sympathetic to its objectives, even though many industrial unions were integrated and union leaders lobbied for civil rights legislation in Washington. Indeed, one of the reasons for the rise of a Black Power movement was the unwillingness of craft unions at the local level to open their ranks to more African-Americans. The continuing exclusion was especially noticeable in the case of apprentice programs.[6] Moreover, many white workers expressed their displeasure with the Civil Rights Movement by voting for the third-party candidacy of George Wallace for president in 1968, and then for Nixon in 1972. Later they became known as "Reagan Democrats."[7]

Other issues were divisive as well. The labor movement was not very friendly to the women's movement because it saw women as competitors for the good jobs that white male trade unionists already held. The raw sexism used to keep women out of the high-paying skilled trades was widely noted at the time, and even in the 1990s there are few women in such jobs. Even more hostility was expressed toward the environmental movement because it was seen as a threat to jobs. Finally, many trade union members intensely disliked those who opposed the Vietnam War. Some union leaders worked openly and proudly against the liberal Democratic candidate for president in 1972, helping Nixon to a landslide victory. As the current president of the AFL-CIO, John Sweeney, later wrote:

> Too often, we kept our heads down, our minds closed, and our mouths shut during the great debates that shaped our nation's social and economic policies. Too often, we refused to reach out to potential allies who could have helped us build a coalition for challenging corporate priorities and offering positive alternatives.[8]

While the unions were doing battle with liberals on several issues, the corporate-conservative coalition carried out its counteroffensive against unions through appointments to the National Labor Relations Board, as explained in chapter 2. This counteroffensive, in combination with the movement of some American factories overseas and increasing automobile and steel imports from Germany and

Japan, led to the large decline of industrial unions after 1975, which is illustrated in chapter 1, table 1.1. This decline dramatically reduced the labor movement's ability to challenge large Northern corporations. In effect, the unions went into battle with the corporations without their traditional liberal allies, who were focused on affirmative action, gender equality, and the environment, and this contributed to their failures. In 1960, when unions were in their heyday, corporate chief executives made 44 times as much as the average worker; in 1995, as the unions continued to decline in numbers and power, the chief executives made 145 times as much as workers.[9]

In the twenty years after 1975, there were changes within the union movement even as its membership declined. Insurgent forces in several unions were successful in democratizing previously oligarchic or crime-dominated structures. More emphasis was put on organizing women and minorities. New leadership slowly rose to the top. Sweeney, elected president in 1995, is the son of recent blue-collar Irish immigrants. The executive vice president is the daughter of Latino sharecroppers in Texas. The executive council is composed of 27 percent women and minorities.[10] As noted in chapter 6, the new leadership put $35 million into its own television ads for the 1996 elections. Whether these changes can have any effect in the face of a well-organized and highly confident power elite is a separate question. There are now about 1,500 consultants, including those at public relations firms, who earn approximately $500 million each year advising corporations on how to keep unions out of their offices and factories.[11] Between 1995 and 1997, union membership dropped another 500,000.

IDENTITY POLITICS: THE FRAGMENTATION OF LIBERALISM

Not only were liberals in conflict with labor because of the movements of the 1960s, but they became divided among themselves when they turned to "identity politics"—meaning that different groups organized separately around the specific areas in which they were excluded and discriminated against. Those who previously would have been known as liberals or social democrats were now called feminists, minority activists, gay rights activists, and environmentalists.

The rise of identity politics was a source of great frustration for those liberals and leftists who wanted to challenge corporate power in an attempt to redistribute wealth and income. But the appeal of identity groups must be understood in terms of the fact that it is very rare for people to take a separate path unless they are excluded by those with greater privilege and power. Those who turned to identity politics were being excluded by white males of all social classes, not just those in the power elite. As already noted, the unions by and large tried to restrict the best jobs to white males, excluding women and minorities, but here it can be added that white male liberals in the Democratic Party often seemed little better to those seeking greater access and involvement. Perhaps the most dramatic example of this point was the unwillingness of very many white liberals to aid the integrated insurgent group called the Mississippi Freedom Democratic Party in its effort to unseat the racist Mississippi delegation at the 1964 Democratic Party convention. Many civil rights activists left that convention extremely disappointed with white liberals and turned toward the separatist politics of Black Power.[12]

By the late 1990s, however, there were three indications that the identity groups might be looking for ways to create a new liberal-labor coalition. First, a certain degree of success in their struggle for inclusion had made economic issues more salient to them. The number of women and minorities in the professions, in positions of authority, and in the workforce in general had risen, however gradually, and tolerance toward the lifestyles of gays and lesbians had grown (despite attempts by ultraconservatives to use civil rights for homosexuals as a wedge issue in Democratic-leaning religious groups). Second, many members of the identity groups came to believe they could not advance their agendas any further with a Republican in the White House. In 1992 they therefore lowered their profiles so they would be less visible to centrist voters and quietly aided the successful Democratic presidential campaign. Clinton then rewarded all the identity groups with the most visible appointments any of them had ever received and with some policy victories as well. Third, feminists and minority activists responded positively to the rise of new leadership in the AFL-CIO. They were heartened by the fact that women and minorities were moving closer to top-level positions and by the new efforts to organize women and minorities in low-paying jobs.

THE TRANSFORMATION OF SOUTHERN POLITICS

The Civil Rights Movement had a profound effect on all aspects of American politics. First, and most importantly, it transformed the lives of African-Americans in the South, who are now able to elect thousands of local officials in their areas of greatest residential concentration and live with less fear of arbitrary police and civilian violence. Second, it led to the collapse of the New Deal coalition that had governed for most of the years since 1932 and the ascendancy of a nationwide conservative Republican majority. That is, the "Solid Democratic South," however conservative it was in so many ways, was in fact as essential as liberals and labor in the North to Democratic success at the national level. For purposes of this chapter, however, the most critical point is the Civil Rights Movement's effect on the Southern Democrats.

The Voting Rights Act of 1965 made it possible for African-Americans to defeat open segregationists and other ultraconservatives in Democratic primaries, thereby pushing them into the Republican Party and providing an opportunity to remake the Democratic Party as an expression of the liberal-labor coalition. The pressure on conservative Democrats from black voters was complemented by the fact that the gradual industrialization of the South since World War II has made the economic base of the Southern segment of the dominant class even more similar to that of its Northern counterpart. When the Democratic Party could no longer fulfill its main historical function—namely, keeping African-Americans powerless—it was relatively easy for wealthy white conservatives to become Republicans.

The exodus did not happen faster primarily because the seniority enjoyed by congressional Southern Democrats gave them considerable power in national politics as long as the Democratic Party remained a majority in Congress. Wherever possible, then, Southern whites continued to control the Democratic Party at the local level even while usually voting Republican at the national level. The result was a split-party system in the South that gave the dominant class the best of both possible worlds while it lasted.[13]

It is only gradually and through the retirement of senior Democrats that the white Democratic South is becoming Republican. The dam may have broken in 1994 when the Republicans unexpectedly took control of both houses of Congress and then held on to them in 1996. Now there is even less reason for wealthy white Southerners and their young politicians to remain Democrats. After the 1994 election one Southern Democratic senator and five Southern members of the House announced they were switching parties. The Republicans picked up two more senatorial seats and three more House seats in the South in 1996.

All this said, there will not be a transformation of the Democrats into a liberal-labor party in the South without a transcendence of racial resentments and a platform that can change the thinking of a considerable number of white voters. This point is best demonstrated in a study of six special congressional elections in the South between 1981 and 1993, all made necessary by deaths and resignations. Surprisingly, all six were won by white conservative Democrats who took several steps to defeat even more conservative Republicans: (1) they first established their conservatism on key social issues like school prayer, the death penalty, and gun control; (2) then they pointed out that the extraordinarily antigovernment stance of the Republicans could be bad for the South if it led to a reduction in federal subsidies of various kinds; (3) they emphasized their long-standing local ties; and (4) they quietly cultivated the African-American vote by advertising on black radio stations, visiting black churches in the company of black campaign workers, and saying they would uphold civil rights legislation.[14]

In the short run, then, there has been very little trend toward a more liberal politics in the South, which has two-thirds of the electoral votes needed to win the presidency and nearly one-third of all congressional seats. All of the Southern Republicans in the Senate and House are conservatives, as are all but one or two of the Democratic senators and eight to ten of the remaining white Democrats in the House. The major change has been the election of sixteen African-Americans to the House, all from majority black districts when they were originally elected. (Two of the districts were changed to majority white due to a court ruling in 1996, but the two incumbents were reelected.) All sixteen, six of whom are women, are liberals, and seven of them joined the Progressive Caucus, which was discussed at the end of chapter 6.[15]

The continuing conservatism of Southern politics aside, the main point about the movement of conservative whites to the Republicans is that it provides the opportunity to turn the Democratic Party into an organizational base for developing and popularizing a liberal-labor program. Just as the black churches were the organizational basis of the Civil Rights Movement, and white fundamentalist churches are a key organizational basis for the New Right, so too could the Democratic Party now become an organizational base for the liberal-labor coalition in the South, with black leaders in a position to play a central role in that coalition. In other words, the roughly 20 percent of the Southern population that is black, and the 40 percent of the white population who would have to join them to create a majority, would enter into the coalition on an equal basis. It may be that the necessary 40 percent of white Southerners are unlikely to join a liberal-labor coalition where they would have to share power with African-Americans, but it is nonetheless the case that the Democratic Party and its primary elections now provide the basis for making an attempt to convince them to take a more liberal voting stance.

The potential for a liberal-labor takeover of the Democratic Party provides the basis for bringing together the other transformations that were mentioned earlier in the chapter. With the outside threat of Soviet communism removed, it might be possible to put more emphasis on economic and social welfare issues. By the same token, leaders within single-issue identity movements might find it in their interest to join a larger coalition if it favored civil rights for everyone. Moreover, some of the leftist activists who previously supported third parties might provide the organizing energies that would be greatly needed in the South. As for the labor movement, it is already engaged in such a strategy and searching for allies.

Taking over the Democratic Party, however, would not be without its tensions and conflicts. It would mean challenging moderate and conservative Democrats on a new platform in party primaries, just as ultraconservative Republicans challenge moderate Republicans in that party's primaries. Challenges to moderate and conservative incumbents would not sit well with them, and they would fight back bitterly. Even if the liberals won the primaries, they might well lose the regular election, of course, but the important point is that the party is now available as an educational vehicle for use in future elections.

POLITICAL PARTIES AS STATE AGENCIES

The end of segregation in the South would not have opened up the Democratic Party without the simultaneous increase in the use of primaries to select candidates. State-sponsored primaries, as noted in chapter 6, began in Wisconsin in 1903, but they did not become a predominant feature of the electoral system until the 1970s. It has now reached the point where the use of primaries, when combined with long-standing government control of party registration, in essence has transformed the parties into the official office-filling agencies of the state. Since anyone can register with the government to be a member of a party, party leaders cannot exclude people from membership based on political beliefs. In the same fashion, since any voter registered in the party can run in its primaries for any office, party leaders and party conventions have very little influence on the policy image projected by the party. In effect, a party stands for what the successful candidates in primaries say that it stands for. Party leaders can protest, and donors can withhold campaign funds, but the winners in the primaries are "the party" for all intents and purposes.

The laws leading to an emphasis on primaries could be changed, of course, just as the election laws were changed at the local level in the Progressive Era to ward off Democratic and socialist challengers, as explained in chapter 6. But an attempt to close the parties in the face of a liberal-labor mobilization might backfire if primaries are now seen as an established tradition and right.

THE CORPORATE-CONSERVATIVE RESPONSE

The corporate-conservative coalition, rather obviously, would not sit back in the face of a liberal-labor challenge through the Democratic Party. Working primarily through the Republican Party, it would play on the general antigovernment ideology that is shared by a majority of Americans. It would stress those few social issues in which a majority of Americans remain conservative, creating a dilemma for social-issue liberals. It would play the race card in subtle and not-so-subtle ways, trying to hold on to the Reagan Democrats who left the party in 1968 and 1972 and only rarely came back after that. It would try to paint the Democrats as atheists, libertines, and bleeding hearts, and it would try to make the words *collectivism* and *liberalism* into the fear-inducing equivalents of *communism* and *socialism*. It would say that more jobs would move overseas if the Democrats won, and that taxes would increase exorbitantly.

The Republicans would raise massive sums of money in order to broadcast their message. Corporations would give far less to Democrats than they have in the past. It would soon be apparent that Republicans have not even come close to realizing their potential when it comes to raising money for political campaigns.

At the same time, the corporate-conservative coalition would face some liabilities within the Republican Party. The New Right may have painted the coalition into a corner on women's issues, especially the right to an abortion. Its program on women's issues, which won it many anti-abortion activists in the 1970s and 1980s, has reached the point at which it may be too threatening to college-educated career women, who usually join with upper-middle-class homemakers in voting solidly Republican. If such women continue to see the New Right program on women in a negative light, they might vote for moderate Democrats, providing that party with just enough votes to win elections, as they did for Clinton in 1996.

But it is not only Republican women who might support moderate Democrats. If a New Right takeover of the Republican Party threatened the policy preferences of the corporate rich, many of them might move into the Democratic Party, where they would provide an immediate challenge to the liberal-labor coalition by supporting mainstream Democrats in primaries. Since the highly emotional social issues are not a primary concern for them, they could easily back "new Democrats" of the Clinton and Albert Gore mold, who are conservative on the important economic issues. That is, centrists in both parties could form a solid enough coalition within the Democrats to defeat liberal-labor candidates in primaries and then defeat ultraconservative Republicans in the regular election. Something very similar to this happened in 1996 in two California House districts, where two businesswomen, Ellen Tauscher and Loretta Sanchez, switched their registration to Democrat and defeated ultraconservative Republican incumbents.

The possibilities that are represented by successful business-oriented Democrats like Tauscher and Sanchez can be seen in the New Democratic Coalition organized in the House in 1997. Its members are described in one business publication as "right of center on fiscal and economic issues and just left of center on social issues."[16] With thirty-seven members, mostly from suburban and rural districts outside the South, it is already a formidable alternative to the fifty-five-member Progressive Caucus.

Despite the moderate possibilities in the Democratic Party, moderate Republicans are likely to remain in their current party. They still have the ability to fend off the most extreme of the New Rightists, who are not likely to challenge the corporate rich on economic issues in any case. It is therefore highly probable that the Democratic leadership coalition will remain roughly as it is today unless there is a major liberal-labor challenge.

WHICH SIDE WOULD WIN?

If the liberal-labor coalition were to succeed in taking over the Democratic Party, could it win enough elections to legislate its policy preferences? The theory presented in this book and recent historical experience suggest that the corporate-conservative coalition is likely—but not certain—to prevail even if it faces a united liberal-labor coalition based in a nationwide Democratic Party free of its Southern conservatives. A majority of people probably would continue to defer to the economic success and expertise that are embodied in the corporate community and policy-formation network, to vote on the basis of their conservative social values, or to be impressed by corporate-conservative arguments about the dangers of big government, higher taxes, and the regulation of the market. Most Christian whites probably would decide that they want to be in the party of the establishment, not the party of minorities, labor unions, feminists, environmentalists, and liberals. Many people may complain about the current leaders, and wish they had a higher income and more job security, but in the end they are seldom ready to risk what they have and know unless they see an excellent chance of succeeding.

SOCIAL CHANGE AND VIOLENCE

Violence is a topic that makes everyone nervous. Most books on power in democratic countries do not even discuss it, preferring to imply that politics is strictly a matter of civilized discussion and compromise. But not to do so is to ignore the fact that Southern slaveholders decided to fight rather than face the prospect of perhaps losing their slaves someday, that employers hired people to attack union organizers in the 1890s and 1930s, and that some Southern whites reacted with violence to the Civil Rights Movement. Indeed, so much violence by property owners is a difficult problem for pluralists, but it is in many ways support for a class-dominance theory. It is not inevitable, but it is a possibility.

Faced with the possibility of violence by property owners, many revolutionary leftists believe that violence is a justifiable and necessary aspect of any large-scale social movement, but they also believe that it makes no sense to talk about that claim until a movement is far enough along that people allegedly would think of it themselves. Also, violent overthrow of the government cannot be openly advocated because it is against the law, but the belief in the eventual need for violence is made clear with calls for change "by any means necessary."

To reduce the possibility of violence, any large-scale social movement would have to begin, as the Civil Rights Movement did, by renouncing violence explicitly in order to address the underlying fears of many citizens who might otherwise resist any changes. Such a stance also would have the advantage of isolating those leftists whose implicit message is the need for violence at some point in the future. But even a nonviolent movement still faces the question: How would the power elite react to a movement that challenged its prerogatives and privileges?

Despite corporate rich protestations of powerlessness in the face of a government dominated by liberals, environmentalists, minorities, and unions, they have not been seriously challenged in the United States since World War II ended the Great Depression and gave them an opportunity to reassert their leadership. It is therefore not clear how they would react to a growing liberal-labor movement that wanted to raise their taxes, provide support to union organizing, and use the government to create more jobs and social benefits.

The likelihood of violence by the corporate rich would be reduced, of course, if opposition was fully and completely nonviolent. Such a stance makes it very hard for any power elite to legitimate violence to the large number of neutrals and moderates in any country. Also, the likelihood of violence is reduced if the movement is not trying to socialize corporations or abolish the market system, which are red flags for the corporate-conservative coalition.

Although the corporate rich have a set of deeply held beliefs about free markets and individualism that could lead them to extreme actions when challenged, some of them also have had the experience of dealing with unions or have seen unions operate in other democratic countries. They know that Canada and countries in Western Europe have prospered with unions and a welfare state—at least until restrictive monetary policies and competition from low-wage countries increased unemployment in the past several years. In the end, it is not possible to make predictions about violence, but the issue does have to be discussed whenever power is at stake.

CONCLUSION

The short-term prospects for modest challenges to the American power elite cannot be known with any degree of certainty. Social scientists and historians can identify patterns and trends, but there are too many factors interacting with each other in not-yet-understood ways for anyone to provide blueprints for the alteration of history. At the most general level, Western history suggests that major events like wars and depressions set in motion the forces that lead to social change. In hindsight, the Great Depression was the starting point for both the New Deal and the Civil Rights Movement, and both the unions and the Civil Rights Movement were aided by World War II.

Casting a wider net, World War I made the Bolshevik Revolution possible by weakening the Czarist power structure. World War II aided the communist revolution in China in the same fashion, along with nationalist movements in many parts of the world. The Vietnam War and the resistance to it in the United States unleashed forces that took many years to play themselves out; they combined with the Civil Rights Movement to create a generation of consumer, environmental, gender, and other activists who were jolted out of conventional career paths and conventional social bonds. A failing economy sank the Soviet Union.

Whether the transformation of the South, the resurgence of the union movement, the coalescence of the identity politics movements, and the fall of the Soviet Union have set loose forces that are strong enough to alter the American power structure is not immediately apparent and not likely to be known for another decade.

NOTES

1. For evidence that the leaders of the American Communist Party followed instructions from Moscow, especially on crucial foreign policy issues, see Harvey Klehr, John Haynes, and Fridrikh Igorevich Firsov, *The Secret World of American Communism* (New Haven, CT: Yale University Press, 1995). For a balanced treatment of the relationship of the Communist Party to other leftists, see James Weinstein, *Ambiguous Legacy: The Left*

in American Politics (New York: Franklin Watts, 1975). Although the efforts of the Communist Party had little or no effect on government policy, I think that they had a negative influence on American leftist policy stances, especially concerning foreign policy, which is another reason why the American left has not been very effective.

2. Although Charles Lindblom, *Politics and Markets* (New York: Basic Books, 1977), remains a good source on this issue, an even more detailed and empirical analysis based on recent economic research can be found in Robert Kuttner, *Everything for Sale: The Virtues and Limits of Markets* (New York: Alfred A. Knopf, 1997). For the best theoretical critique of conventional economic theorizing about the efficiency of markets, see Joseph E. Stiglitz, *Whither Socialism?* (Cambridge, MA: MIT Press, 1994). Stiglitz argues that the less centrally planned "market socialisms" that were tried to some extent in Eastern Europe failed because they were based on the faulty assumptions concerning markets in mainstream economics.

3. See Martin Carnoy and Derek Shearer, *Economic Democracy* (White Plains, NY: M. E. Sharpe, 1980), for the first major attempt to bridge this gap. See also Robin Archer, *Economic Democracy: The Politics of a Feasible Socialism* (New York: Oxford University Press, 1995), and Kuttner, op. cit.

4. James O'Connor, *Accumulation Crisis* (New York: Blackwell, 1984), p. 188. The history of this idea in the writings of Marx, Engels, and Lenin has been traced by Stanley Moore, *A Critique of Capitalist Democracy* (New York: Monthly Review Press, 1957).

    The idea of the economic market as inherently exploitative combines with the belief that "bourgeois freedoms" are a thin veil for repression of the working class to generate a moral anger and contempt for liberalism and democracy that, in my view, is the root problem in the failure of Marxism as politics. For an insightful analysis of what he calls the "elitist dimension of the left tradition" (p. 267), along with plausible ways to overcome it, see Richard Flacks, *Making History: The Radical Tradition in American Life* (New York: Columbia University Press, 1988), pp. 243–247, 267–275.

5. For a succinct statement of the problems with the Marxian conception of freedom, see Andrzej Walicki, "Marx and Freedom," *New York Review* (Nov. 24, 1983): 50–55. Walicki concludes that "the Marxian legacy has become the most fertile ground for breeding different kinds of myths, some of them intellectually inspiring but most of them generating a millennarian faith in early salvation and, therefore, dangerous and destructive of the relative but more tangible achievements of human progress" (p. 55). He closes with this important question:

    > On the one hand it is undeniable that Marxism gave birth to a fruitful and academically respectable methodological approach to the social sciences; that it provided, and continues to provide, some valuable insights for the criticism of modern civilization and culture. We should ask therefore: is it possible to preserve Marxism as a part of our cultural heritage, to assimilate it, and, at the same time, to be immune to its myth-creating political influence? (p. 55)

6. Herbert Hill, "Race, Ethnicity, and Organized Labor: The Opposition to Affirmative Action," *New Politics*, 1 (1987): 31–82; Herbert Hill, "The Importance of Race in American Labor History," *International Journal of Politics, Culture, and Society*, 9 (1995): 317–343. For the argument that white workers benefited from the segregation of African-Americans and therefore played an active role in maintaining antiblack sentiments and discrimination, see Alexander Saxton, *The Rise and Fall of the White Republic* (New York: Verso Books, 1990); David Roediger, *The Wages of Whiteness* (New York: Verso Books, 1991); and Noel Ignatiev, *How the Irish Became White* (New York: Routledge, 1995).

7. Dan T. Carter, *The Politics of Rage: George Wallace, the Origins of the New Conservatism, and the Transformation of American Politics* (New York: Simon & Schuster, 1995), chapter 13, shows the centrality of the antibusing theme in the 1972 presidential elections. On the day Wallace was crippled in an assassination attempt, he won 51 percent of the vote in the Democratic primary in Michigan, partly because of "crossover" votes by suburban Republicans who opposed busing (p. 445).

8. John Sweeney, *America Needs a Raise* (Boston: Houghton-Mifflin, 1996), p. 57.

9. Ibid., p. 40.

10. Ibid., pp. 93, 95.

11. David Kusnet, "A Dirty Business," *Commonweal* (Feb. 24, 1989): 107–108; Martin Jay Levitt, *Confessions of a Union Buster* (New York: Crown Publishers, 1993). For a detailed analysis of labor's political problems, see William Form, *Segmented Labor, Fractured Politics* (New York: Plenum Press, 1995). For the lack of progress in building up union strength despite the efforts of the new leadership, see Steven Greenhouse, "A Union Comeback? Tell It to Sweeney," *New York Times* (June 8, 1997): E4. For an excellent analysis of the challenges facing union organizers, see Richard Rothstein, "Toward a More Perfect Union," *The American Prospect*, May–June 1996: 47–53.

12. Clayborne Carson, *In Struggle: SNCC and the Black Awakening of the 1960s* (Cambridge: Harvard University Press, 1995); William Van Deburg, *New Day in Babylon* (Chicago: University of Chicago Press, 1992).

13. Chandler Davidson and Bernard Grofman, eds., *Quiet Revolution in the South* (Princeton, NJ: Princeton University Press, 1994), discusses both the large number of black elected officials in the South (over 5,000 at the local, county, and state levels) and the persistence of white dominance in any electoral district at any level of the governmental system in which whites are the majority (through the early 1990s). See also Alexander Lamis, *The Two-Party South* (New York: Oxford University Press, 1984), especially pages 231–232, where he discusses the potential for a liberal Democratic Party in the South.

14. James Glaser, *Race, Campaign Politics, and Realignment in the South* (New Haven, CT: Yale University Press, 1996). Glaser also shows the way in which Republican candidates make subtle and not-so-subtle racial appeals in districts where there is a solid white majority.

15. For a detailed quantitative study showing the importance of a simple liberal-conservative dimension in explaining congressional voting since the 1790s, and placing African-American and women Democrats at the liberal end of the Democratic Party spectrum in 1995, see Keith Poole and Howard Rosenthal, *Congress: A Political-Economic History of Roll Call Voting* (New York: Oxford University Press, 1997), p. 231. The liberal-conservative polarization between Democrats and Republicans is now at a very high level (p. 232).

16. Jim McTague, "New Dogs: Moderate Democrats Tug at the Party's Leash, Help Shape Budget Deal, Threaten Fight over Trade," *Barron's* (Aug. 18, 1997): 25–29. Quote appears on page 26.

Appendix

Social Registers and Blue Books

The Social Register
Detroit Social Secretary
New Orleans Social Register
Seattle Blue Book

Private Schools

Agnes Irwin (Rosemont, PA)[1]
Annie Wright (Tacoma, WA)[1]
Asheville (Asheville, NC)
Ashley Hall (Charleston, SC)[1]
Baldwin (Bryn Mawr, PA)[1]
Berkeley Carroll (Brooklyn, NY)
Bishops School (La Jolla, CA)
Branson (Ross, CA)
Brearley (New York, NY)[1]
Brimmer and May (Chestnut Hill, MA)
Bryn Mawr (Baltimore, MD)[1]
Buckley (New York, NY)[2]
Cate (Carpenteria, CA)
Catlin Gable (Portland, OR)
Chapin (New York, NY)[1]
Chatham Hall (Chatham, VA)[1]
Choate Rosemary Hall (Wallingford, CT)
Collegiate (Richmond, VA)
Concord Academy (Concord, MA)
Convent of the Sacred Heart (New York, NY)[1]
Cranbrook (Bloomfield Hills, MI)
Dalton (New York, NY)
Dana Hall (Wellesley, MA)[1]
Deerfield (Deerfield, MA)
Emma Willard (Troy, NY)[1]
Episcopal High (Alexandria, VA)
Ethel Walker (Simsbury, CT)[1]

Note: Schools are coeducational unless followed by a "1" (girls only) or "2" (boys only).

Foxcroft (Middlebury, VA)[1]
Garrison Forest (Owings Mills, MD)[1]
Gilman (Baltimore, MD)[2]
Groton (Groton, MA)
Hathaway Brown (Shaker Heights, OH)[1]
Head-Royce (Oakland, CA)
Hewitt (New York, NY)[1]
Hill (Pottstown, PA)[2]
Hockaday (Dallas, TX)[1]
Hotchkiss (Lakeview, CT)
Kent (Kent, CT)
Kinkaid (Houston, TX)
Lake Forest (Lake Forest, IL)
Lakeside (Seattle, WA)
Laurel (Shaker Heights, OH)[1]
Lawrenceville (Lawrenceville, NJ)
Louise S. McGehee (New Orleans, LA)[1]
Madeira (McLean, VA)[1]
Marlborough (Los Angeles, CA)[1]
Mary Institute and Saint Louis Country Day (St. Louis, MO)
Masters (Dobbs Ferry, NY)
Middlesex (Concord, MA)
Milton (Milton, MA)
Miss Hall's (Pittsfield, MA)[1]
Miss Porter's (Farmington, CT)[1]
Pomfret (Pomfret, CT)
Portsmouth Abbey (Portsmouth, RI)
Punahou (Honolulu, HI)
Salem Academy (Winston-Salem, NC)[1]
Shattuck-St. Mary's (Fairbault, MN)
Shipley (Bryn Mawr, PA)
Spence (New York, NY)[1]
St. Andrew's (Middlebury, DE)
St. Catherine's (Richmond, VA)[1]
St. Christopher's (Richmond, VA)[2]
St. Paul's (Concord, NH)
St. Timothy's (Stevenson, MD)[1]
Stuart Hall (Staunton, VA)[1]
Taft (Watertown, CT)
Thatcher (Ojai, CA)
University School (Hunting Valley, OH)[2]
Walnut Hill (Natick, MA)
Webb (Bell Buckle, TN)
Westminster (Atlanta, GA)
Westover (Middlebury, CT)[1]
Westridge (Pasadena, CA)[1]
Woodberry Forest (Woodberry Forest, VA)[2]

Country and Men's Clubs

Arlington (Portland, OR)
Bohemian (San Francisco, CA)

Boston (New Orleans, LA)
Brook (New York, NY)
Burlingame Country Club (San Francisco, CA)
California (Los Angeles, CA)
Casino (Chicago, IL)
Century (New York, NY)
Chagrin Valley Hunt (Cleveland, OH)
Charleston (Charleston, SC)
Chicago (Chicago, IL)
Cuyamuca (San Diego, CA)
Denver (Denver, CO)
Detroit (Detroit, MI)
Eagle Lake (Houston, TX)
Everglades (Palm Beach, CA)
Hartford (Hartford, CT)
Hope (Providence, RI)
Idlewild (Dallas, TX)
Knickerbocker (New York, NY)
Links (New York, NY)
Maryland (Baltimore, MD)
Milwaukee (Milwaukee, WI)
Minneapolis (Minneapolis, WI)
New Haven Lawn Club (New Haven, CT)
Pacific Union (San Francisco, CA)
Philadelphia (Philadelphia, PA)
Piedmont Driving (Atlanta, GA)
Piping Rock (New York, NY)
Racquet Club (St. Louis, MO)
Rainier (Seattle, WA)
Richmond German (Richmond, VA)
Rittenhouse (Philadelphia, PA)
River (New York, NY)
Rolling Rock (Pittsburgh, PA)
Saturn (Buffalo, NY)
St. Cecelia (Charleston, SC)
St. Louis County Club (St. Louis, MO)
Somerset (Boston, MA)
Union, Cleveland, OH)
Woodhill Country Club (Minneapolis, MN)

Women's Clubs

Mt. Vernon Club (Baltimore, MD)
Society of Colonial Dames
Sulgrave (Washington, DC)
Sunset (Seattle, WA)
Vincent (Boston, MA)
Acorn (Philadelphia, PA)
Chilton (Boston, MA)
Colony (New York, NY)
Fortnightly (Chicago, IL)
Friday (Chicago, IL)

Index

321